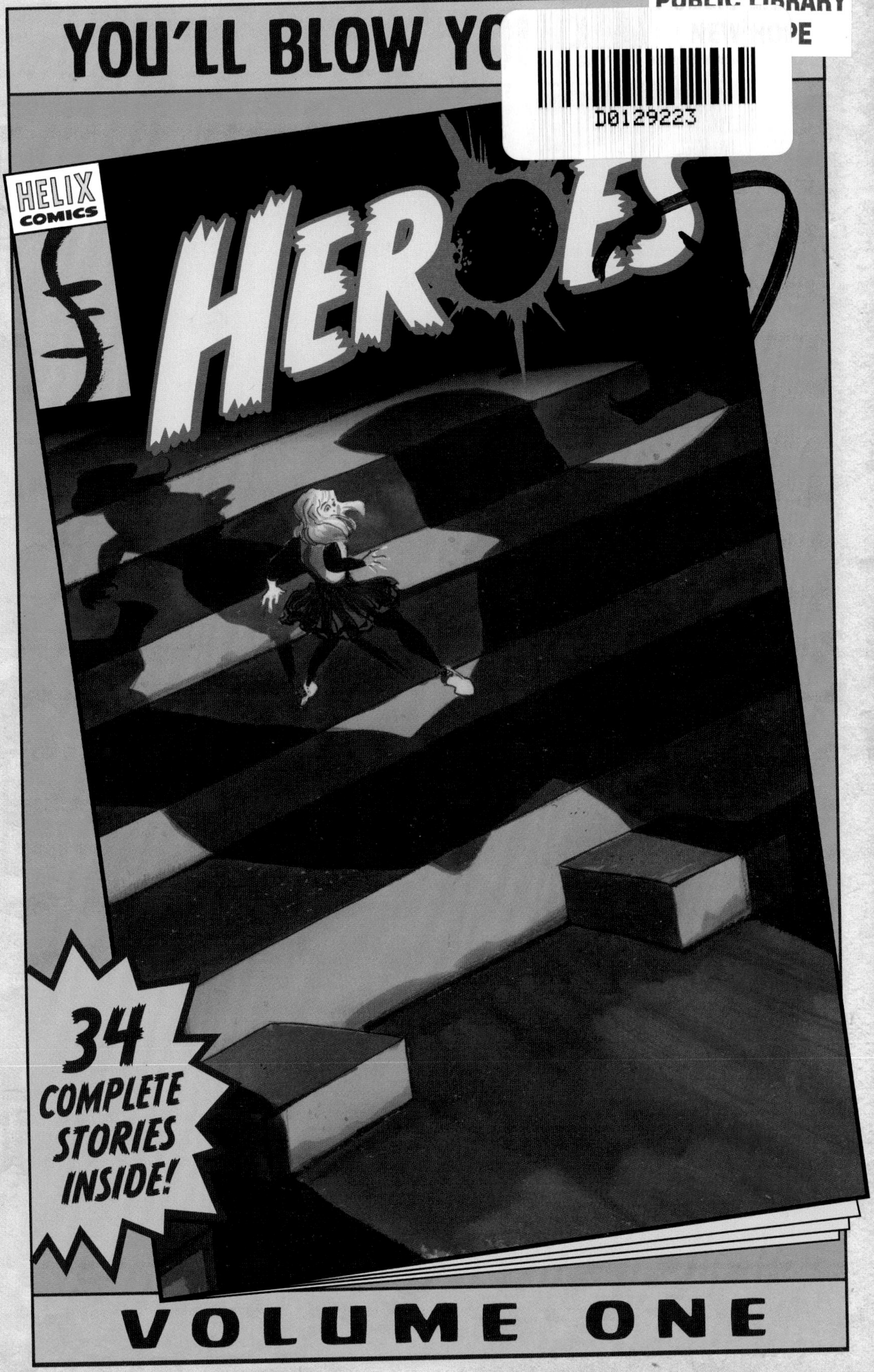
YOU'LL BLOW YO
HELIX COMICS
HEROES
34 COMPLETE STORIES INSIDE!
VOLUME ONE

CONTENTS

CREDITS

MONSTERS

Written by
ARON ELI COLEITE
Pencils by
MICHAEL TURNER
& KOI TURNBULL
Inks by PETER
STEIGERWALD
& DAVID MORAN
Colors by
MARK ROSLAN

CHAP. 1
PAGE
6

THE CRANE

Written by ARON ELI COLEITE
Art by MICAH GUNNELL
Digital inks by MARK ROSLAN
Colors by DAVID MORAN

Chapter 2..................Page 13

TRIAL BY FIRE

Chapter 3
PAGE 19

Written by CHUCK KIM
Pencils by MARCUS TO
Digital inks by MARK ROSLAN
Colors by DAVID MORAN

AFTERMATH

Written by
JOE POKASKI
Pencils by
MICAH
GUNNELL
Digital inks by
MARK ROSLAN
Colors by PETER STEIGERWALD

EASIER THAN YOU THINK!

Chapter 4..........................Page 25

SNAPSHOTS

Written by JOE POKASKI
Pencils by MARCUS TO
Digital inks and
colors by PETER
STEIGERWALD

Chapter 5
...Page 32

STOLEN TIME

Written by
JOE POKASKI
Pencils by
MARCUS TO
Digital inks
MARK ROSLAN
Colors by PETER STEIGERWALD

Chapter 6...............Page 39

TREASURE CHEST OF STORIES!

CONTROL

Written by OLIVER GRIGSBY
Art by MICAH GUNNELL
Digital inks by MARK ROSLAN
Colors by PETER STEIGERWALD

Chapter 7...............Page 45

ISAAC'S FIRST TIME

Written by ARON ELI COLEITE
Art by MICAH GUNNELL
Digital inks by
MARK ROSLAN
Colors by
DAVID MORAN

Chapter 8....................Page 51

LIFE BEFORE EDEN

Written by
PIERLUIGI
COTHRAN
Art by
MARCUS TO
Digital inks by
MARK ROSLAN
Colors by PETER STEIGERWALD

Chapter 9:........................Page 57

TURNING POINT

Written by CHRISTOPHER ZATTA
Art by MICAH GUNNELL
& MARCUS TO
Digital inks by MARK ROSLAN
Colors by DAVID MORAN

Chapter 10...........Page 63

SUPER-HEROICS

Written by
HARRISON WILCOX
Art by
MICAH GUNNELL
Digital Inks by
PETER STEIGERWALD
Colors by
BETH SOTELO
& DAVID MORAN

Chapter 12...Page 75

FATHERS & DAUGHTERS

Written by ANDREW CHAMBLISS
Art by TRAVIS KOTZEBUE & MICAH GUNNELL
Digital Inks by PETER STEIGERWALD
Colors by DAVID MORAN & JOHN STARR

Chapter 11....................................Page 69

CONTENTS

WIRELESS

Chapter 13: Page 82
Written by ARON ELI COLEITE
Art by MICAH GUNNELL
Guest art by PHIL JIMENEZ
Digital inks by MARK ROSLAN
Colors by BETH SOTELO
& PETER STEIGERWALD

Chapter 14: Page 90
Written by ARON ELI COLEITE
& JOE POKASKI
Art by MICAH GUNNELL
Digital inks by MARK ROSLAN
Colors by BETH SOTELO
& PETER STEIGERWALD

Chapter 15: Page 96
Written by ARON ELI COLEITE
& JOE POKASKI
Art by MICAH GUNNELL
Digital inks by MARK ROSLAN
Colors by BETH SOTELO
& PETER STEIGERWALD

Chapter 16: Page 102
Written by ARON ELI COLEITE
& JOE POKASKI
Art by MICAH GUNNELL
Digital inks by MARK ROSLAN
Colors by BETH SOTELO
& PETER STEIGERWALD

HOW DO YOU STOP AN EXPLODING MAN?

Chapter 17: Page 108
Written by
JESSE ALEXANDER
& ARON ELI COLEITE
Pencils by TRAVIS KOTZEBUE
Digital inks by
MARK ROSLAN
Colors by BETH SOTELO

Chapter 18: Page 114
Written by
JESSE ALEXANDER
& ARON ELI COLEITE
Pencils by JORDAN KOTZEBUE
Digital inks by
MARK ROSLAN
Colors by BETH SOTELO

BULLY

Written by CHUCK KIM
Art by MICAH GUNNELL
Digital inks by MARK ROSLAN
Colors by BETH SOTELO
& PETER STEIGERWALD
Chapter 19.........Page 120

HELL'S ANGEL

Written by JESSE ALEXANDER
Art by MICHAEL GAYDOS
Colors by EDGAR @ STUDIO F

ROAD KILL

**CHAPTER 20
PAGE 126**

Written by
JOE POKASKI
Art by
JASON BADOWER
Colors by
ANNETTE KWOK

The Path of the Righteous

**CHAPTER 21
PAGE 133**

Written by ARON ELI COLEITE
Art by STAZ JOHNSON
Colors by CHRIS SOTOMAYOR

12 MODELS
3 TO 5 HP

**Chapter 22
Page 139**

FAMILY MAN

Written by JESSE ALEXANDER
Art by STAZ JOHNSON
Colors by RICHARD ISANOVE

Chapter 23............Page 145

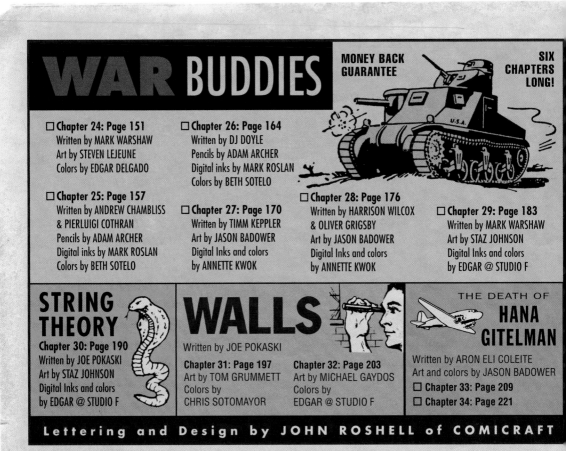

WAR BUDDIES

MONEY BACK GUARANTEE

SIX CHAPTERS LONG!

☐ **Chapter 24: Page 151**
Written by MARK WARSHAW
Art by STEVEN LEJEUNE
Colors by EDGAR DELGADO

☐ **Chapter 25: Page 157**
Written by ANDREW CHAMBLISS
& PIERLUIGI COTHRAN
Pencils by ADAM ARCHER
Digital inks by MARK ROSLAN
Colors by BETH SOTELO

☐ **Chapter 26: Page 164**
Written by DJ DOYLE
Pencils by ADAM ARCHER
Digital inks by MARK ROSLAN
Colors by BETH SOTELO

☐ **Chapter 27: Page 170**
Written by TIMM KEPPLER
Art by JASON BADOWER
Digital Inks and colors
by ANNETTE KWOK

☐ **Chapter 28: Page 176**
Written by HARRISON WILCOX
& OLIVER GRIGSBY
Art by JASON BADOWER
Digital Inks and colors
by ANNETTE KWOK

☐ **Chapter 29: Page 183**
Written by MARK WARSHAW
Art by STAZ JOHNSON
Digital Inks and colors
by EDGAR @ STUDIO F

STRING THEORY

Chapter 30: Page 190
Written by JOE POKASKI
Art by STAZ JOHNSON
Digital Inks and colors
by EDGAR @ STUDIO F

WALLS

Written by JOE POKASKI

Chapter 31: Page 197
Art by TOM GRUMMETT
Colors by
CHRIS SOTOMAYOR

Chapter 32: Page 203
Art by MICHAEL GAYDOS
Colors by
EDGAR @ STUDIO F

THE DEATH OF HANA GITELMAN

Written by ARON ELI COLEITE
Art and colors by JASON BADOWER
☐ **Chapter 33: Page 209**
☐ **Chapter 34: Page 221**

Lettering and Design by JOHN ROSHELL of COMICRAFT

Collected Edition Cover by **ALEX ROSS**   Paintings by **TIM SALE & DAVE STEWART**

Special thanks to FRANK MASTROMAURO & NANCI QUESADA

The Folks From Helix Comics:

**Aron Eli Coleite • Joe Pokaski • Jesse Alexander
Jeph Loeb • Chuck Kim • Mark Warshaw**

MASSIVELY MIGHTY MASTHEAD:

JIM LEE
Editorial Director

JOHN NEE
VP—Business Development

HANK KANALZ
VP—General Manager:
WildStorm and
Collected Edition Editor

KRISTY QUINN and
MICHAEL McCALISTER
Collected Edition
Assistant Editors

ED ROEDER
Art Director

PAUL LEVITZ
President & Publisher

GEORG BREWER
VP—Design & DC Direct
Creative

RICHARD BRUNING
Senior VP—
Creative Director

PATRICK CALDON
Executive VP—
Finance & Operations

CHRIS CARAMALIS
VP—Finance

JOHN CUNNINGHAM
VP—Marketing

ALISON GILL
VP—Manufacturing

PAULA LOWITT
Senior VP—Business &
Legal Affairs

MARYELLEN McLAUGHLIN
VP—Advertising & Custom
Publishing

GREGORY NOVECK
Senior VP—Creative Affairs

SUE POHJA
VP—Book Trade Sales

CHERYL RUBIN
Senior VP—
Brand Management

JEFF TROJAN
VP—Business Development:
DC Direct

BOB WAYNE
VP—Sales

NATURALLY NIFTY, NEWSY, NONDESCRIPT NONSENSE ABOUT OUR NUTTY NON-ENTITIES!

HEROES, published by WildStorm Productions. 888 Prospect St. #240, La Jolla, CA 92037. Compilation, cover art, chapter break art, interview and introduction copyright © 2007 Universal Studios Licensing LLLP. Heroes is a trademark and copyright of NBC Studios, Inc. All rights reserved. SUPERMAN #1 is ™ and © DC Comics. Used with permission. Originally published at www.nbc. com/Heroes/novels © 2006, 2007, NBC Studios, Inc.

WildStorm and logo are trademarks of DC Comics. The stories, characters, and incidents mentioned in this magazine are entirely fictional. Printed on recyclable paper. WildStorm does not read or accept unsolicited submissions of ideas, stories or artwork. Printed in the United States. THIRD PRINTING

DC Comics, a Warner Bros. Entertainment Company.

ISBN: 978-1-4012-1711-2

A FEW WORDS FROM MASI OKA • A FEW WORDS FROM MASI OKA

JUMP, MAGAZINE, SUNDAY.

THESE THREE WORDS describe a big part of my childhood and my imagination. They are three manga magazines published weekly in Japan. Even after coming to America at the age of six, I read the imported magazines and they defined a good part of my adolescence. These magazines printed stories by everyone from great classical authors like Osamu Tezuka and Fujio Akatsuka, to contemporary masters like Naoki Urasawa, Akira Toriyama, and Rumiko Takahashi, just to name a few. The artists always brought stories and characters that reflected our current culture and times to the page. We grew with them and they grew with us.

Manga, like graphic novels or any piece of art, has many unique powers. It can unite us and inspire us. Through these art forms, we share a common bond, a passion that we could all lose ourselves in. It was always fascinating to me that every Tuesday when the weekly SHONEN JUMP came out, all the businessmen, in their suits and ties, would pick up a JUMP from a kiosk. They would ride the subways or buses, all silent, just immersing themselves in the world of manga. At that moment, these grown men were all experiencing the same thing. Manga is part of the Japanese culture and it defines a lot of who I am. At times it would be my romantic consultant, reading stories about a shy boy who is trying to muster the courage to ask a girl out. It would be my teacher as it pontificated on potential disruptions to the space/time continuum. It would be my hero as it continued to inspire me with journeys and tales of bravery and adventure. Sure, at lot of what I've "learned" isn't too applicable in real life, or would sometimes invite a slap in the face, but it enhanced my imagination and enriched our creativity.

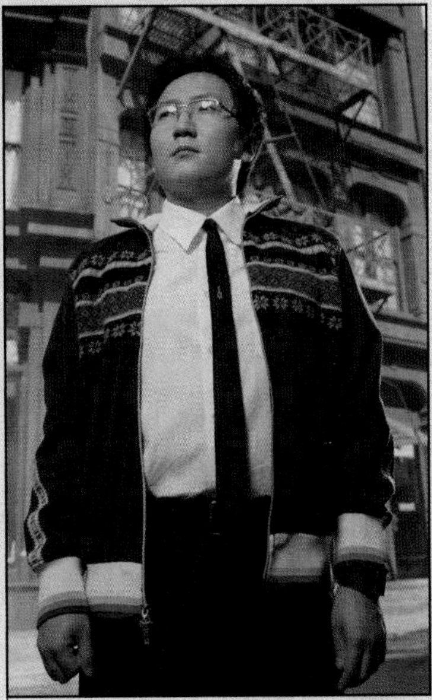

We've all been affected by graphic novels in one form or another. As we grow, become adults, and gain responsibility, mangas are where I can find sanctuary and still be a kid. Imagination flows and it's a comfort to know that there are many, many others out there—from all walks of life—enjoying the same experience. If you're a kid, enjoy it. Savor it. Hold on to your imagination and your dreams. You can make a world a different place—but it begins with you. If you're an adult, enjoy. Relax. Let yourself be a kid again. Take a vacation and let your mind wander in the magical world of graphic novels. No one can stop us from learning. No one can stop us from dreaming. No one can stop us from believing.

Tim Kring created a beautiful world, laden with rich stories and deep characters. Many artists came together under his vision to create a fantastical piece of television called HEROES. What you see on television is a reflection of all the hard work put in by hundreds of people. But a mere television show couldn't contain us. There still are more stories to tell, that we *wanted* to tell but couldn't given the medium. Fortunately, we can share and expand through a different medium. We present you these graphic novels to help add another dimension to the HEROES universe. We hope you enjoy it and let yourself get lost in the HEROES world.

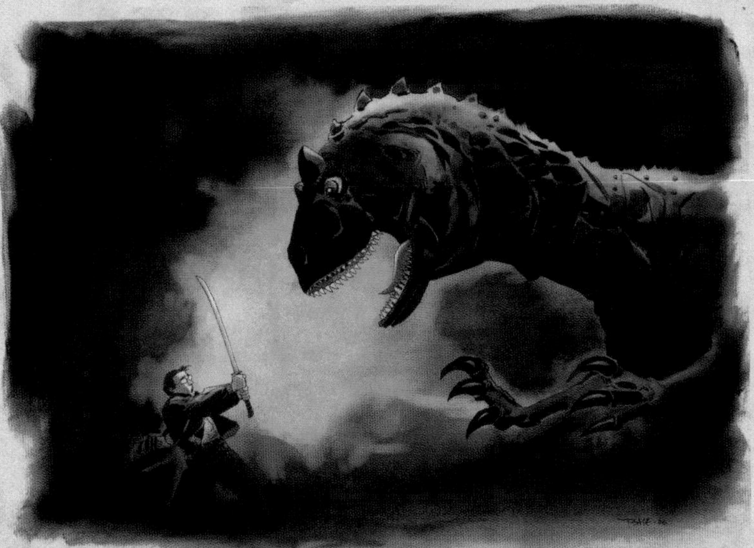

For Charlie,
Hiro Nakamura
(Masi Oka)

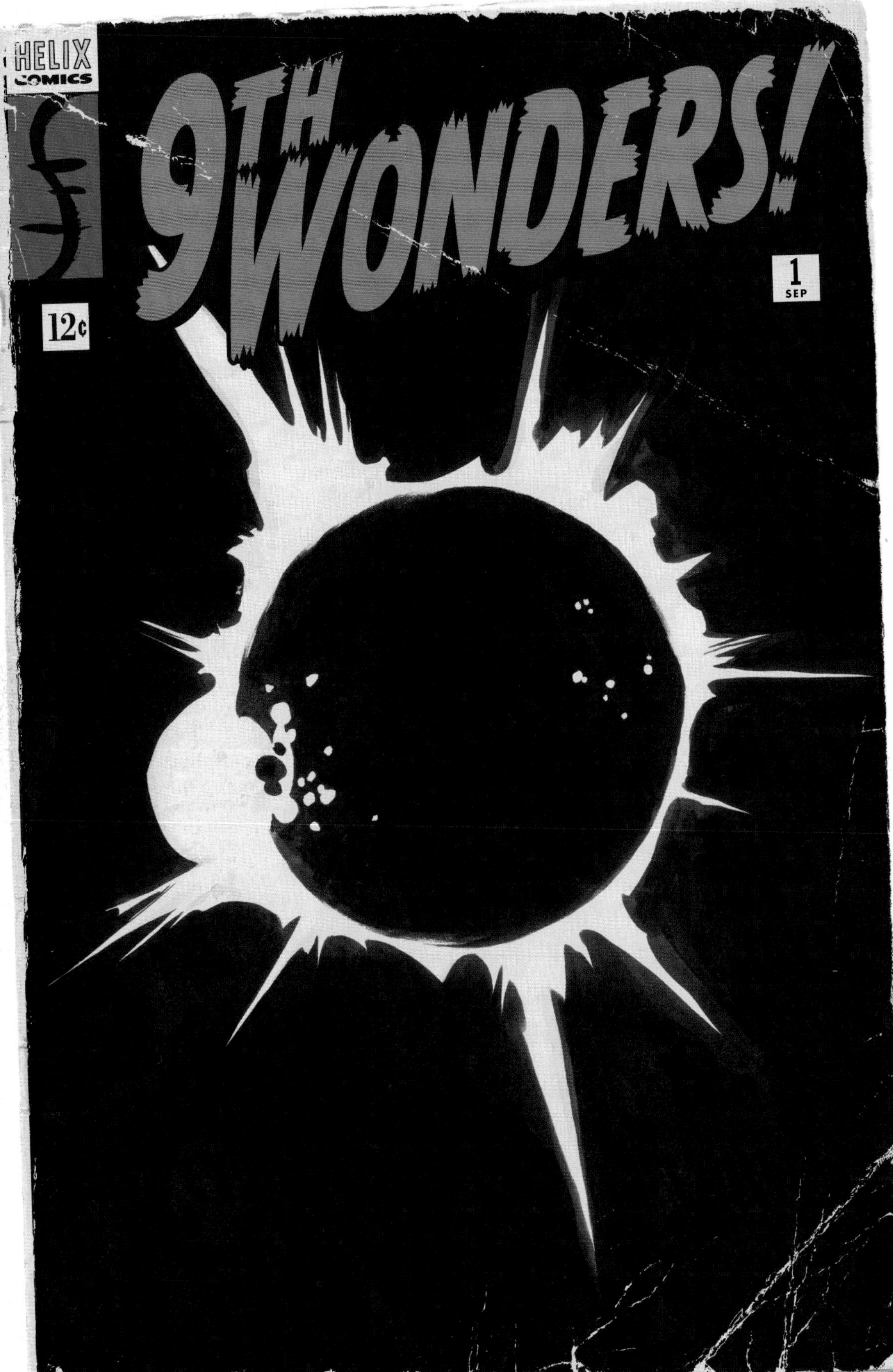
HELIX COMICS
12¢
9TH WONDERS!
1 SEP

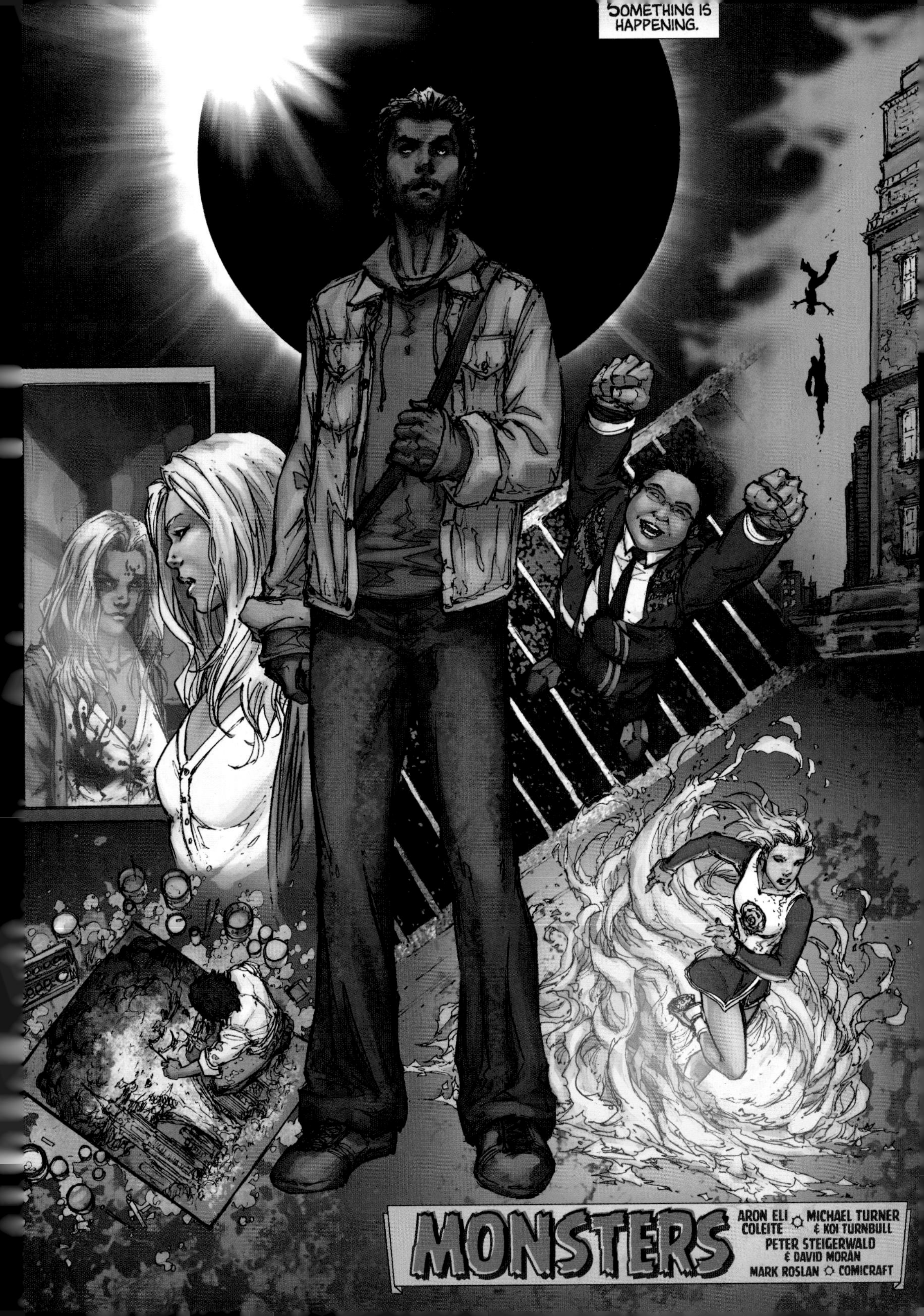
SOMETHING IS HAPPENING.
MONSTERS
ARON ELI COLEITE
MICHAEL TURNER & KOI TURNBULL
PETER STEIGERWALD & DAVID MORÁN
MARK ROSLAN
COMICRAFT

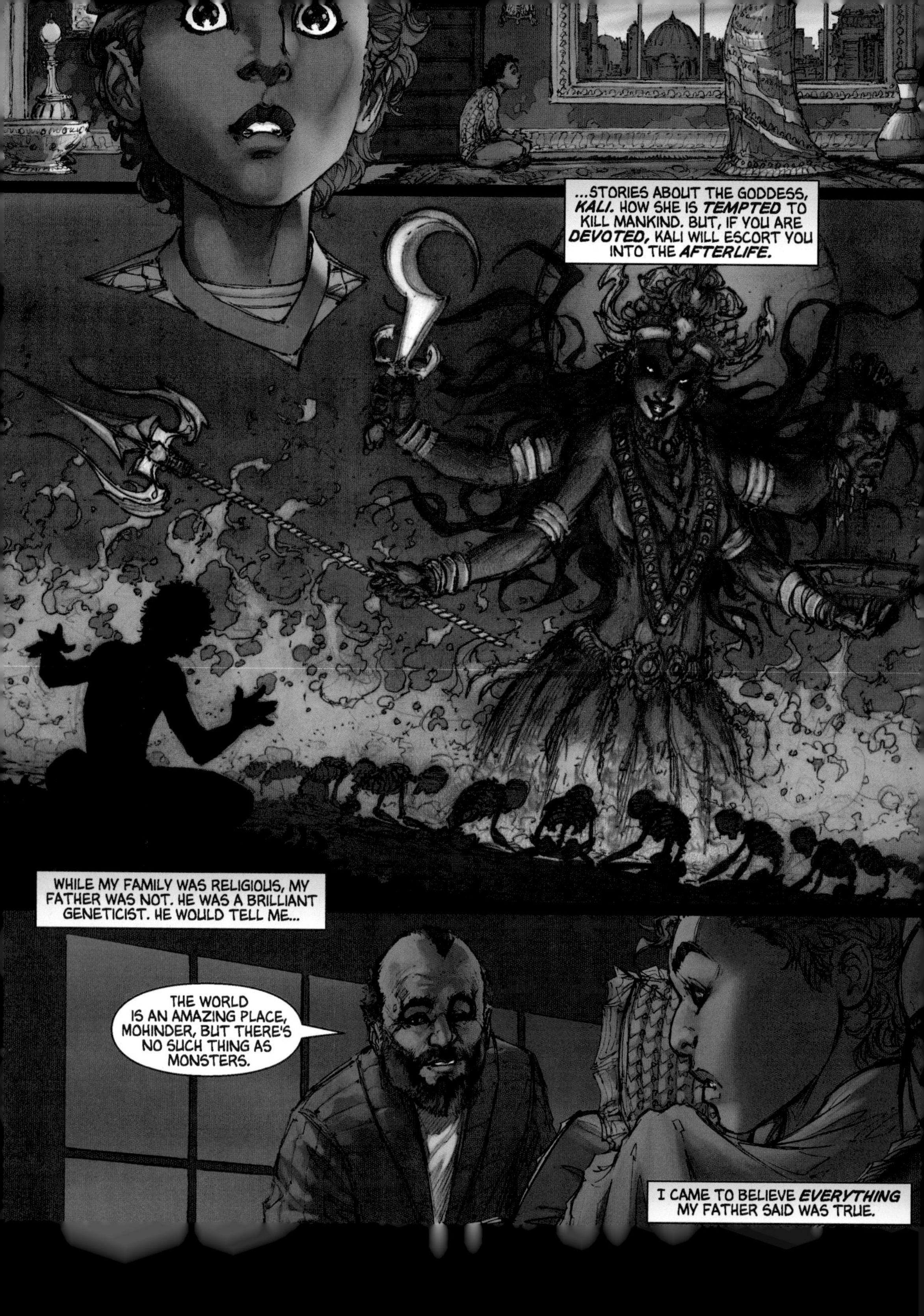
...STORIES ABOUT THE GODDESS, KALI. HOW SHE IS TEMPTED TO KILL MANKIND. BUT, IF YOU ARE DEVOTED, KALI WILL ESCORT YOU INTO THE AFTERLIFE.
WHILE MY FAMILY WAS RELIGIOUS, MY FATHER WAS NOT. HE WAS A BRILLIANT GENETICIST. HE WOULD TELL ME...
THE WORLD IS AN AMAZING PLACE, MOHINDER, BUT THERE'S NO SUCH THING AS MONSTERS.
I CAME TO BELIEVE EVERYTHING MY FATHER SAID WAS TRUE.

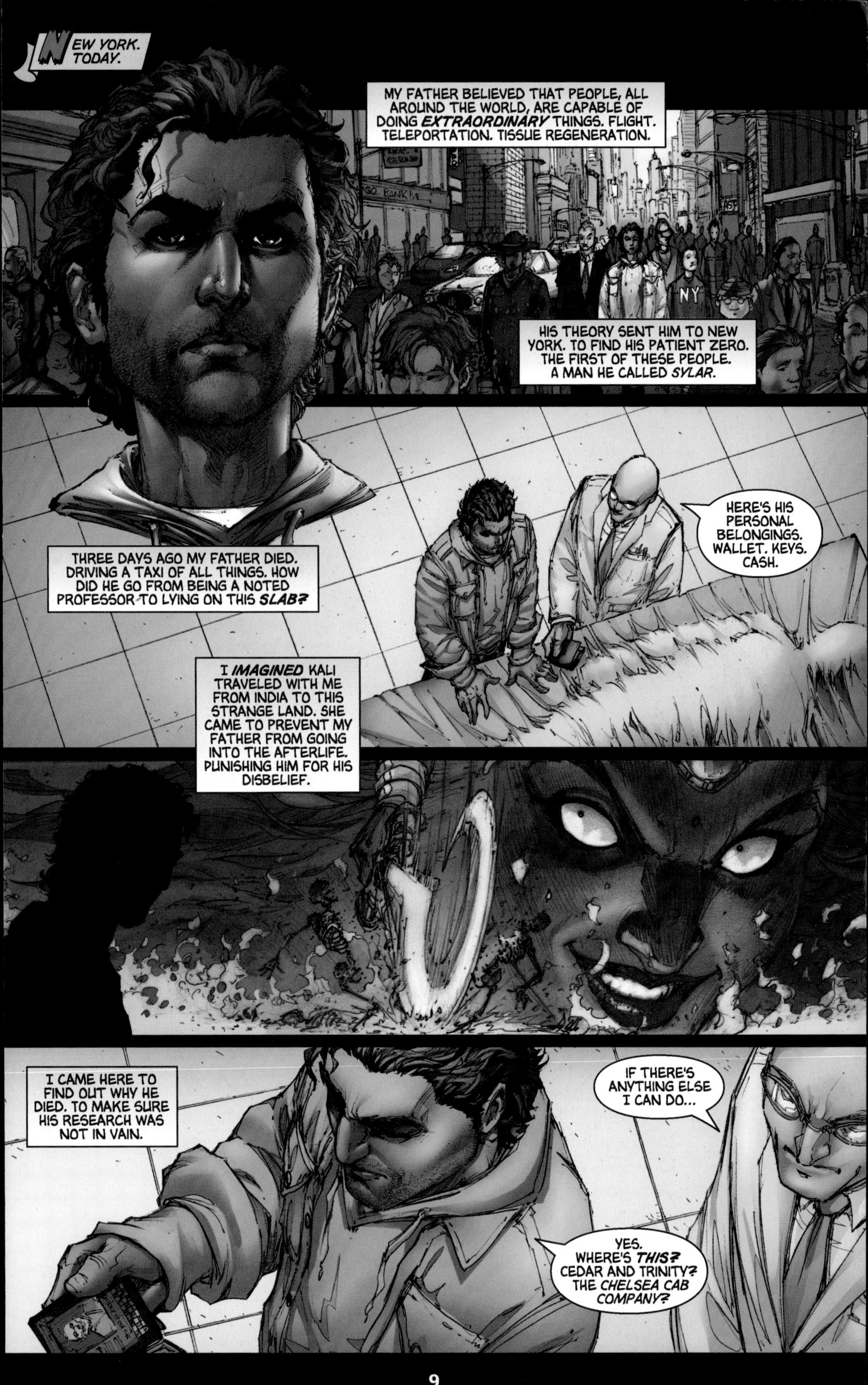
NEW YORK. TODAY.
MY FATHER BELIEVED THAT PEOPLE, ALL AROUND THE WORLD, ARE CAPABLE OF DOING EXTRAORDINARY THINGS. FLIGHT. TELEPORTATION. TISSUE REGENERATION.
HIS THEORY SENT HIM TO NEW YORK. TO FIND HIS PATIENT ZERO. THE FIRST OF THESE PEOPLE. A MAN HE CALLED SYLAR.
THREE DAYS AGO MY FATHER DIED. DRIVING A TAXI OF ALL THINGS. HOW DID HE GO FROM BEING A NOTED PROFESSOR TO LYING ON THIS SLAB?
HERE'S HIS PERSONAL BELONGINGS. WALLET. KEYS. CASH.
I IMAGINED KALI TRAVELED WITH ME FROM INDIA TO THIS STRANGE LAND. SHE CAME TO PREVENT MY FATHER FROM GOING INTO THE AFTERLIFE. PUNISHING HIM FOR HIS DISBELIEF.
I CAME HERE TO FIND OUT WHY HE DIED. TO MAKE SURE HIS RESEARCH WAS NOT IN VAIN.
IF THERE'S ANYTHING ELSE I CAN DO...
YES. WHERE'S THIS? CEDAR AND TRINITY? THE CHELSEA CAB COMPANY?

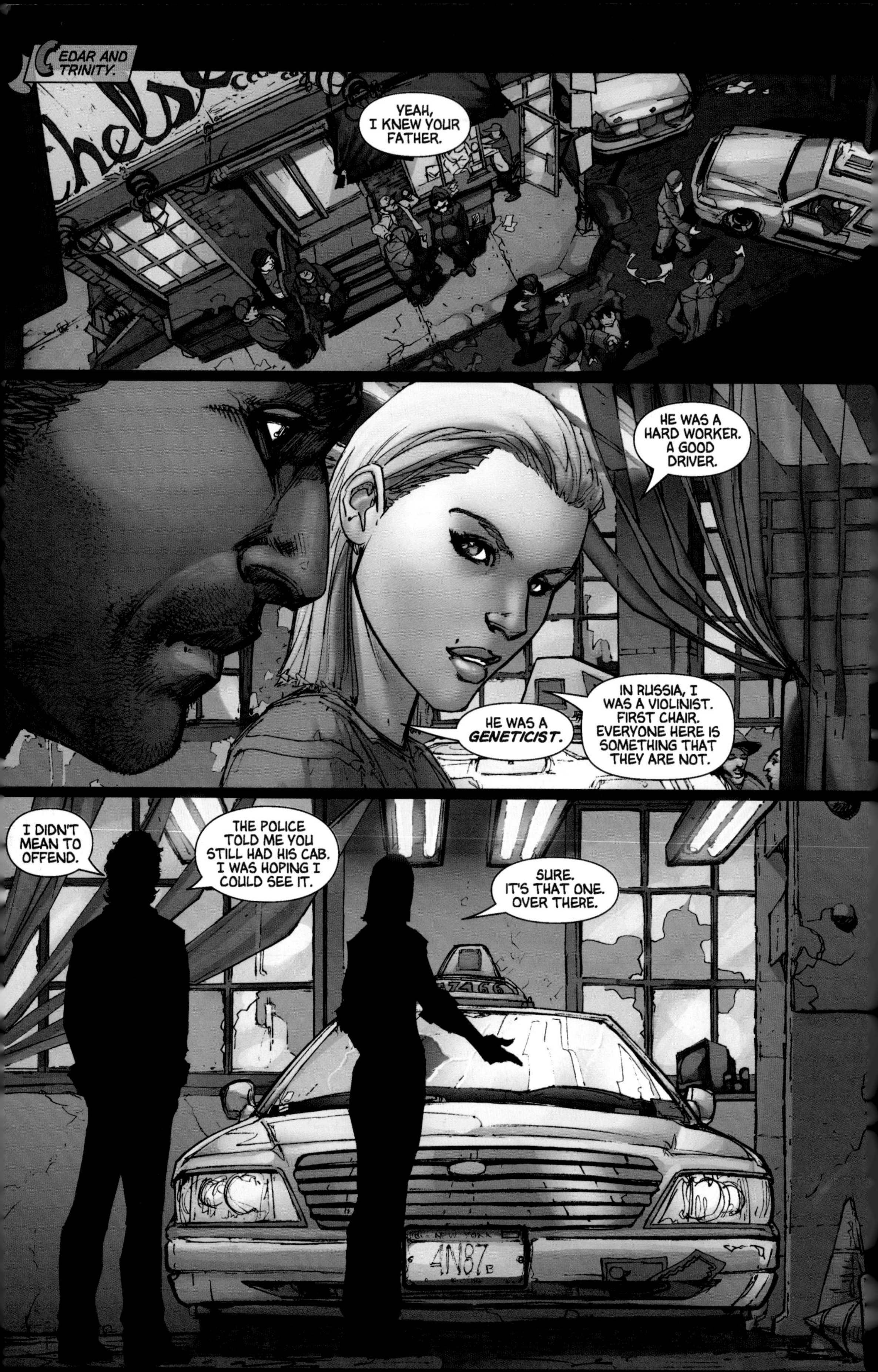
CEDAR AND TRINITY.
YEAH, I KNEW YOUR FATHER.
HE WAS A HARD WORKER. A GOOD DRIVER.
HE WAS A *GENETICIST*.
IN RUSSIA, I WAS A VIOLINIST. FIRST CHAIR. EVERYONE HERE IS SOMETHING THAT THEY ARE NOT.
I DIDN'T MEAN TO OFFEND.
THE POLICE TOLD ME YOU STILL HAD HIS CAB. I WAS HOPING I COULD SEE IT.
SURE. IT'S THAT ONE. OVER THERE.

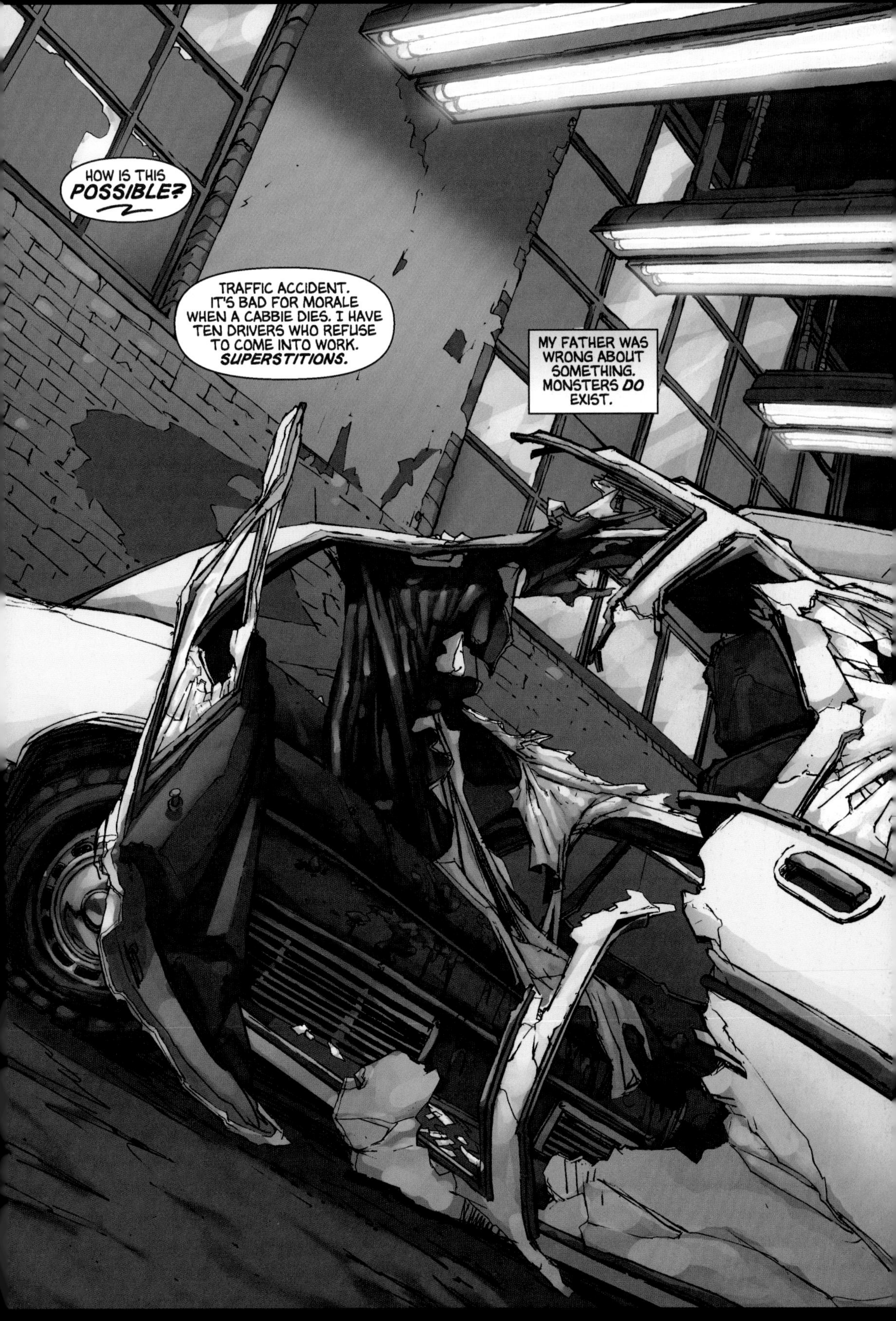
HOW IS THIS POSSIBLE?
TRAFFIC ACCIDENT. IT'S BAD FOR MORALE WHEN A CABBIE DIES. I HAVE TEN DRIVERS WHO REFUSE TO COME INTO WORK. SUPERSTITIONS.
MY FATHER WAS WRONG ABOUT SOMETHING. MONSTERS DO EXIST.

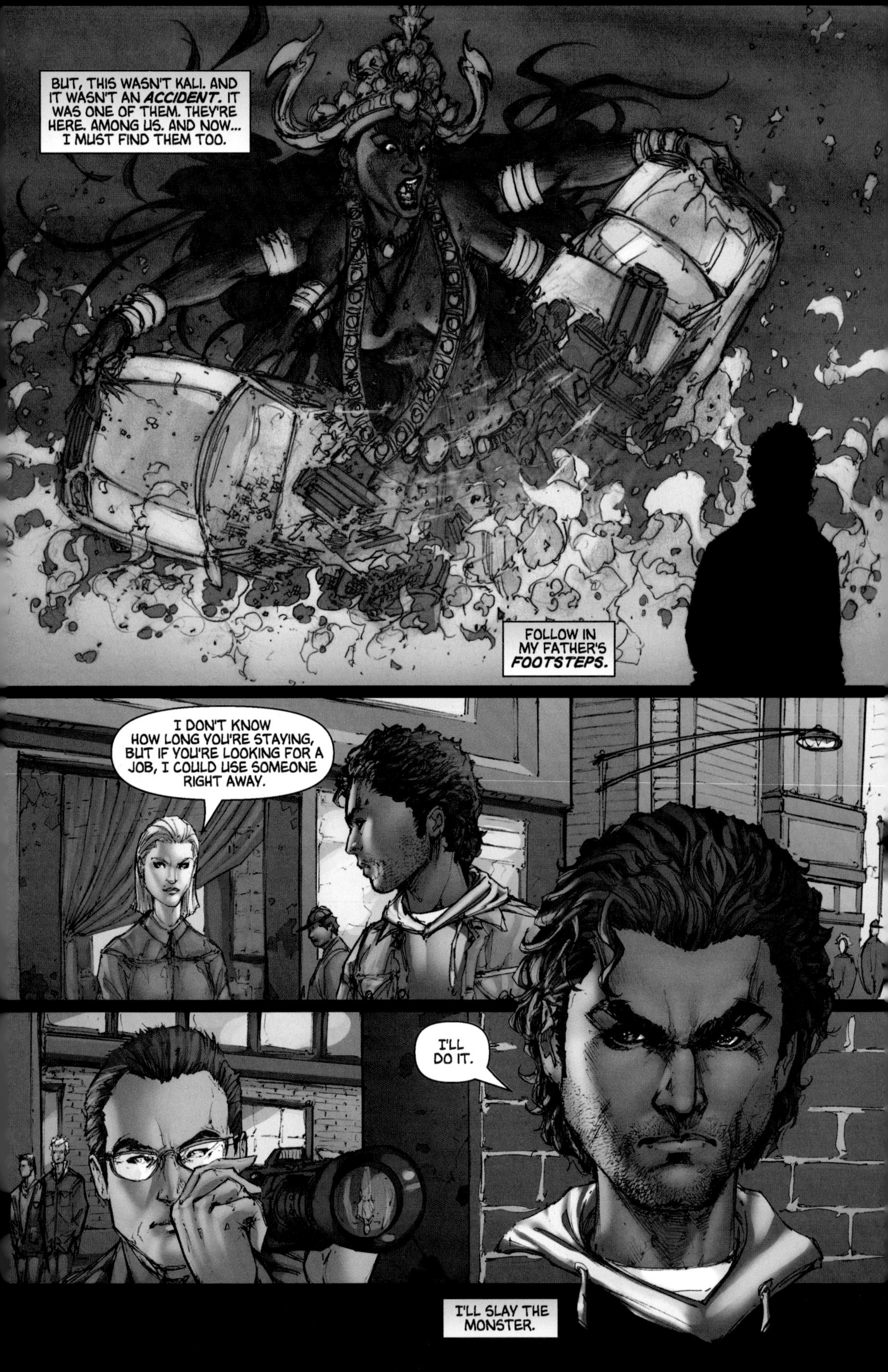
BUT, THIS WASN'T KALI. AND IT WASN'T AN ACCIDENT. IT WAS ONE OF THEM. THEY'RE HERE. AMONG US. AND NOW... I MUST FIND THEM TOO.
FOLLOW IN MY FATHER'S FOOTSTEPS.
I DON'T KNOW HOW LONG YOU'RE STAYING, BUT IF YOU'RE LOOKING FOR A JOB, I COULD USE SOMEONE RIGHT AWAY.
I'LL DO IT.
I'LL SLAY THE MONSTER.

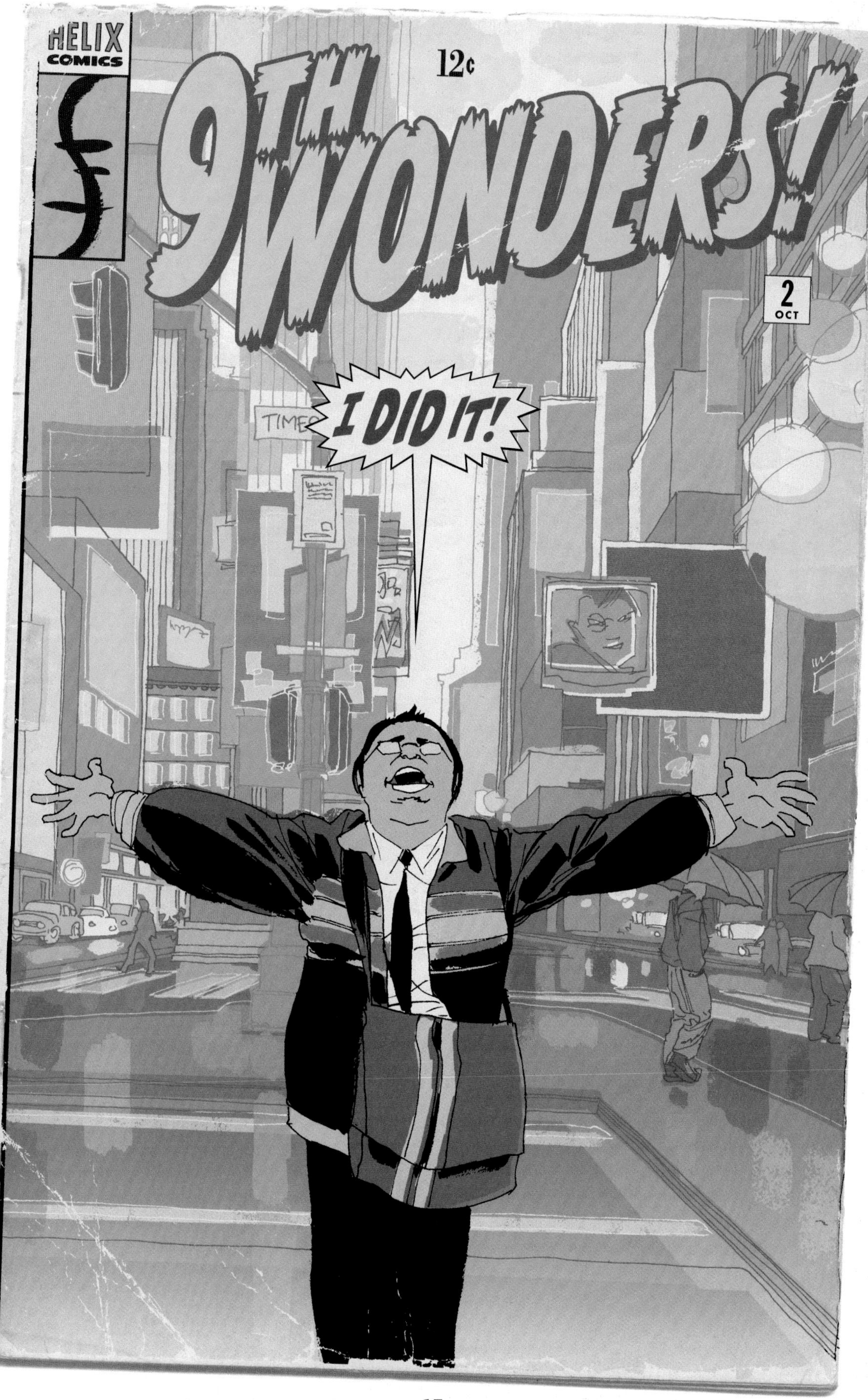
HELIX COMICS
12¢
9TH WONDERS!
2 OCT
TIMES
I DID IT!

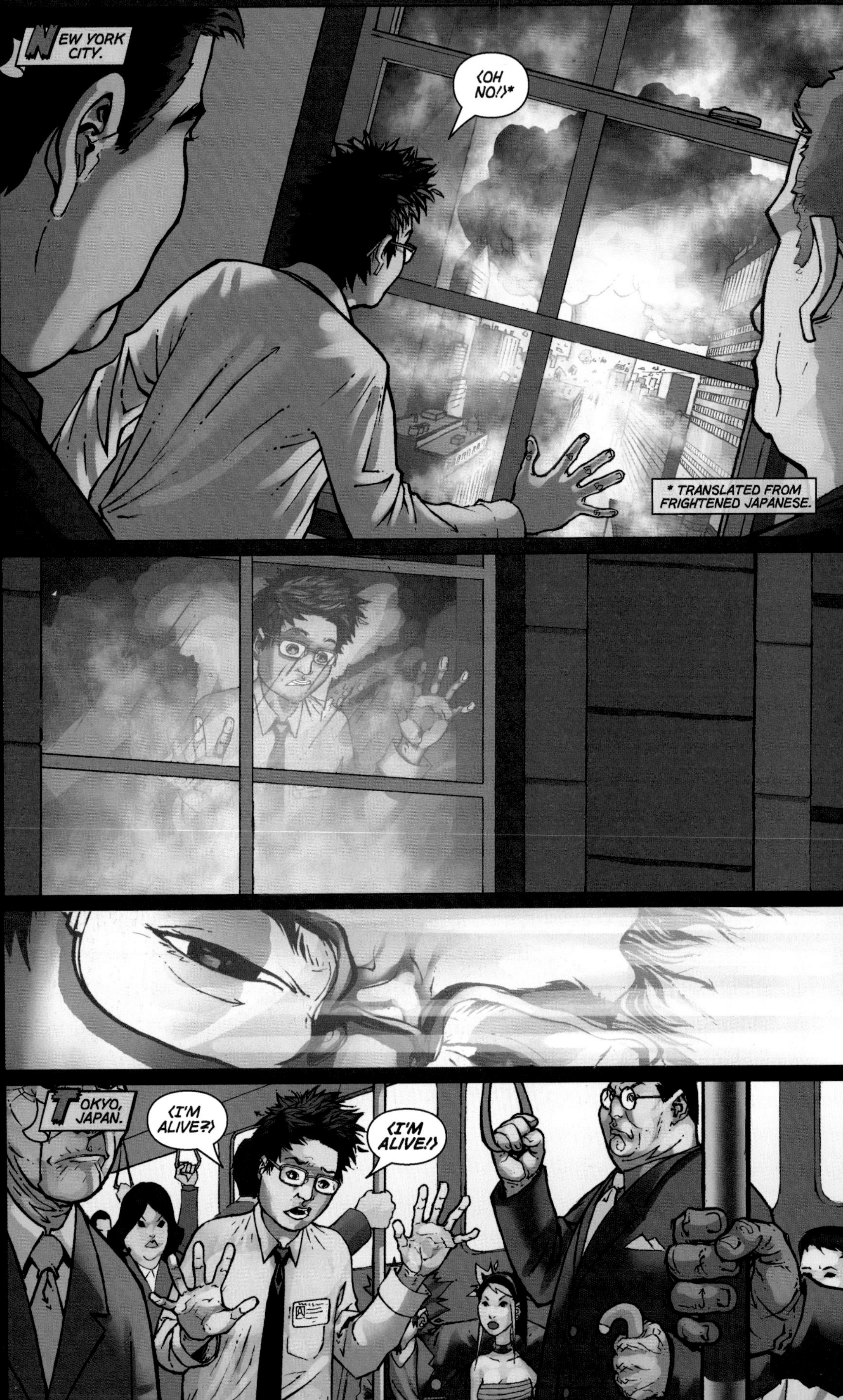
NEW YORK CITY.
‹OH NO!›*
* TRANSLATED FROM FRIGHTENED JAPANESE.
TOKYO, JAPAN.
‹I'M ALIVE?›
‹I'M ALIVE!›

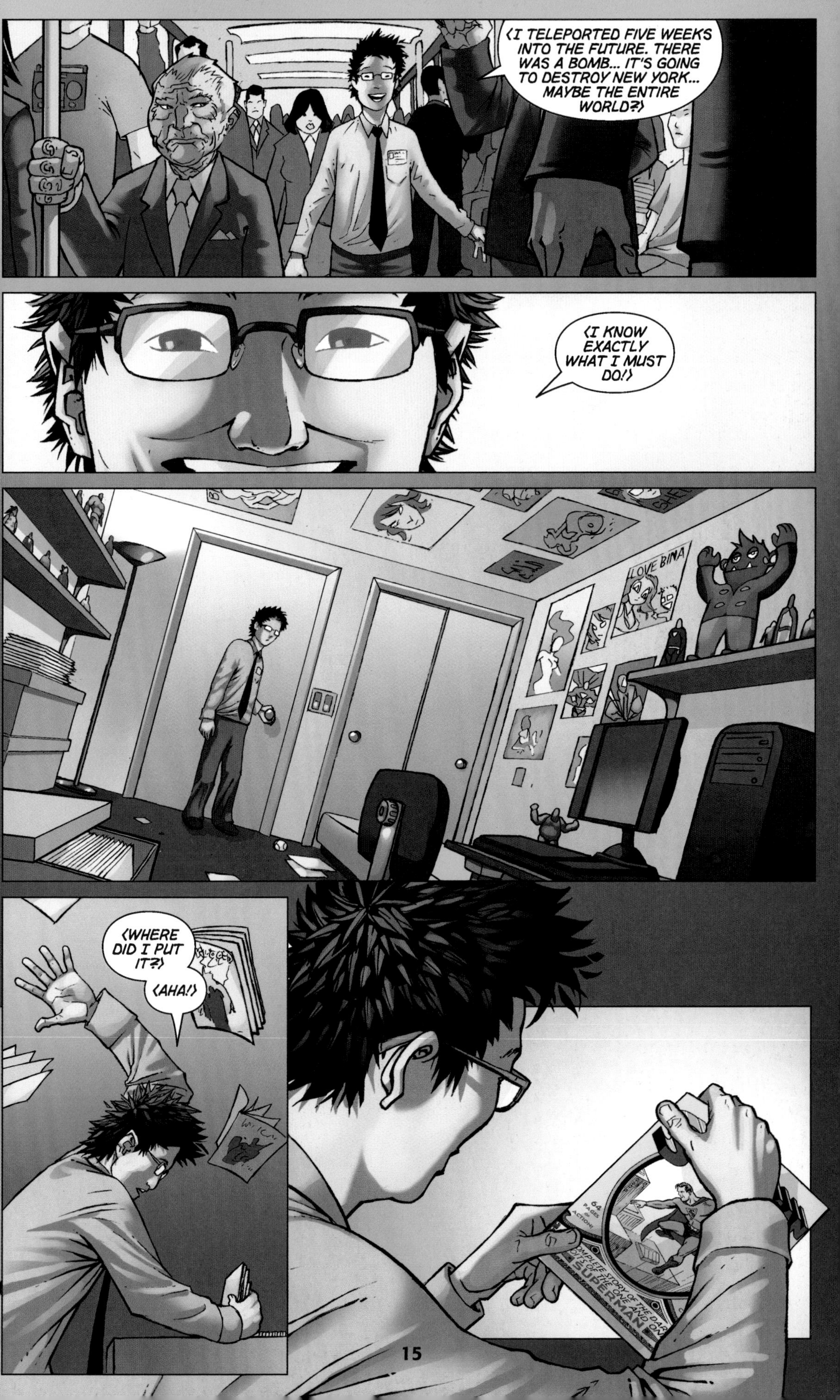

〈I TELEPORTED FIVE WEEKS INTO THE FUTURE. THERE WAS A BOMB... IT'S GOING TO DESTROY NEW YORK... MAYBE THE ENTIRE WORLD?〉
〈I KNOW EXACTLY WHAT I MUST DO!〉
LOVE BINA
〈WHERE DID I PUT IT?〉
〈AHA!〉
64 PAGES OF ACTION!
COMPLETE STORY OF THE DARING EXPLOITS OF THE ONE AND ONLY SUPERMAN

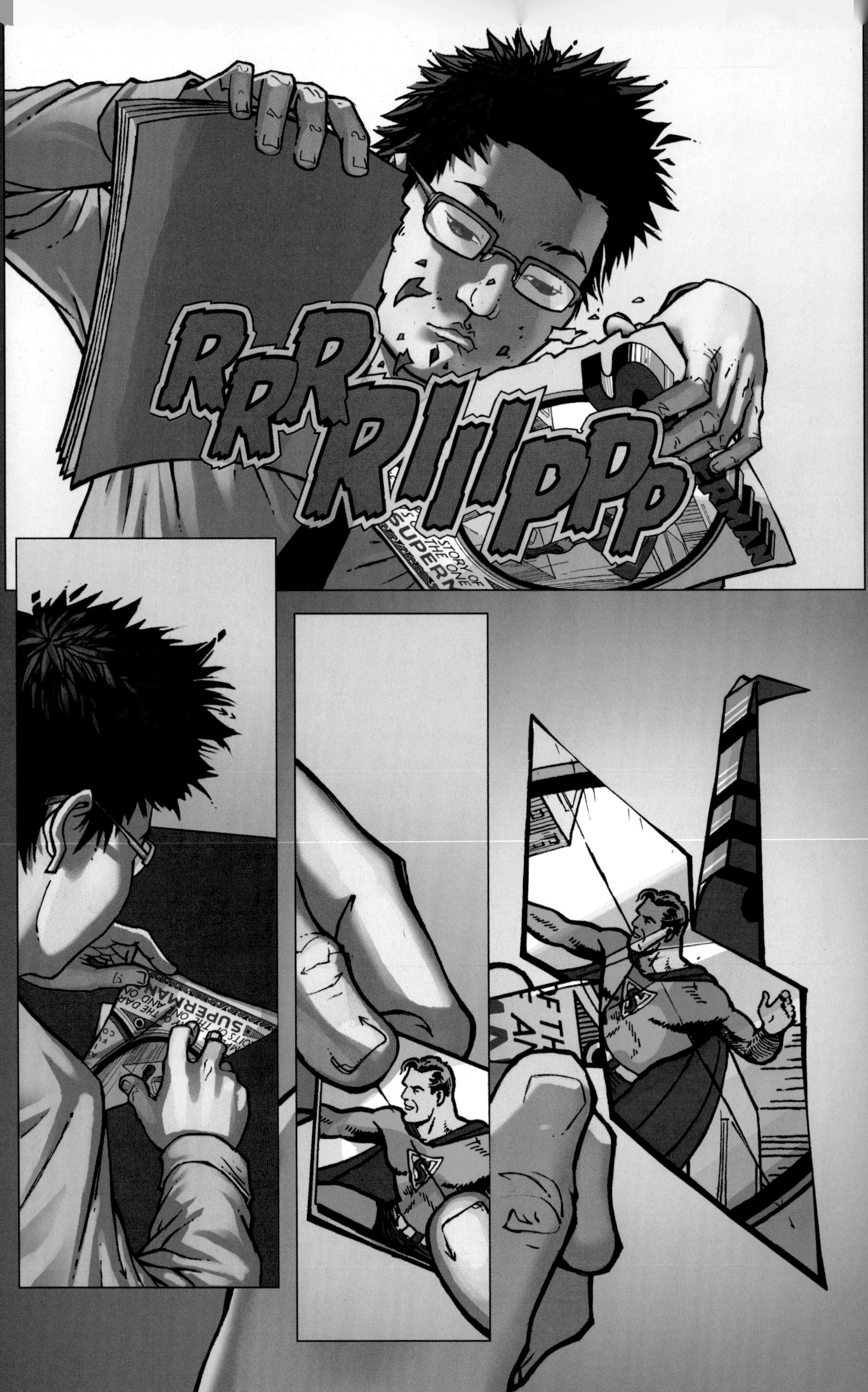
RRRRIIPPP

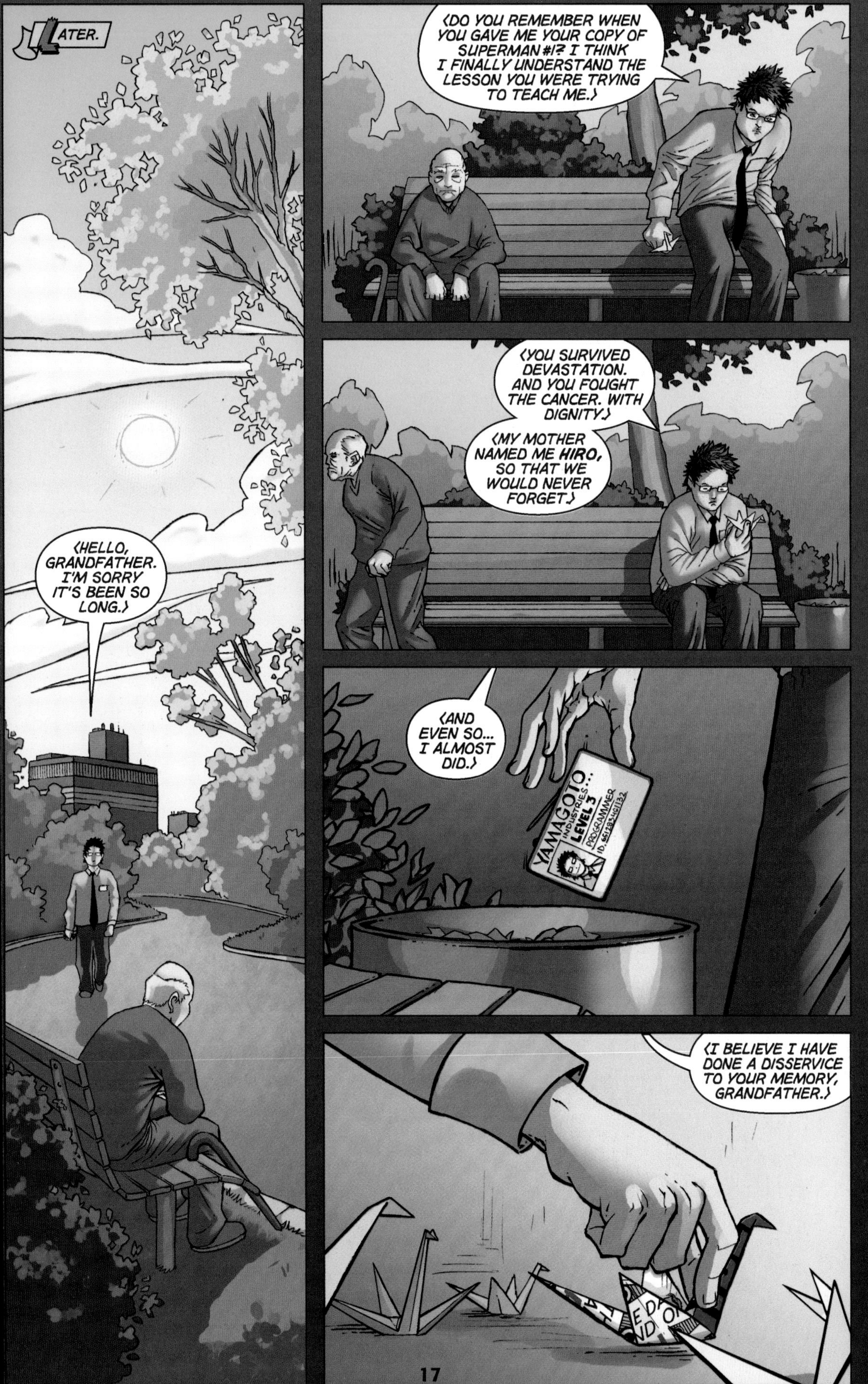
LATER.
‹HELLO, GRANDFATHER. I'M SORRY IT'S BEEN SO LONG.›
‹DO YOU REMEMBER WHEN YOU GAVE ME YOUR COPY OF SUPERMAN #1? I THINK I FINALLY UNDERSTAND THE LESSON YOU WERE TRYING TO TEACH ME.›
‹YOU SURVIVED DEVASTATION. AND YOU FOUGHT THE CANCER. WITH DIGNITY.›
‹MY MOTHER NAMED ME HIRO, SO THAT WE WOULD NEVER FORGET.›
‹AND EVEN SO... I ALMOST DID.›
YAMAGOTO INDUSTRIES... LEVEL 3 PROGRAMMER
‹I BELIEVE I HAVE DONE A DISSERVICE TO YOUR MEMORY, GRANDFATHER.›

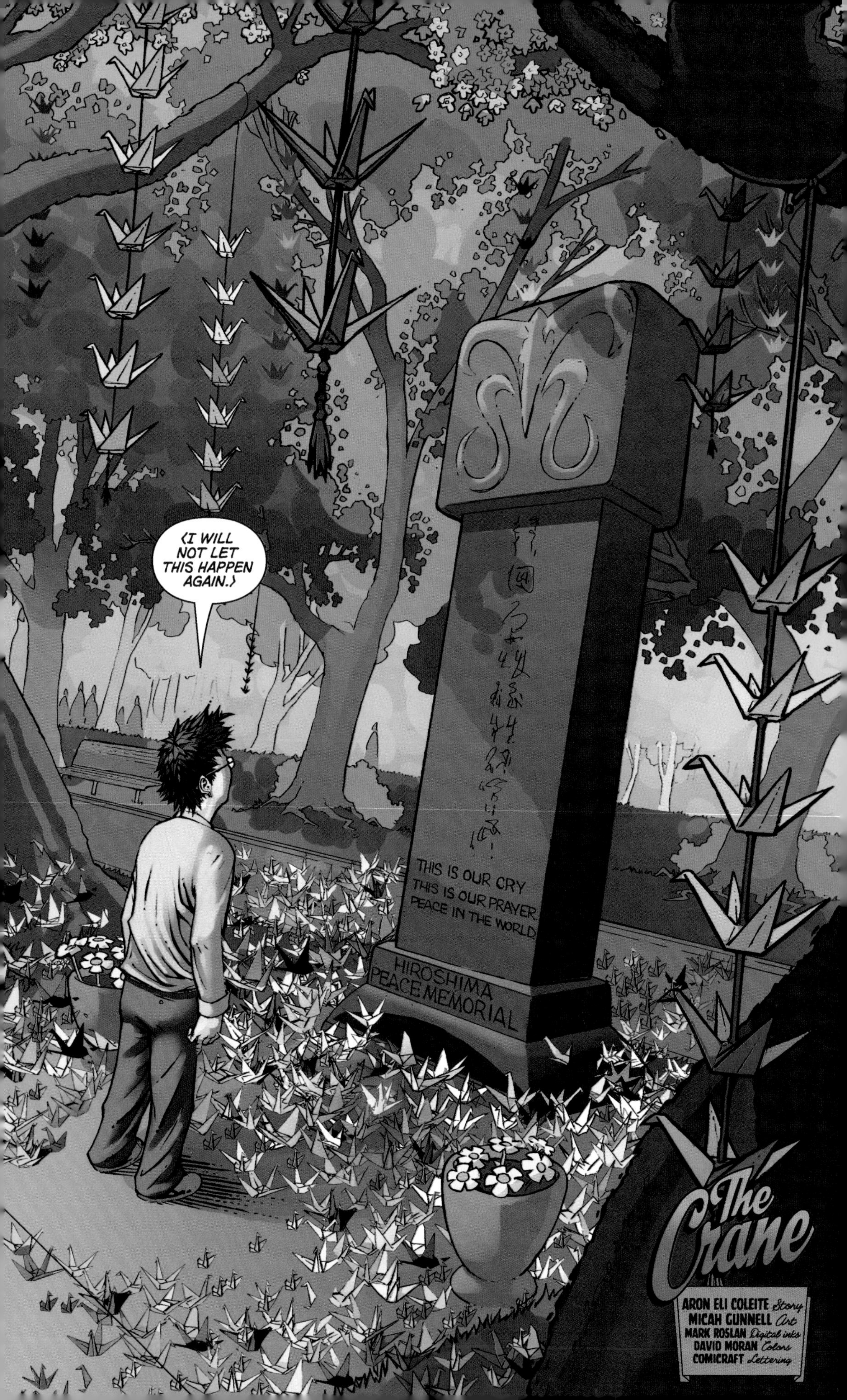
‹I WILL NOT LET THIS HAPPEN AGAIN.›
THIS IS OUR CRY
THIS IS OUR PRAYER
PEACE IN THE WORLD
HIROSHIMA PEACE MEMORIAL
The Crane
ARON ELI COLEITE Story
MICAH GUNNELL Art
MARK ROSLAN Digital inks
DAVID MORAN Colors
COMICRAFT Lettering

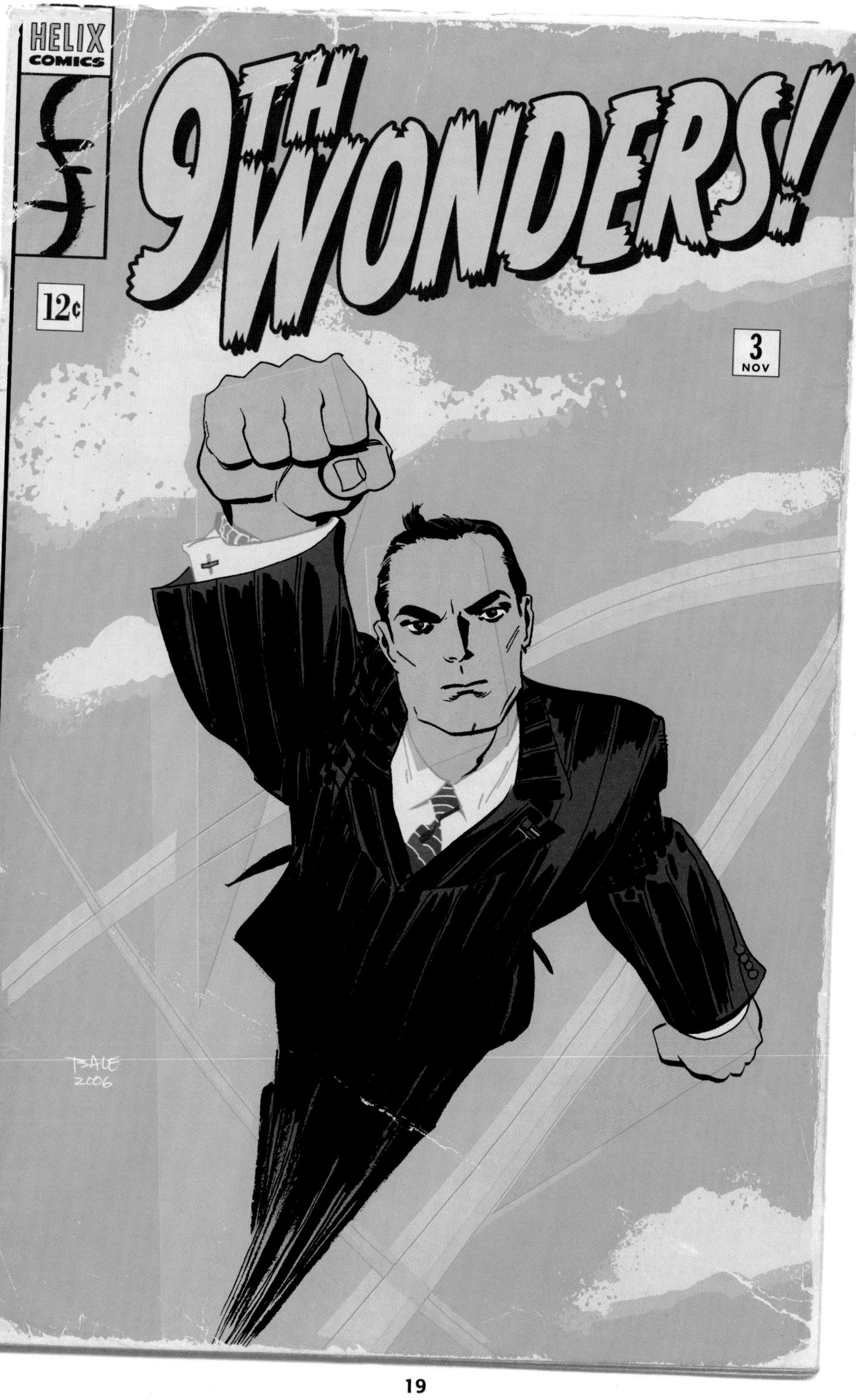
HELIX COMICS
9TH WONDERS!
12¢
3 NOV
BALE 2006

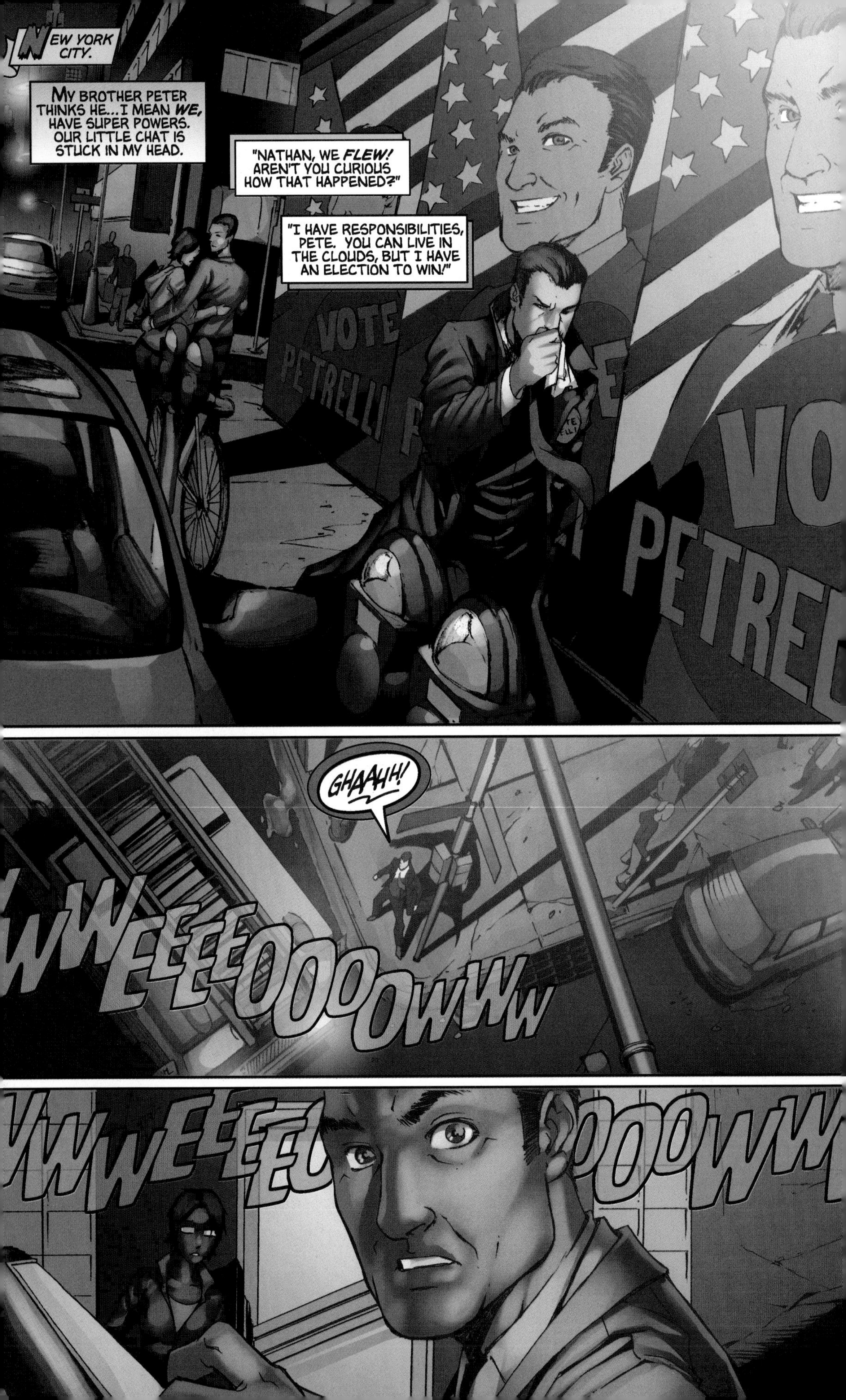
NEW YORK CITY.
MY BROTHER PETER THINKS HE...I MEAN WE, HAVE SUPER POWERS. OUR LITTLE CHAT IS STUCK IN MY HEAD.
"NATHAN, WE FLEW! AREN'T YOU CURIOUS HOW THAT HAPPENED?"
"I HAVE RESPONSIBILITIES, PETE. YOU CAN LIVE IN THE CLOUDS, BUT I HAVE AN ELECTION TO WIN!"
VOTE PETRELLI
GHAAHH!
WWEEEEOOOOWWW
WWWEEEEOOOOWWW

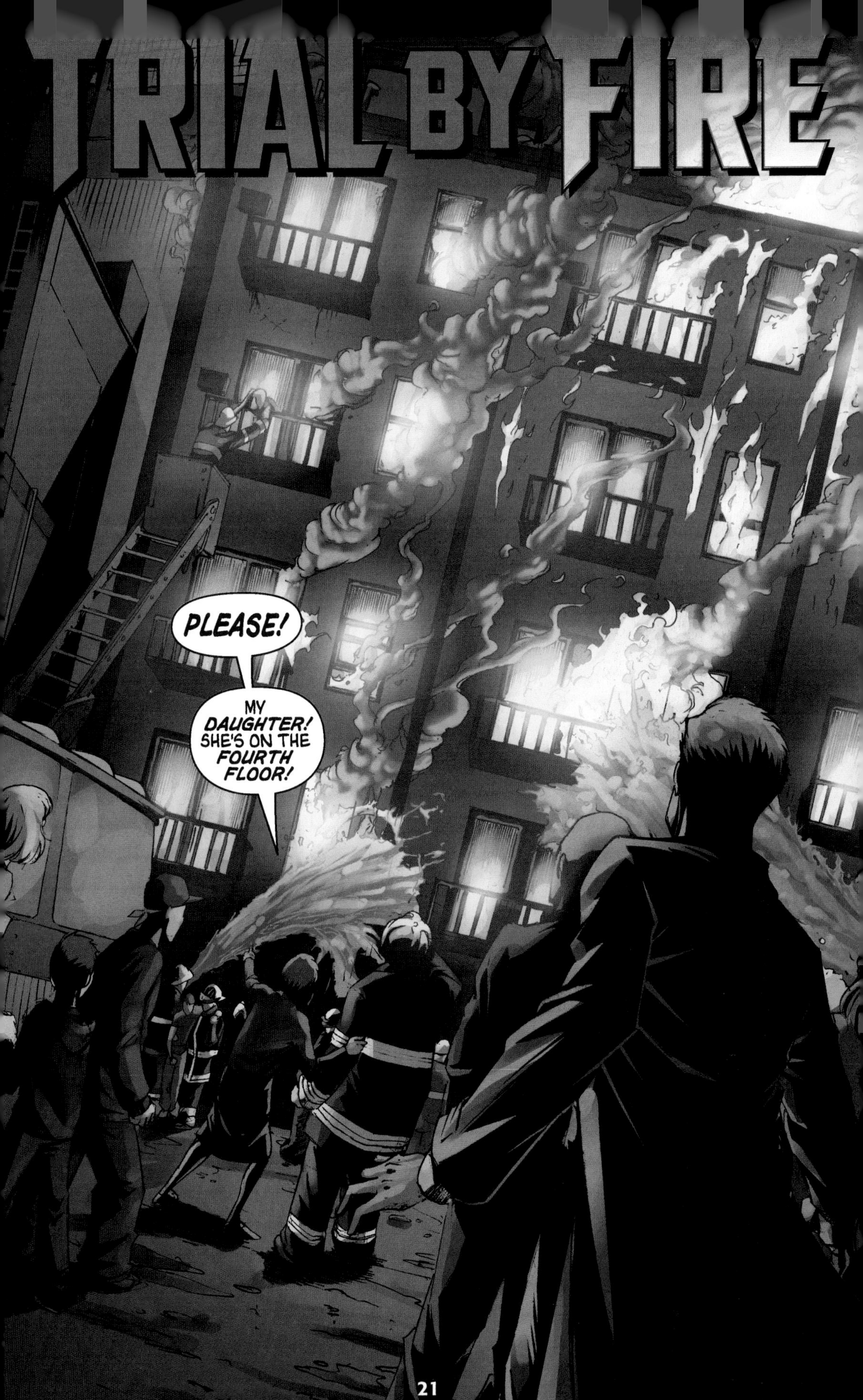
TRIAL BY FIRE
PLEASE!
MY DAUGHTER! SHE'S ON THE FOURTH FLOOR!

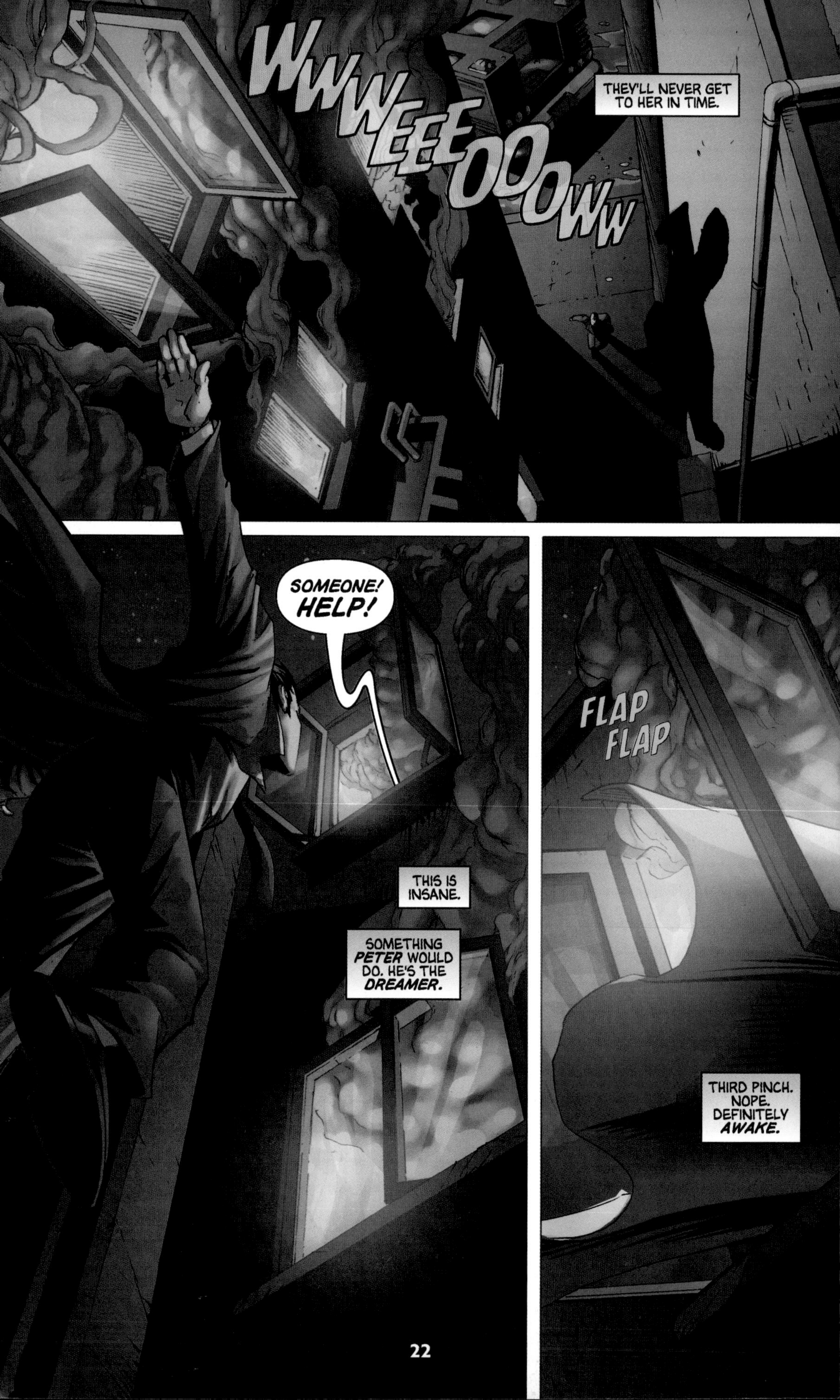
WWWEEEOOOWW
THEY'LL NEVER GET TO HER IN TIME.
SOMEONE! HELP!
THIS IS INSANE.
SOMETHING PETER WOULD DO. HE'S THE DREAMER.
FLAP FLAP
THIRD PINCH. NOPE. DEFINITELY AWAKE.

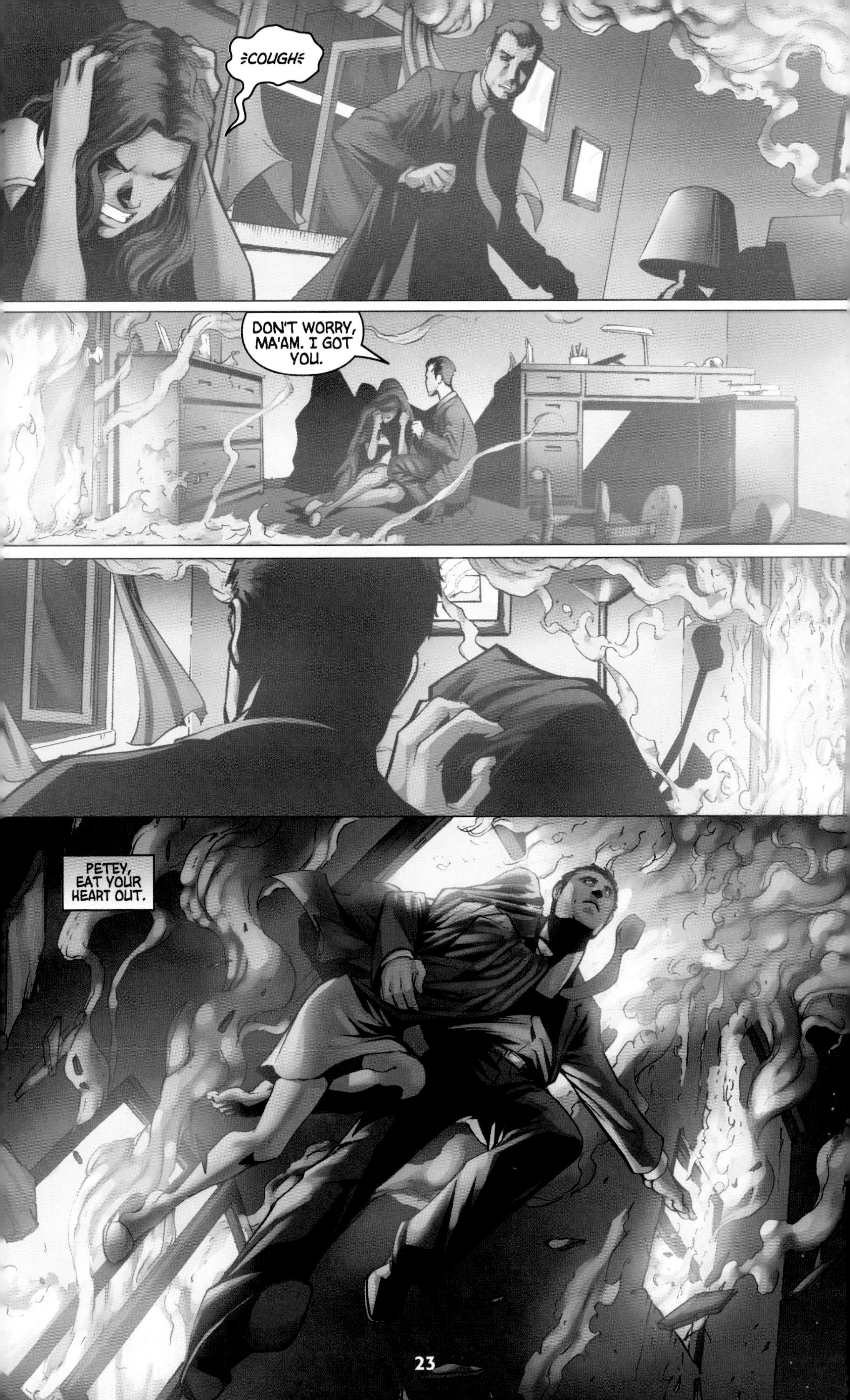
COUGH
DON'T WORRY, MA'AM. I GOT YOU.
PETEY, EAT YOUR HEART OUT.

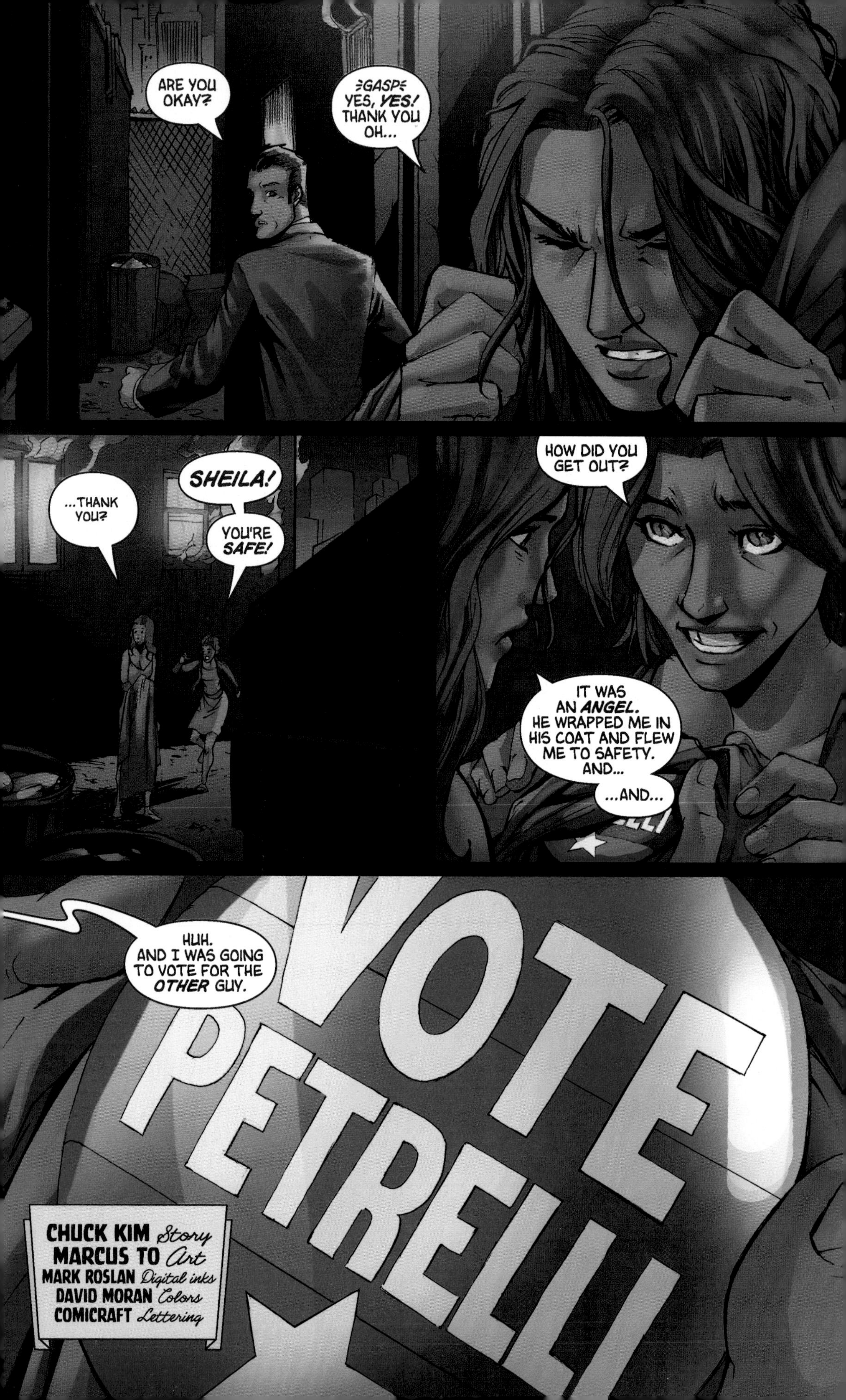
ARE YOU OKAY?
GASP YES, YES! THANK YOU OH...
...THANK YOU?
SHEILA!
YOU'RE SAFE!
HOW DID YOU GET OUT?
IT WAS AN ANGEL. HE WRAPPED ME IN HIS COAT AND FLEW ME TO SAFETY. AND...
...AND...
HUH. AND I WAS GOING TO VOTE FOR THE OTHER GUY.
VOTE PETRELLI
CHUCK KIM Story
MARCUS TO Art
MARK ROSLAN Digital inks
DAVID MORAN Colors
COMICRAFT Lettering

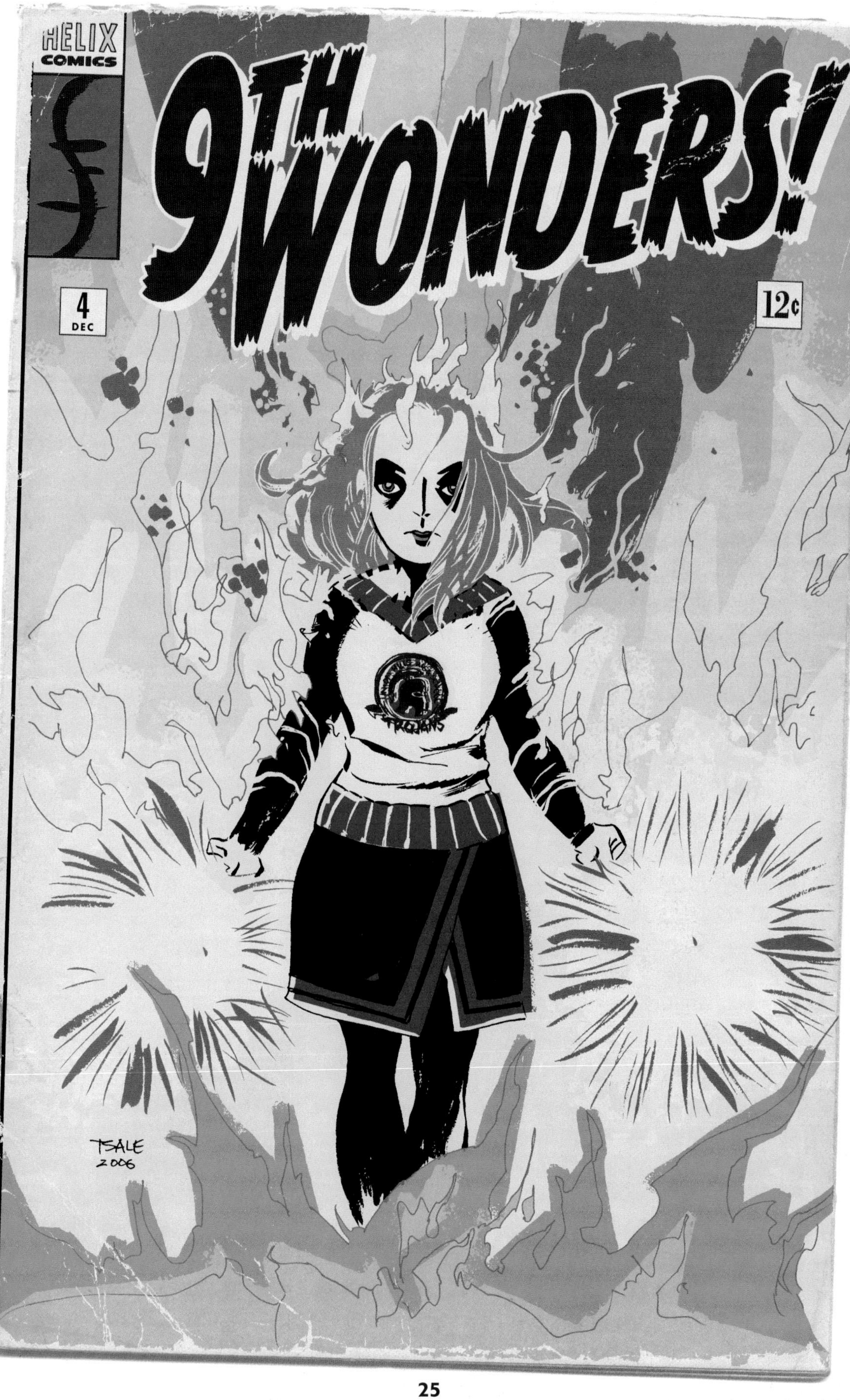
HELIX
COMICS
9TH WONDERS!
4
DEC
12¢
TSALE
2006

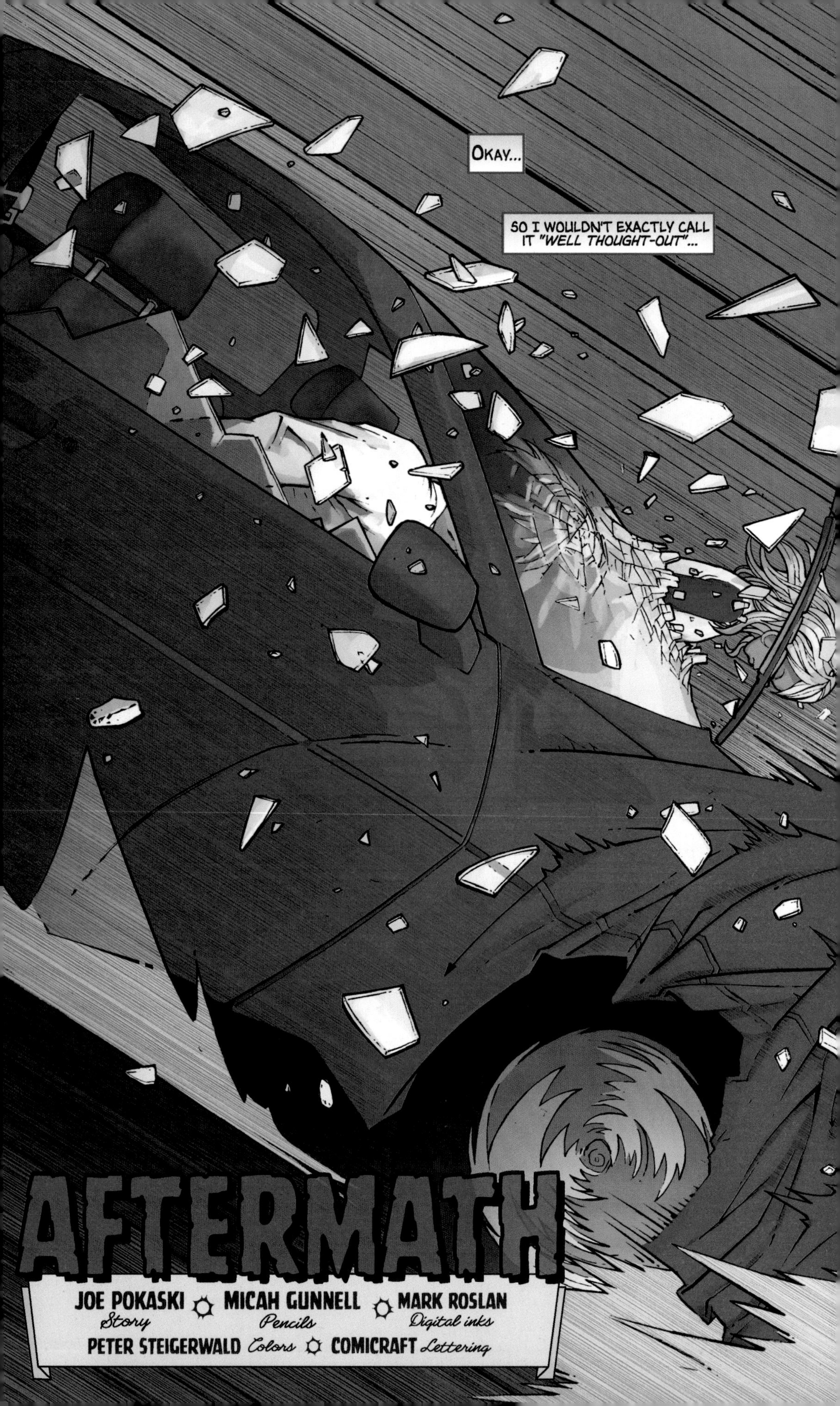
OKAY...
SO I WOULDN'T EXACTLY CALL IT "WELL THOUGHT-OUT"...
AFTERMATH
JOE POKASKI Story
MICAH GUNNELL Pencils
MARK ROSLAN Digital inks
PETER STEIGERWALD Colors
COMICRAFT Lettering

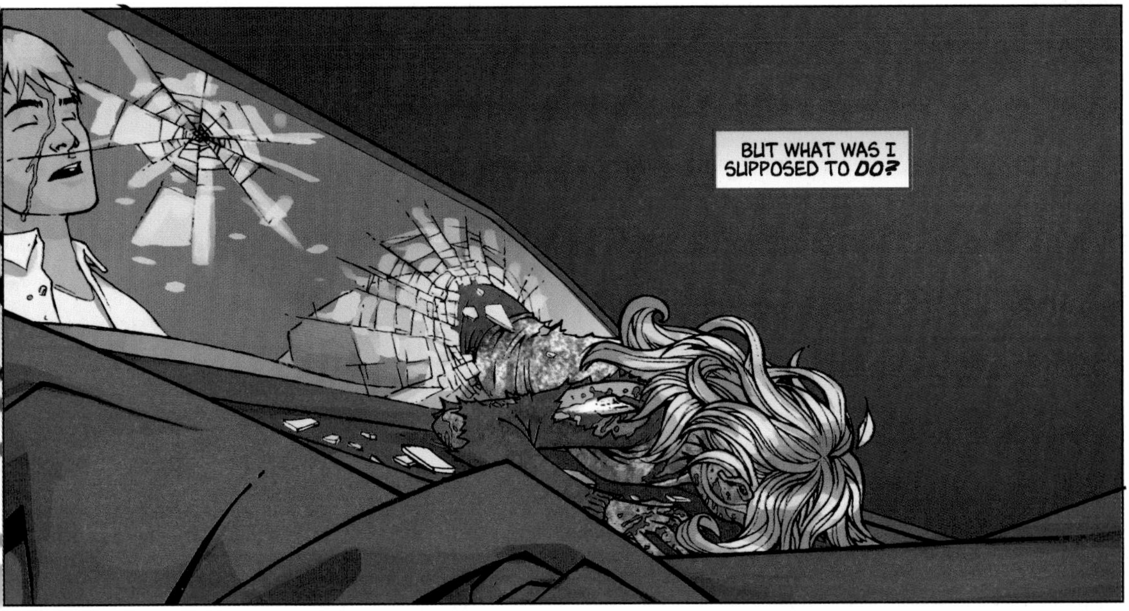
BUT WHAT WAS I SUPPOSED TO *DO?*

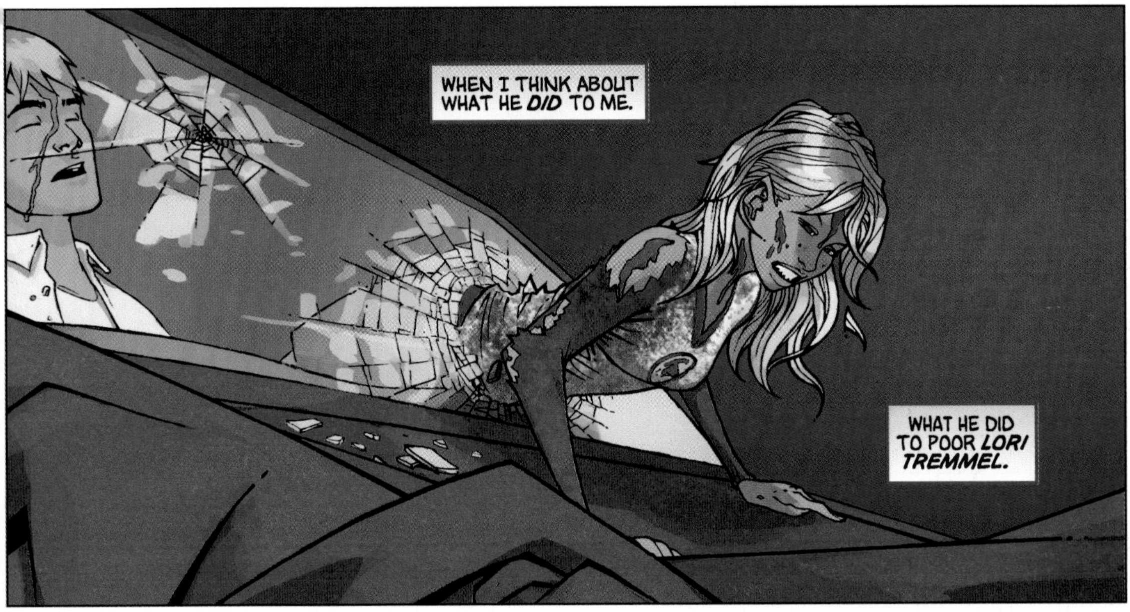
WHEN I THINK ABOUT WHAT HE *DID* TO ME.
WHAT HE DID TO POOR *LORI TREMMEL.*

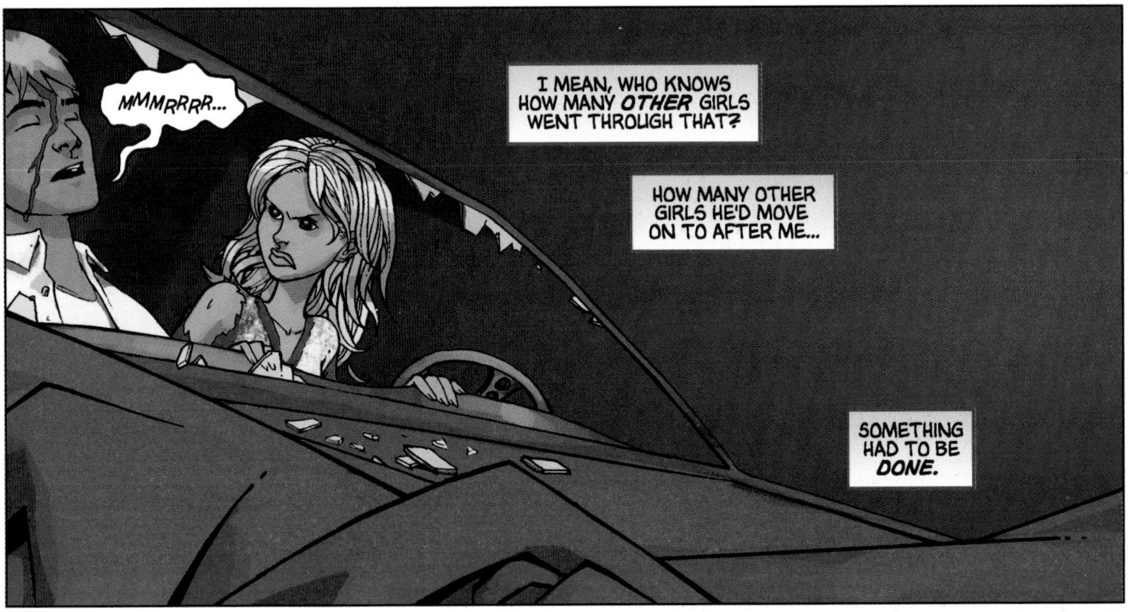
MMMRRRR...
I MEAN, WHO KNOWS HOW MANY *OTHER* GIRLS WENT THROUGH THAT?
HOW MANY OTHER GIRLS HE'D MOVE ON TO AFTER ME...
SOMETHING HAD TO BE *DONE.*

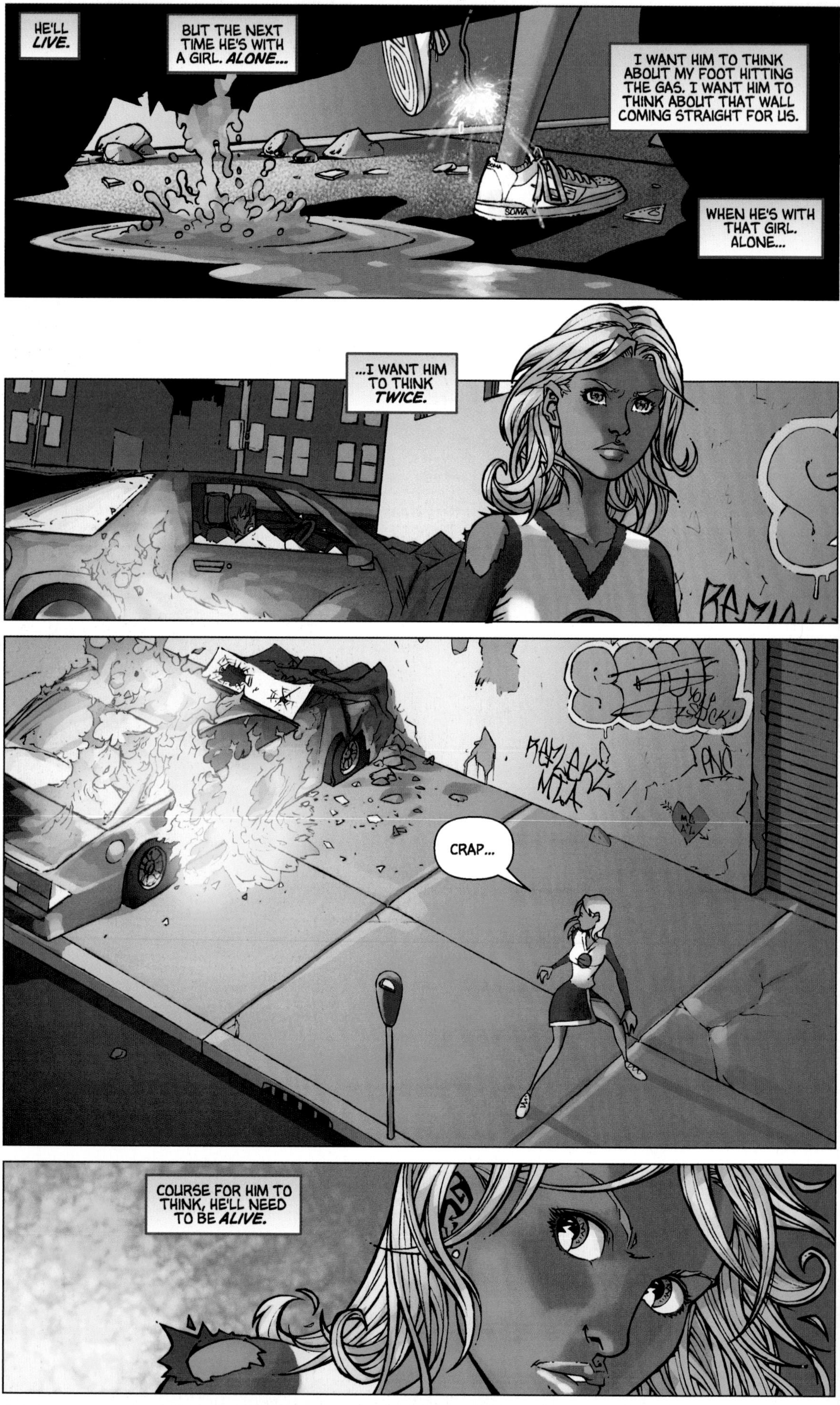

HE'LL *LIVE.*
BUT THE NEXT TIME HE'S WITH A GIRL. *ALONE...*
I WANT HIM TO THINK ABOUT MY FOOT HITTING THE GAS. I WANT HIM TO THINK ABOUT THAT WALL COMING STRAIGHT FOR US.
WHEN HE'S WITH THAT GIRL. ALONE...
...I WANT HIM TO THINK *TWICE.*
CRAP...
COURSE FOR HIM TO THINK, HE'LL NEED TO BE *ALIVE.*

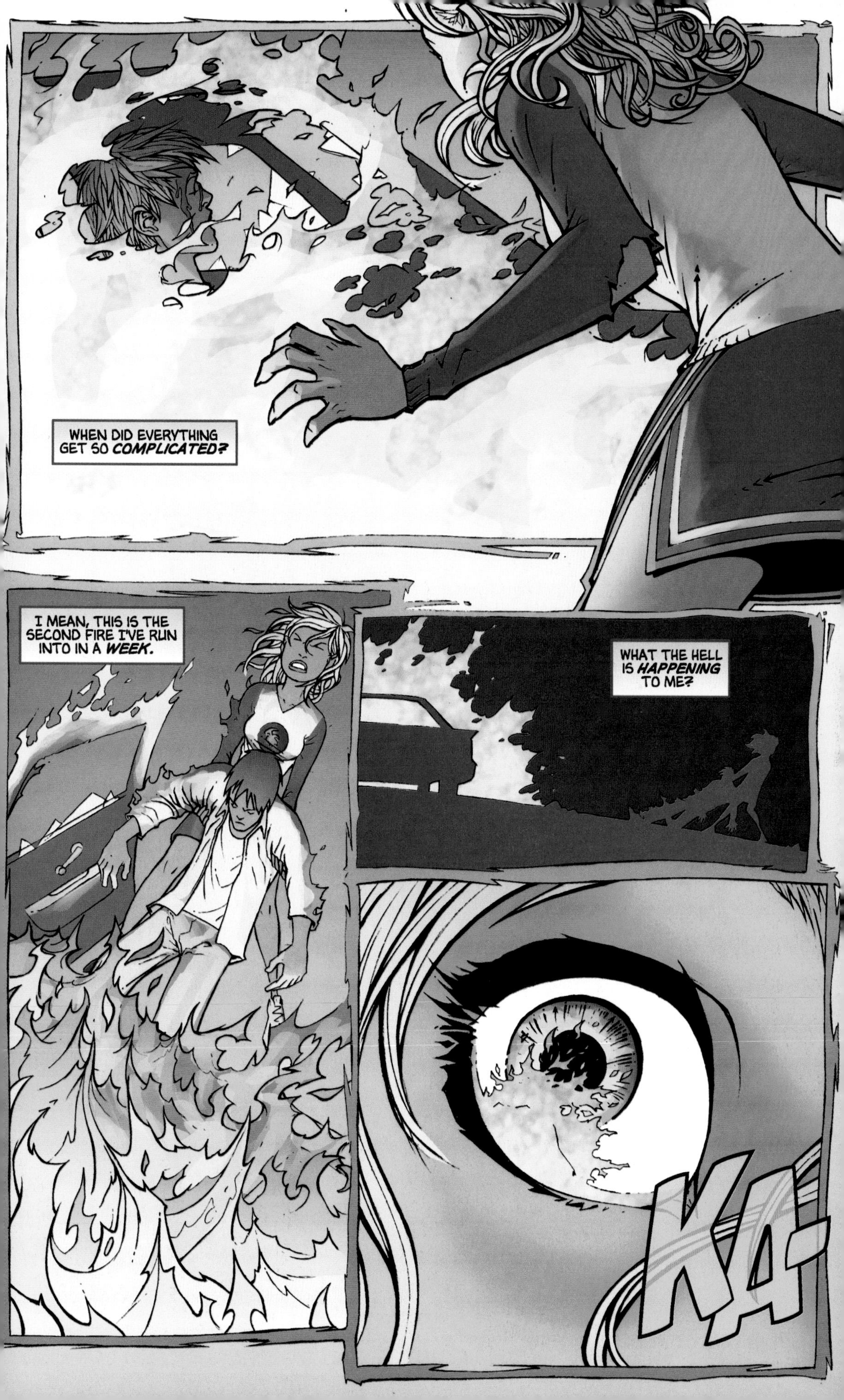
WHEN DID EVERYTHING GET SO *COMPLICATED?*
I MEAN, THIS IS THE SECOND FIRE I'VE RUN INTO IN A *WEEK.*
WHAT THE HELL IS *HAPPENING* TO ME?
KA-

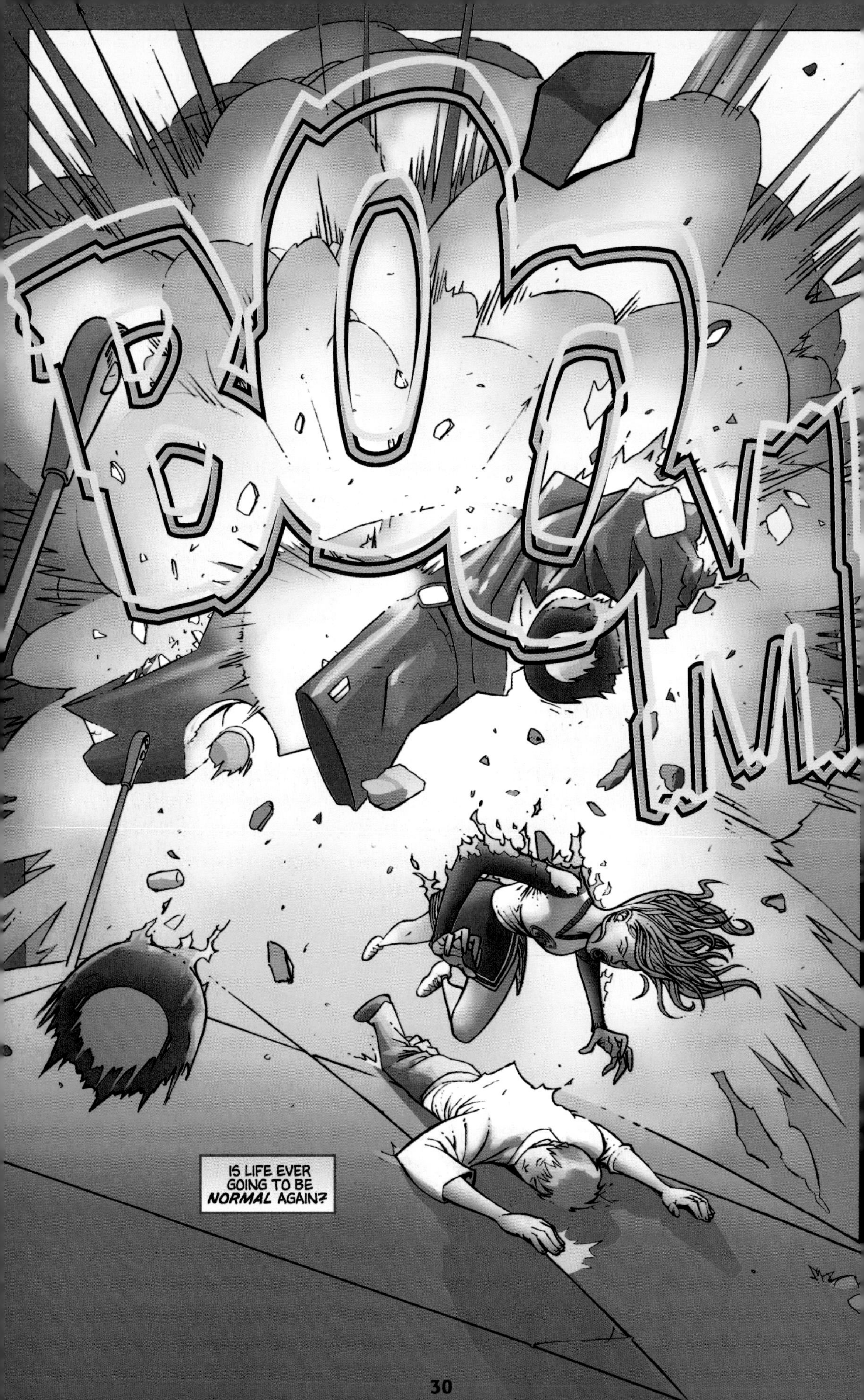
BOOOM
IS LIFE EVER GOING TO BE NORMAL AGAIN?

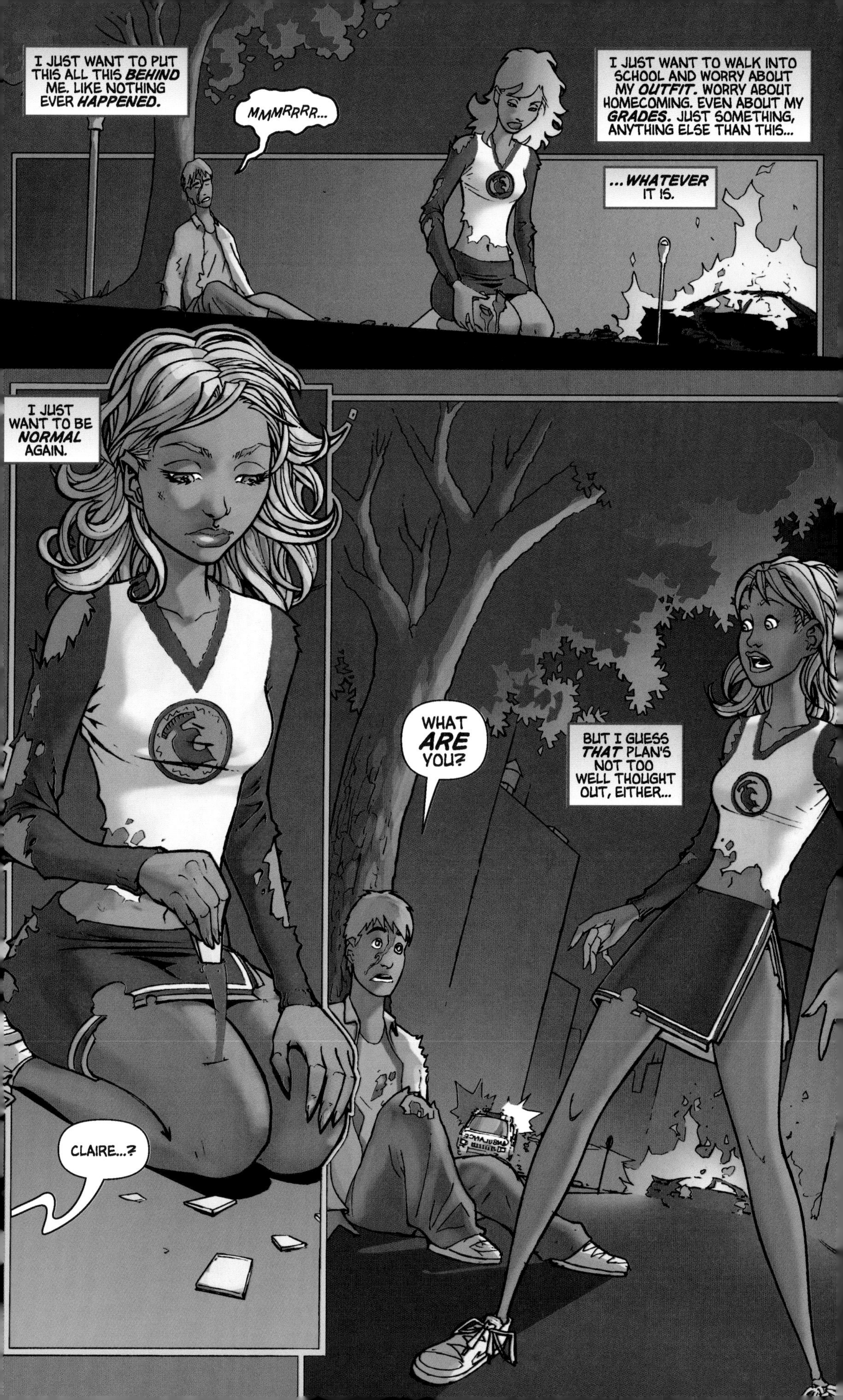
I JUST WANT TO PUT THIS ALL THIS *BEHIND* ME. LIKE NOTHING EVER *HAPPENED.*
MMMRRRR...
I JUST WANT TO WALK INTO SCHOOL AND WORRY ABOUT MY *OUTFIT*. WORRY ABOUT HOMECOMING. EVEN ABOUT MY *GRADES*. JUST SOMETHING, ANYTHING ELSE THAN THIS...
...*WHATEVER* IT IS.
I JUST WANT TO BE *NORMAL* AGAIN.
CLAIRE...?
WHAT *ARE* YOU?
BUT I GUESS *THAT* PLAN'S NOT TOO WELL THOUGHT OUT, EITHER...

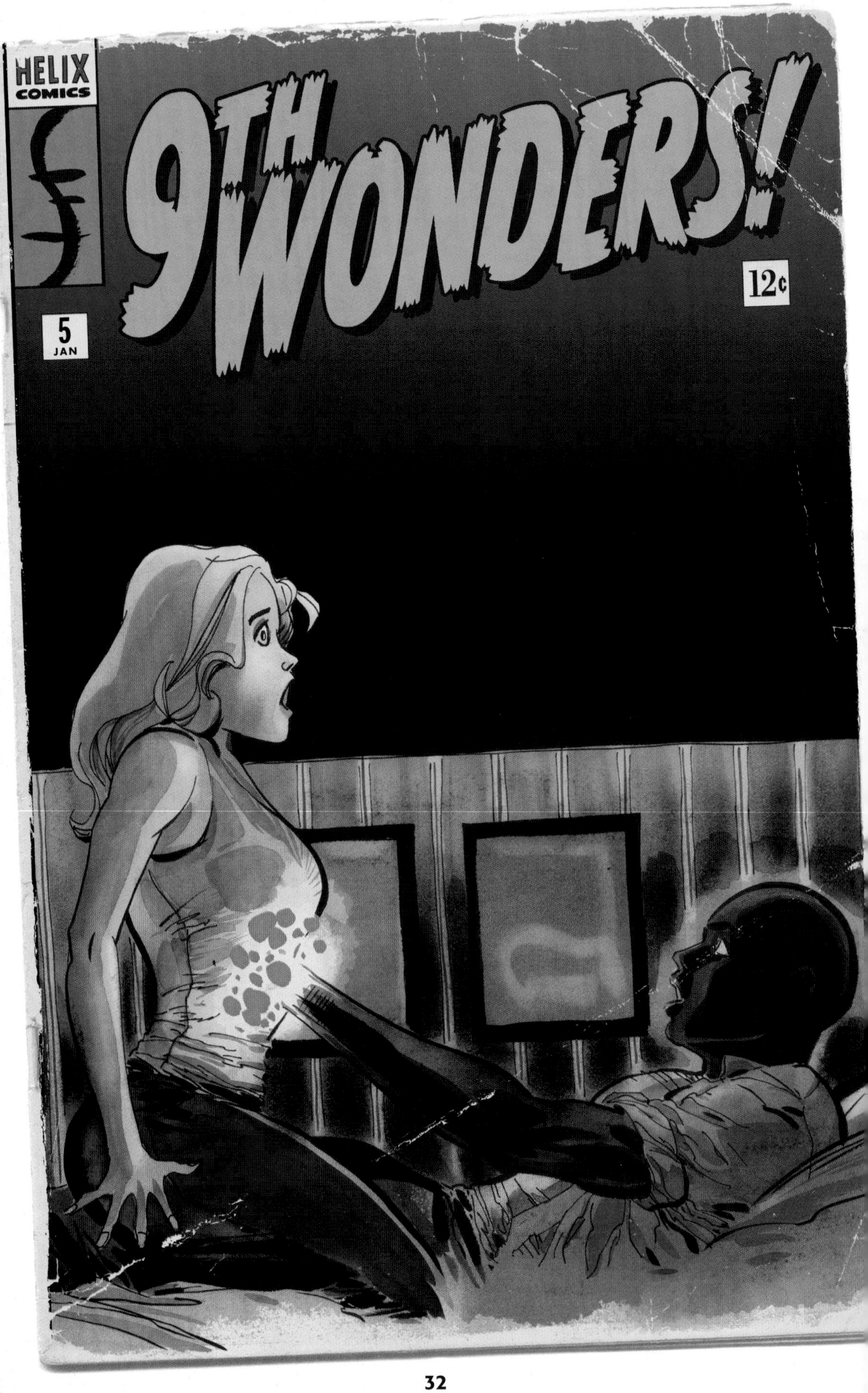
HELIX COMICS
9TH WONDERS!
12¢
5
JAN

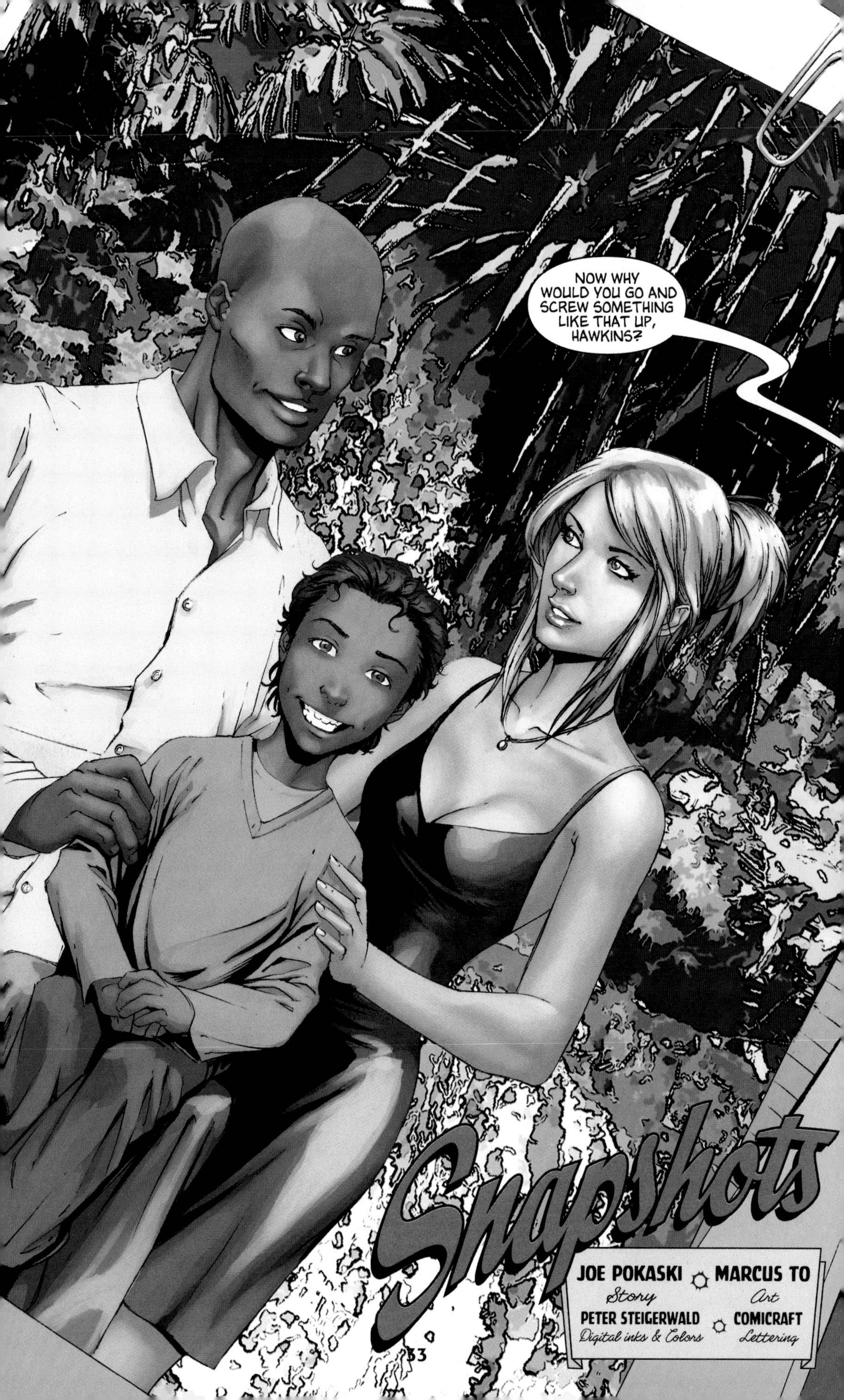
NOW WHY WOULD YOU GO AND SCREW SOMETHING LIKE THAT UP, HAWKINS?
Snapshots
JOE POKASKI Story
MARCUS TO Art
PETER STEIGERWALD Digital inks & Colors
COMICRAFT Lettering

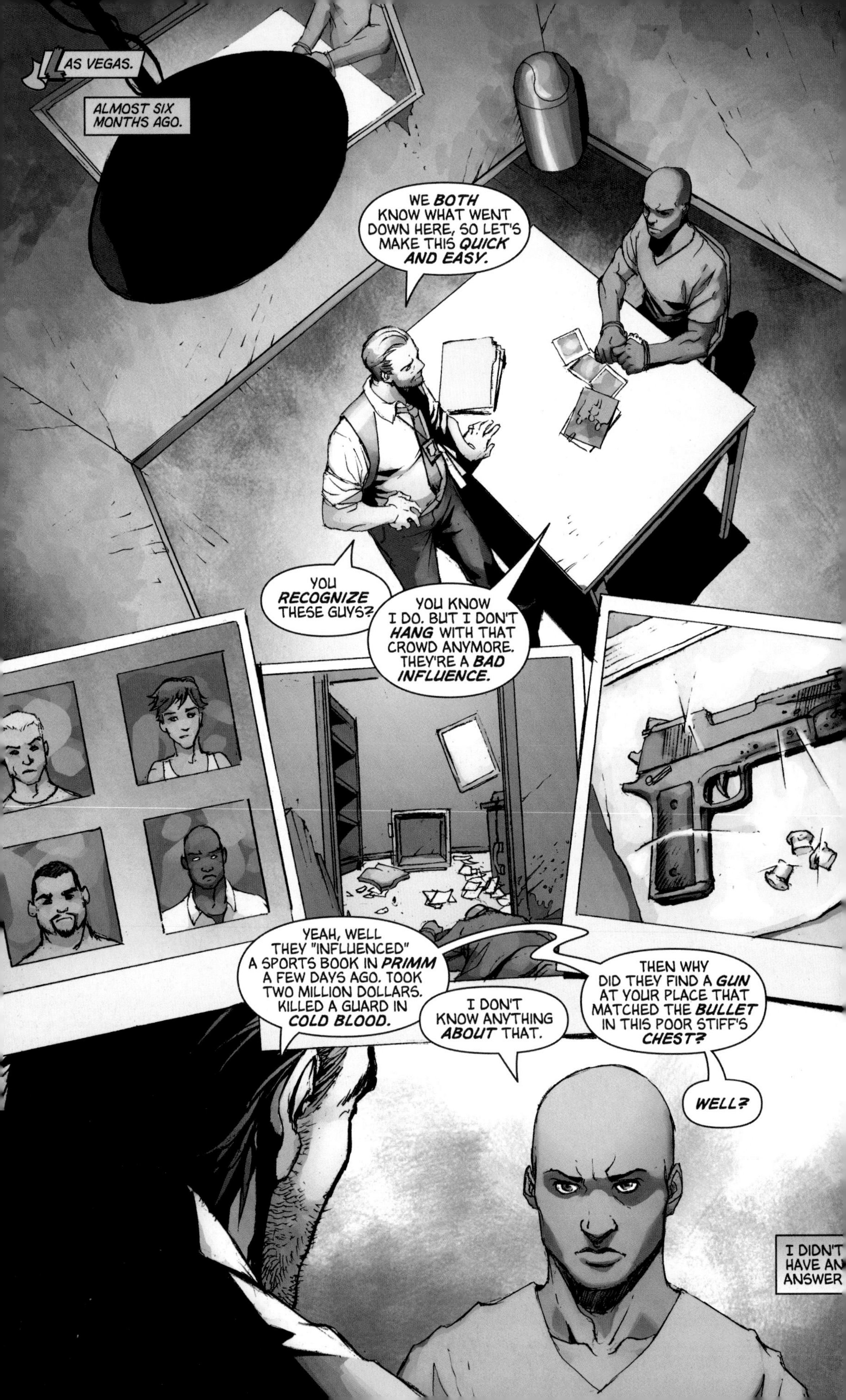
AS VEGAS.
ALMOST SIX MONTHS AGO.
WE BOTH KNOW WHAT WENT DOWN HERE, SO LET'S MAKE THIS QUICK AND EASY.
YOU RECOGNIZE THESE GUYS?
YOU KNOW I DO. BUT I DON'T HANG WITH THAT CROWD ANYMORE. THEY'RE A BAD INFLUENCE.
YEAH, WELL THEY "INFLUENCED" A SPORTS BOOK IN PRIMM A FEW DAYS AGO. TOOK TWO MILLION DOLLARS. KILLED A GUARD IN COLD BLOOD.
I DON'T KNOW ANYTHING ABOUT THAT.
THEN WHY DID THEY FIND A GUN AT YOUR PLACE THAT MATCHED THE BULLET IN THIS POOR STIFF'S CHEST?
WELL?
I DIDN'T HAVE AN ANSWER

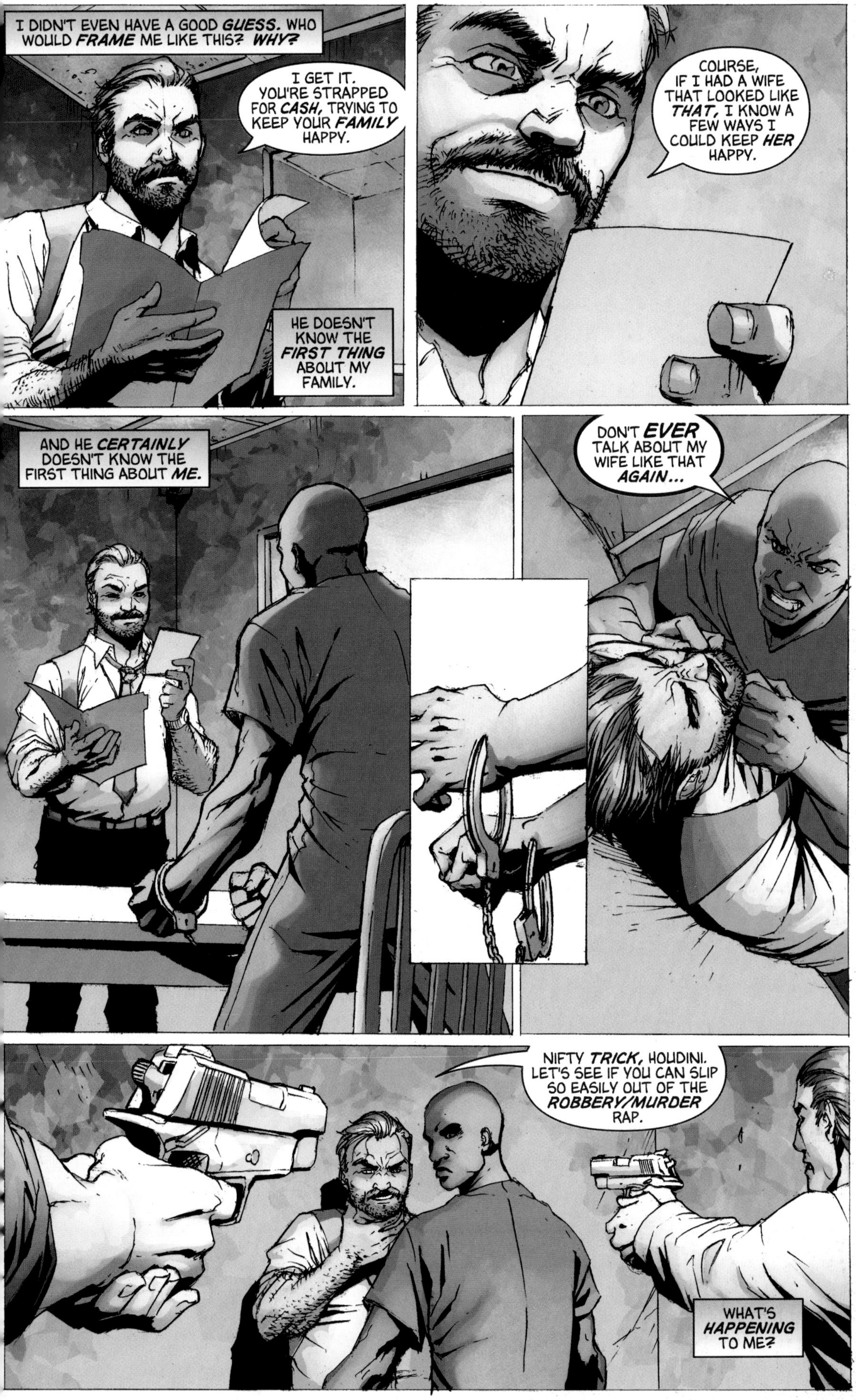
I DIDN'T EVEN HAVE A GOOD GUESS. WHO WOULD FRAME ME LIKE THIS? WHY?
I GET IT. YOU'RE STRAPPED FOR CASH, TRYING TO KEEP YOUR FAMILY HAPPY.
HE DOESN'T KNOW THE FIRST THING ABOUT MY FAMILY.
COURSE, IF I HAD A WIFE THAT LOOKED LIKE THAT, I KNOW A FEW WAYS I COULD KEEP HER HAPPY.
AND HE CERTAINLY DOESN'T KNOW THE FIRST THING ABOUT ME.
DON'T EVER TALK ABOUT MY WIFE LIKE THAT AGAIN...
NIFTY TRICK, HOUDINI. LET'S SEE IF YOU CAN SLIP SO EASILY OUT OF THE ROBBERY/MURDER RAP.
WHAT'S HAPPENING TO ME?

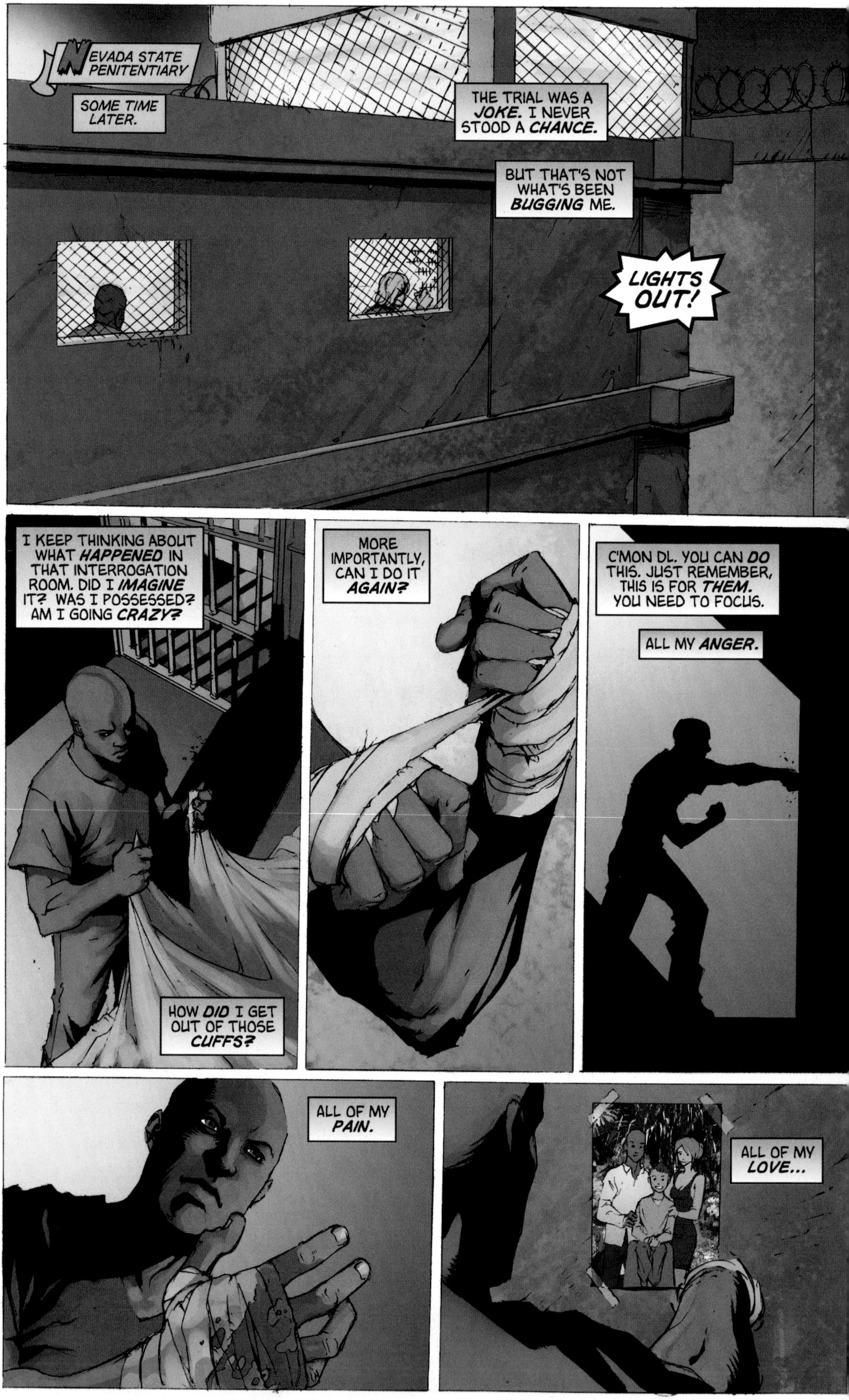
NEVADA STATE PENITENTIARY
SOME TIME LATER.
THE TRIAL WAS A JOKE. I NEVER STOOD A CHANCE.
BUT THAT'S NOT WHAT'S BEEN BUGGING ME.
LIGHTS OUT!
I KEEP THINKING ABOUT WHAT HAPPENED IN THAT INTERROGATION ROOM. DID I IMAGINE IT? WAS I POSSESSED? AM I GOING CRAZY?
HOW DID I GET OUT OF THOSE CUFFS?
MORE IMPORTANTLY, CAN I DO IT AGAIN?
C'MON DL. YOU CAN DO THIS. JUST REMEMBER, THIS IS FOR THEM. YOU NEED TO FOCUS.
ALL MY ANGER.
ALL OF MY PAIN.
ALL OF MY LOVE...

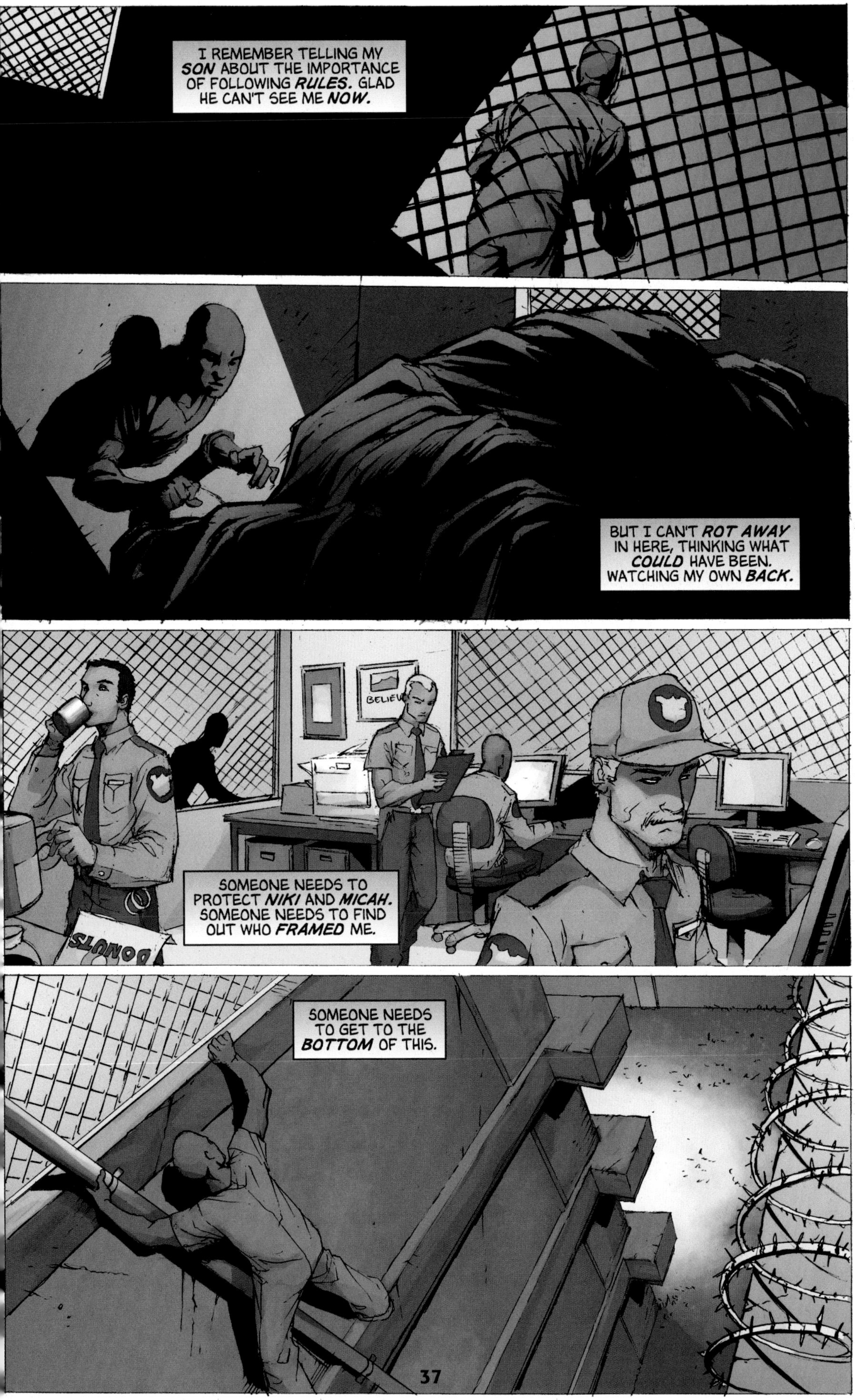
I REMEMBER TELLING MY SON ABOUT THE IMPORTANCE OF FOLLOWING RULES. GLAD HE CAN'T SEE ME NOW.
BUT I CAN'T ROT AWAY IN HERE, THINKING WHAT COULD HAVE BEEN. WATCHING MY OWN BACK.
BELIEV
SOMEONE NEEDS TO PROTECT NIKI AND MICAH. SOMEONE NEEDS TO FIND OUT WHO FRAMED ME.
DONUTS
SOMEONE NEEDS TO GET TO THE BOTTOM OF THIS.

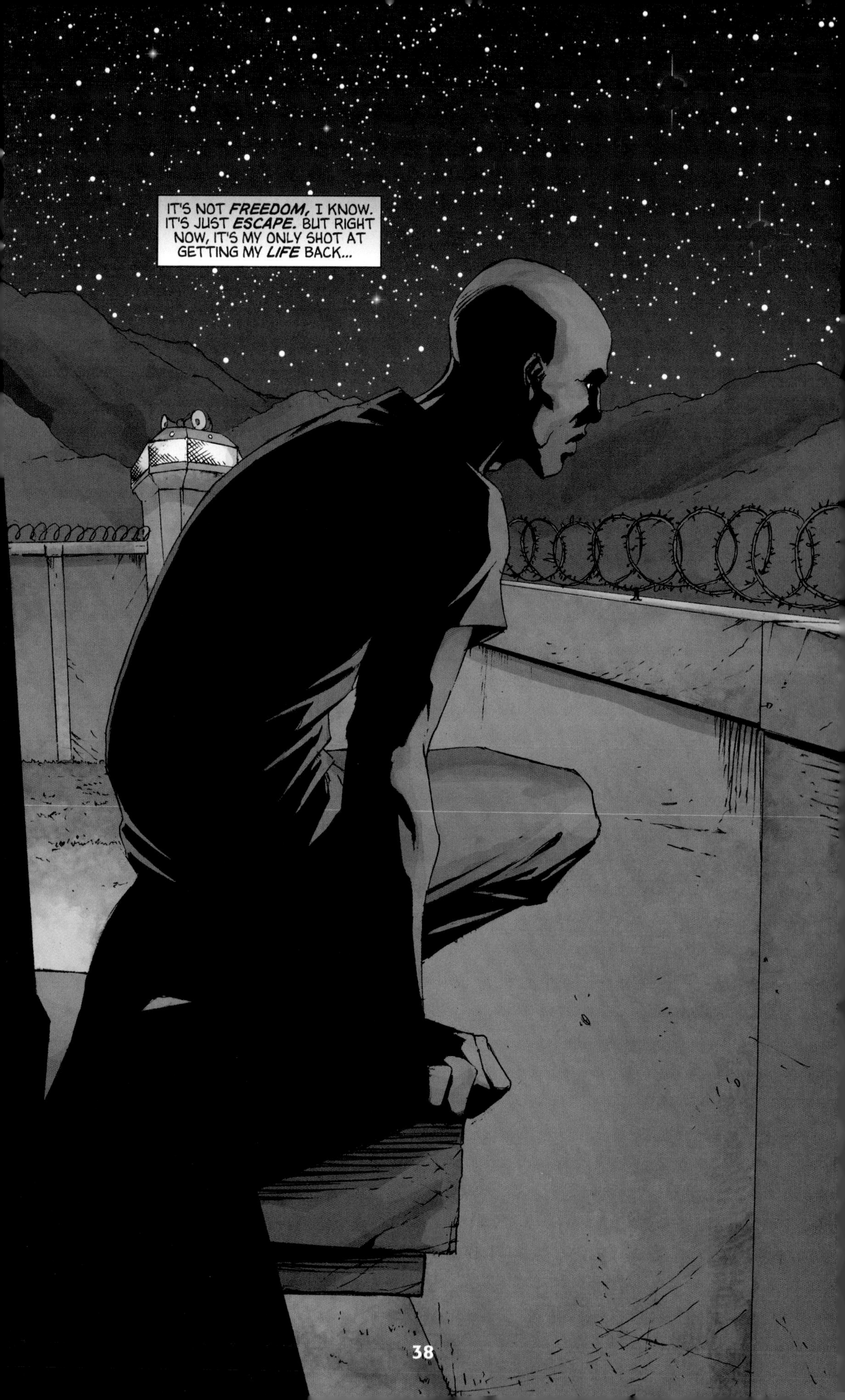
IT'S NOT FREEDOM, I KNOW. IT'S JUST ESCAPE. BUT RIGHT NOW, IT'S MY ONLY SHOT AT GETTING MY LIFE BACK...

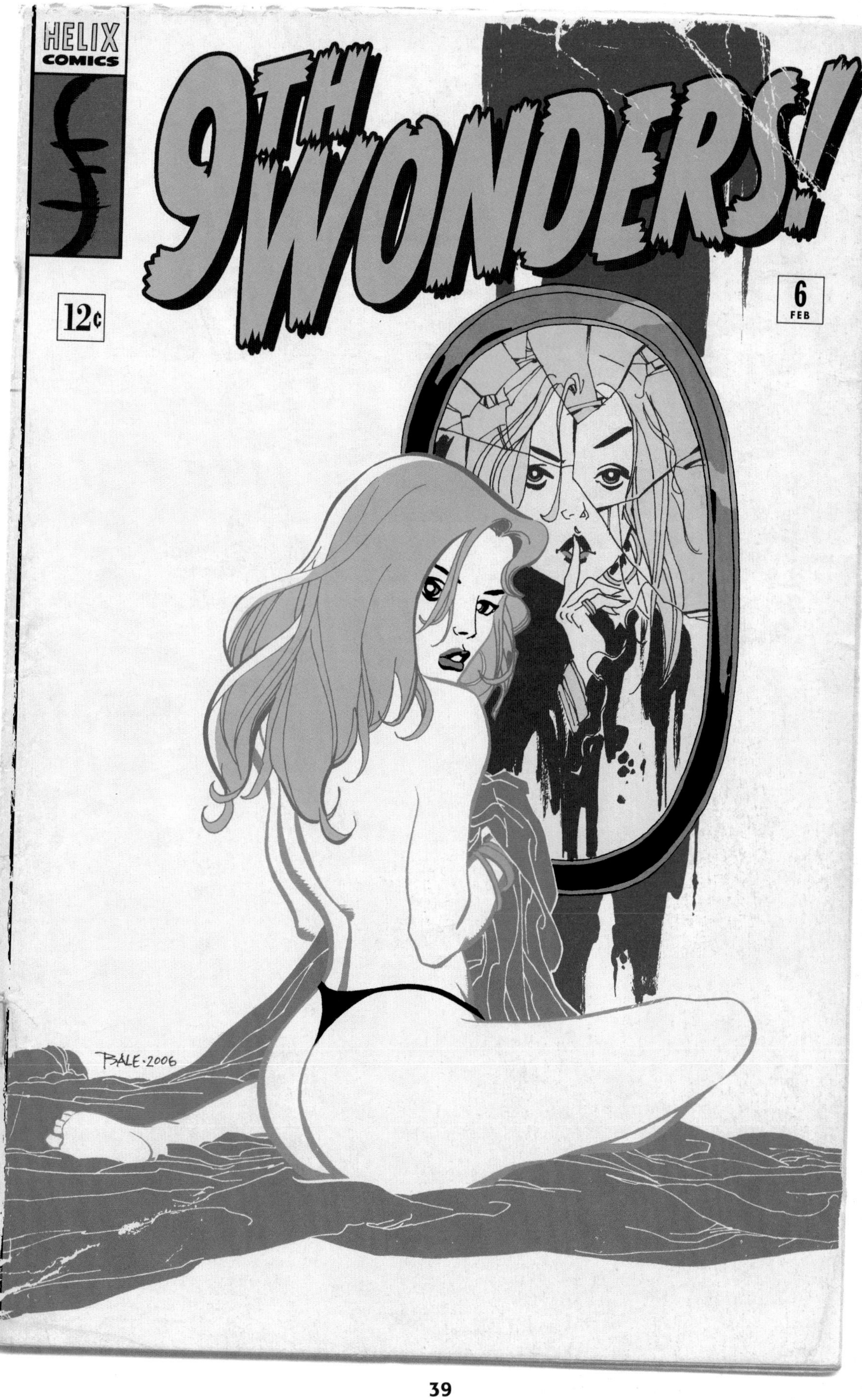
HELIX COMICS
9TH WONDERS!
12¢
6 FEB
BALE·2006

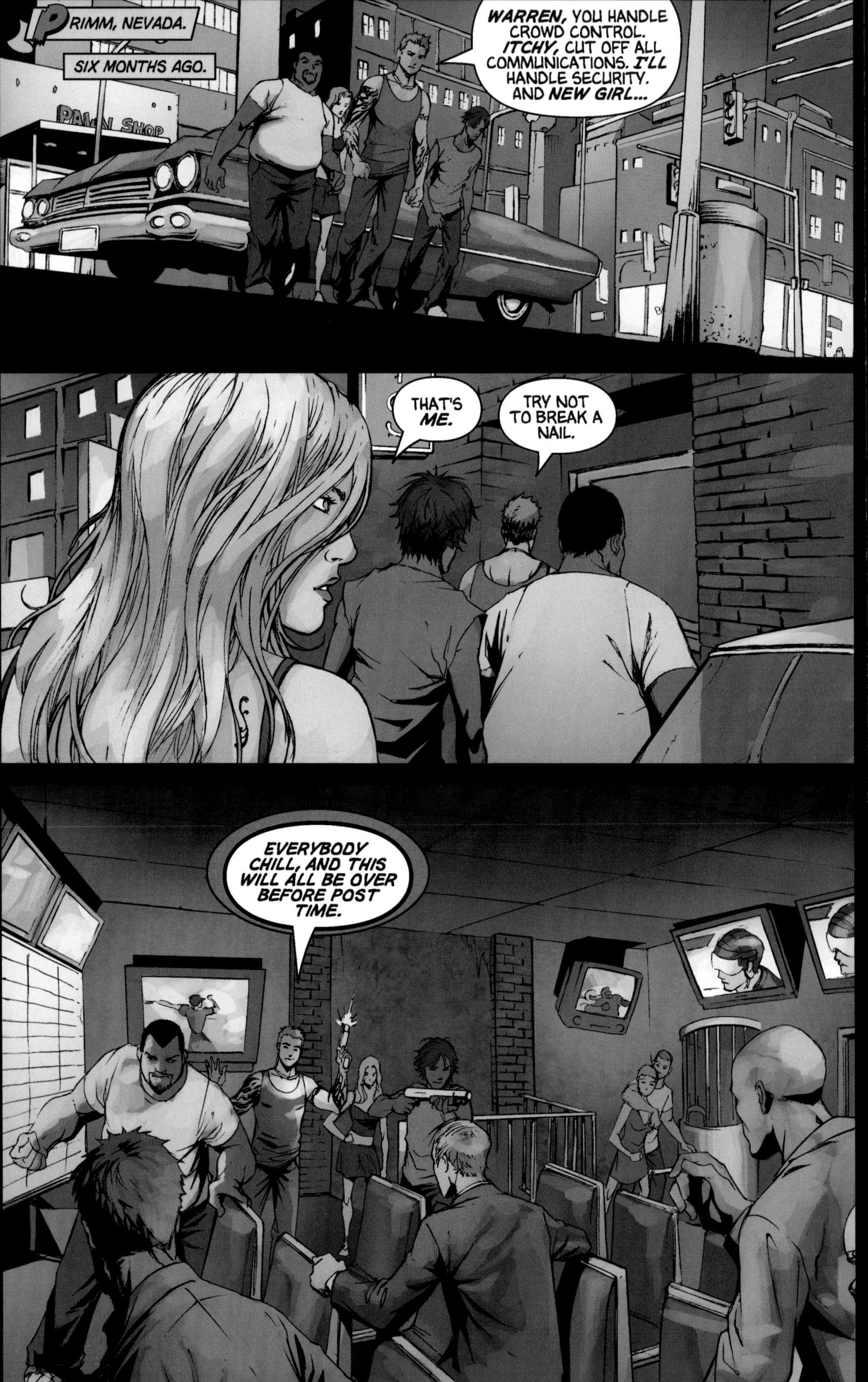
PRIMM, NEVADA.
SIX MONTHS AGO.
WARREN, YOU HANDLE CROWD CONTROL. ITCHY, CUT OFF ALL COMMUNICATIONS. I'LL HANDLE SECURITY. AND NEW GIRL...
PAWN SHOP
THAT'S ME.
TRY NOT TO BREAK A NAIL.
EVERYBODY CHILL, AND THIS WILL ALL BE OVER BEFORE POST TIME.

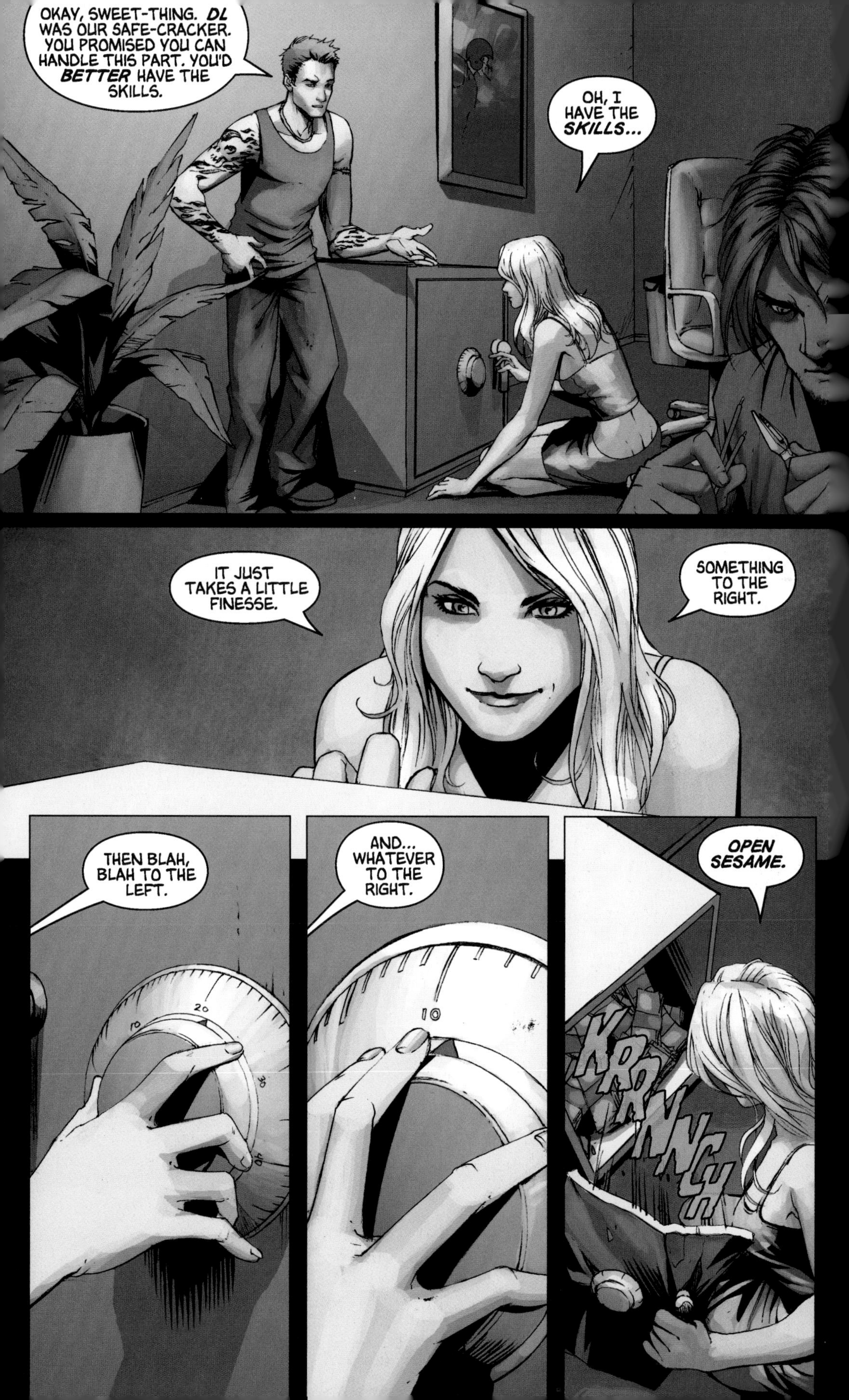
OKAY, SWEET-THING. DL WAS OUR SAFE-CRACKER. YOU PROMISED YOU CAN HANDLE THIS PART. YOU'D BETTER HAVE THE SKILLS.
OH, I HAVE THE SKILLS...
IT JUST TAKES A LITTLE FINESSE.
SOMETHING TO THE RIGHT.
THEN BLAH, BLAH TO THE LEFT.
AND... WHATEVER TO THE RIGHT.
OPEN SESAME.
KRRNNCH

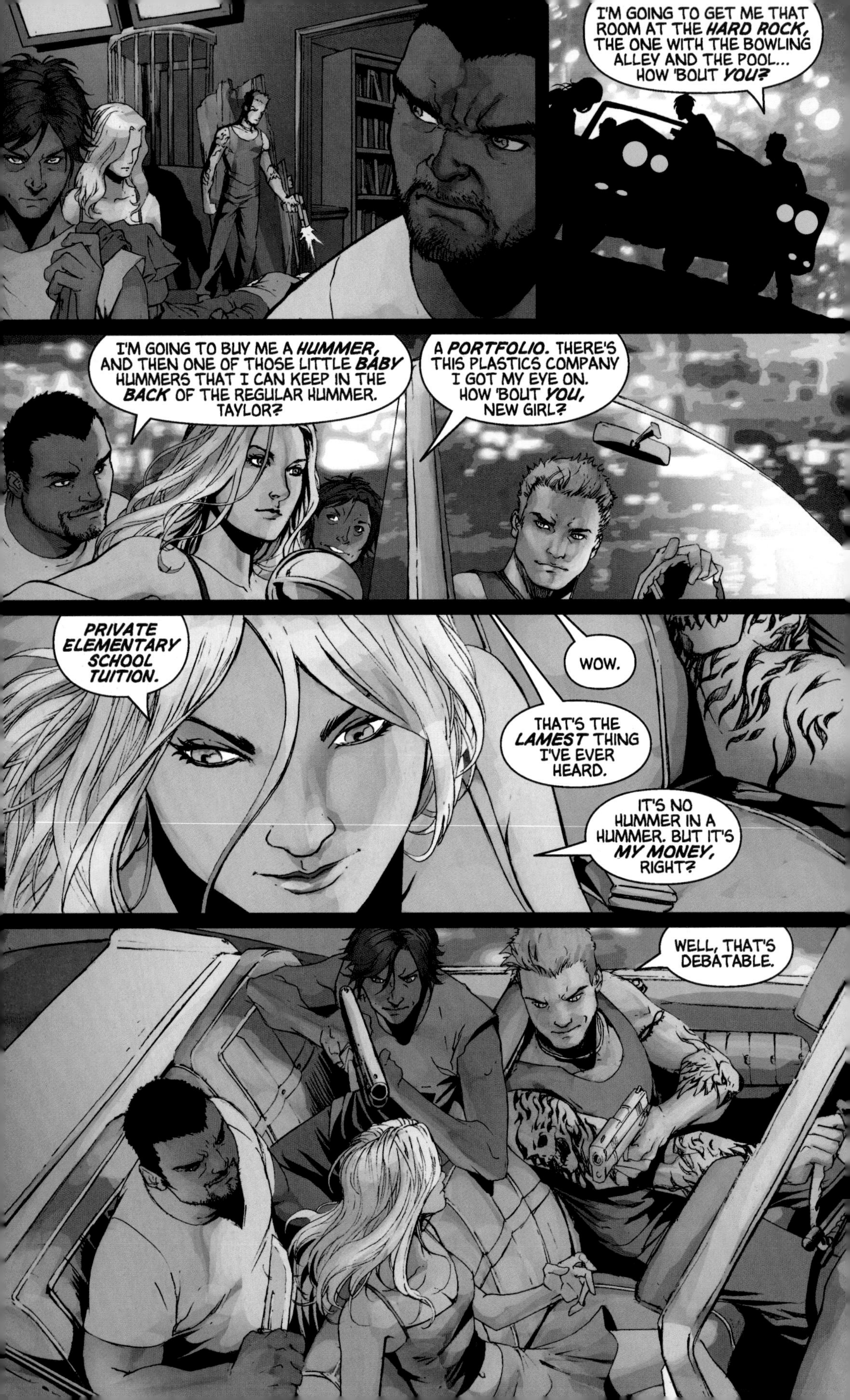
I'M GOING TO GET ME THAT ROOM AT THE HARD ROCK, THE ONE WITH THE BOWLING ALLEY AND THE POOL... HOW 'BOUT YOU?
I'M GOING TO BUY ME A HUMMER, AND THEN ONE OF THOSE LITTLE BABY HUMMERS THAT I CAN KEEP IN THE BACK OF THE REGULAR HUMMER. TAYLOR?
A PORTFOLIO. THERE'S THIS PLASTICS COMPANY I GOT MY EYE ON. HOW 'BOUT YOU, NEW GIRL?
PRIVATE ELEMENTARY SCHOOL TUITION.
WOW.
THAT'S THE LAMEST THING I'VE EVER HEARD.
IT'S NO HUMMER IN A HUMMER. BUT IT'S MY MONEY, RIGHT?
WELL, THAT'S DEBATABLE.

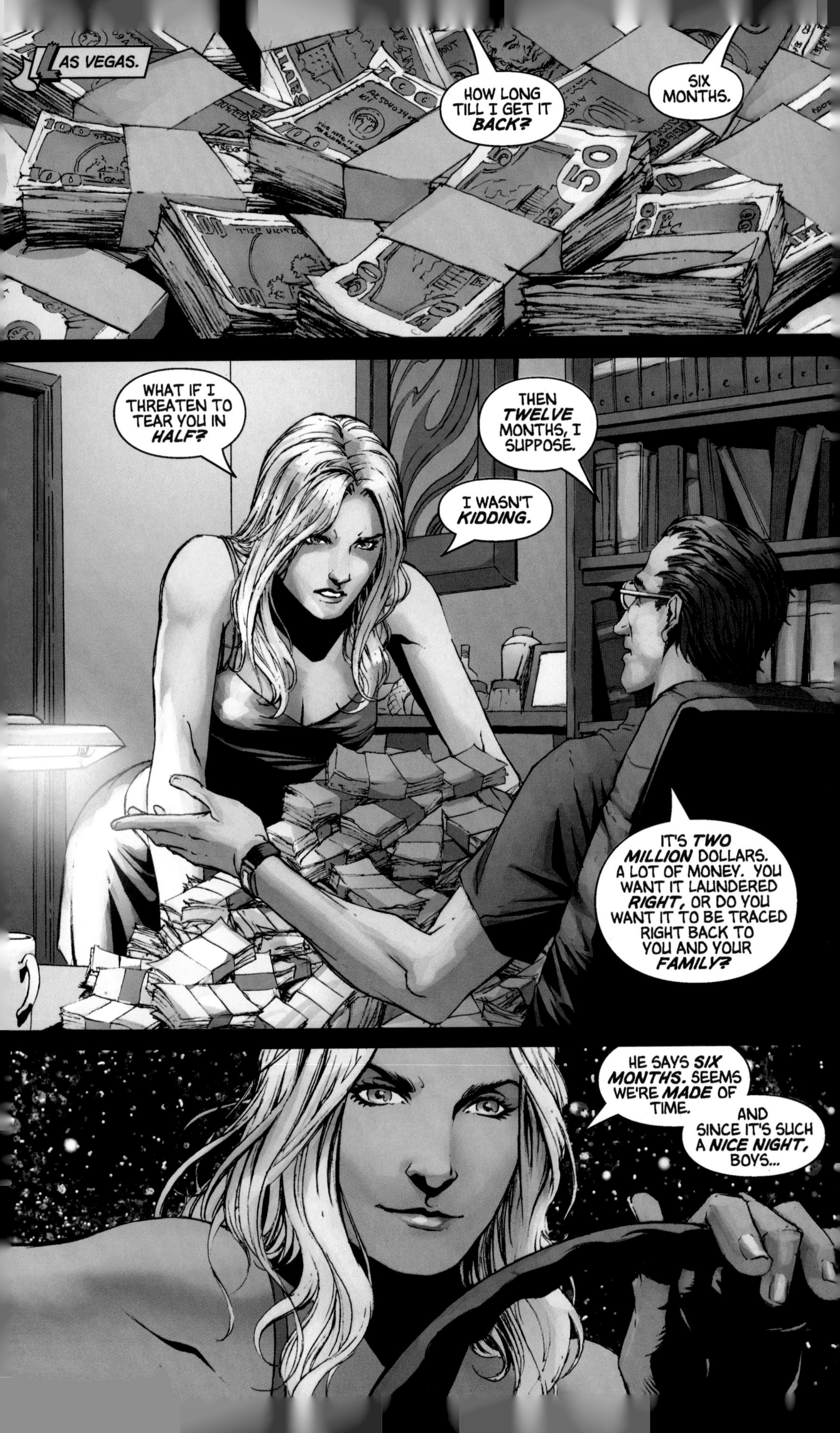
LAS VEGAS.
HOW LONG TILL I GET IT BACK?
SIX MONTHS.
WHAT IF I THREATEN TO TEAR YOU IN HALF?
THEN TWELVE MONTHS, I SUPPOSE.
I WASN'T KIDDING.
IT'S TWO MILLION DOLLARS. A LOT OF MONEY. YOU WANT IT LAUNDERED RIGHT, OR DO YOU WANT IT TO BE TRACED RIGHT BACK TO YOU AND YOUR FAMILY?
HE SAYS SIX MONTHS. SEEMS WE'RE MADE OF TIME.
AND SINCE IT'S SUCH A NICE NIGHT, BOYS...

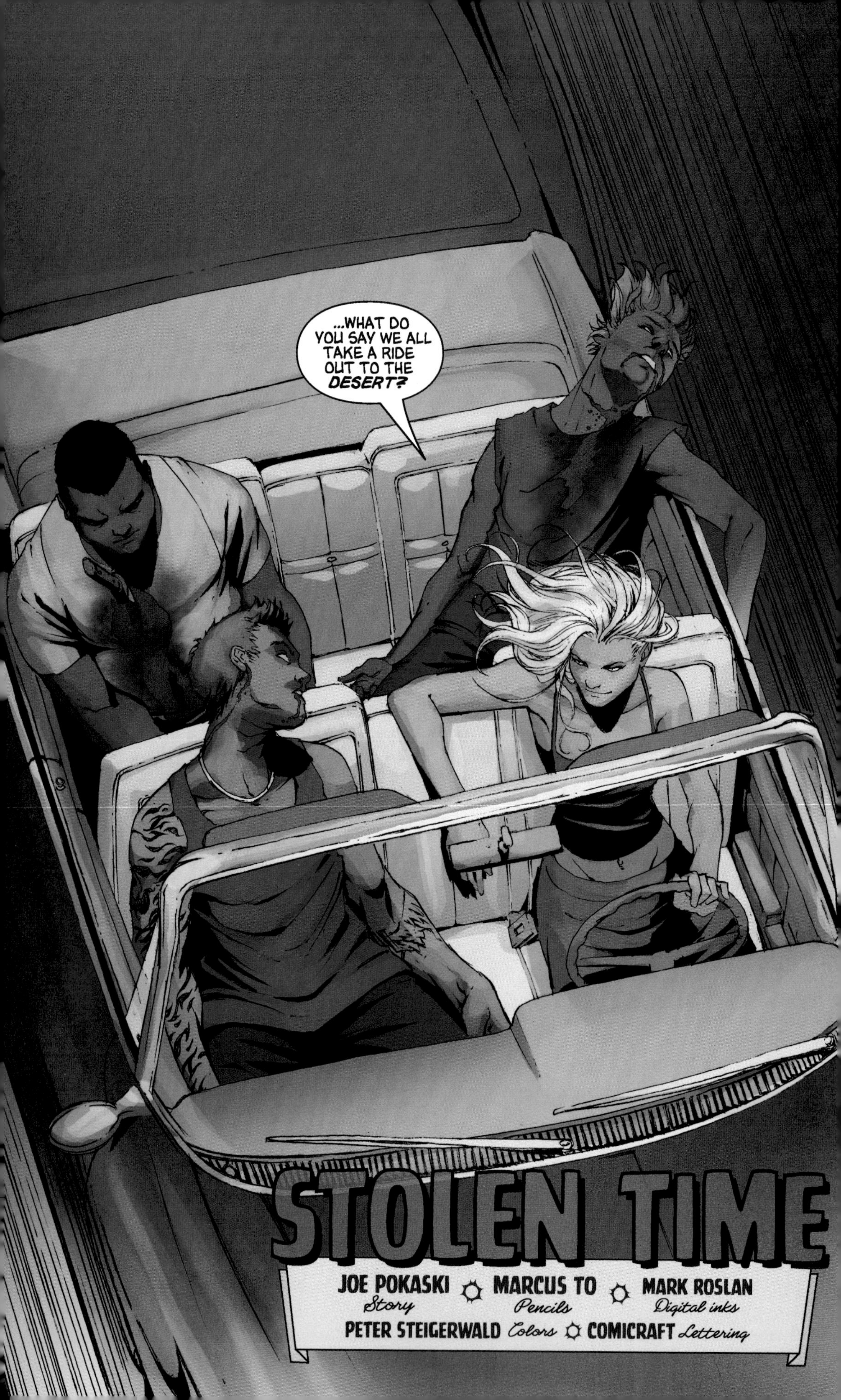
...WHAT DO YOU SAY WE ALL TAKE A RIDE OUT TO THE DESERT?
STOLEN TIME
JOE POKASKI Story
MARCUS TO Pencils
MARK ROSLAN Digital inks
PETER STEIGERWALD Colors
COMICRAFT Lettering

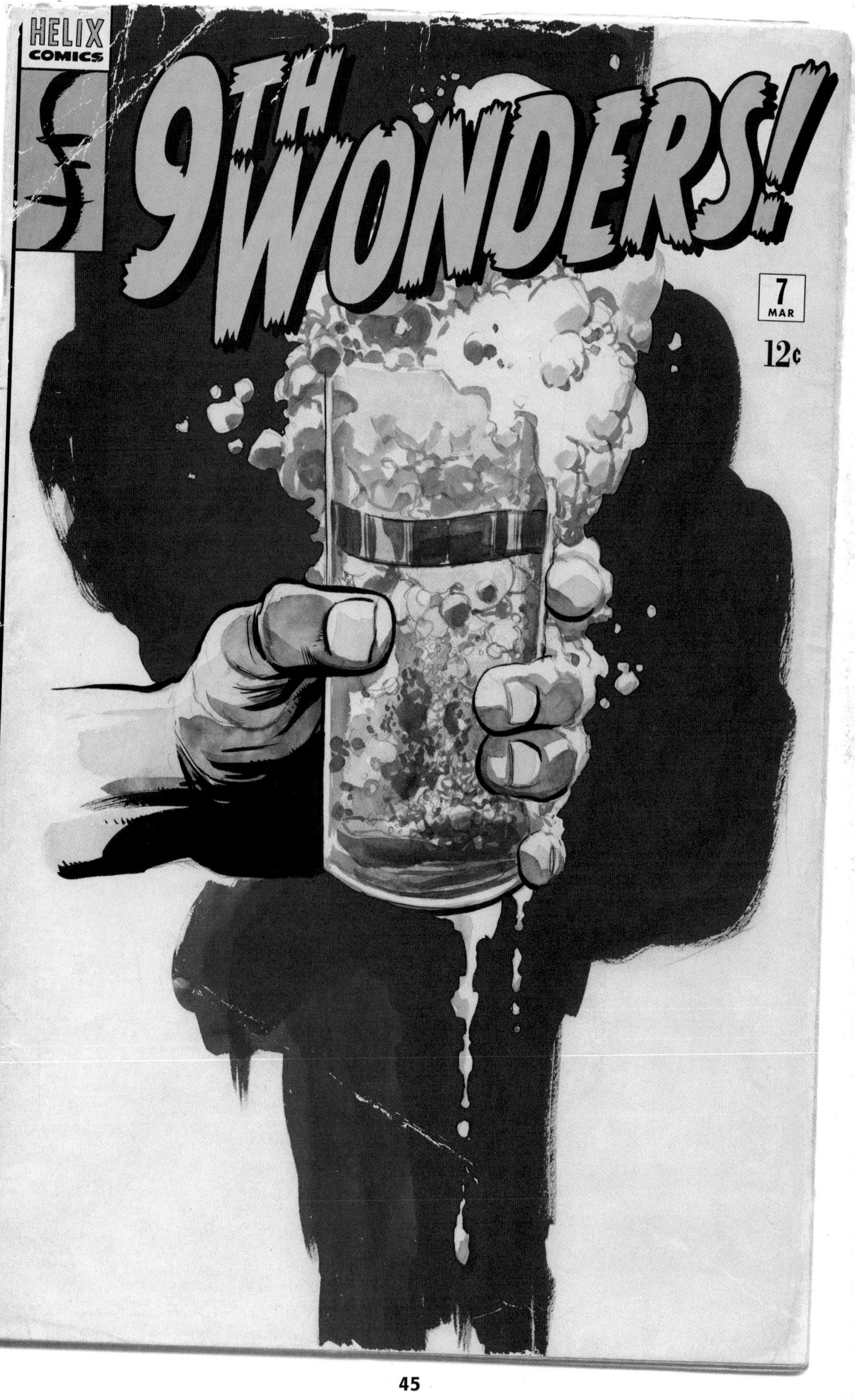
HELIX
COMICS
9TH WONDERS!
7
MAR
12¢

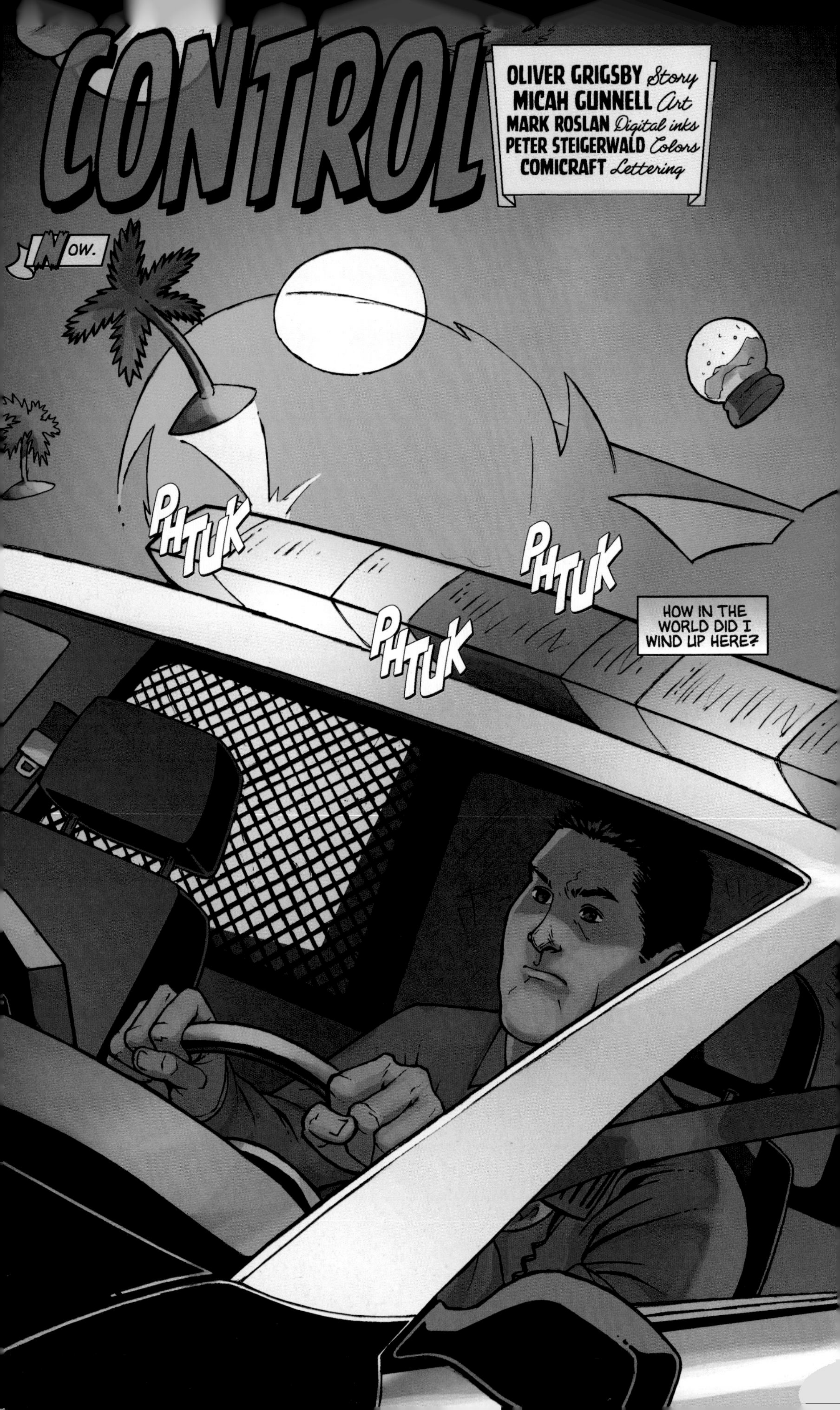
CONTROL
OLIVER GRIGSBY Story
MICAH GUNNELL Art
MARK ROSLAN Digital inks
PETER STEIGERWALD Colors
COMICRAFT Lettering
NOW.
PHTUK
PHTUK
PHTUK
HOW IN THE WORLD DID I WIND UP HERE?

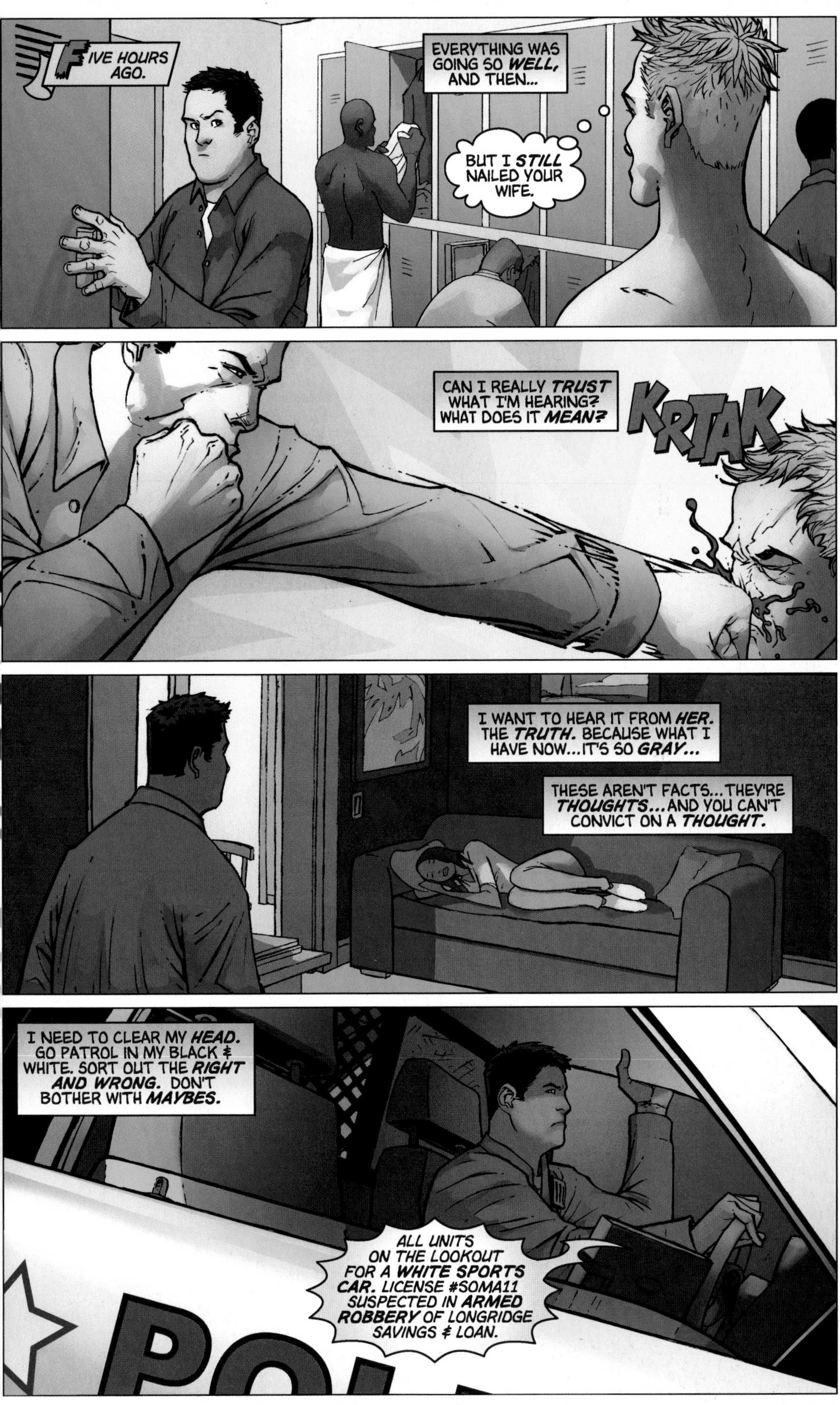
FIVE HOURS AGO.
EVERYTHING WAS GOING SO WELL, AND THEN...
BUT I STILL NAILED YOUR WIFE.
CAN I REALLY TRUST WHAT I'M HEARING? WHAT DOES IT MEAN?
KRTAK
I WANT TO HEAR IT FROM HER. THE TRUTH. BECAUSE WHAT I HAVE NOW...IT'S SO GRAY...
THESE AREN'T FACTS...THEY'RE THOUGHTS...AND YOU CAN'T CONVICT ON A THOUGHT.
I NEED TO CLEAR MY HEAD. GO PATROL IN MY BLACK & WHITE. SORT OUT THE RIGHT AND WRONG. DON'T BOTHER WITH MAYBES.
ALL UNITS ON THE LOOKOUT FOR A WHITE SPORTS CAR. LICENSE #SOMA11 SUSPECTED IN ARMED ROBBERY OF LONGRIDGE SAVINGS & LOAN.

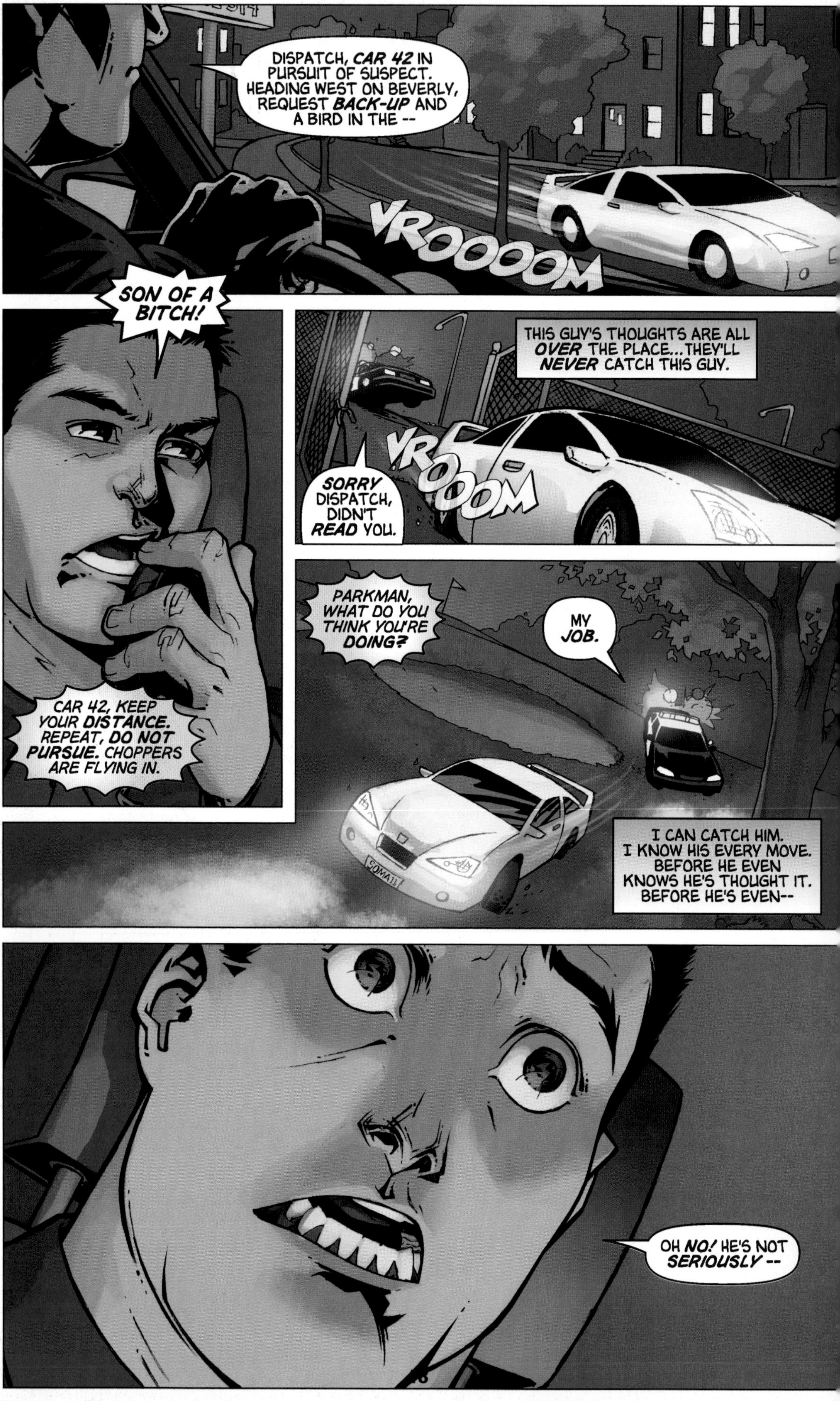
DISPATCH, CAR 42 IN PURSUIT OF SUSPECT. HEADING WEST ON BEVERLY, REQUEST BACK-UP AND A BIRD IN THE --
VROOOOM
SON OF A BITCH!
CAR 42, KEEP YOUR DISTANCE. REPEAT, DO NOT PURSUE. CHOPPERS ARE FLYING IN.
THIS GUY'S THOUGHTS ARE ALL OVER THE PLACE...THEY'LL NEVER CATCH THIS GUY.
VROOOM
SORRY DISPATCH, DIDN'T READ YOU.
PARKMAN, WHAT DO YOU THINK YOU'RE DOING?
MY JOB.
I CAN CATCH HIM. I KNOW HIS EVERY MOVE. BEFORE HE EVEN KNOWS HE'S THOUGHT IT. BEFORE HE'S EVEN--
OH NO! HE'S NOT SERIOUSLY --

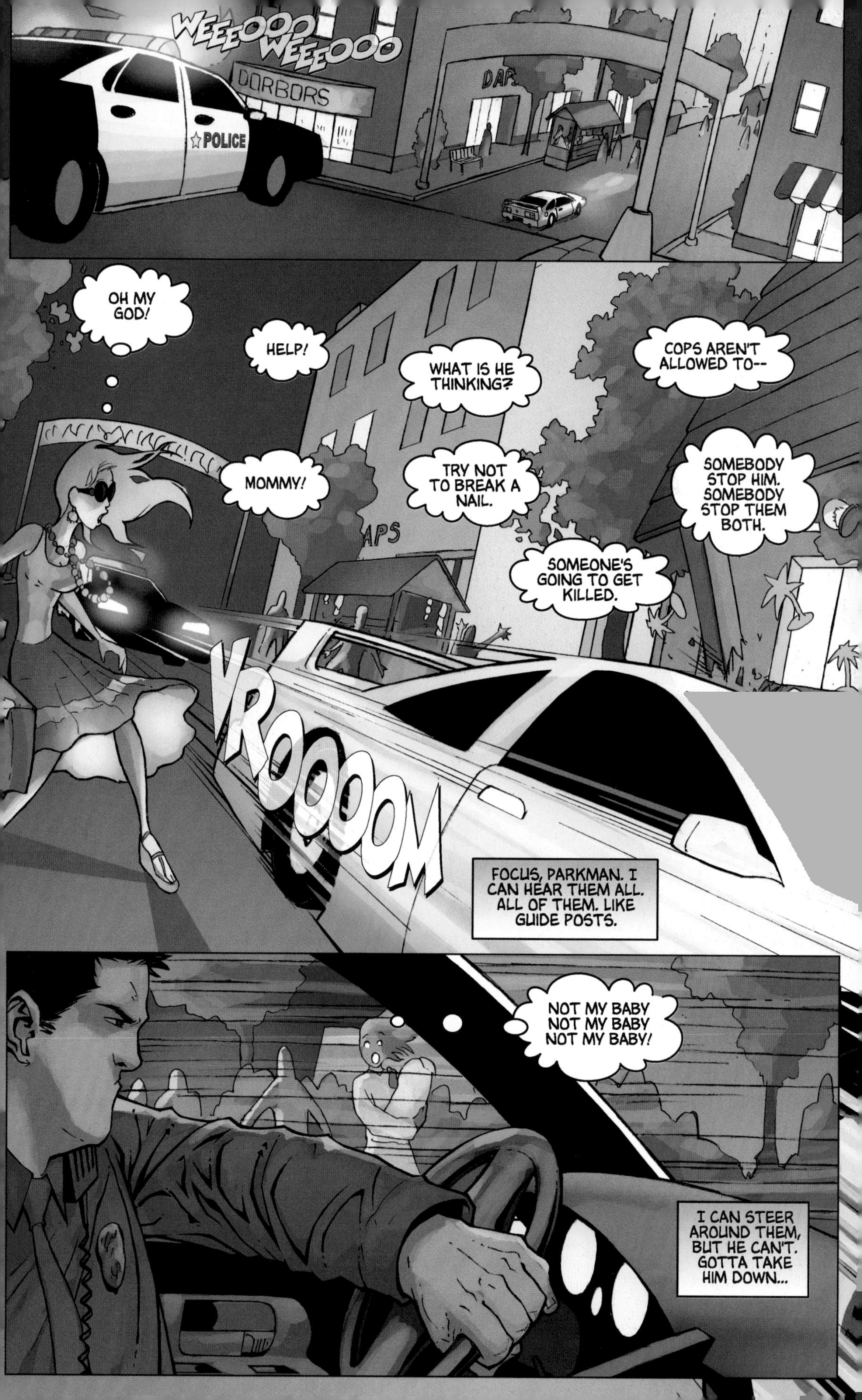
WEEEOOO WEEEOOO
DORBORS
POLICE
OH MY GOD!
HELP!
WHAT IS HE THINKING?
COPS AREN'T ALLOWED TO--
MOMMY!
TRY NOT TO BREAK A NAIL.
SOMEBODY STOP HIM. SOMEBODY STOP THEM BOTH.
SOMEONE'S GOING TO GET KILLED.
VROOOOOM
FOCUS, PARKMAN. I CAN HEAR THEM ALL. ALL OF THEM. LIKE GUIDE POSTS.
NOT MY BABY NOT MY BABY NOT MY BABY!
I CAN STEER AROUND THEM, BUT HE CAN'T. GOTTA TAKE HIM DOWN...

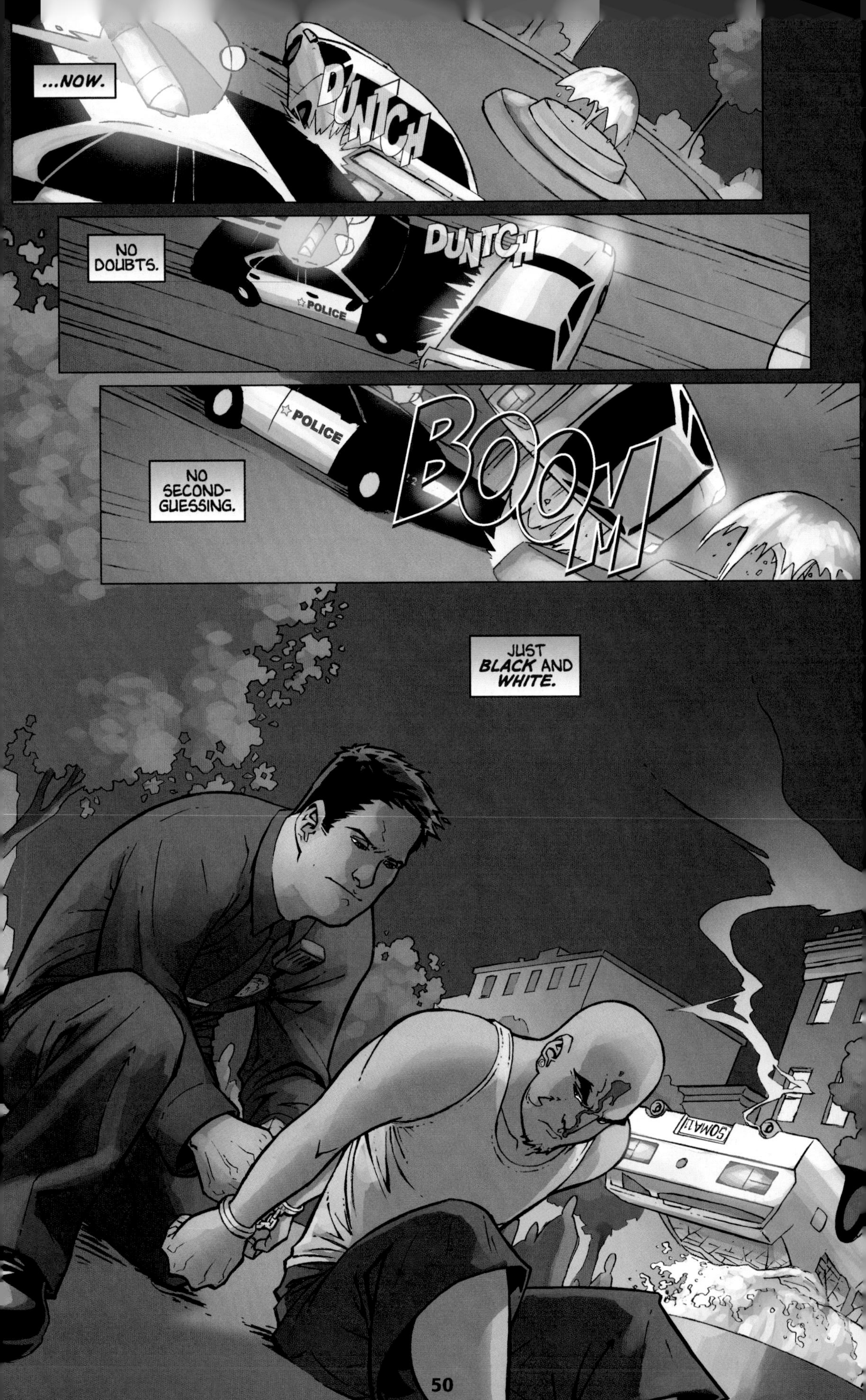
...NOW.
DUNTCH
NO DOUBTS.
DUNTCH
NO SECOND-GUESSING.
BOOM
JUST *BLACK* AND *WHITE*.

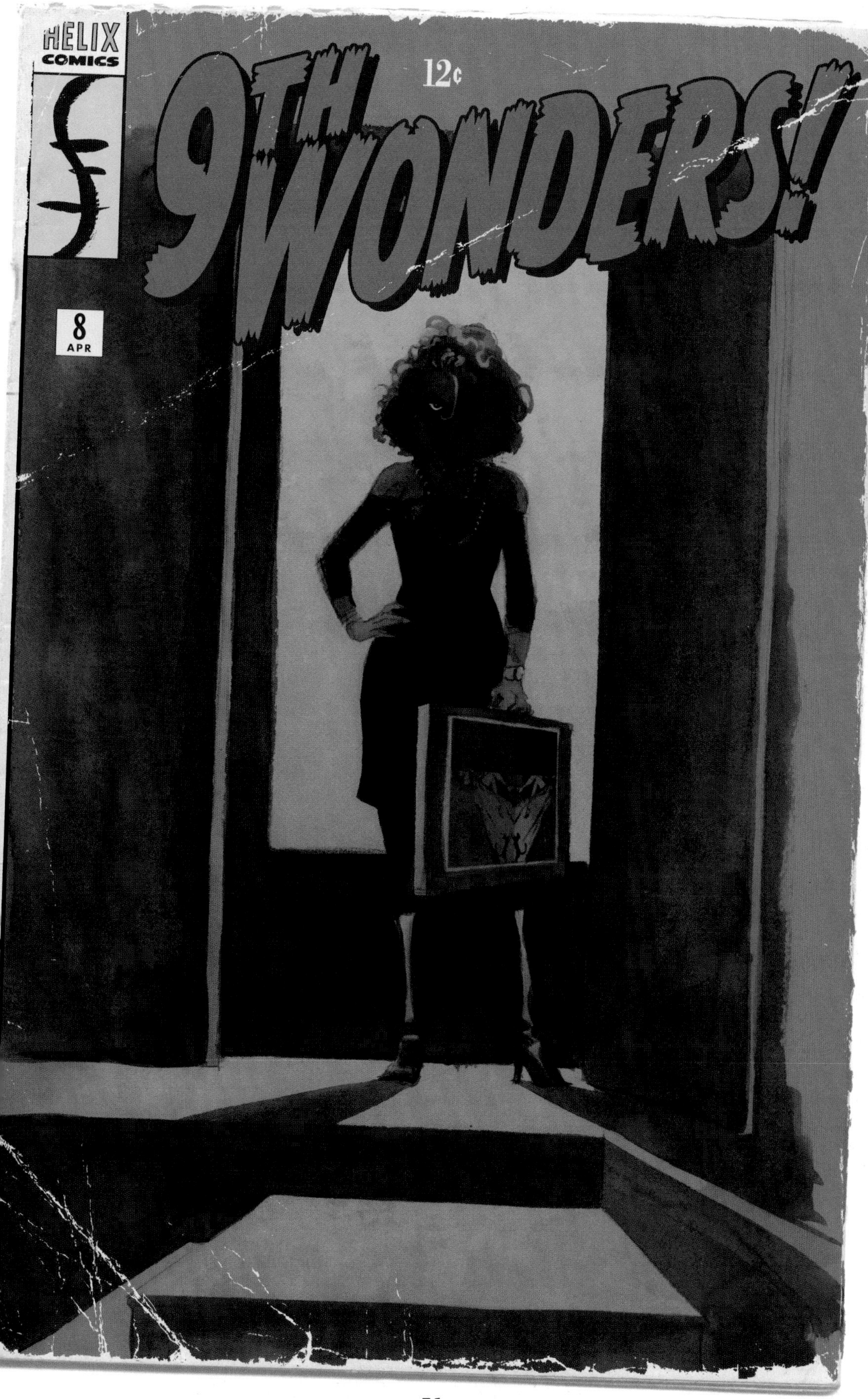
HELIX
COMICS
12¢
9TH WONDERS!
8
APR

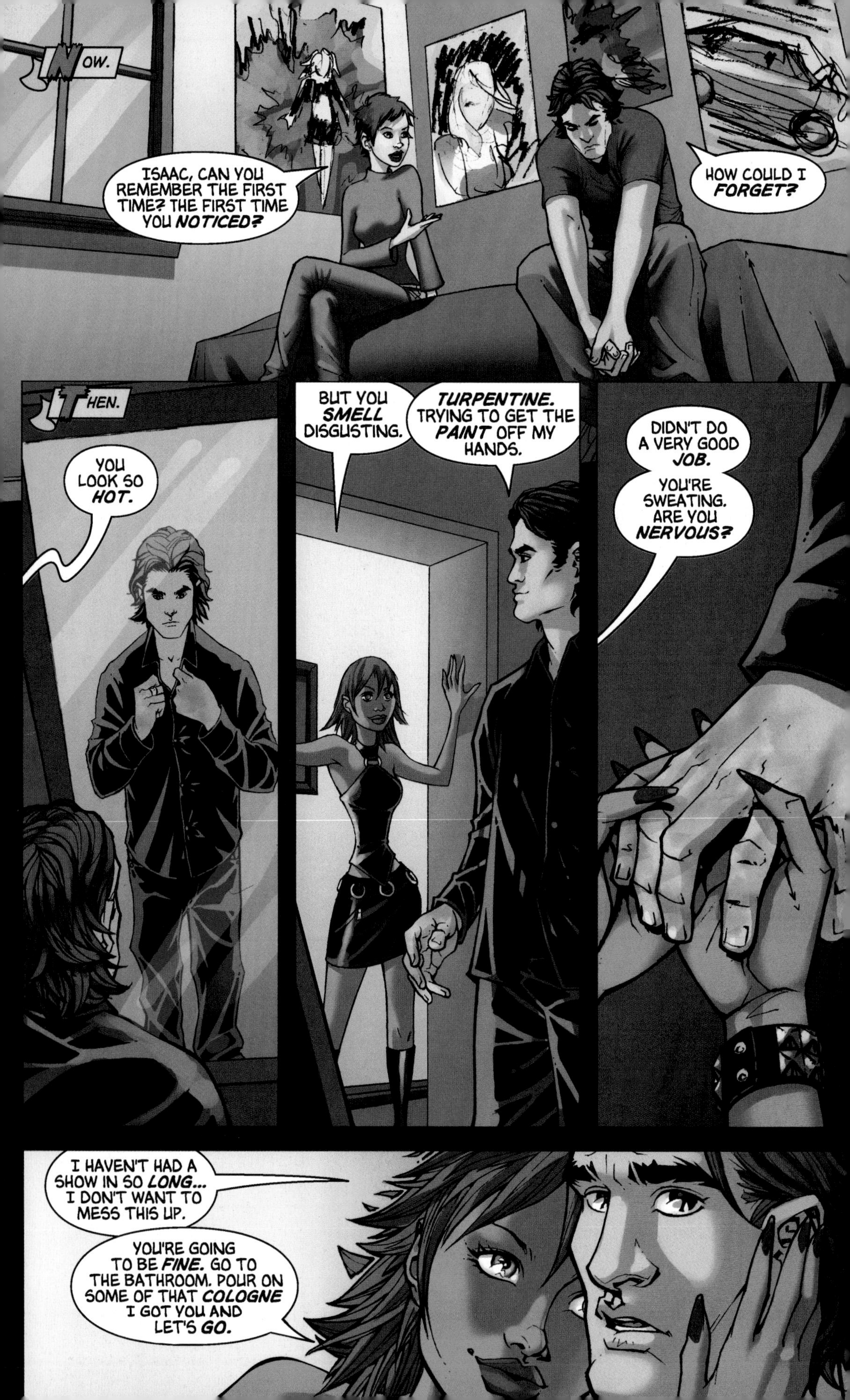
NOW.
ISAAC, CAN YOU REMEMBER THE FIRST TIME? THE FIRST TIME YOU NOTICED?
HOW COULD I FORGET?
THEN.
YOU LOOK SO HOT.
BUT YOU SMELL DISGUSTING.
TURPENTINE. TRYING TO GET THE PAINT OFF MY HANDS.
DIDN'T DO A VERY GOOD JOB.
YOU'RE SWEATING. ARE YOU NERVOUS?
I HAVEN'T HAD A SHOW IN SO LONG... I DON'T WANT TO MESS THIS UP.
YOU'RE GOING TO BE FINE. GO TO THE BATHROOM. POUR ON SOME OF THAT COLOGNE I GOT YOU AND LET'S GO.

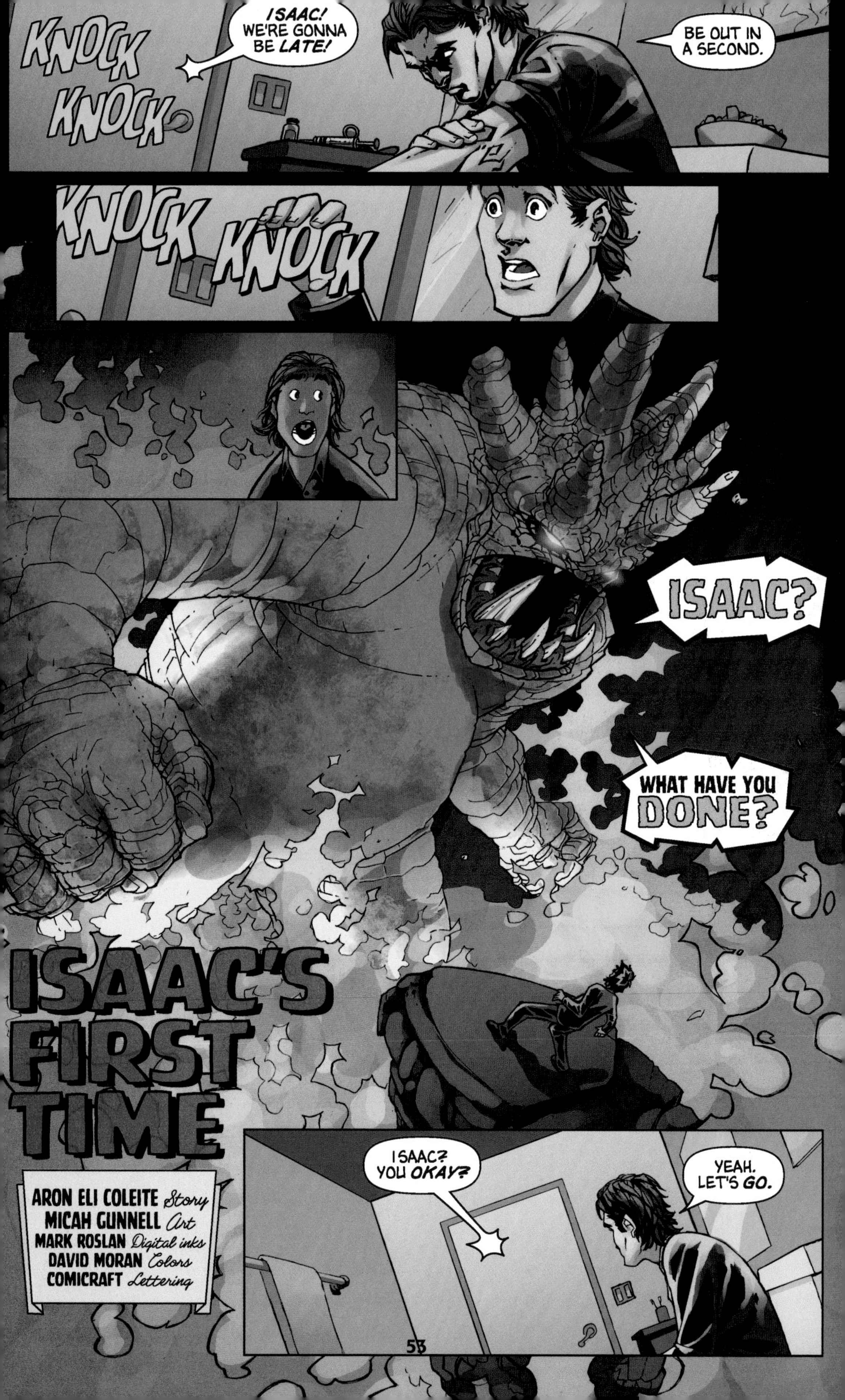
KNOCK KNOCK
ISAAC! WE'RE GONNA BE LATE!
BE OUT IN A SECOND.
KNOCK KNOCK
ISAAC?
WHAT HAVE YOU DONE?
ISAAC'S FIRST TIME
ARON ELI COLEITE Story
MICAH GUNNELL Art
MARK ROSLAN Digital inks
DAVID MORAN Colors
COMICRAFT Lettering
ISAAC? YOU OKAY?
YEAH. LET'S GO.

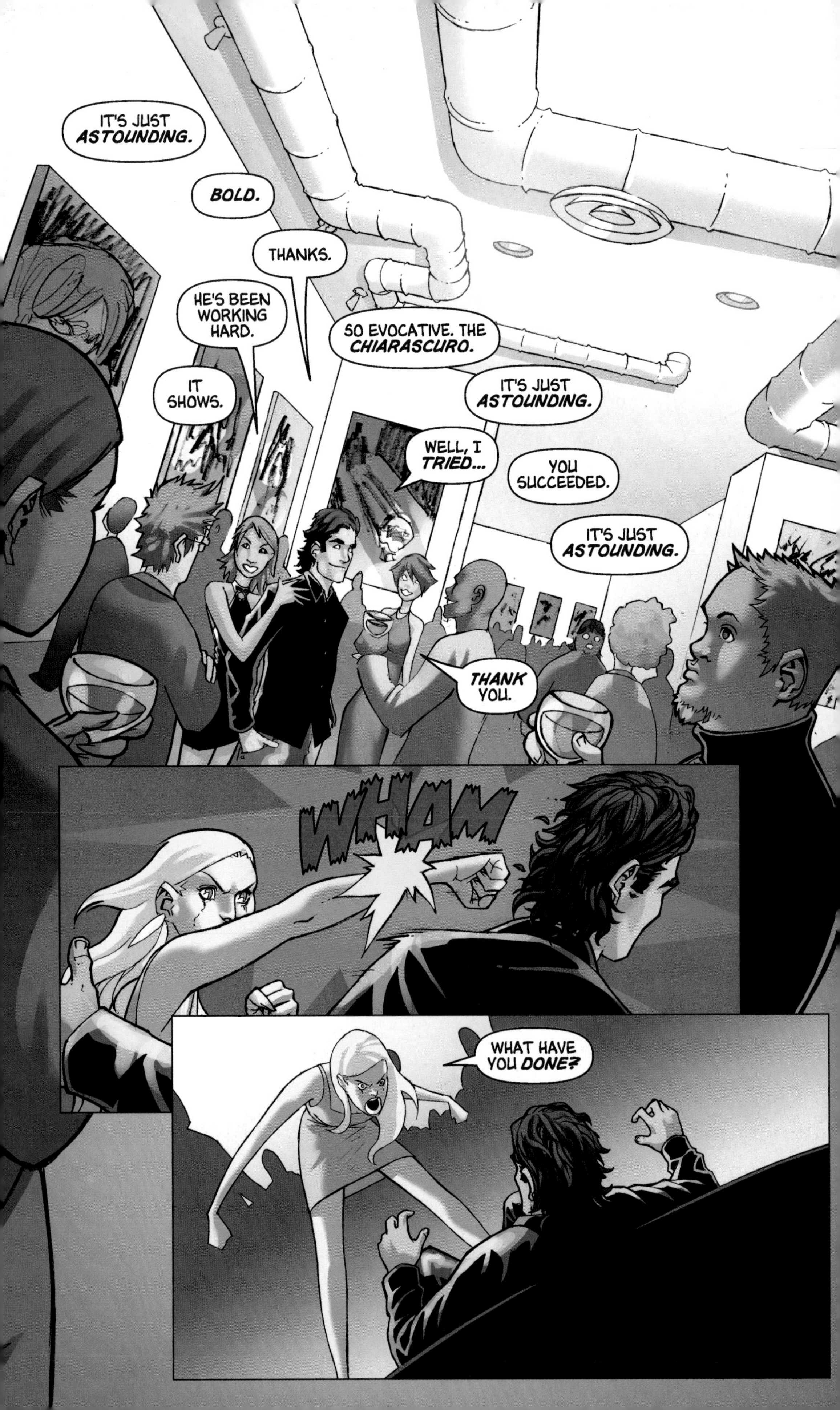

IT'S JUST ASTOUNDING.
BOLD.
THANKS.
HE'S BEEN WORKING HARD.
IT SHOWS.
SO EVOCATIVE. THE CHIARASCURO.
IT'S JUST ASTOUNDING.
WELL, I TRIED...
YOU SUCCEEDED.
IT'S JUST ASTOUNDING.
THANK YOU.
WHAM
WHAT HAVE YOU DONE?

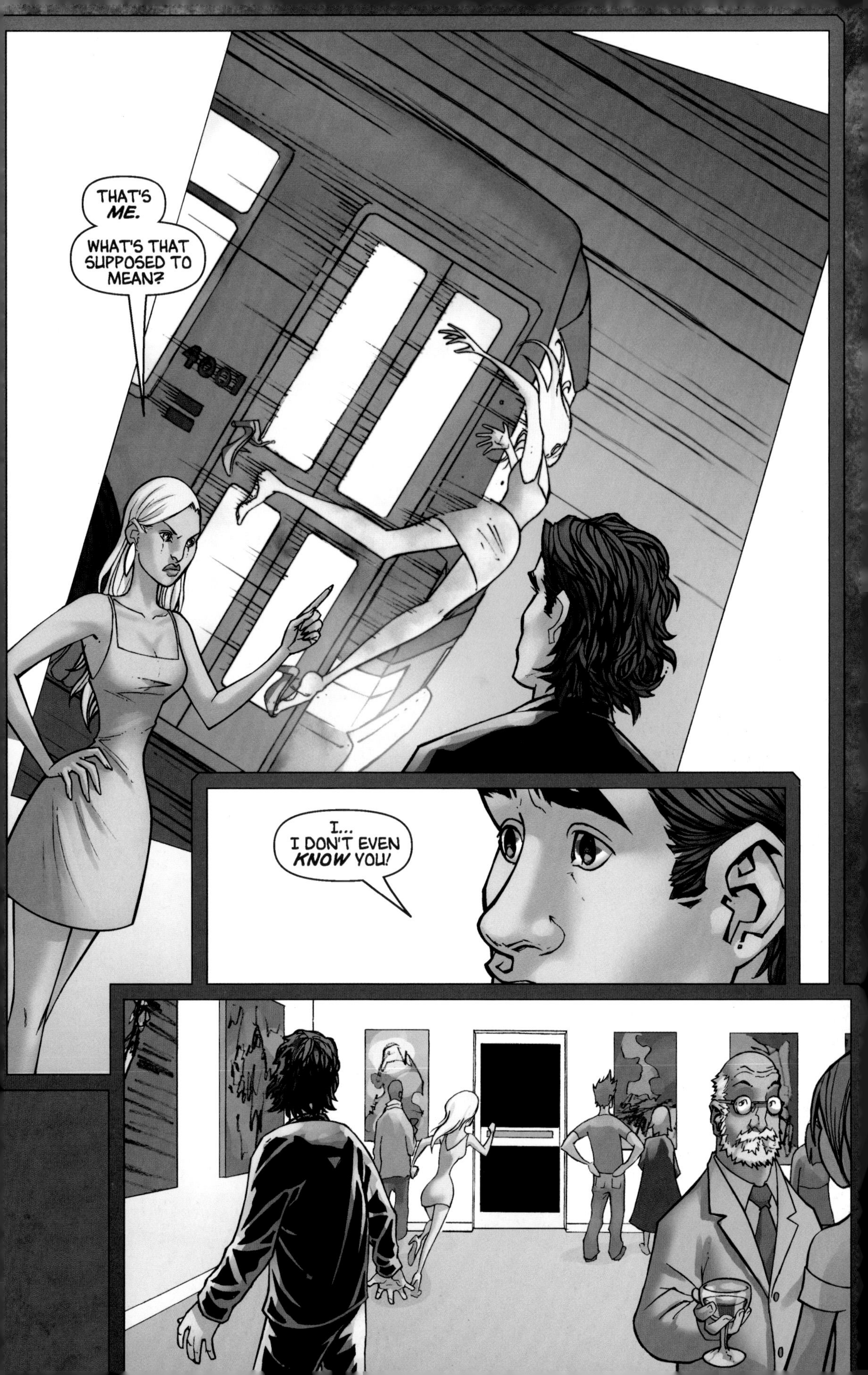
THAT'S *ME.*
WHAT'S THAT SUPPOSED TO MEAN?
I... I DON'T EVEN *KNOW* YOU!

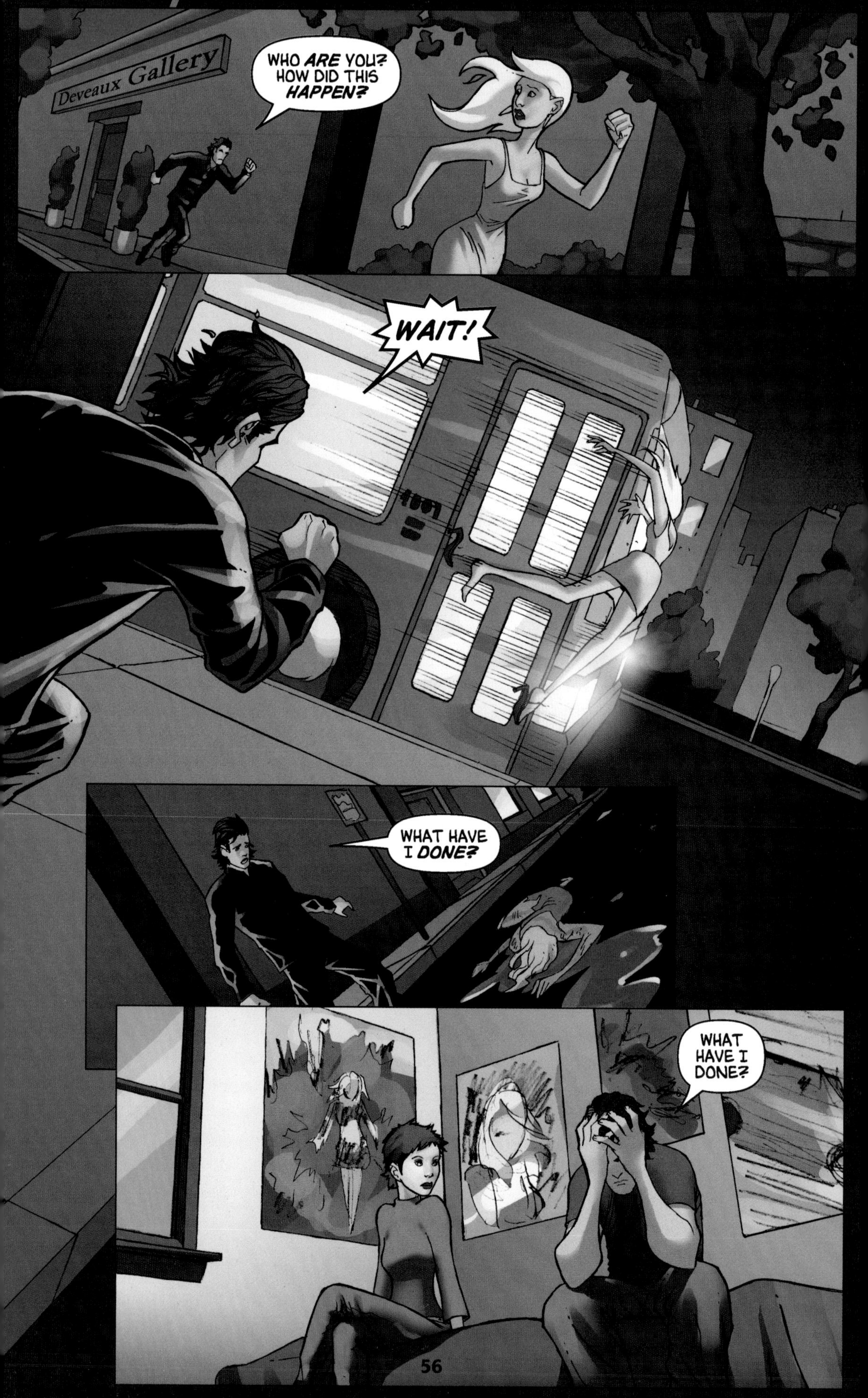
Deveaux Gallery
WHO ARE YOU? HOW DID THIS HAPPEN?
WAIT!
WHAT HAVE I DONE?
WHAT HAVE I DONE?

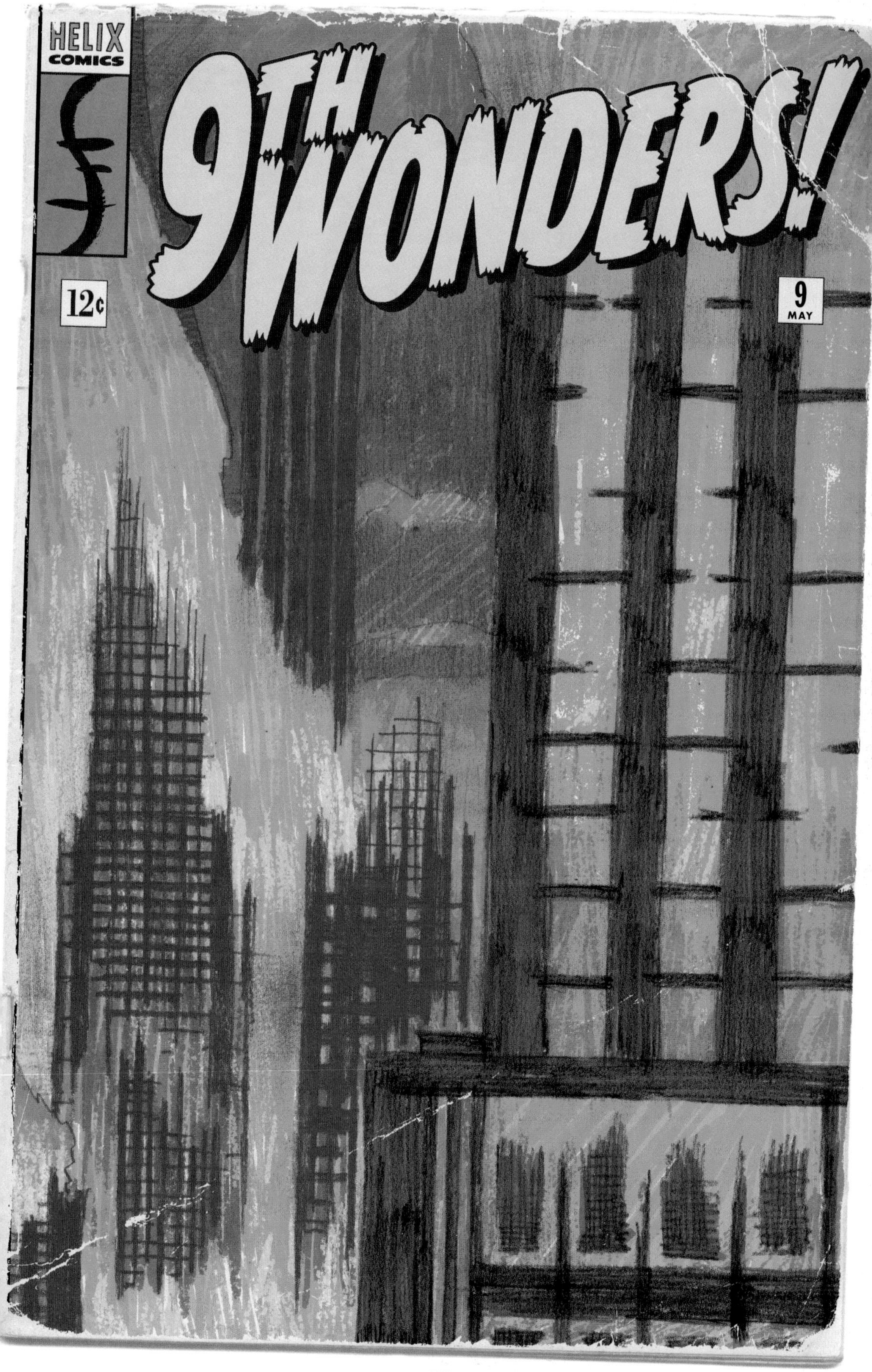
HELIX
COMICS
9TH WONDERS!
12¢
9
MAY

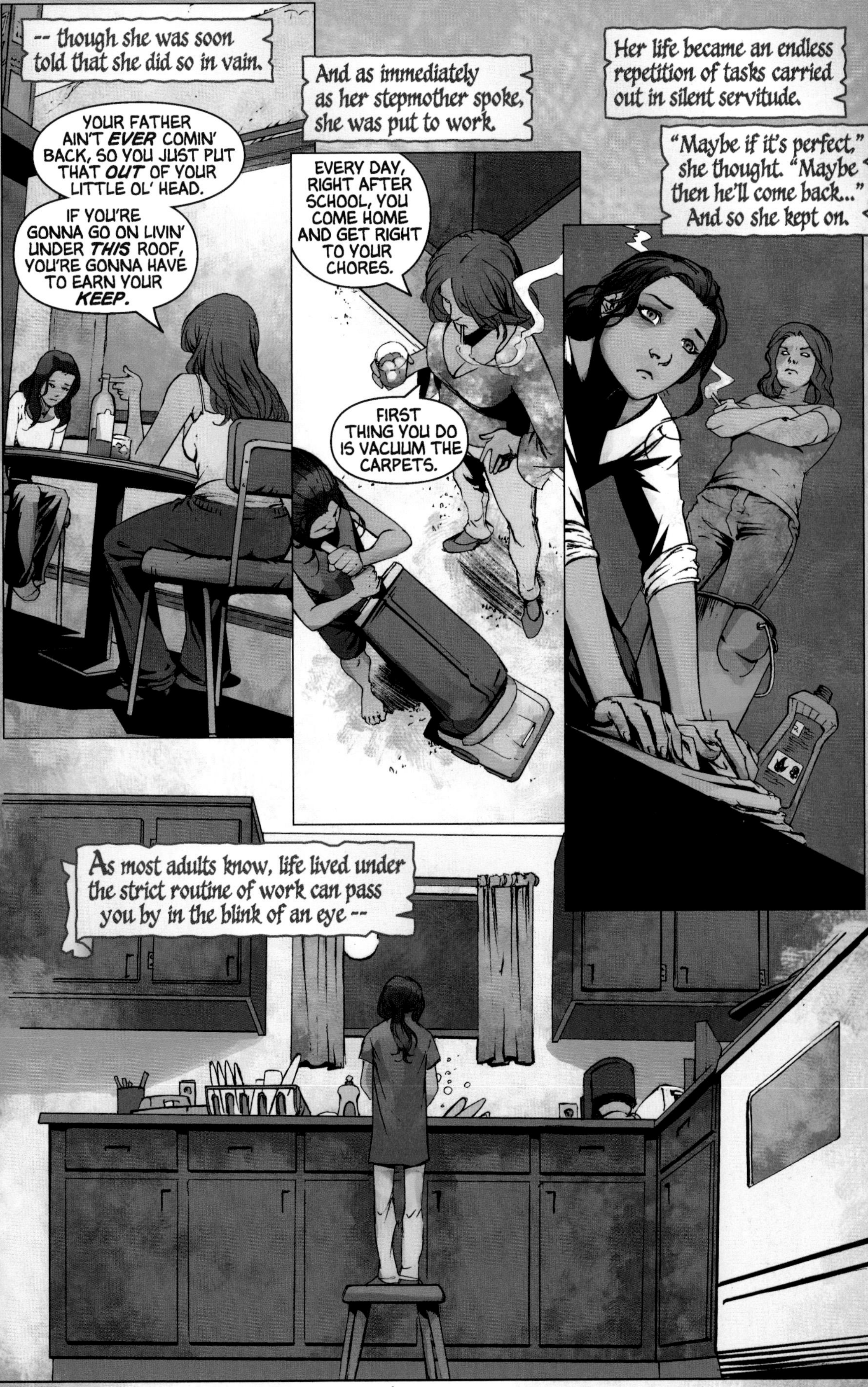
-- though she was soon told that she did so in vain.
YOUR FATHER AIN'T EVER COMIN' BACK, SO YOU JUST PUT THAT OUT OF YOUR LITTLE OL' HEAD.
IF YOU'RE GONNA GO ON LIVIN' UNDER THIS ROOF, YOU'RE GONNA HAVE TO EARN YOUR KEEP.
And as immediately as her stepmother spoke, she was put to work.
EVERY DAY, RIGHT AFTER SCHOOL, YOU COME HOME AND GET RIGHT TO YOUR CHORES.
FIRST THING YOU DO IS VACUUM THE CARPETS.
Her life became an endless repetition of tasks carried out in silent servitude.
"Maybe if it's perfect," she thought. "Maybe then he'll come back..." And so she kept on.
As most adults know, life lived under the strict routine of work can pass you by in the blink of an eye --

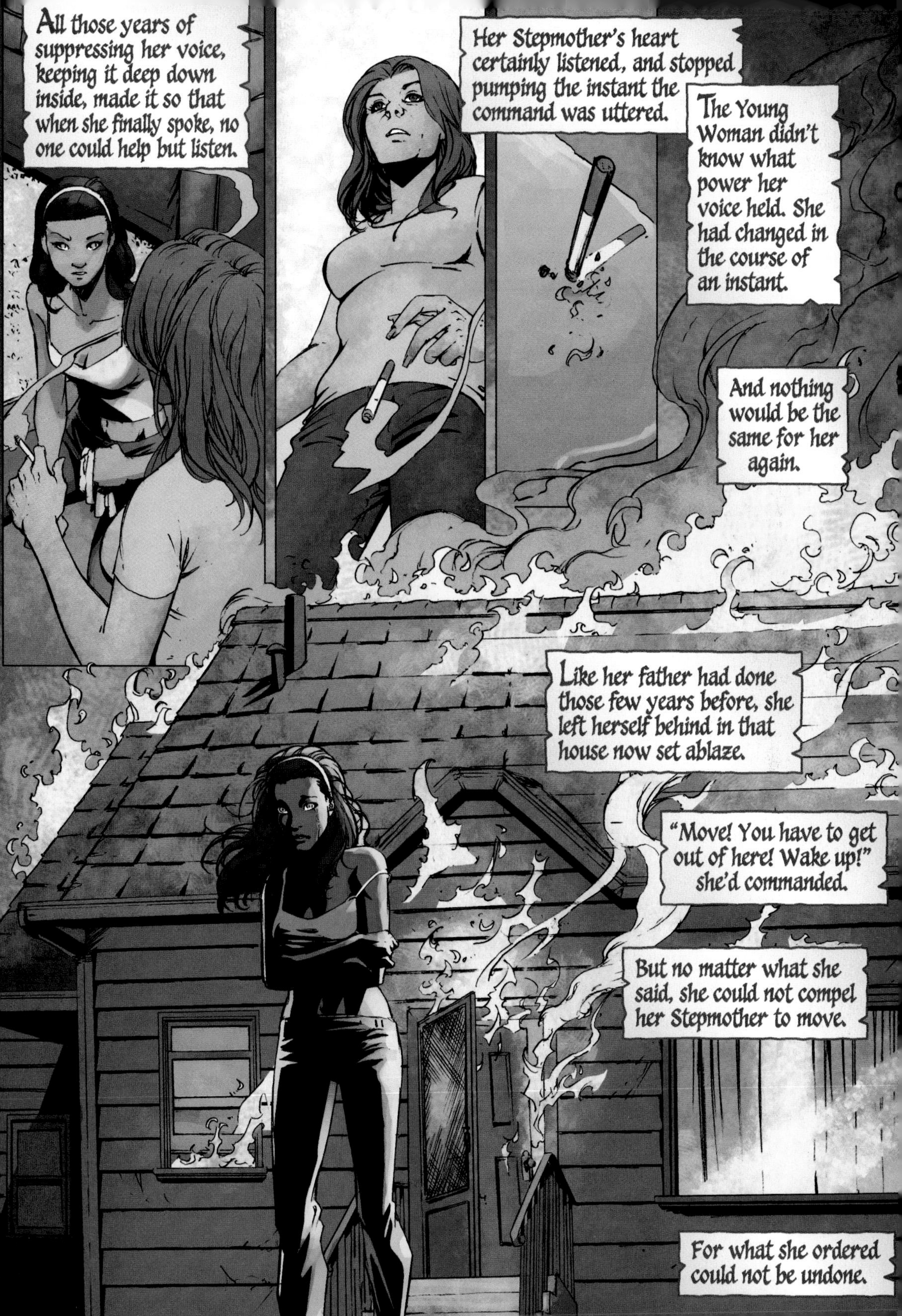
All those years of suppressing her voice, keeping it deep down inside, made it so that when she finally spoke, no one could help but listen.
Her Stepmother's heart certainly listened, and stopped pumping the instant the command was uttered.
The Young Woman didn't know what power her voice held. She had changed in the course of an instant.
And nothing would be the same for her again.
Like her father had done those few years before, she left herself behind in that house now set ablaze.
"Move! You have to get out of here! Wake up!" she'd commanded.
But no matter what she said, she could not compel her Stepmother to move.
For what she ordered could not be undone.

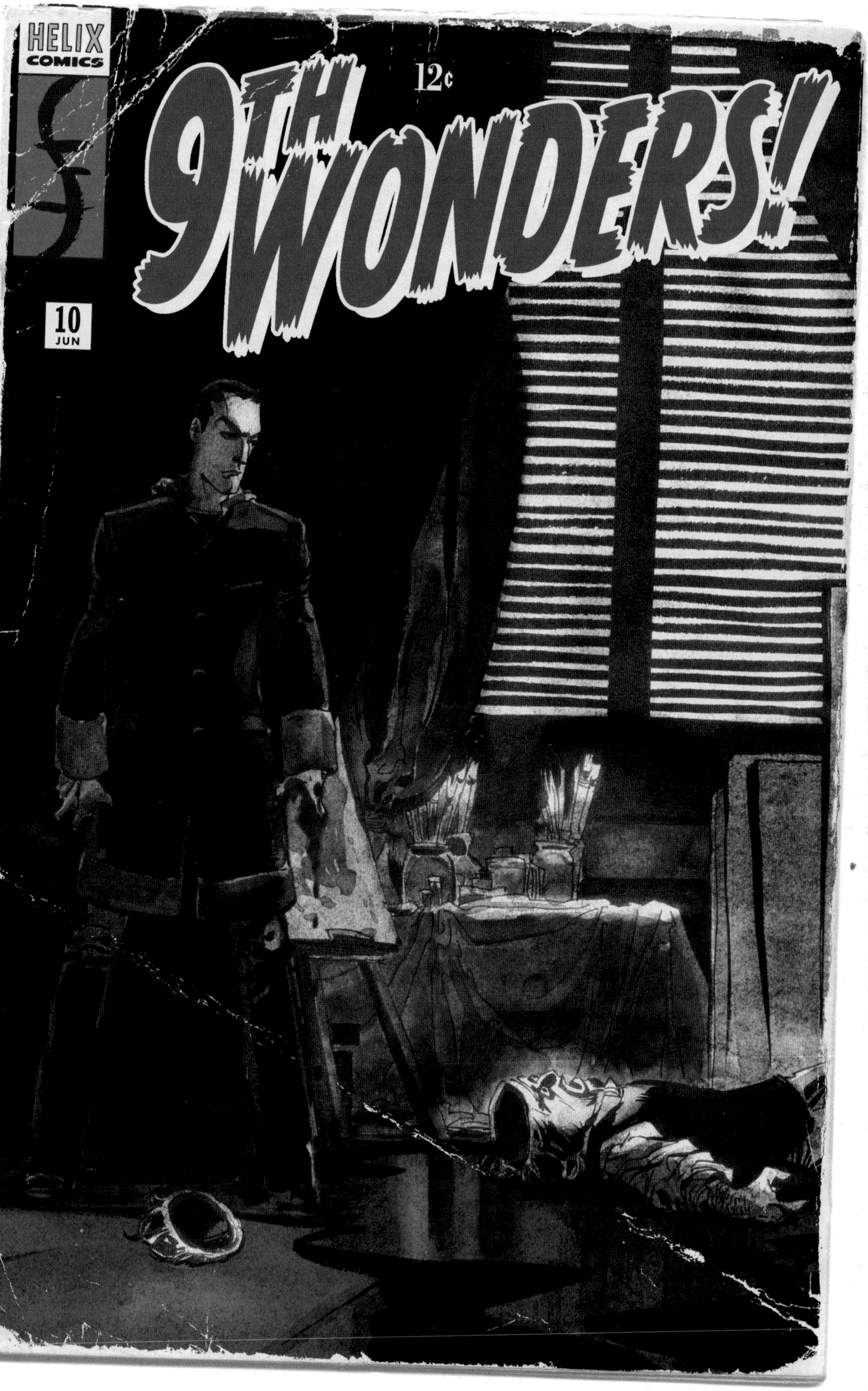
HELIX
COMICS
12¢
9TH WONDERS!
10
JUN

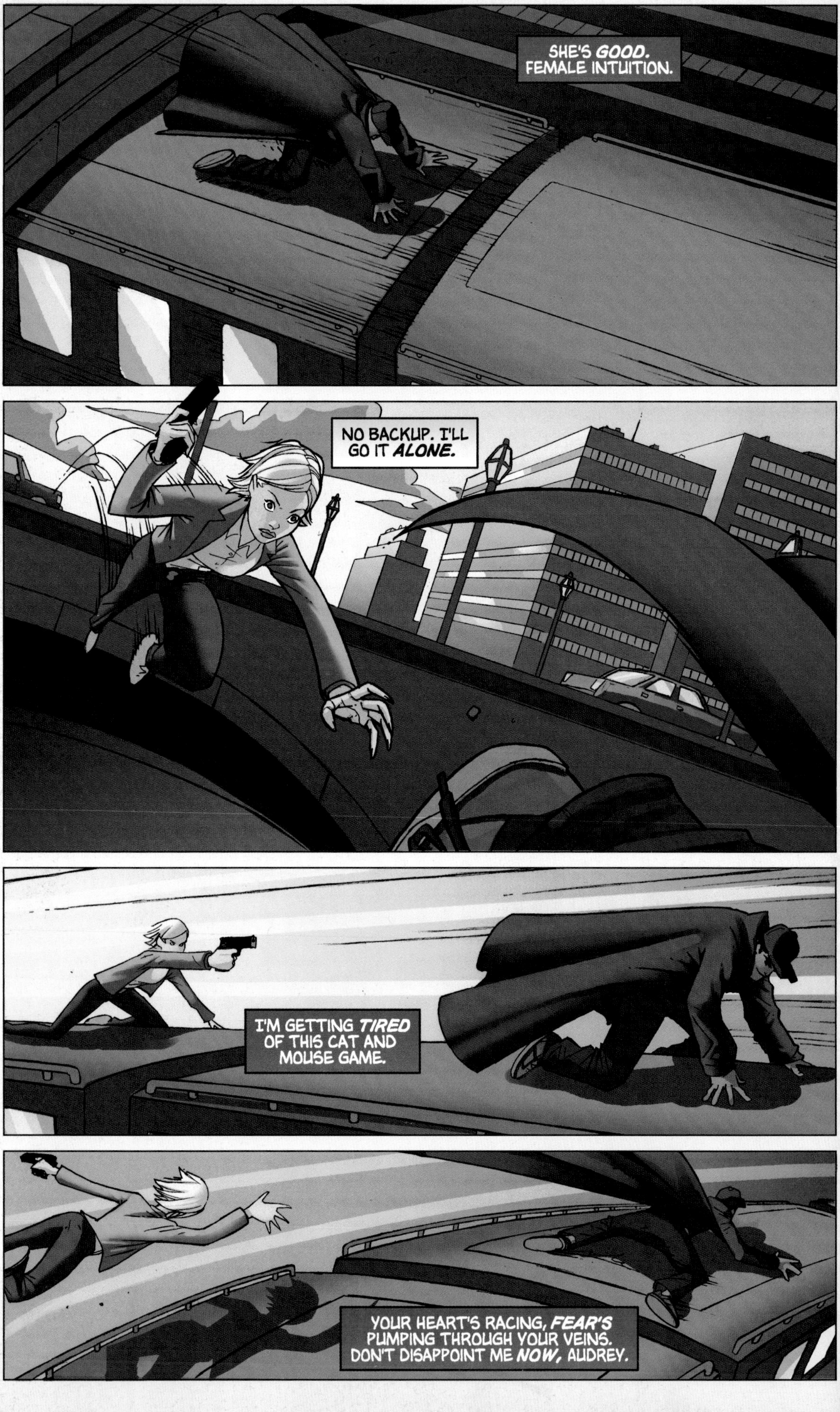
SHE'S GOOD. FEMALE INTUITION.
NO BACKUP. I'LL GO IT ALONE.
I'M GETTING TIRED OF THIS CAT AND MOUSE GAME.
YOUR HEART'S RACING, FEAR'S PUMPING THROUGH YOUR VEINS. DON'T DISAPPOINT ME NOW, AUDREY.

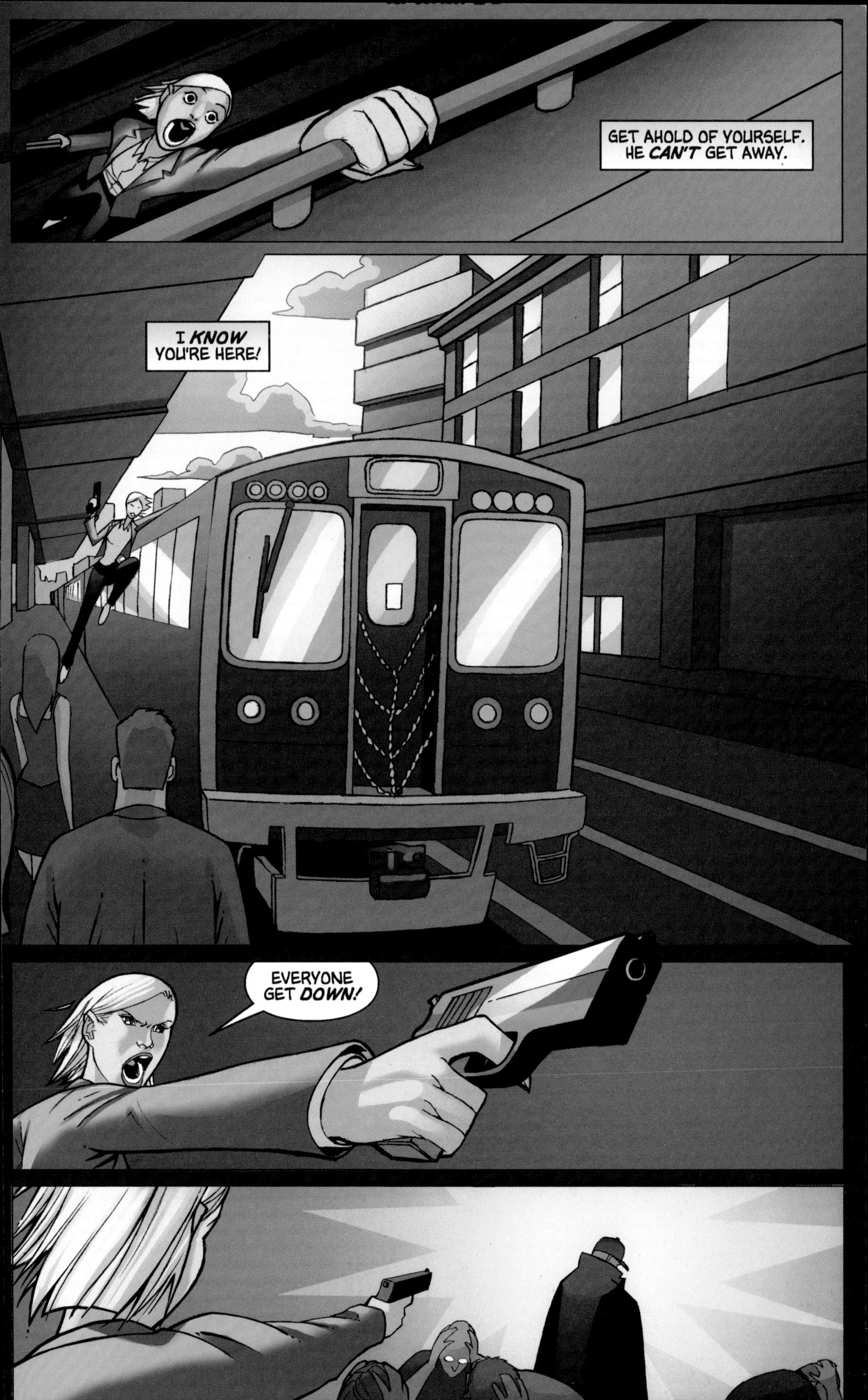
GET AHOLD OF YOURSELF. HE CAN'T GET AWAY.
I KNOW YOU'RE HERE!
EVERYONE GET DOWN!

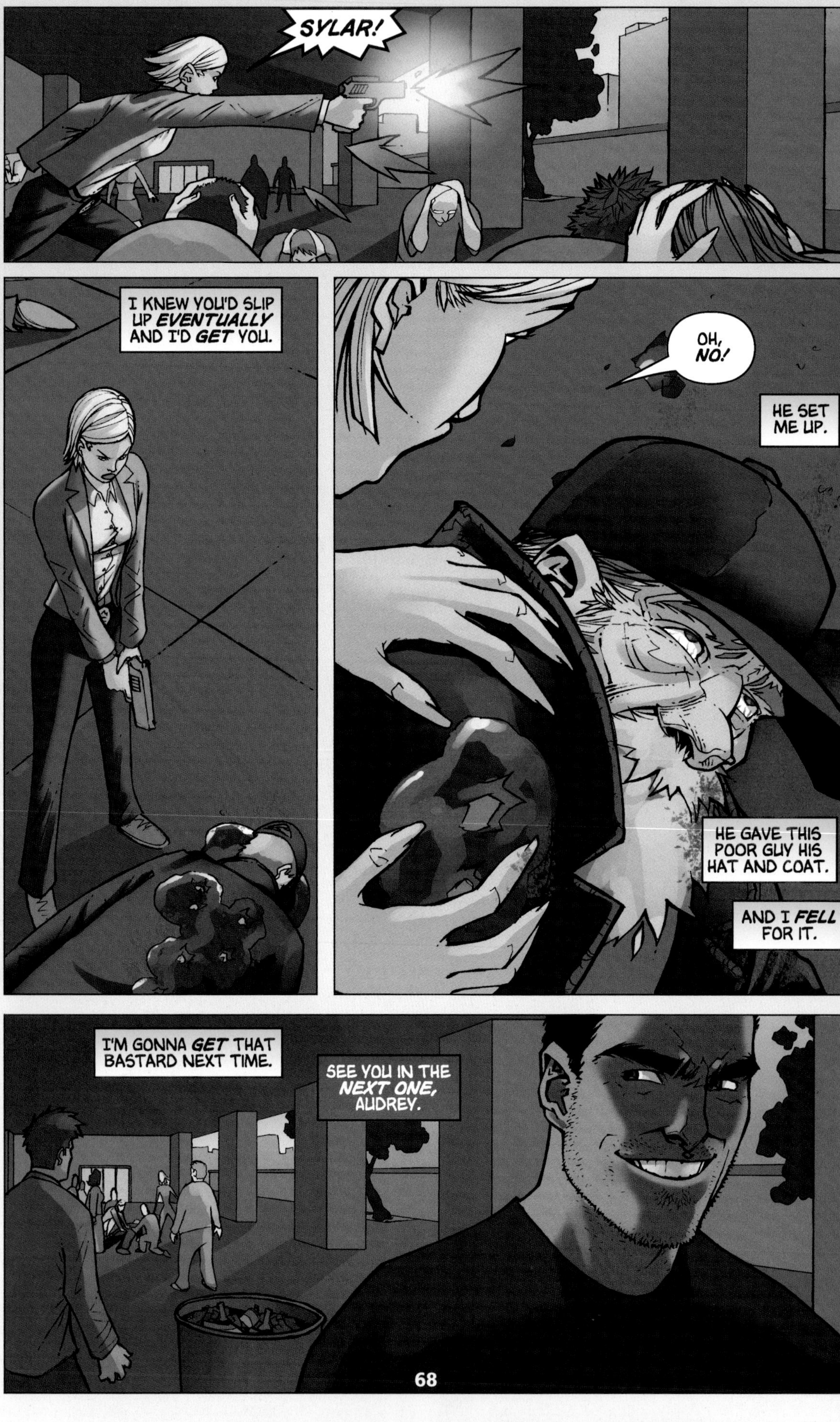
SYLAR!
I KNEW YOU'D SLIP UP *EVENTUALLY* AND I'D *GET* YOU.
OH, *NO!*
HE SET ME UP.
HE GAVE THIS POOR GUY HIS HAT AND COAT.
AND I *FELL* FOR IT.
I'M GONNA *GET* THAT BASTARD NEXT TIME.
SEE YOU IN THE *NEXT ONE,* AUDREY.

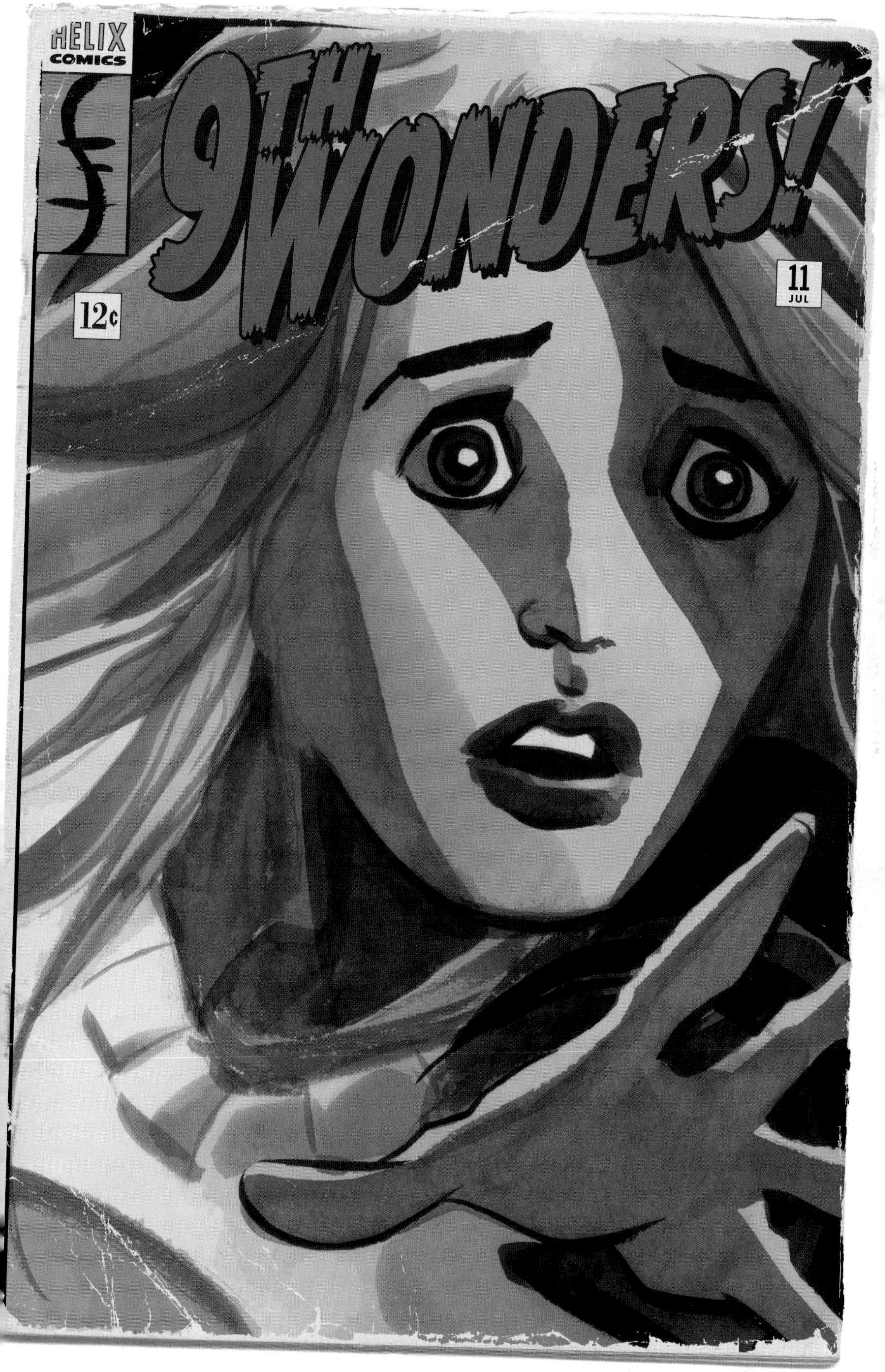
HELIX
COMICS
9TH WONDERS!
12¢
11
JUL

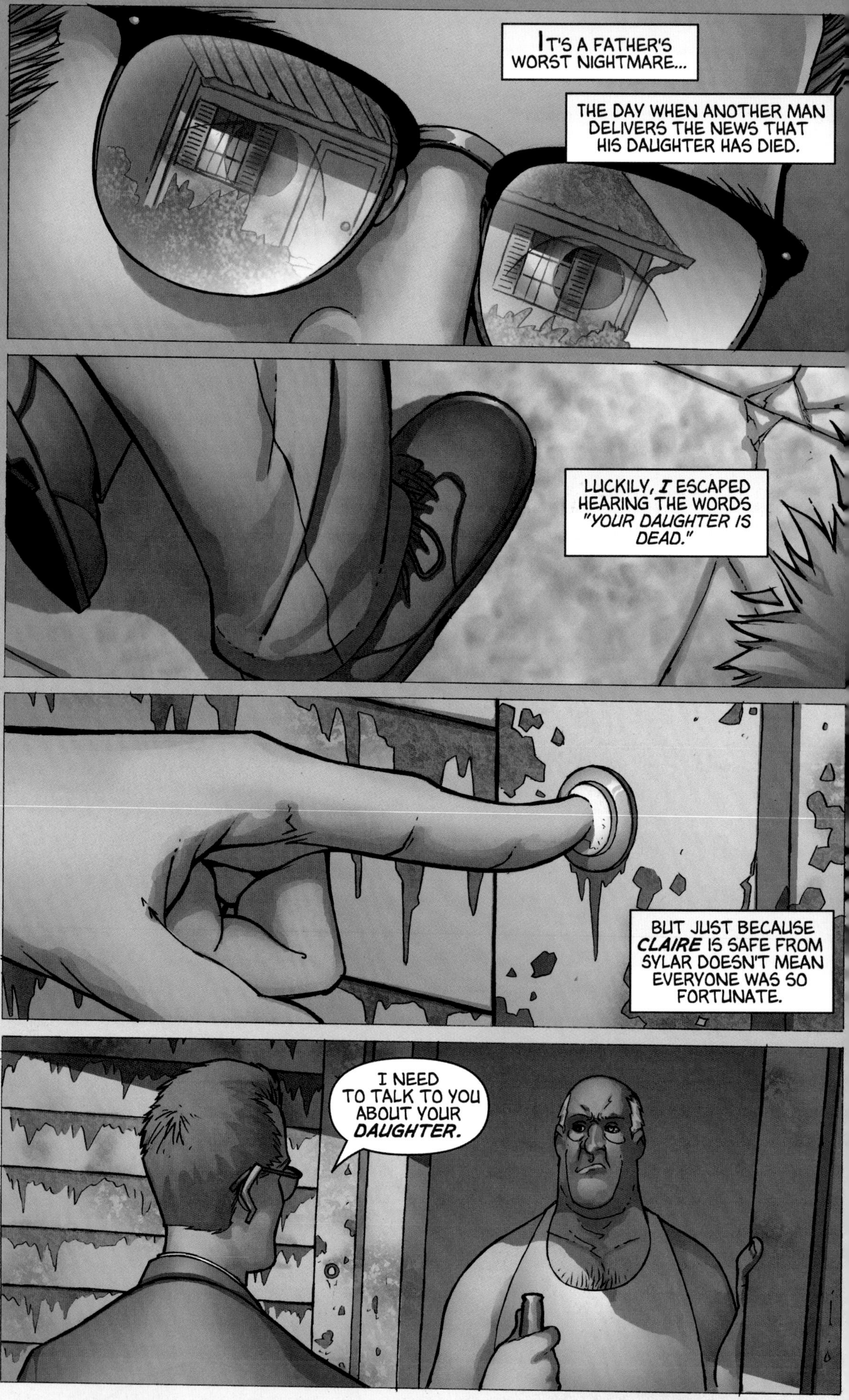
IT'S A FATHER'S WORST NIGHTMARE...
THE DAY WHEN ANOTHER MAN DELIVERS THE NEWS THAT HIS DAUGHTER HAS DIED.
LUCKILY, *I* ESCAPED HEARING THE WORDS *"YOUR DAUGHTER IS DEAD."*
BUT JUST BECAUSE *CLAIRE* IS SAFE FROM SYLAR DOESN'T MEAN EVERYONE WAS SO FORTUNATE.
I NEED TO TALK TO YOU ABOUT YOUR *DAUGHTER*.

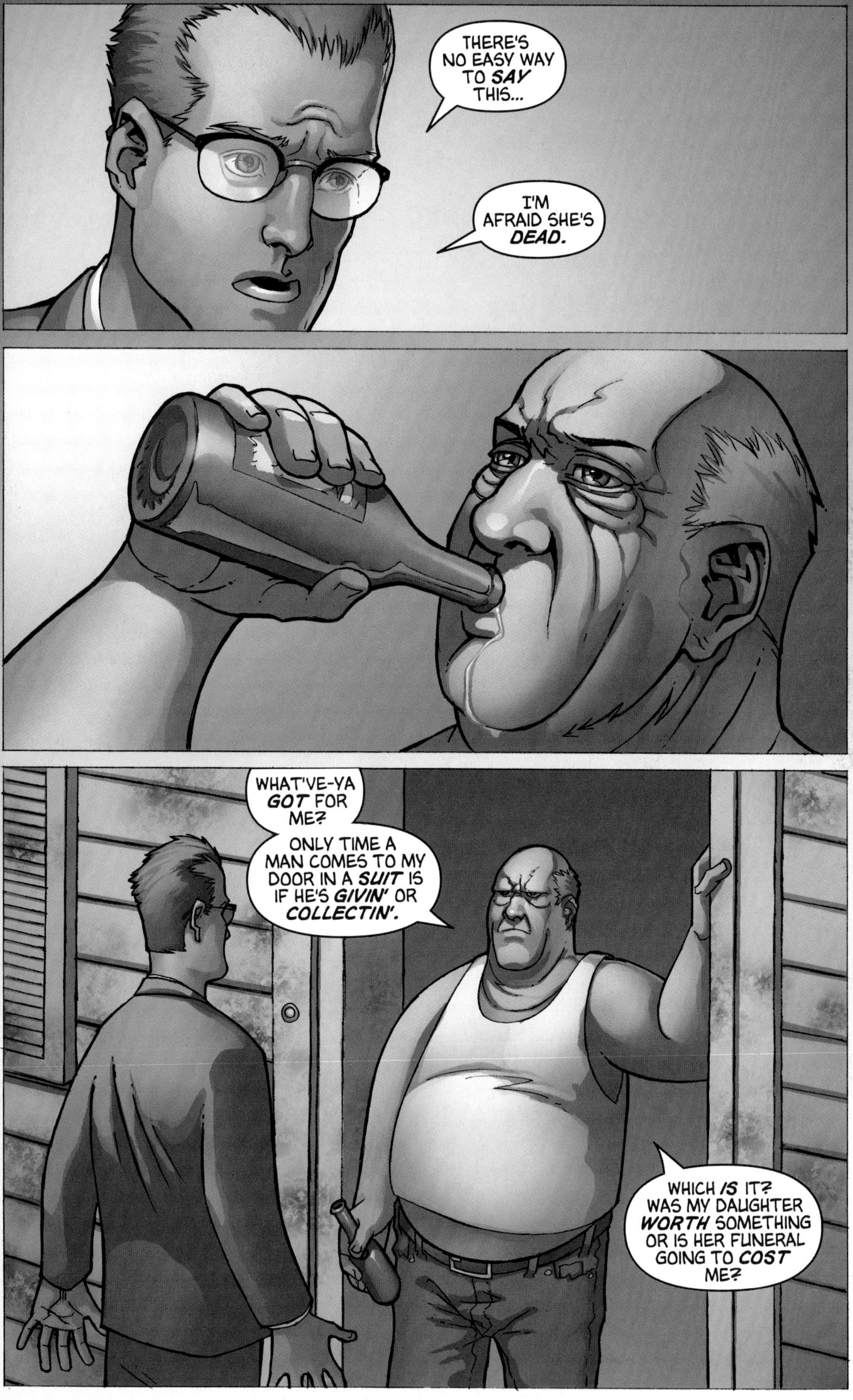
THERE'S NO EASY WAY TO *SAY* THIS...
I'M AFRAID SHE'S *DEAD.*
WHAT'VE-YA *GOT* FOR ME?
ONLY TIME A MAN COMES TO MY DOOR IN A *SUIT* IS IF HE'S *GIVIN'* OR *COLLECTIN'*.
WHICH *IS* IT? WAS MY DAUGHTER *WORTH* SOMETHING OR IS HER FUNERAL GOING TO *COST* ME?

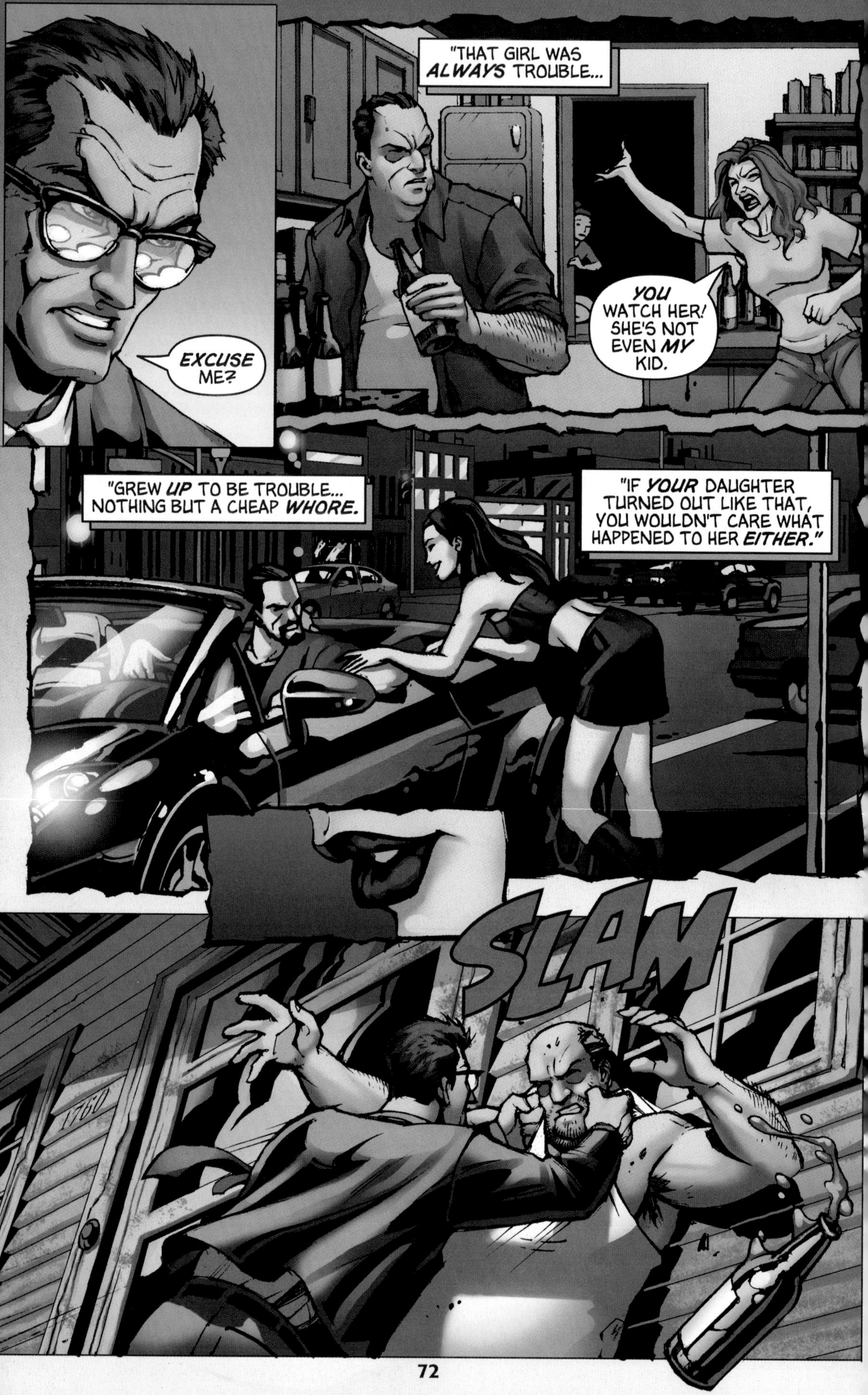

EXCUSE ME?
"THAT GIRL WAS ALWAYS TROUBLE...
YOU WATCH HER! SHE'S NOT EVEN MY KID.
"GREW UP TO BE TROUBLE... NOTHING BUT A CHEAP WHORE.
"IF YOUR DAUGHTER TURNED OUT LIKE THAT, YOU WOULDN'T CARE WHAT HAPPENED TO HER EITHER."
SLAM

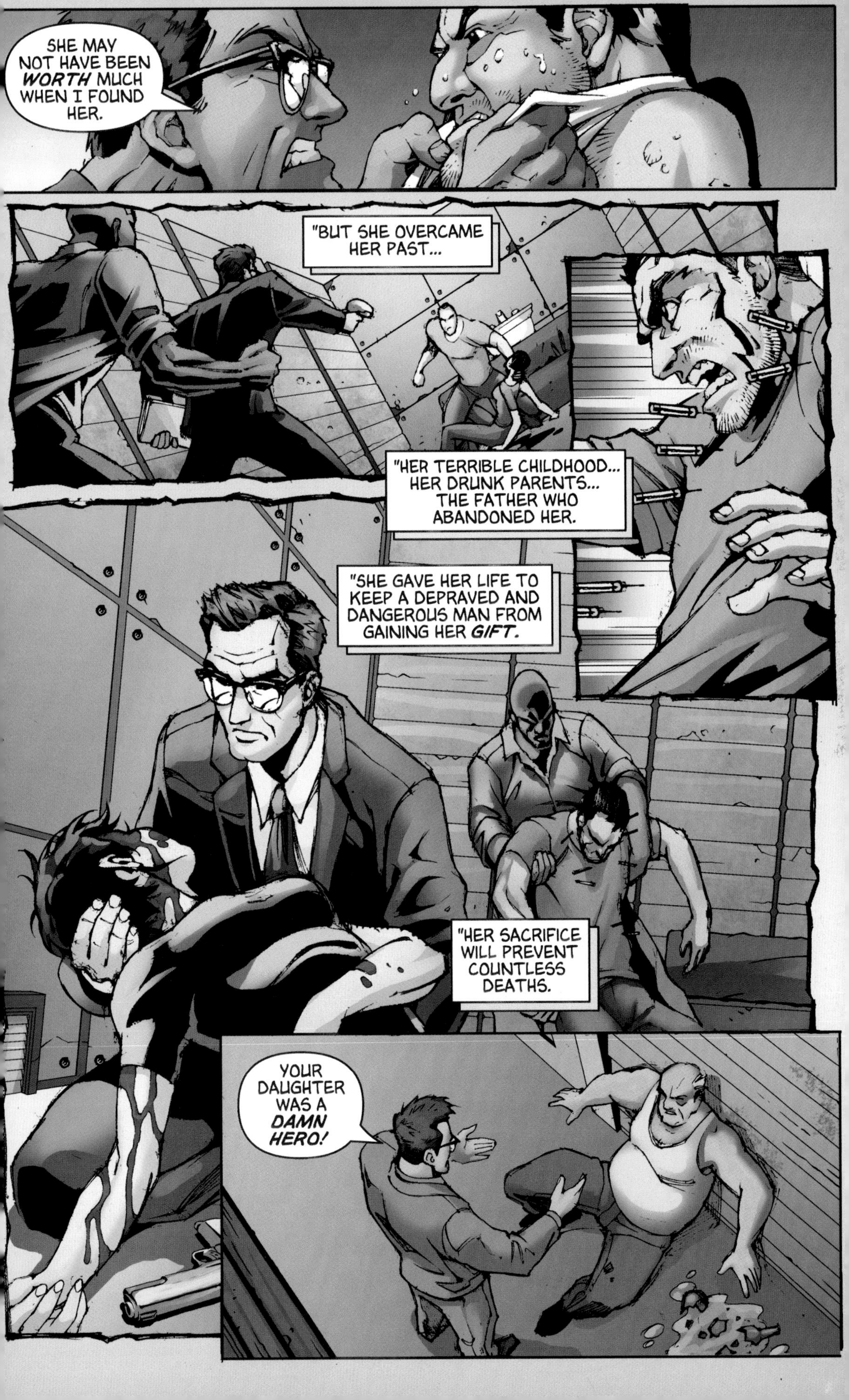
SHE MAY NOT HAVE BEEN WORTH MUCH WHEN I FOUND HER.
"BUT SHE OVERCAME HER PAST...
"HER TERRIBLE CHILDHOOD... HER DRUNK PARENTS... THE FATHER WHO ABANDONED HER.
"SHE GAVE HER LIFE TO KEEP A DEPRAVED AND DANGEROUS MAN FROM GAINING HER GIFT.
"HER SACRIFICE WILL PREVENT COUNTLESS DEATHS.
YOUR DAUGHTER WAS A DAMN HERO!

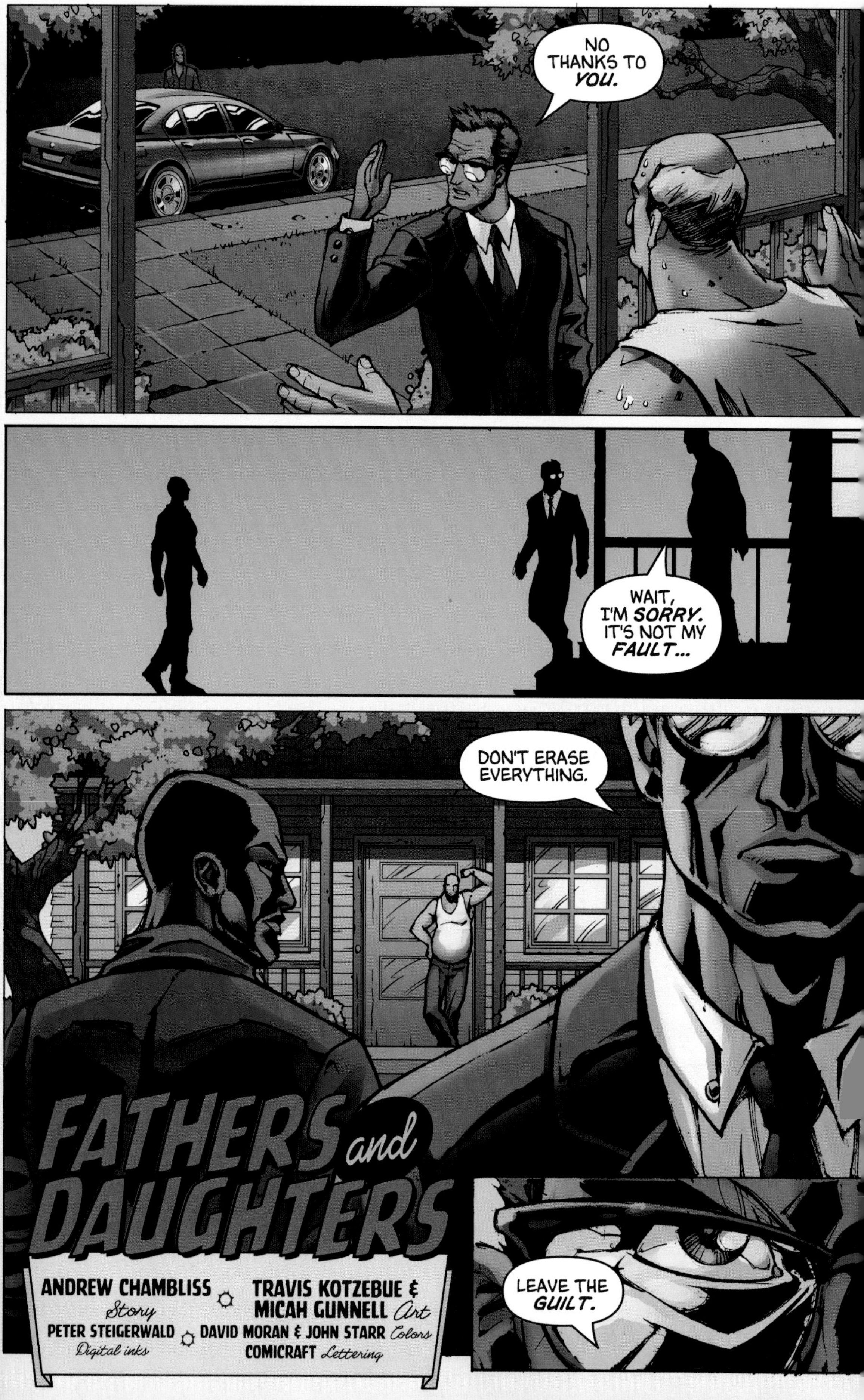

NO THANKS TO *YOU.*
WAIT, I'M *SORRY.* IT'S NOT MY *FAULT...*
DON'T ERASE EVERYTHING.
FATHERS and DAUGHTERS
ANDREW CHAMBLISS Story
TRAVIS KOTZEBUE & MICAH GUNNELL Art
PETER STEIGERWALD Digital inks
DAVID MORAN & JOHN STARR Colors
COMICRAFT Lettering
LEAVE THE *GUILT.*

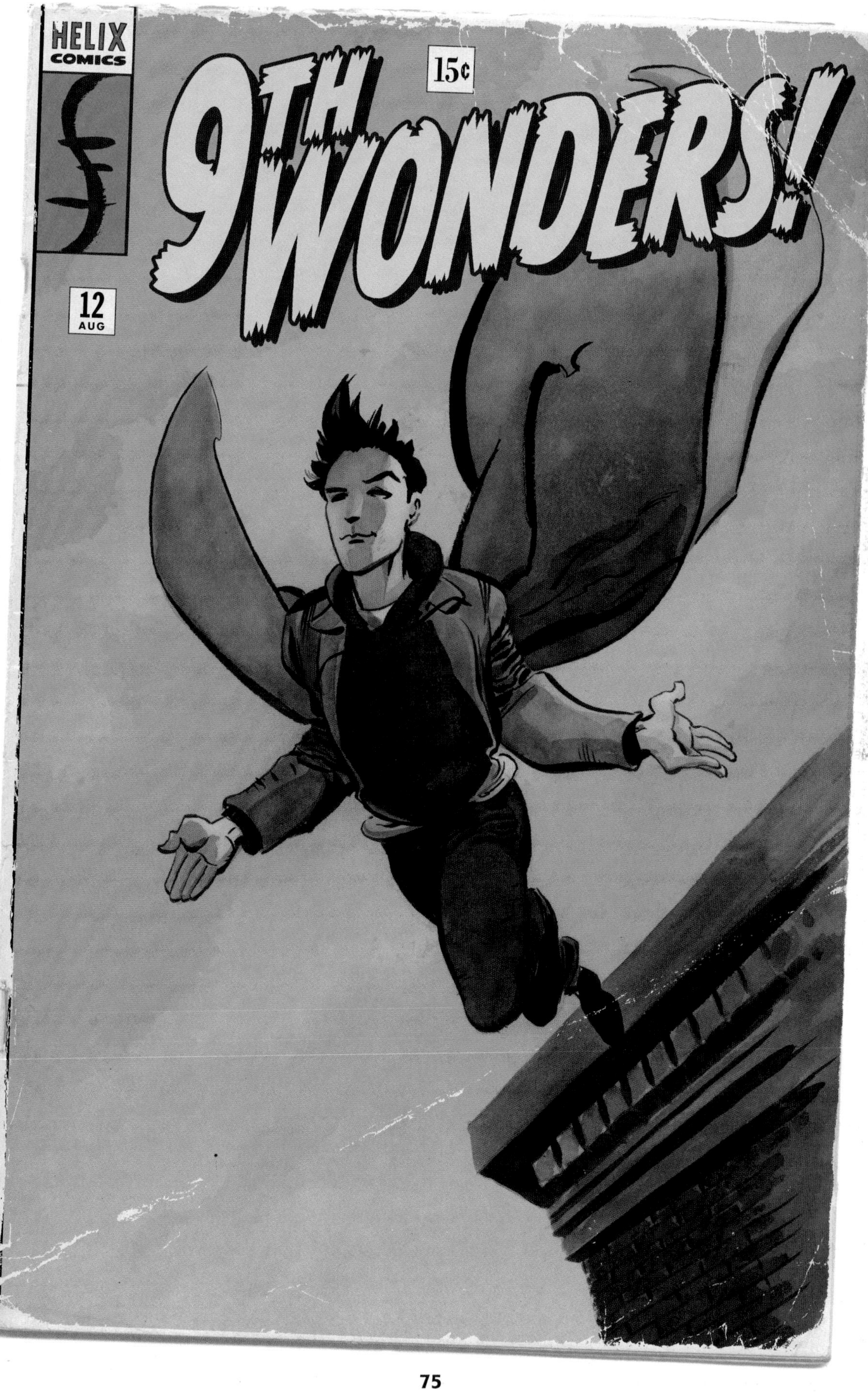
HELIX
COMICS
15¢
9TH WONDERS!
12
AUG

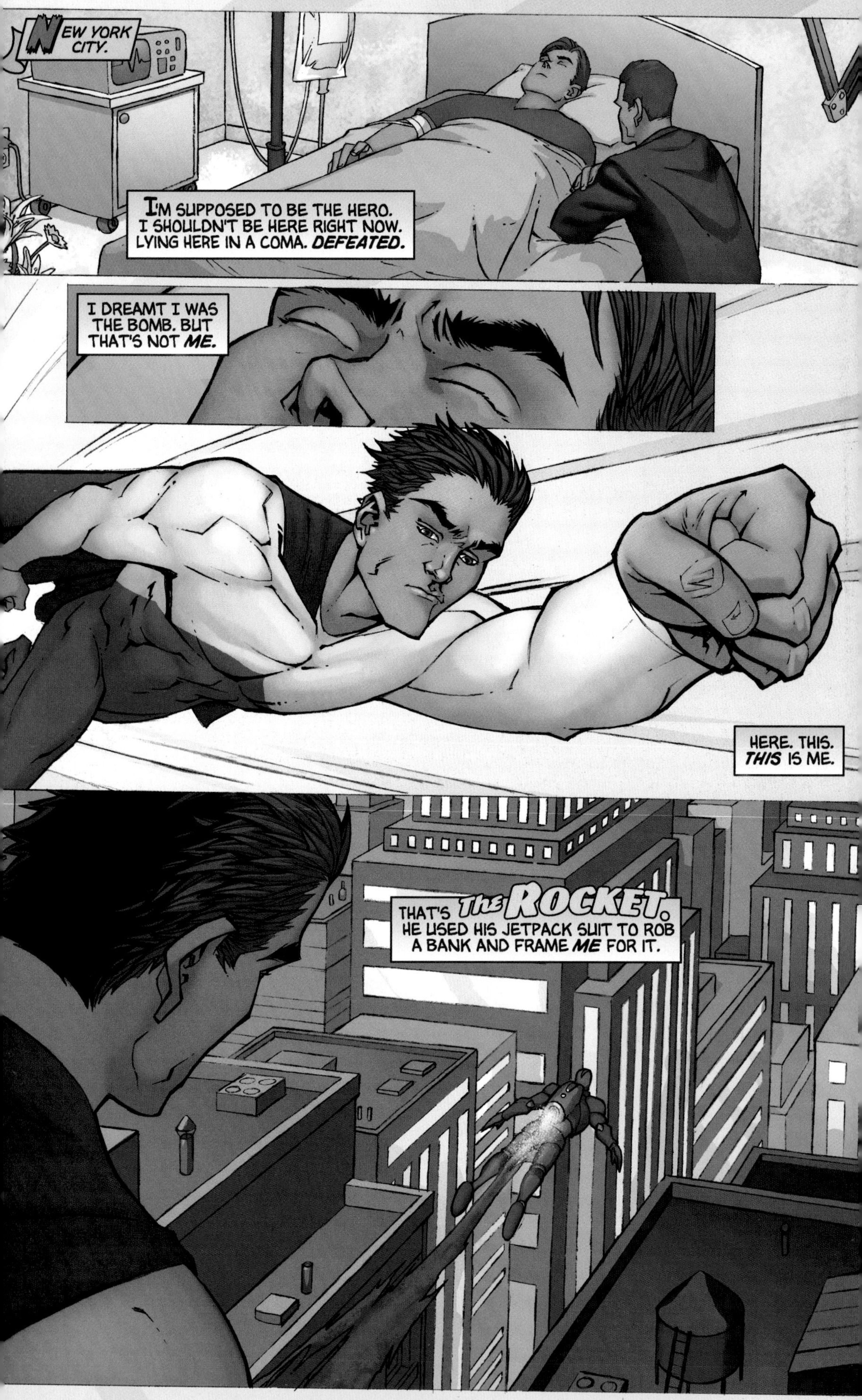
NEW YORK CITY.
I'M SUPPOSED TO BE THE HERO. I SHOULDN'T BE HERE RIGHT NOW. LYING HERE IN A COMA. DEFEATED.
I DREAMT I WAS THE BOMB. BUT THAT'S NOT ME.
HERE. THIS. THIS IS ME.
THAT'S THE ROCKET. HE USED HIS JETPACK SUIT TO ROB A BANK AND FRAME ME FOR IT.

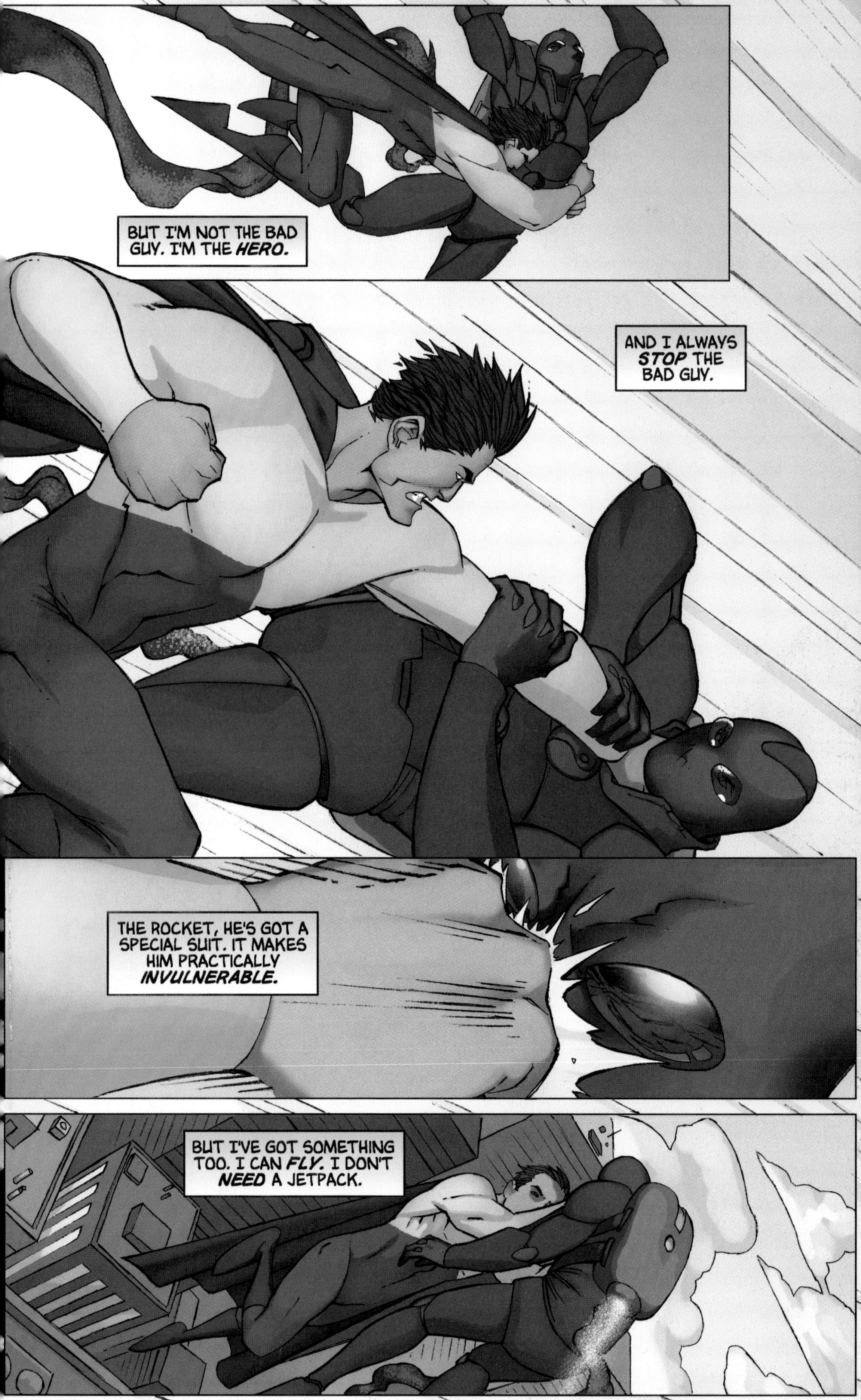
BUT I'M NOT THE BAD GUY. I'M THE *HERO.*
AND I ALWAYS *STOP* THE BAD GUY.
THE ROCKET, HE'S GOT A SPECIAL SUIT. IT MAKES HIM PRACTICALLY *INVULNERABLE.*
BUT I'VE GOT SOMETHING TOO. I CAN *FLY.* I DON'T *NEED* A JETPACK.

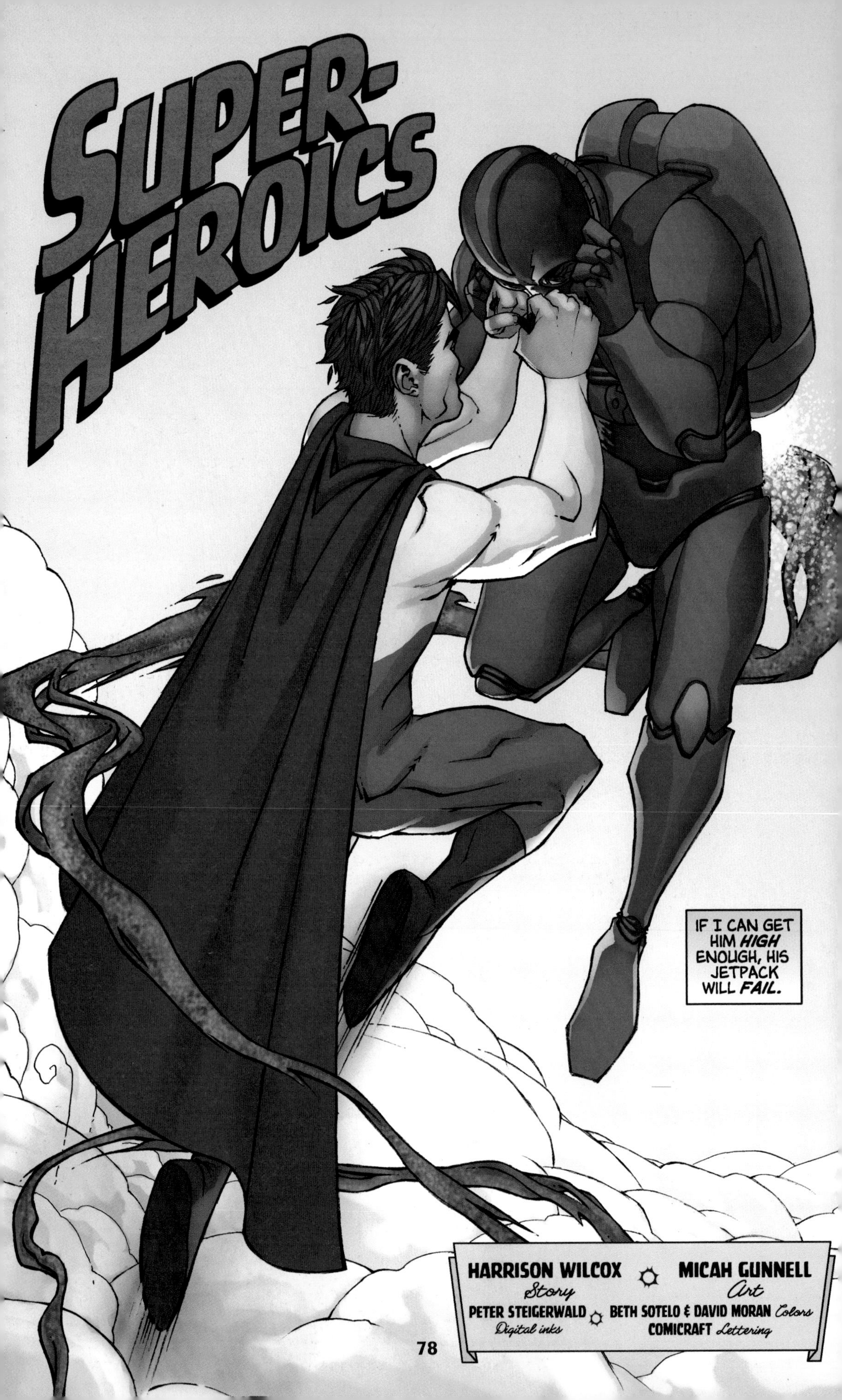
SUPER-HEROICS
IF I CAN GET HIM HIGH ENOUGH, HIS JETPACK WILL FAIL.
HARRISON WILCOX Story
MICAH GUNNELL Art
PETER STEIGERWALD Digital inks
BETH SOTELO & DAVID MORAN Colors
COMICRAFT Lettering

THEN ALL I NEED IS TO HIT HIS SUIT HARD ENOUGH AGAINST SOMETHING TO *BREAK* IT.

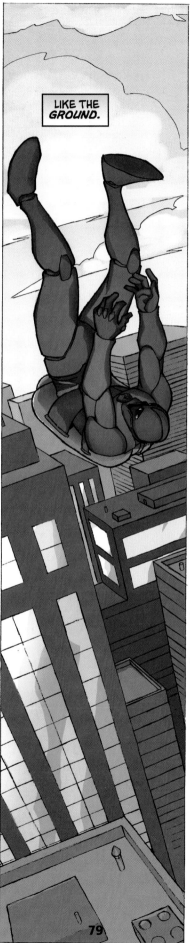

LIKE THE *GROUND.*

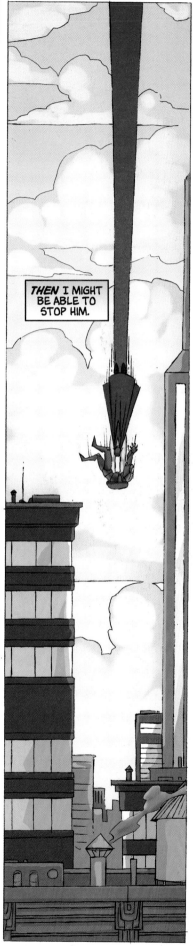

THEN I MIGHT BE ABLE TO STOP HIM.

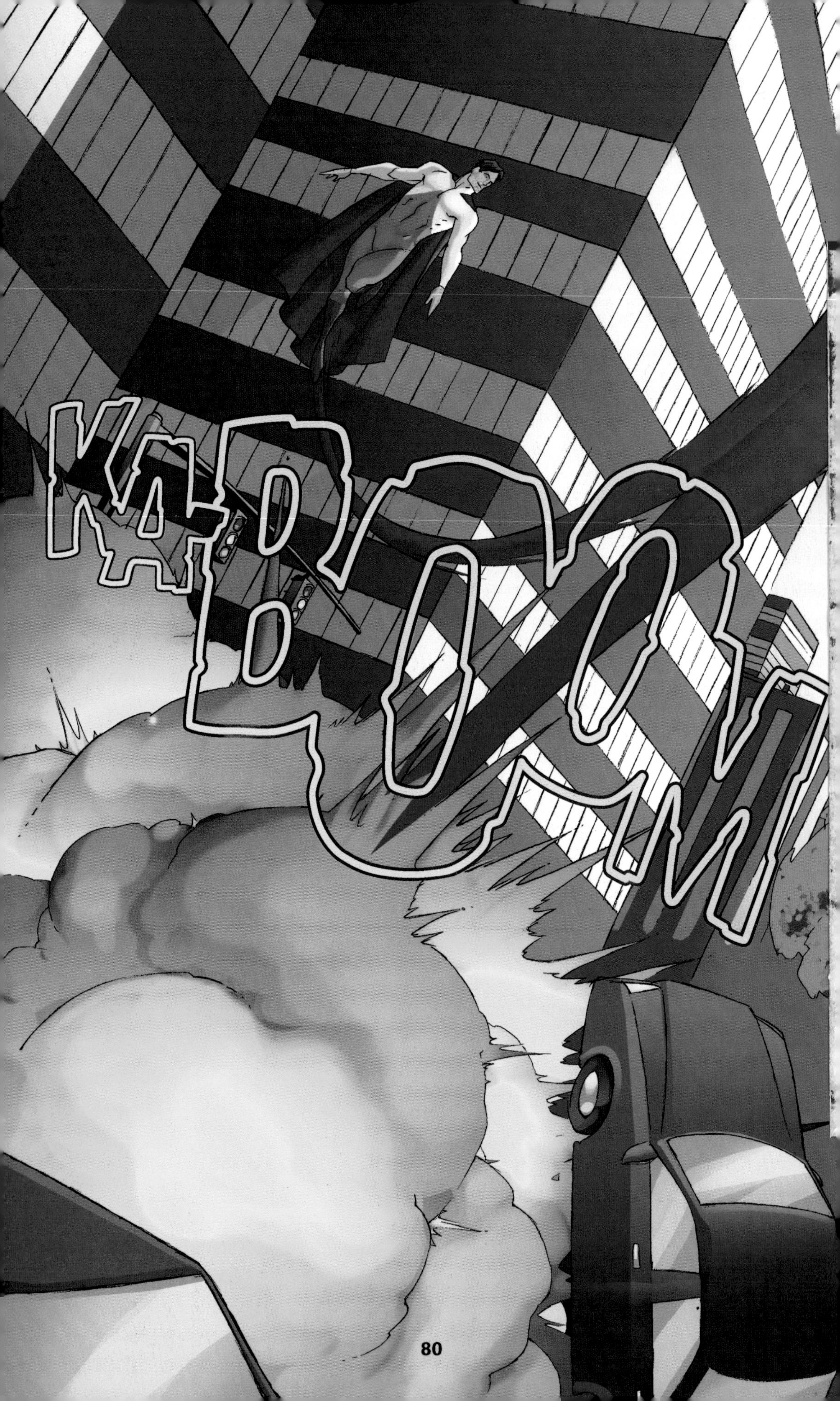
KA-BOOM

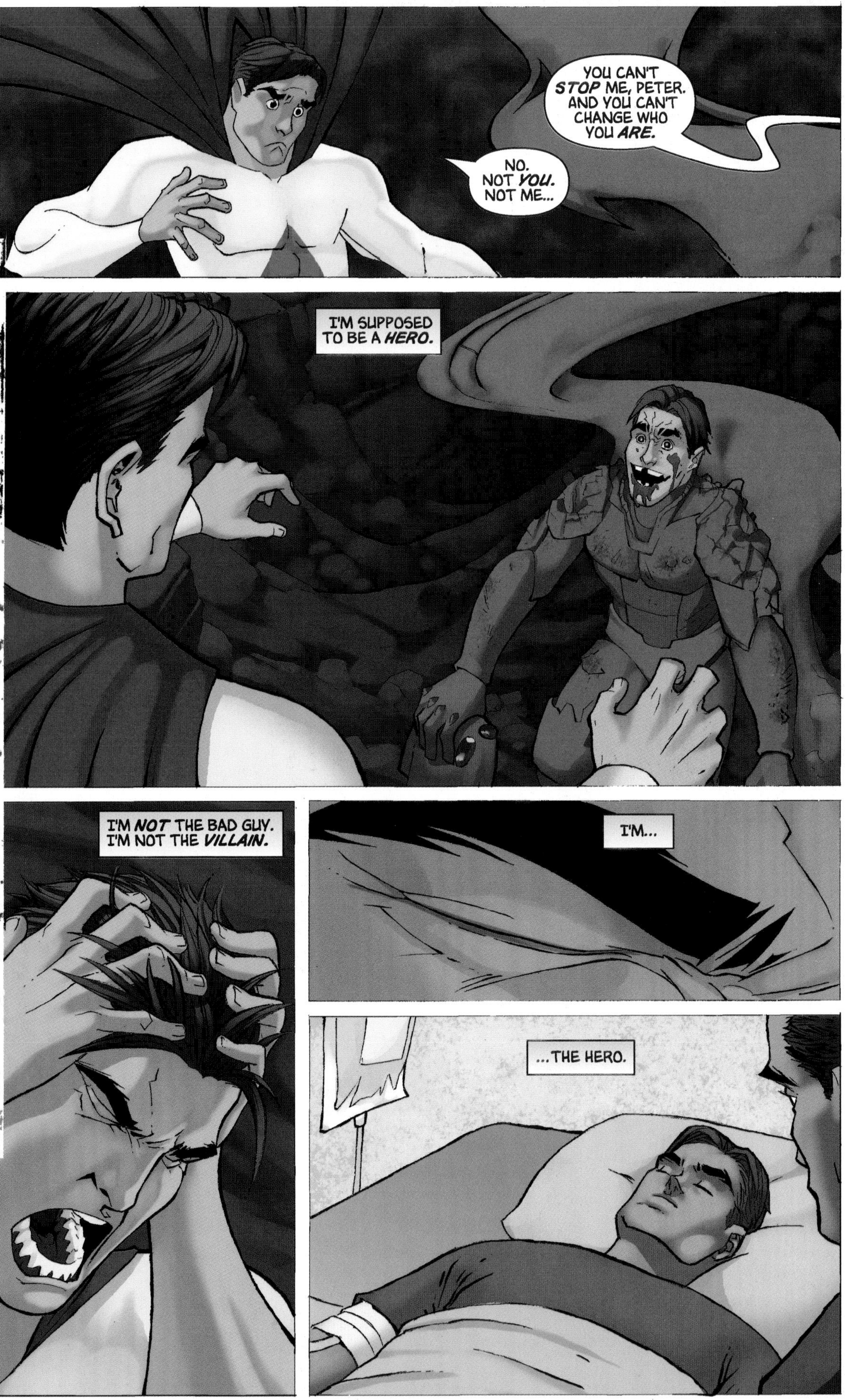
YOU CAN'T STOP ME, PETER. AND YOU CAN'T CHANGE WHO YOU ARE.
NO. NOT YOU. NOT ME...
I'M SUPPOSED TO BE A HERO.
I'M NOT THE BAD GUY. I'M NOT THE VILLAIN.
I'M...
...THE HERO.

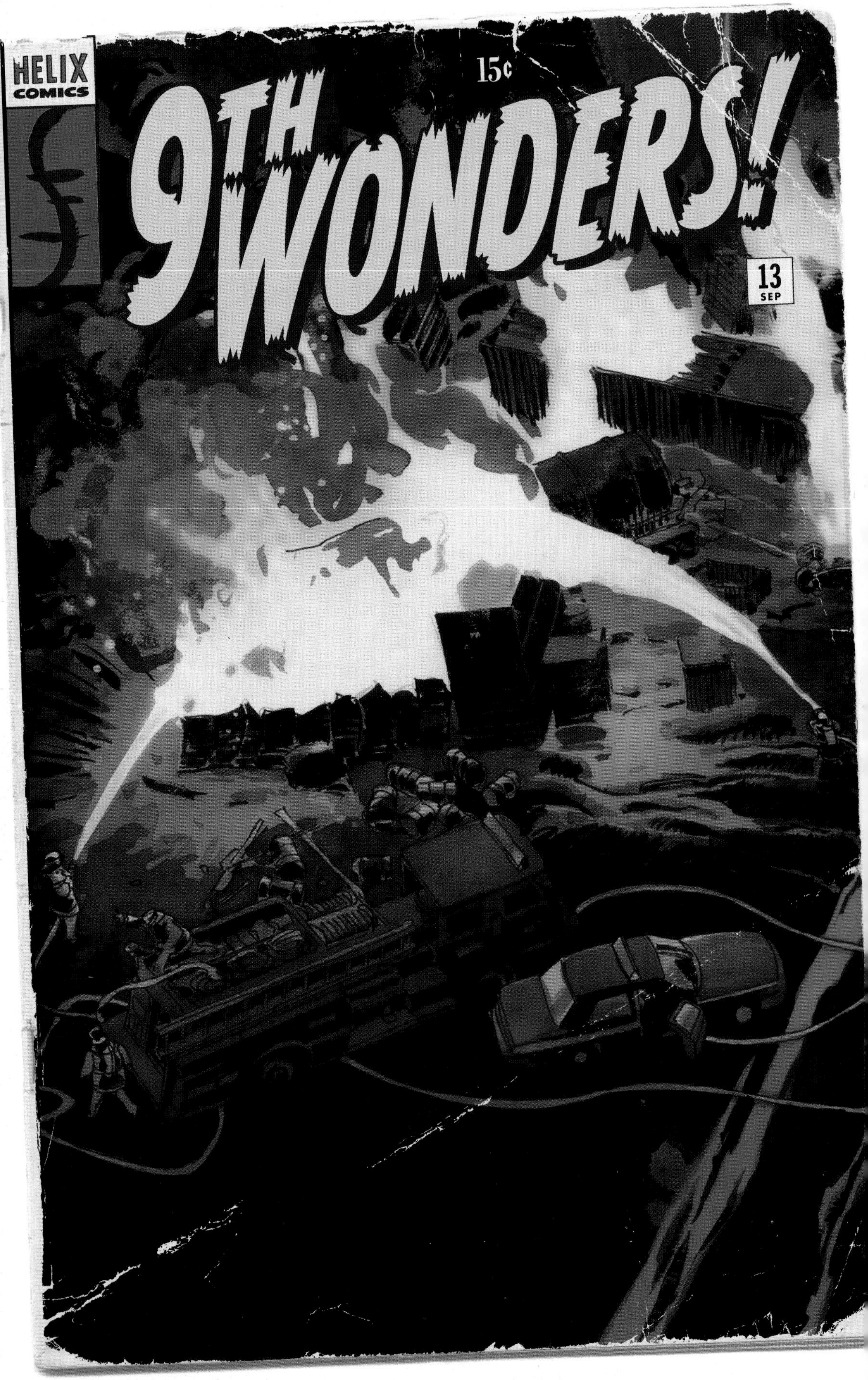
HELIX
COMICS
15¢
9TH WONDERS!
13
SEP

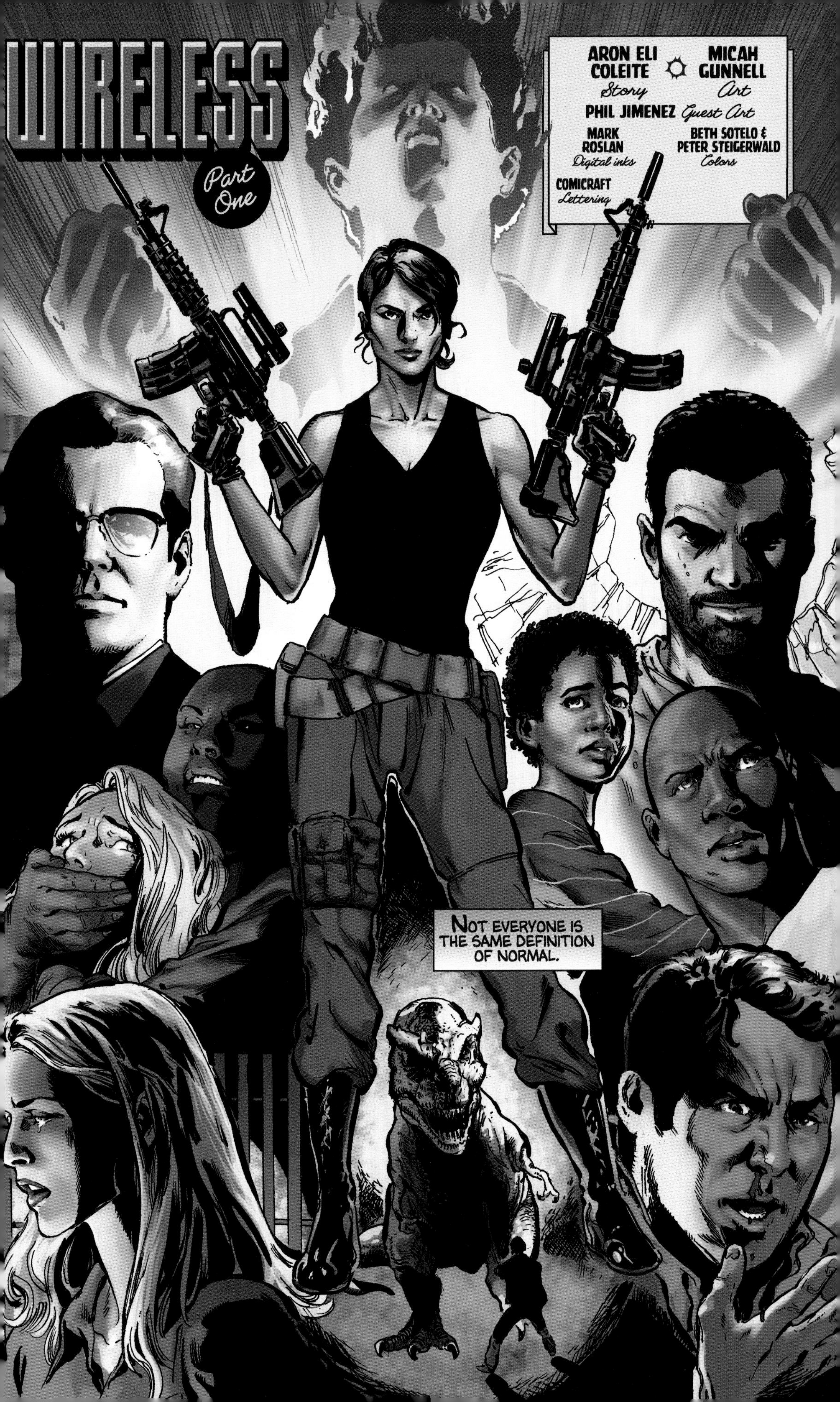
WIRELESS
Part One
ARON ELI COLEITE Story
MICAH GUNNELL Art
PHIL JIMENEZ Guest Art
MARK ROSLAN Digital inks
BETH SOTELO & PETER STEIGERWALD Colors
COMICRAFT Lettering
NOT EVERYONE IS THE SAME DEFINITION OF NORMAL.

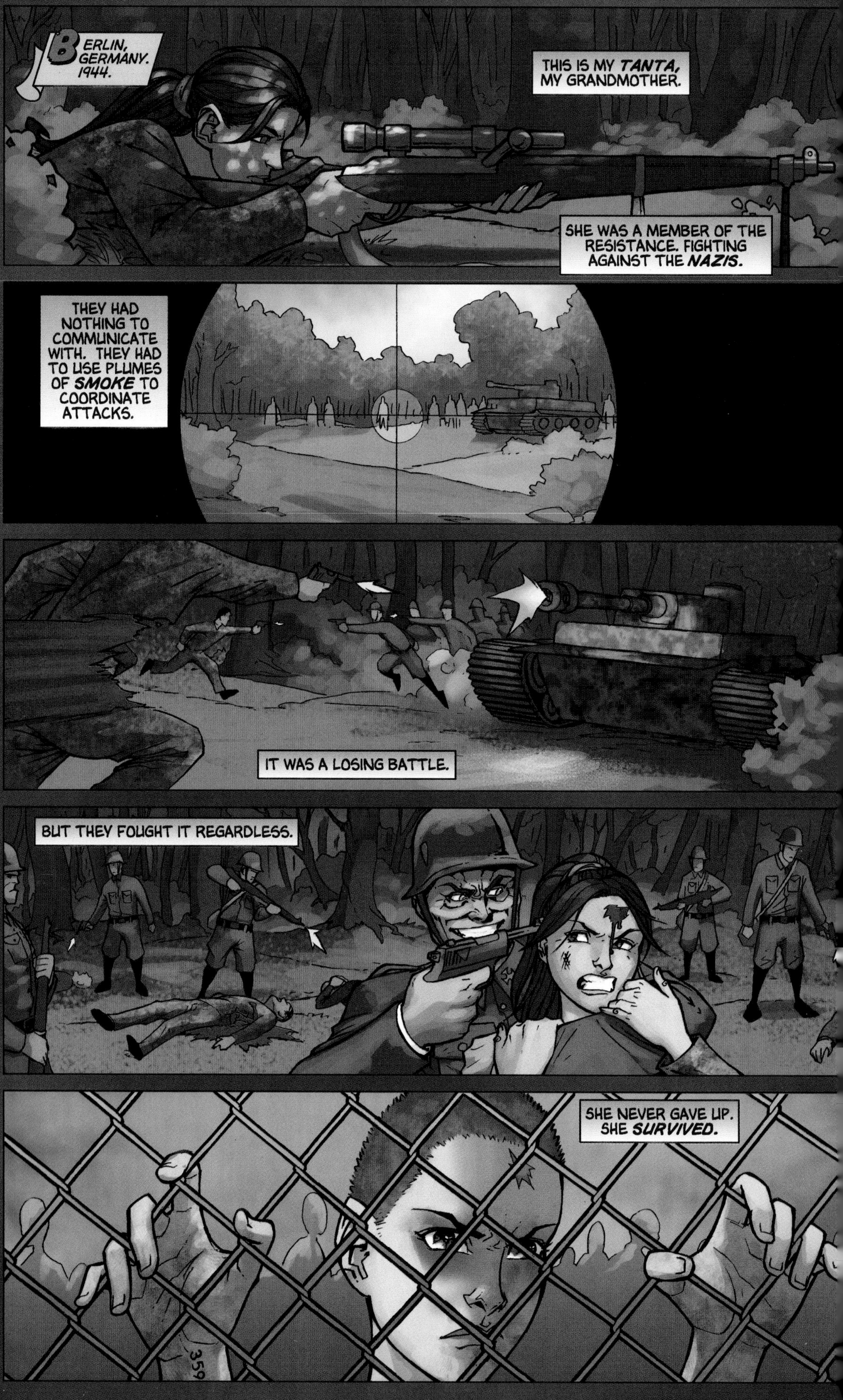
BERLIN, GERMANY. 1944.
THIS IS MY *TANTA*, MY GRANDMOTHER.
SHE WAS A MEMBER OF THE RESISTANCE. FIGHTING AGAINST THE *NAZIS*.
THEY HAD NOTHING TO COMMUNICATE WITH. THEY HAD TO USE PLUMES OF *SMOKE* TO COORDINATE ATTACKS.
IT WAS A LOSING BATTLE.
BUT THEY FOUGHT IT REGARDLESS.
SHE NEVER GAVE UP. SHE *SURVIVED*.
359

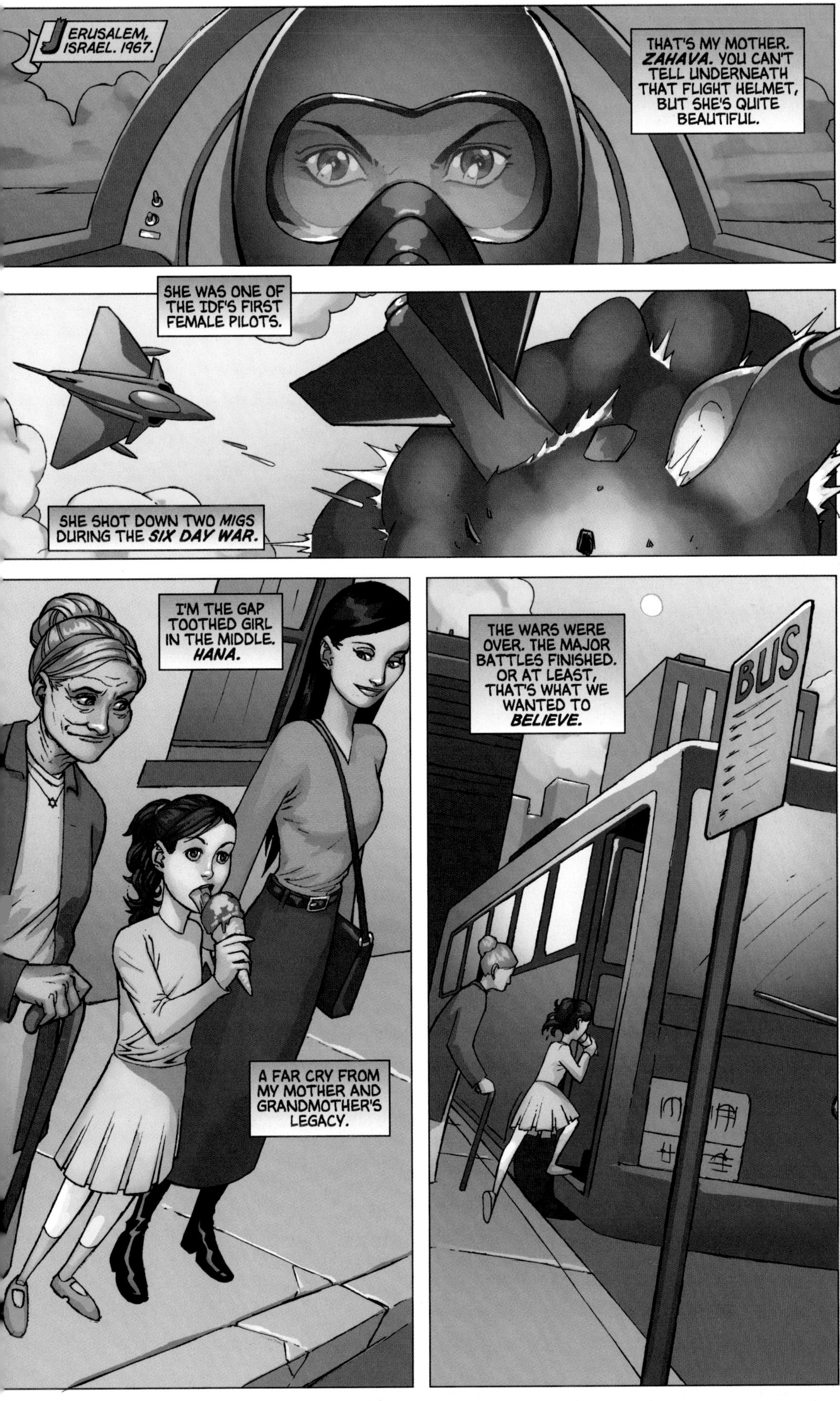
JERUSALEM, ISRAEL. 1967.
THAT'S MY MOTHER. ZAHAVA. YOU CAN'T TELL UNDERNEATH THAT FLIGHT HELMET, BUT SHE'S QUITE BEAUTIFUL.
SHE WAS ONE OF THE IDF'S FIRST FEMALE PILOTS.
SHE SHOT DOWN TWO MIGS DURING THE SIX DAY WAR.
I'M THE GAP TOOTHED GIRL IN THE MIDDLE. HANA.
A FAR CRY FROM MY MOTHER AND GRANDMOTHER'S LEGACY.
THE WARS WERE OVER. THE MAJOR BATTLES FINISHED. OR AT LEAST, THAT'S WHAT WE WANTED TO BELIEVE.
BUS

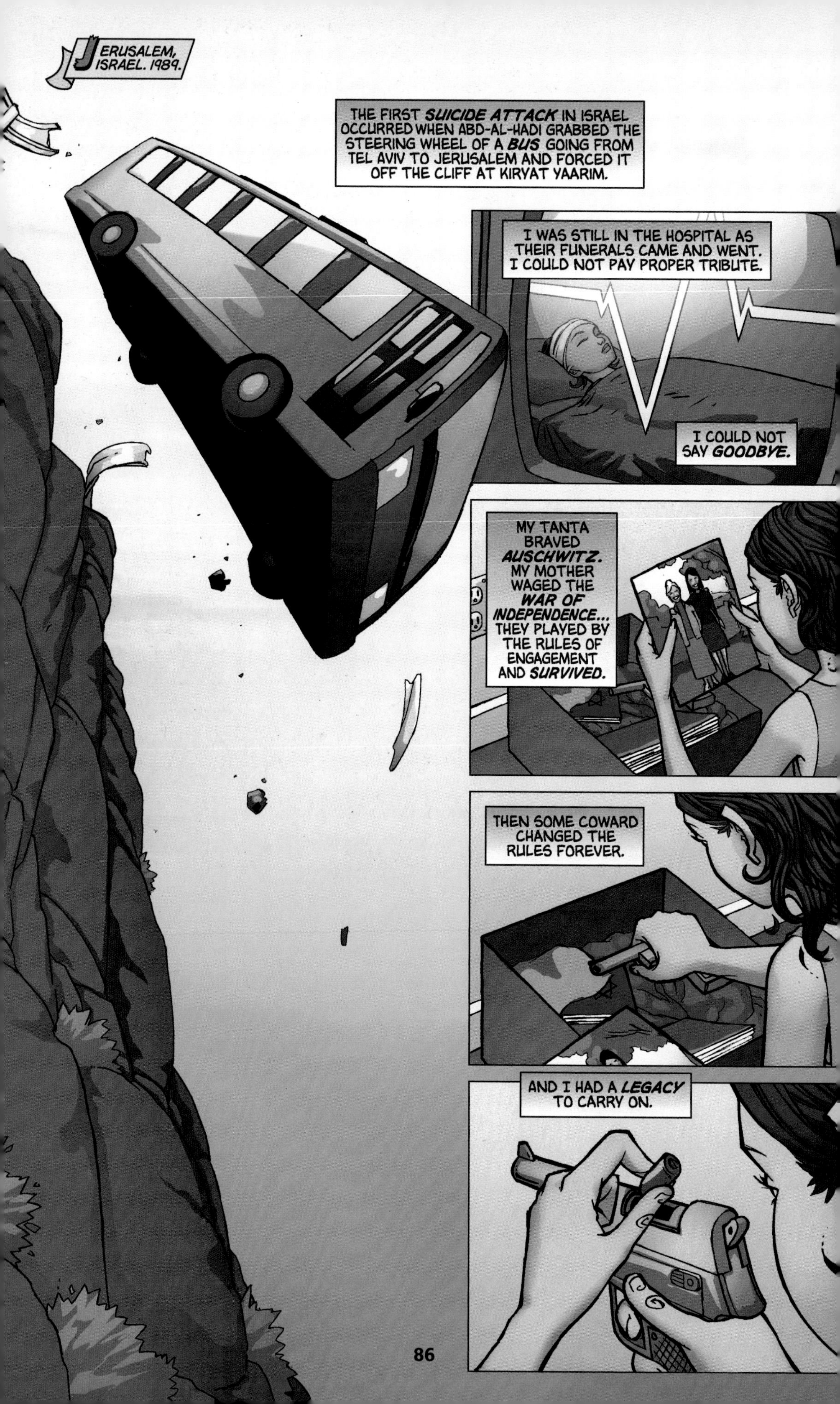
JERUSALEM, ISRAEL. 1989.
THE FIRST SUICIDE ATTACK IN ISRAEL OCCURRED WHEN ABD-AL-HADI GRABBED THE STEERING WHEEL OF A BUS GOING FROM TEL AVIV TO JERUSALEM AND FORCED IT OFF THE CLIFF AT KIRYAT YAARIM.
I WAS STILL IN THE HOSPITAL AS THEIR FUNERALS CAME AND WENT. I COULD NOT PAY PROPER TRIBUTE.
I COULD NOT SAY GOODBYE.
MY TANTA BRAVED AUSCHWITZ. MY MOTHER WAGED THE WAR OF INDEPENDENCE... THEY PLAYED BY THE RULES OF ENGAGEMENT AND SURVIVED.
THEN SOME COWARD CHANGED THE RULES FOREVER.
AND I HAD A LEGACY TO CARRY ON.

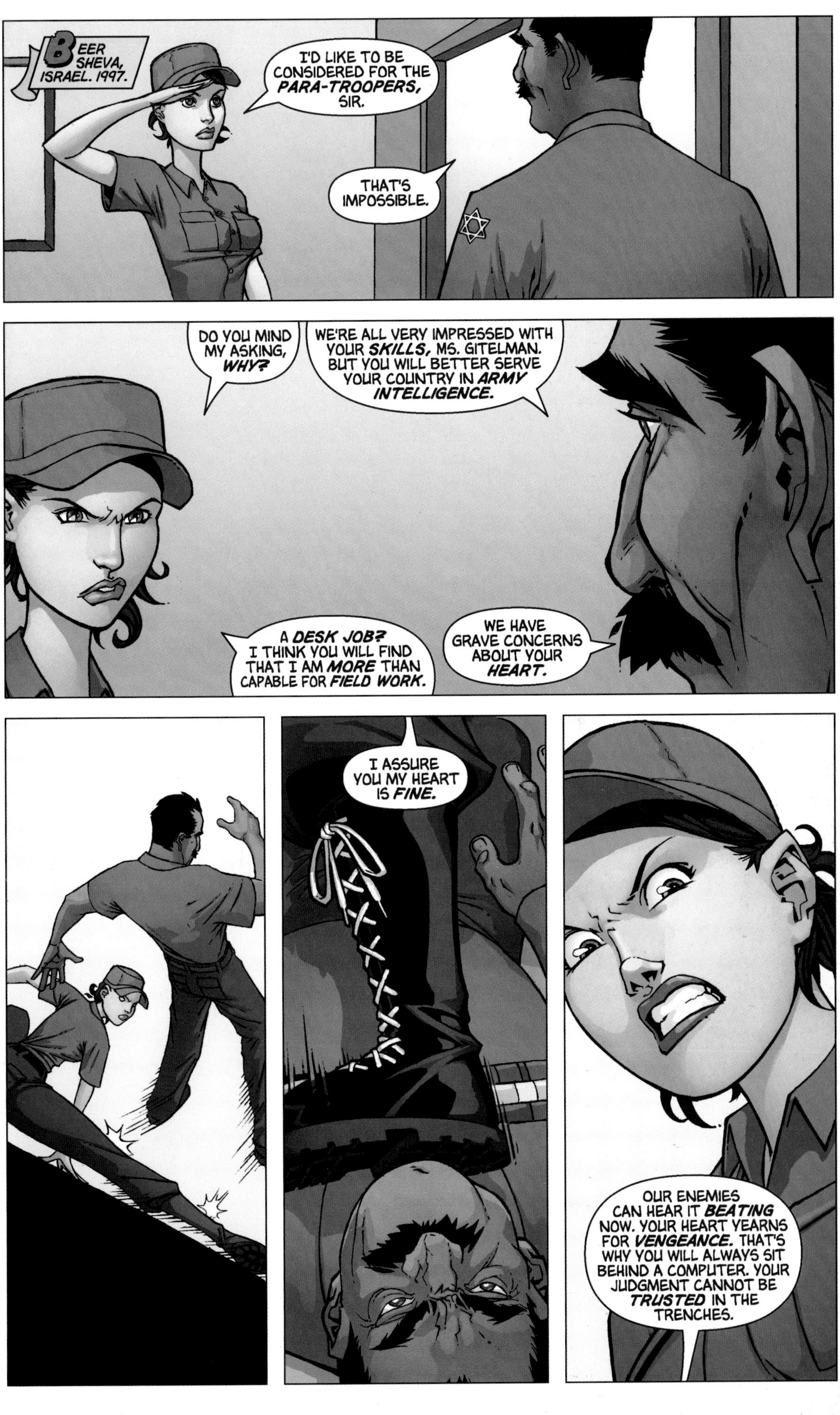
BEER SHEVA, ISRAEL. 1997.
I'D LIKE TO BE CONSIDERED FOR THE PARA-TROOPERS, SIR.
THAT'S IMPOSSIBLE.
DO YOU MIND MY ASKING, WHY?
WE'RE ALL VERY IMPRESSED WITH YOUR SKILLS, MS. GITELMAN. BUT YOU WILL BETTER SERVE YOUR COUNTRY IN ARMY INTELLIGENCE.
A DESK JOB? I THINK YOU WILL FIND THAT I AM MORE THAN CAPABLE FOR FIELD WORK.
WE HAVE GRAVE CONCERNS ABOUT YOUR HEART.
I ASSURE YOU MY HEART IS FINE.
OUR ENEMIES CAN HEAR IT BEATING NOW. YOUR HEART YEARNS FOR VENGEANCE. THAT'S WHY YOU WILL ALWAYS SIT BEHIND A COMPUTER. YOUR JUDGMENT CANNOT BE TRUSTED IN THE TRENCHES.

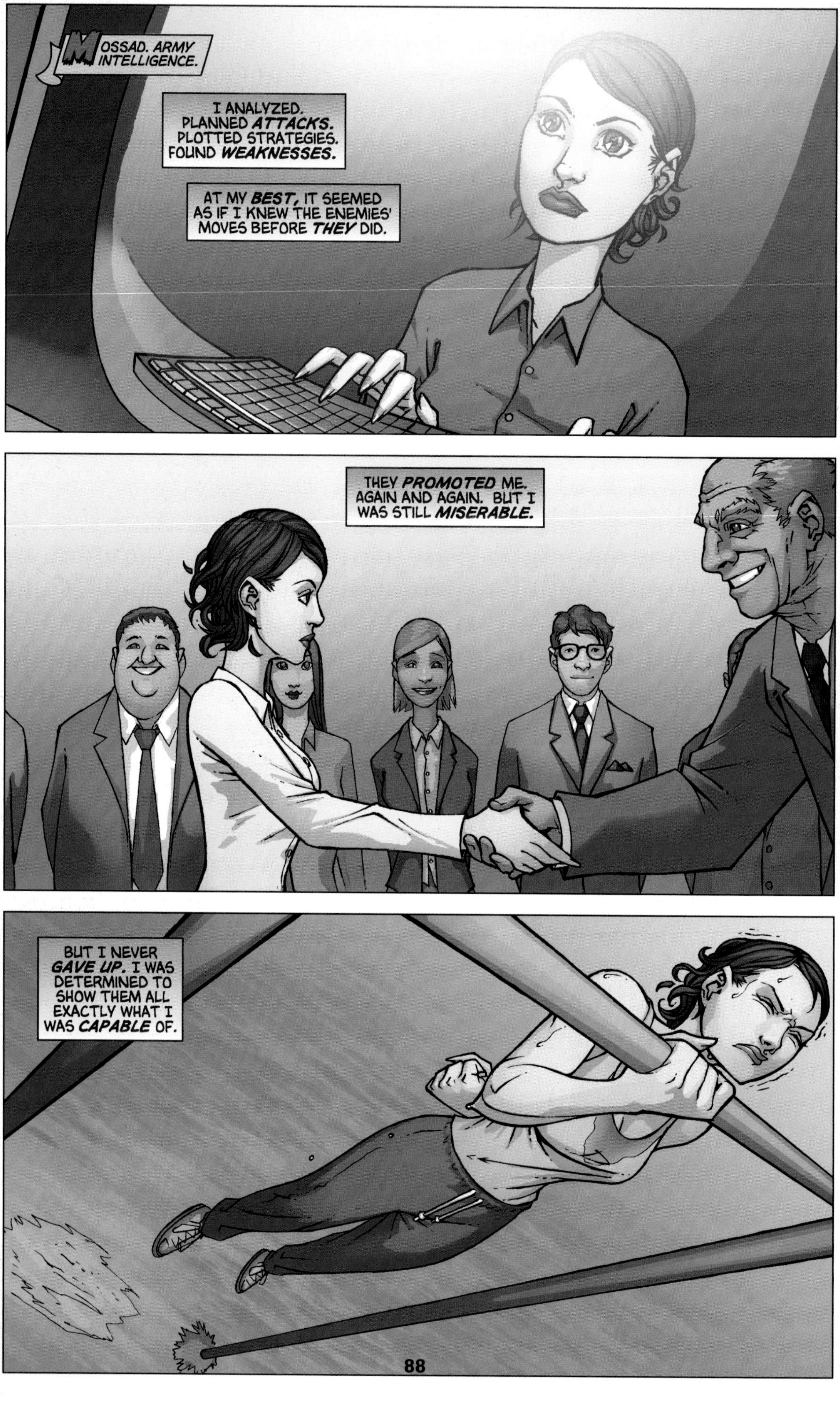
MOSSAD. ARMY INTELLIGENCE.
I ANALYZED. PLANNED ATTACKS. PLOTTED STRATEGIES. FOUND WEAKNESSES.
AT MY BEST, IT SEEMED AS IF I KNEW THE ENEMIES' MOVES BEFORE THEY DID.
THEY PROMOTED ME. AGAIN AND AGAIN. BUT I WAS STILL MISERABLE.
BUT I NEVER GAVE UP. I WAS DETERMINED TO SHOW THEM ALL EXACTLY WHAT I WAS CAPABLE OF.

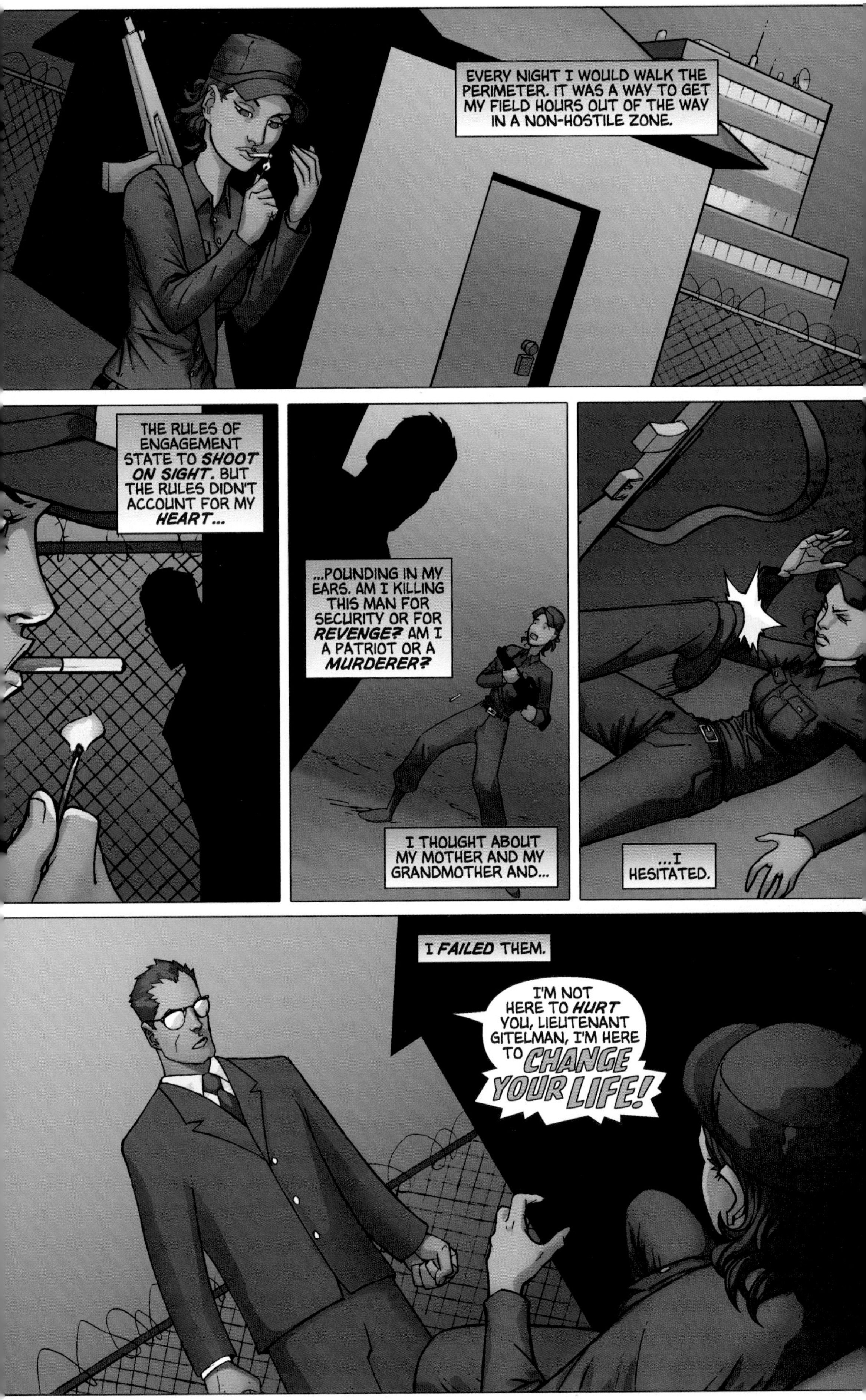

EVERY NIGHT I WOULD WALK THE PERIMETER. IT WAS A WAY TO GET MY FIELD HOURS OUT OF THE WAY IN A NON-HOSTILE ZONE.
THE RULES OF ENGAGEMENT STATE TO *SHOOT ON SIGHT*. BUT THE RULES DIDN'T ACCOUNT FOR MY *HEART*...
...POUNDING IN MY EARS. AM I KILLING THIS MAN FOR SECURITY OR FOR *REVENGE?* AM I A PATRIOT OR A *MURDERER?*
I THOUGHT ABOUT MY MOTHER AND MY GRANDMOTHER AND...
...I HESITATED.
I *FAILED* THEM.
I'M NOT HERE TO *HURT* YOU, LIEUTENANT GITELMAN, I'M HERE TO *CHANGE YOUR LIFE!*

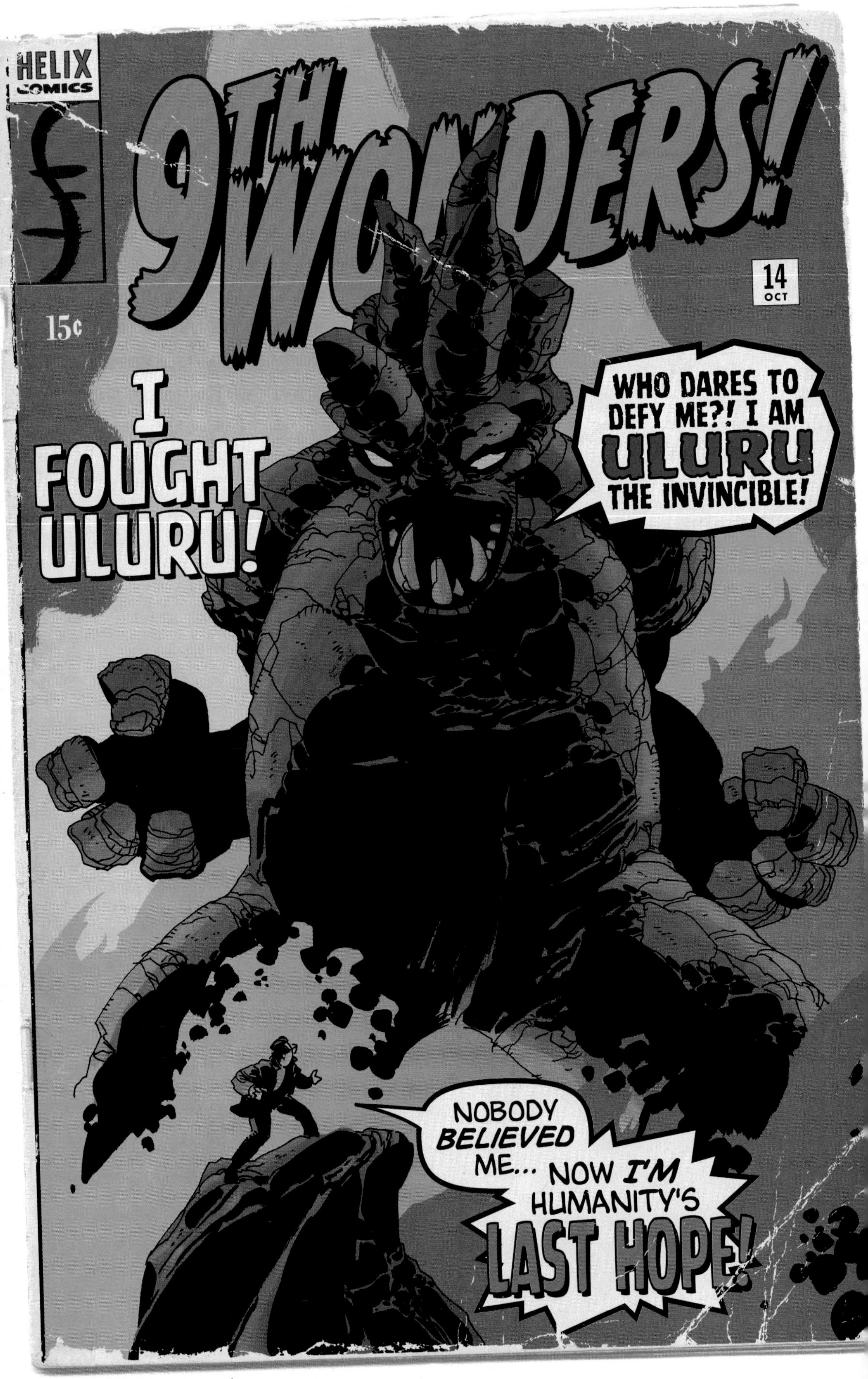
HELIX COMICS
9TH WONDERS!
14 OCT
15¢
I FOUGHT ULURU!
WHO DARES TO DEFY ME?! I AM ULURU THE INVINCIBLE!
NOBODY BELIEVED ME... NOW I'M HUMANITY'S LAST HOPE!

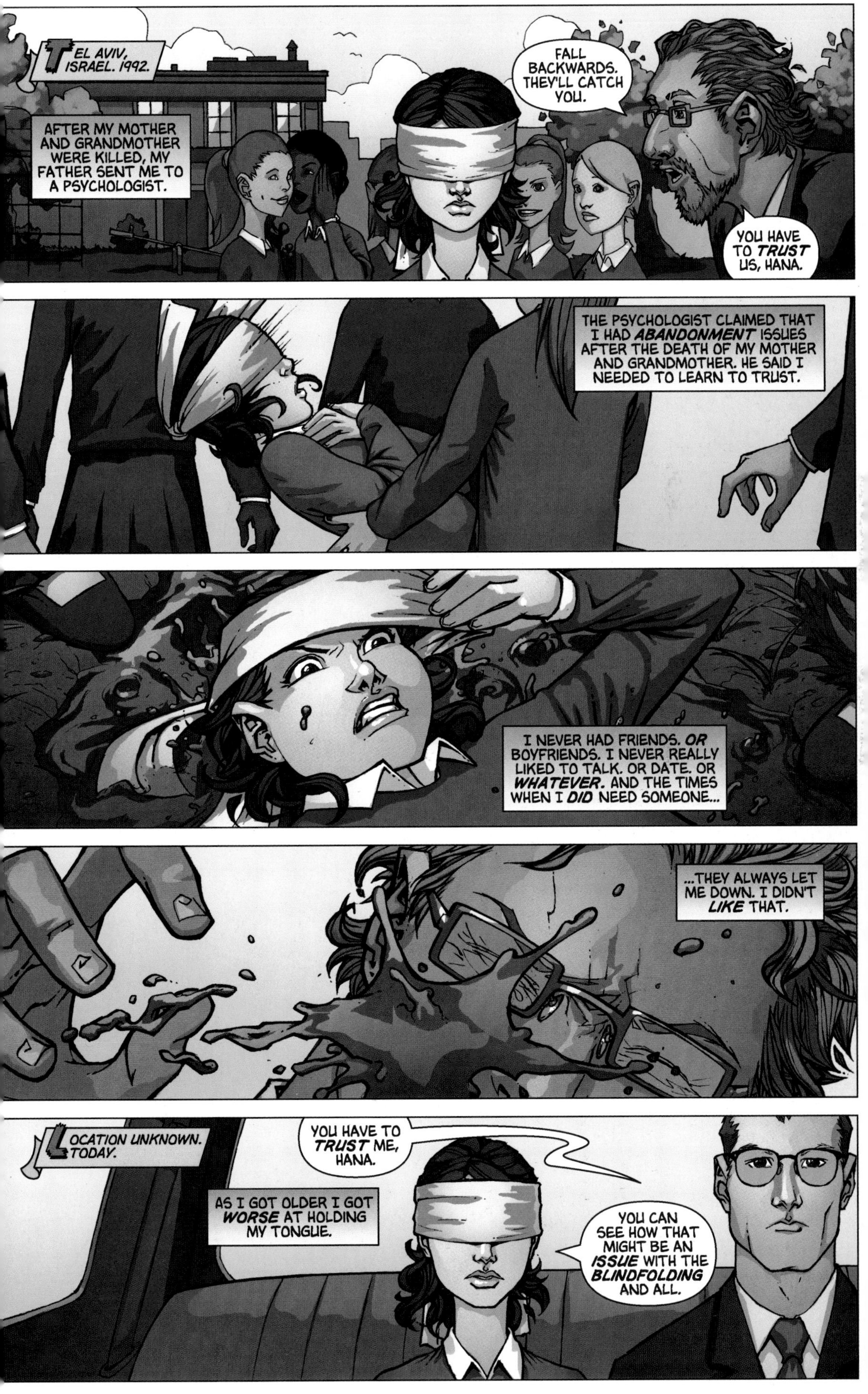
TEL AVIV, ISRAEL. 1992.
AFTER MY MOTHER AND GRANDMOTHER WERE KILLED, MY FATHER SENT ME TO A PSYCHOLOGIST.
FALL BACKWARDS. THEY'LL CATCH YOU.
YOU HAVE TO TRUST US, HANA.
THE PSYCHOLOGIST CLAIMED THAT I HAD ABANDONMENT ISSUES AFTER THE DEATH OF MY MOTHER AND GRANDMOTHER. HE SAID I NEEDED TO LEARN TO TRUST.
I NEVER HAD FRIENDS. OR BOYFRIENDS. I NEVER REALLY LIKED TO TALK. OR DATE. OR WHATEVER. AND THE TIMES WHEN I DID NEED SOMEONE...
...THEY ALWAYS LET ME DOWN. I DIDN'T LIKE THAT.
LOCATION UNKNOWN. TODAY.
YOU HAVE TO TRUST ME, HANA.
AS I GOT OLDER I GOT WORSE AT HOLDING MY TONGUE.
YOU CAN SEE HOW THAT MIGHT BE AN ISSUE WITH THE BLINDFOLDING AND ALL.

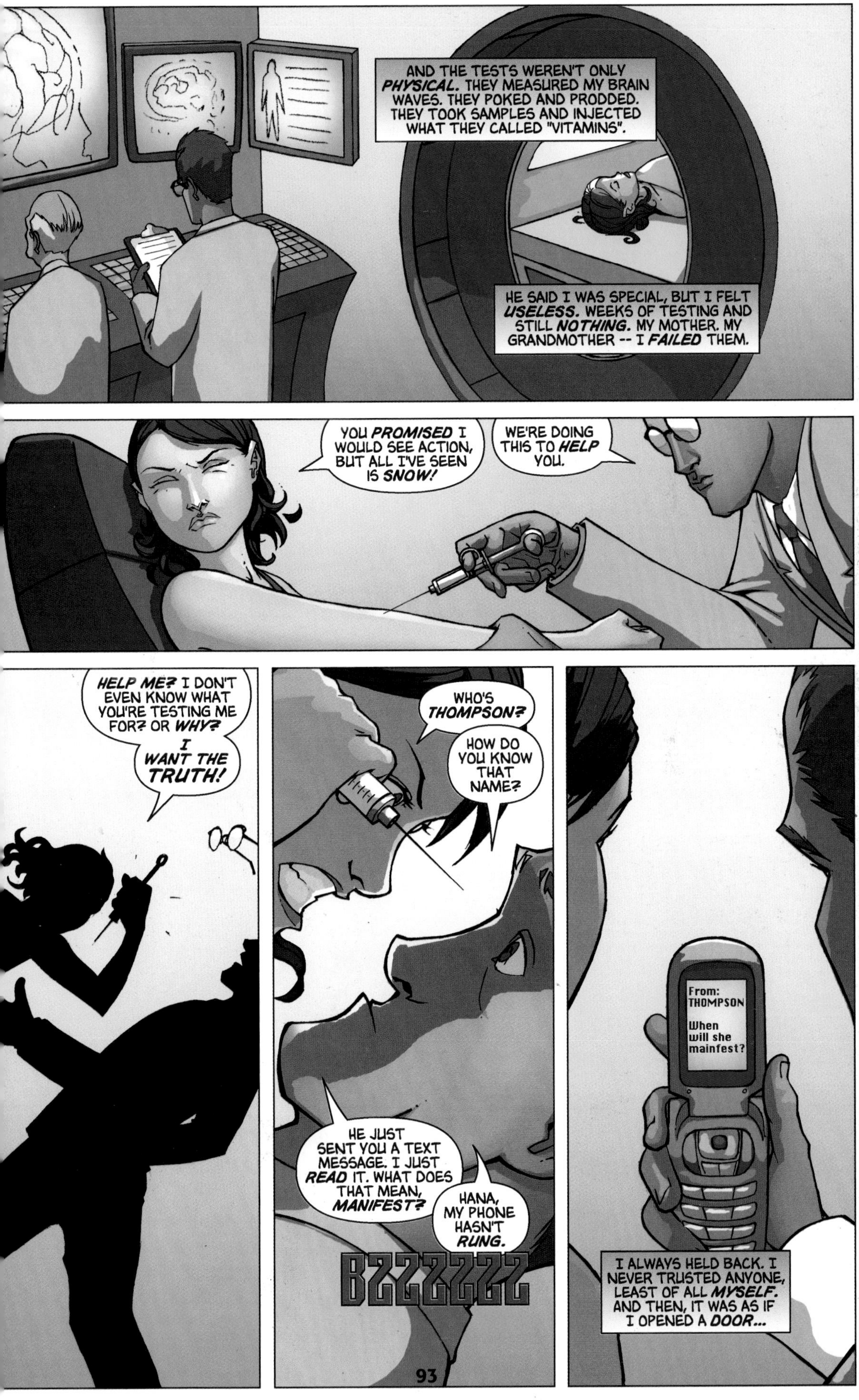
AND THE TESTS WEREN'T ONLY PHYSICAL. THEY MEASURED MY BRAIN WAVES. THEY POKED AND PRODDED. THEY TOOK SAMPLES AND INJECTED WHAT THEY CALLED "VITAMINS".
HE SAID I WAS SPECIAL, BUT I FELT USELESS. WEEKS OF TESTING AND STILL NOTHING. MY MOTHER. MY GRANDMOTHER -- I FAILED THEM.
YOU PROMISED I WOULD SEE ACTION, BUT ALL I'VE SEEN IS SNOW!
WE'RE DOING THIS TO HELP YOU.
HELP ME? I DON'T EVEN KNOW WHAT YOU'RE TESTING ME FOR? OR WHY?
I WANT THE TRUTH!
WHO'S THOMPSON?
HOW DO YOU KNOW THAT NAME?
HE JUST SENT YOU A TEXT MESSAGE. I JUST READ IT. WHAT DOES THAT MEAN, MANIFEST?
HANA, MY PHONE HASN'T RUNG.
BZZZZZZ
From: THOMPSON
When will she mainfest?
I ALWAYS HELD BACK. I NEVER TRUSTED ANYONE, LEAST OF ALL MYSELF. AND THEN, IT WAS AS IF I OPENED A DOOR...

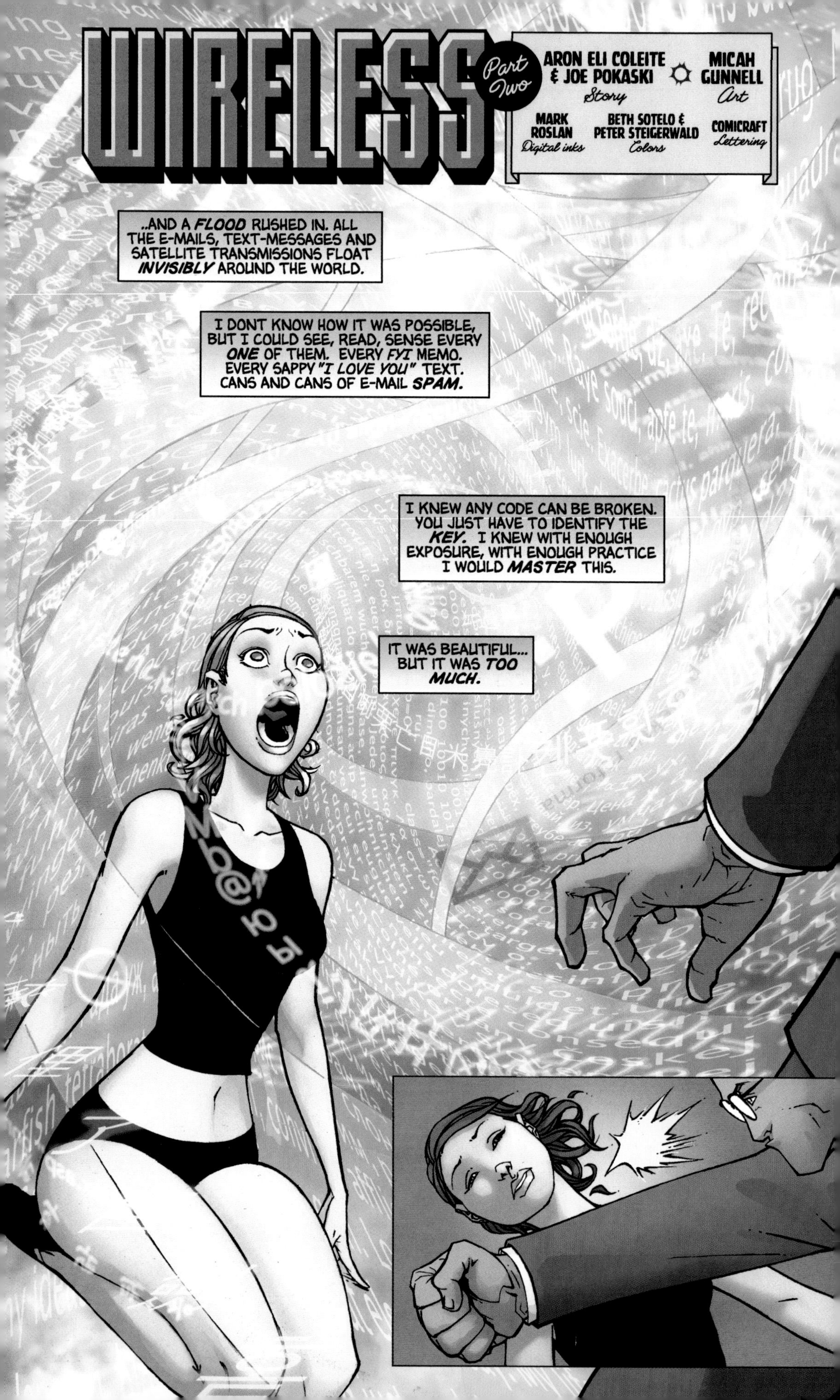
WIRELESS
Part Two
ARON ELI COLEITE & JOE POKASKI Story
MICAH GUNNELL Art
MARK ROSLAN Digital inks
BETH SOTELO & PETER STEIGERWALD Colors
COMICRAFT Lettering
..AND A FLOOD RUSHED IN. ALL THE E-MAILS, TEXT-MESSAGES AND SATELLITE TRANSMISSIONS FLOAT INVISIBLY AROUND THE WORLD.
I DONT KNOW HOW IT WAS POSSIBLE, BUT I COULD SEE, READ, SENSE EVERY ONE OF THEM. EVERY FYI MEMO. EVERY SAPPY "I LOVE YOU" TEXT. CANS AND CANS OF E-MAIL SPAM.
I KNEW ANY CODE CAN BE BROKEN. YOU JUST HAVE TO IDENTIFY THE KEY. I KNEW WITH ENOUGH EXPOSURE, WITH ENOUGH PRACTICE I WOULD MASTER THIS.
IT WAS BEAUTIFUL... BUT IT WAS TOO MUCH.

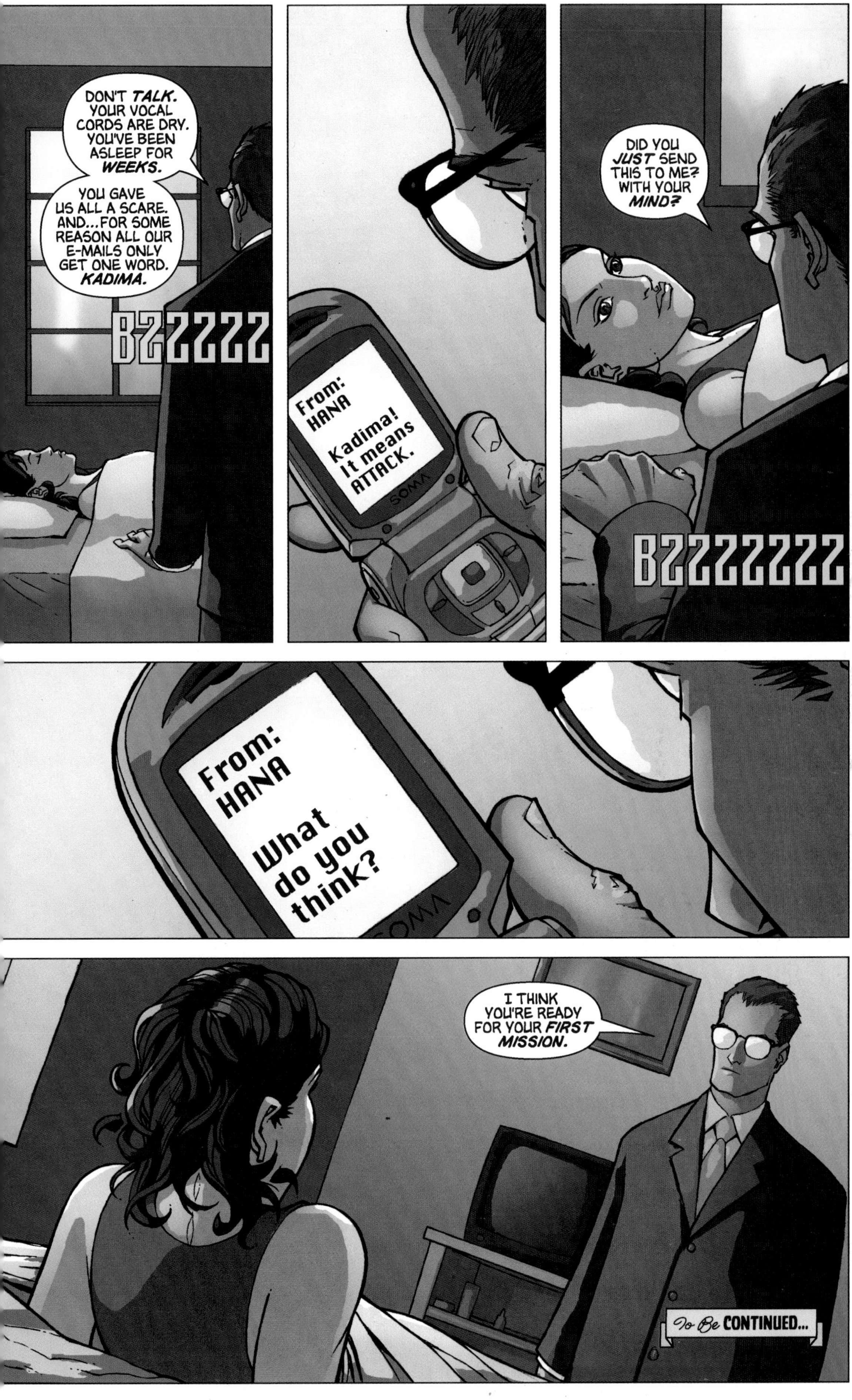

DON'T TALK. YOUR VOCAL CORDS ARE DRY. YOU'VE BEEN ASLEEP FOR WEEKS.
YOU GAVE US ALL A SCARE. AND...FOR SOME REASON ALL OUR E-MAILS ONLY GET ONE WORD. KADIMA.
BZZZZZ
From: HANA Kadima! It means ATTACK.
SOMA
DID YOU JUST SEND THIS TO ME? WITH YOUR MIND?
BZZZZZZZ
From: HANA What do you think?
SOMA
I THINK YOU'RE READY FOR YOUR FIRST MISSION.
To Be CONTINUED...

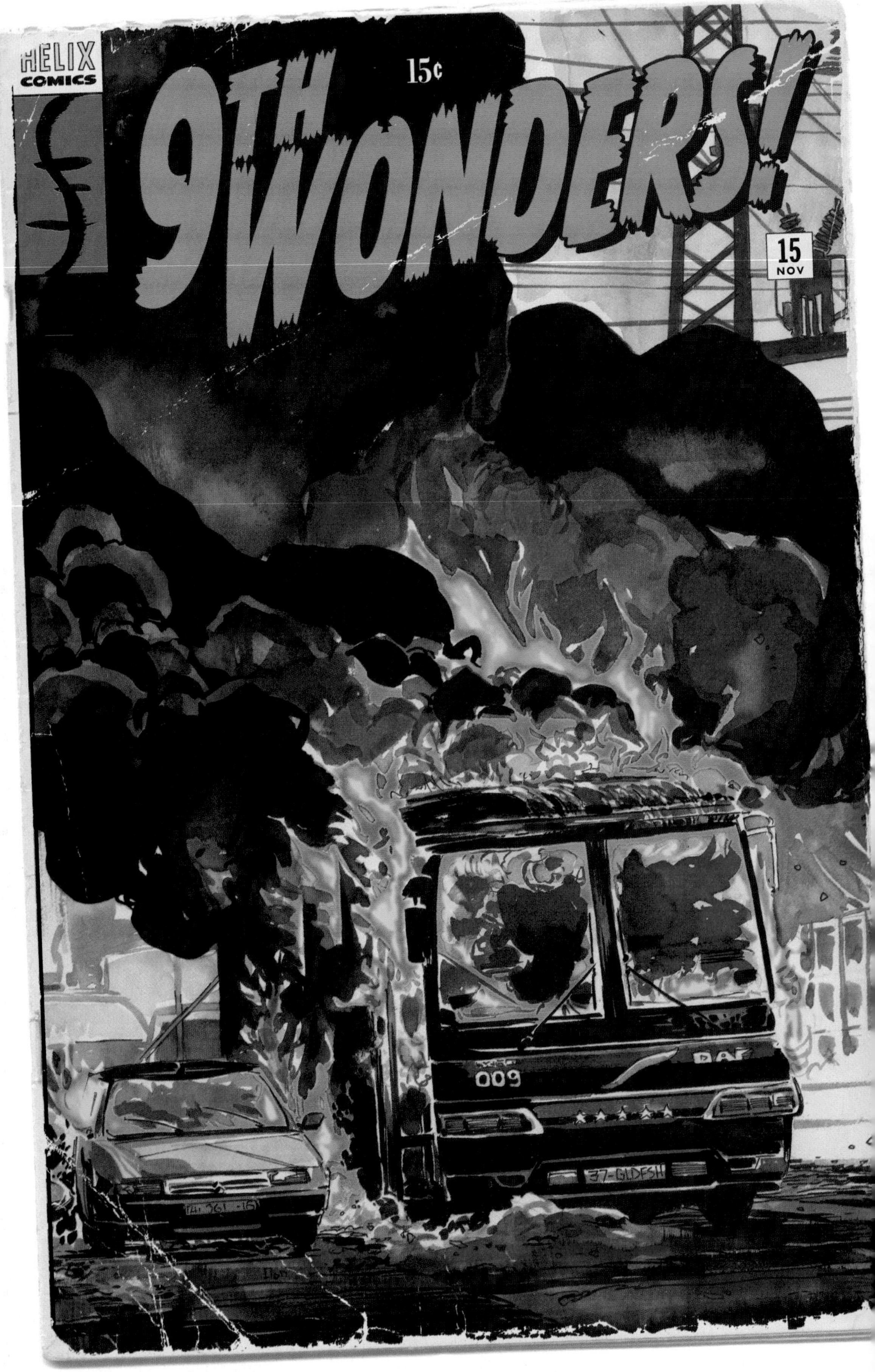
HELIX
COMICS
15¢
9TH WONDERS!
15
NOV
DAF
009
37-GLDFSH
741-361-16

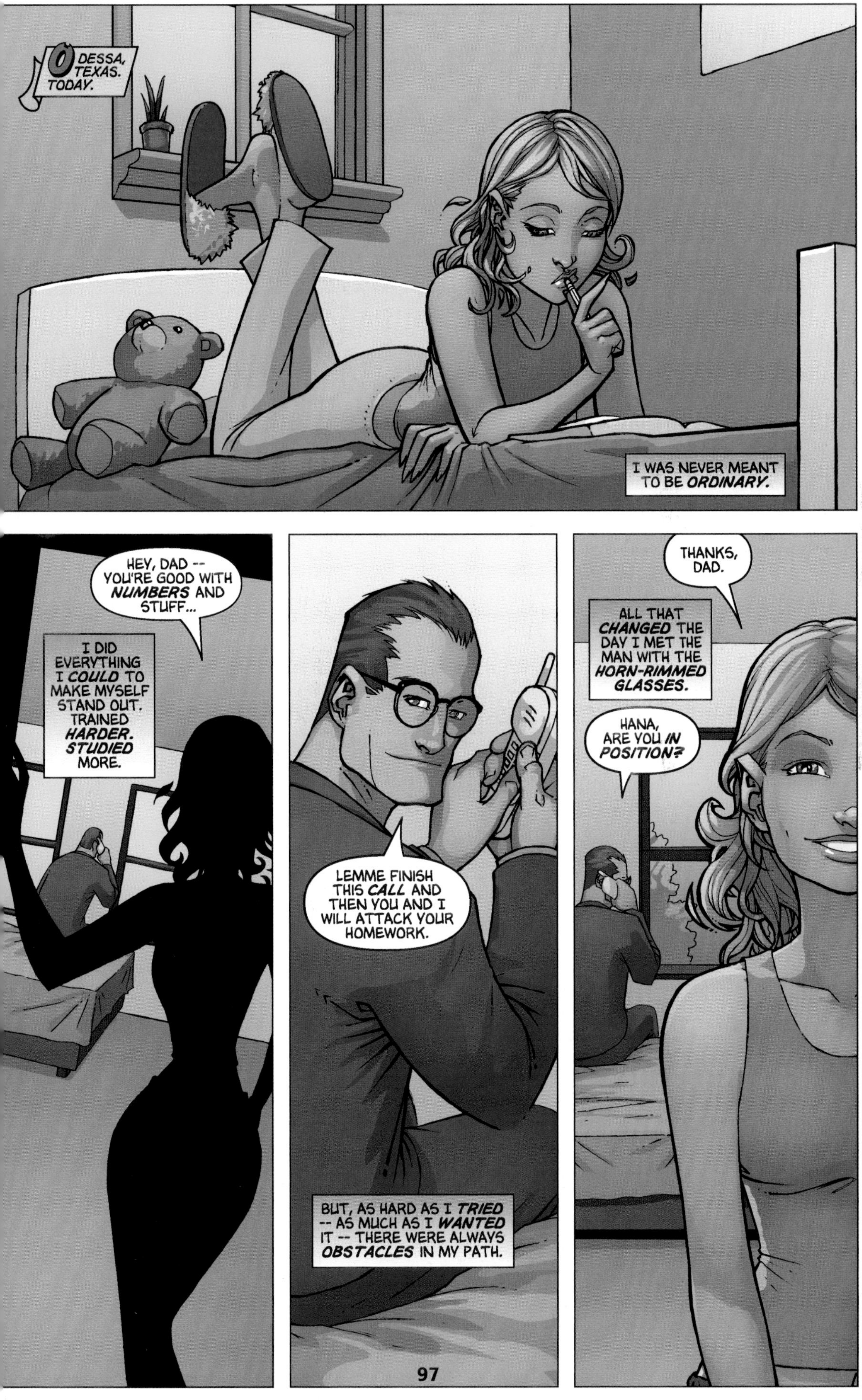
ODESSA, TEXAS. TODAY.
I WAS NEVER MEANT TO BE ORDINARY.
HEY, DAD -- YOU'RE GOOD WITH NUMBERS AND STUFF...
I DID EVERYTHING I COULD TO MAKE MYSELF STAND OUT. TRAINED HARDER. STUDIED MORE.
LEMME FINISH THIS CALL AND THEN YOU AND I WILL ATTACK YOUR HOMEWORK.
BUT, AS HARD AS I TRIED -- AS MUCH AS I WANTED IT -- THERE WERE ALWAYS OBSTACLES IN MY PATH.
THANKS, DAD.
ALL THAT CHANGED THE DAY I MET THE MAN WITH THE HORN-RIMMED GLASSES.
HANA, ARE YOU IN POSITION?

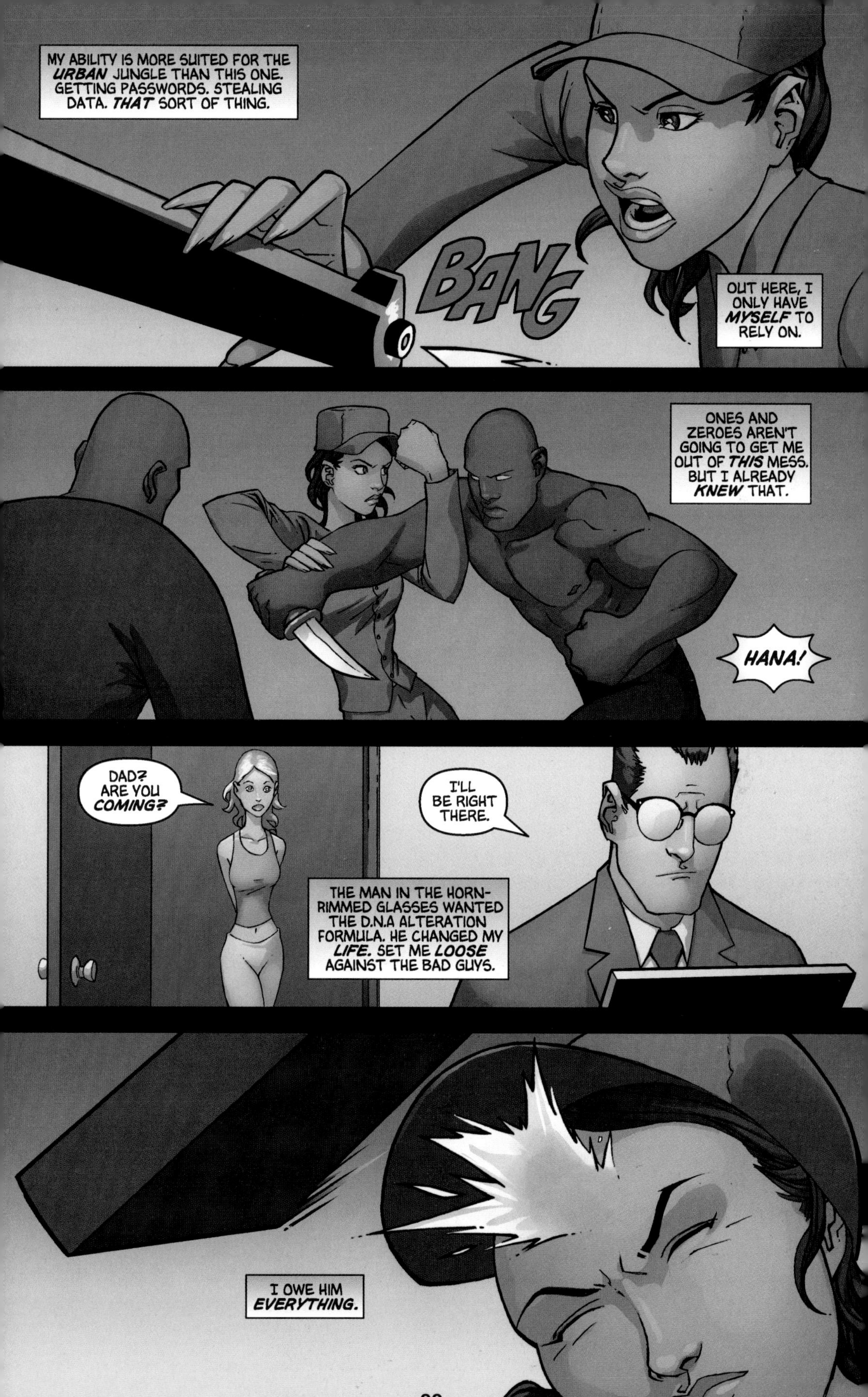
MY ABILITY IS MORE SUITED FOR THE URBAN JUNGLE THAN THIS ONE. GETTING PASSWORDS. STEALING DATA. THAT SORT OF THING.
BANG
OUT HERE, I ONLY HAVE MYSELF TO RELY ON.
ONES AND ZEROES AREN'T GOING TO GET ME OUT OF THIS MESS. BUT I ALREADY KNEW THAT.
HANA!
DAD? ARE YOU COMING?
I'LL BE RIGHT THERE.
THE MAN IN THE HORN-RIMMED GLASSES WANTED THE D.N.A ALTERATION FORMULA. HE CHANGED MY LIFE. SET ME LOOSE AGAINST THE BAD GUYS.
I OWE HIM EVERYTHING.

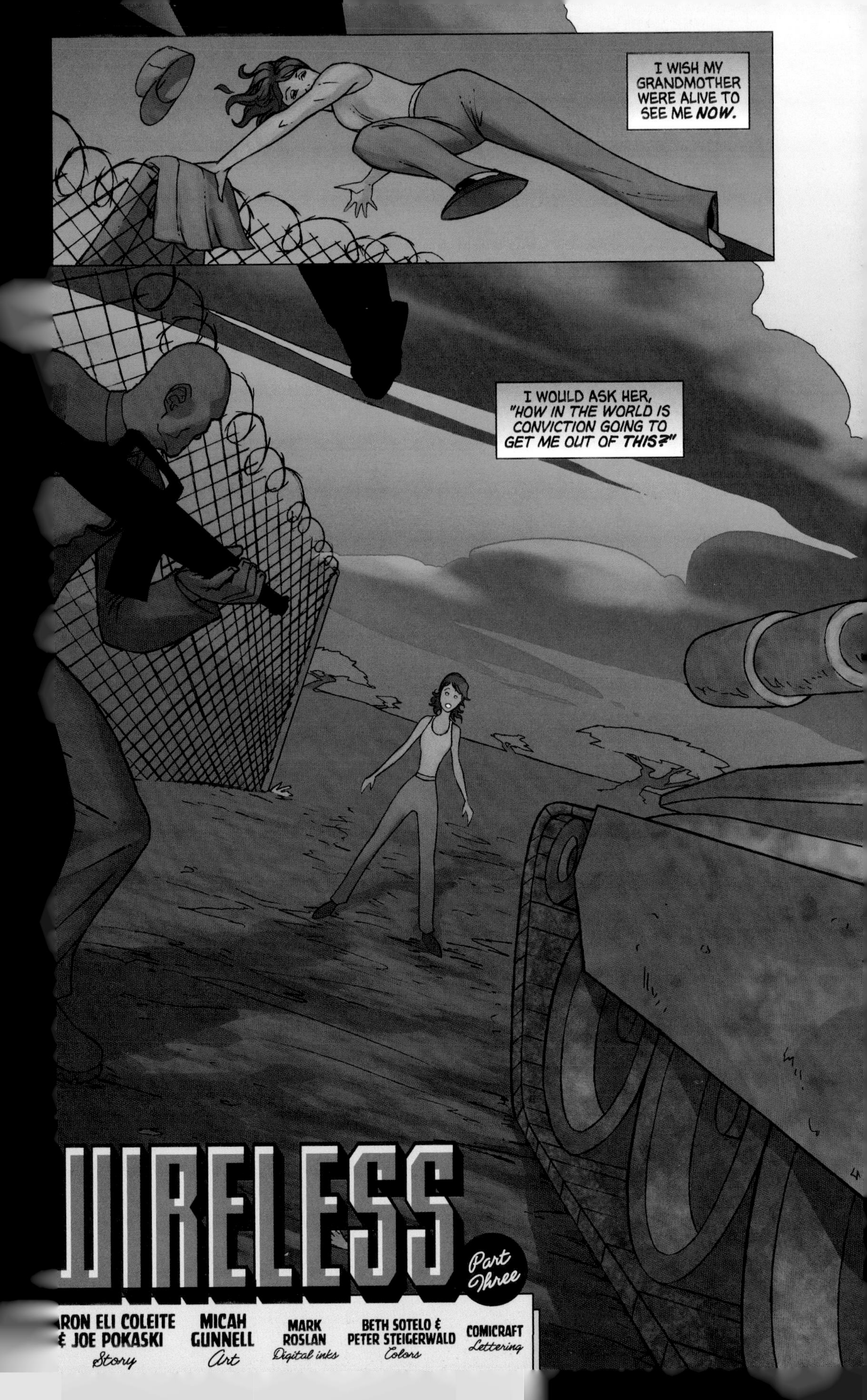

I WISH MY GRANDMOTHER WERE ALIVE TO SEE ME NOW.
I WOULD ASK HER, "HOW IN THE WORLD IS CONVICTION GOING TO GET ME OUT OF THIS?"
WIRELESS
Part Three
ARON ELI COLEITE & JOE POKASKI Story
MICAH GUNNELL Art
MARK ROSLAN Digital inks
BETH SOTELO & PETER STEIGERWALD Colors
COMICRAFT Lettering

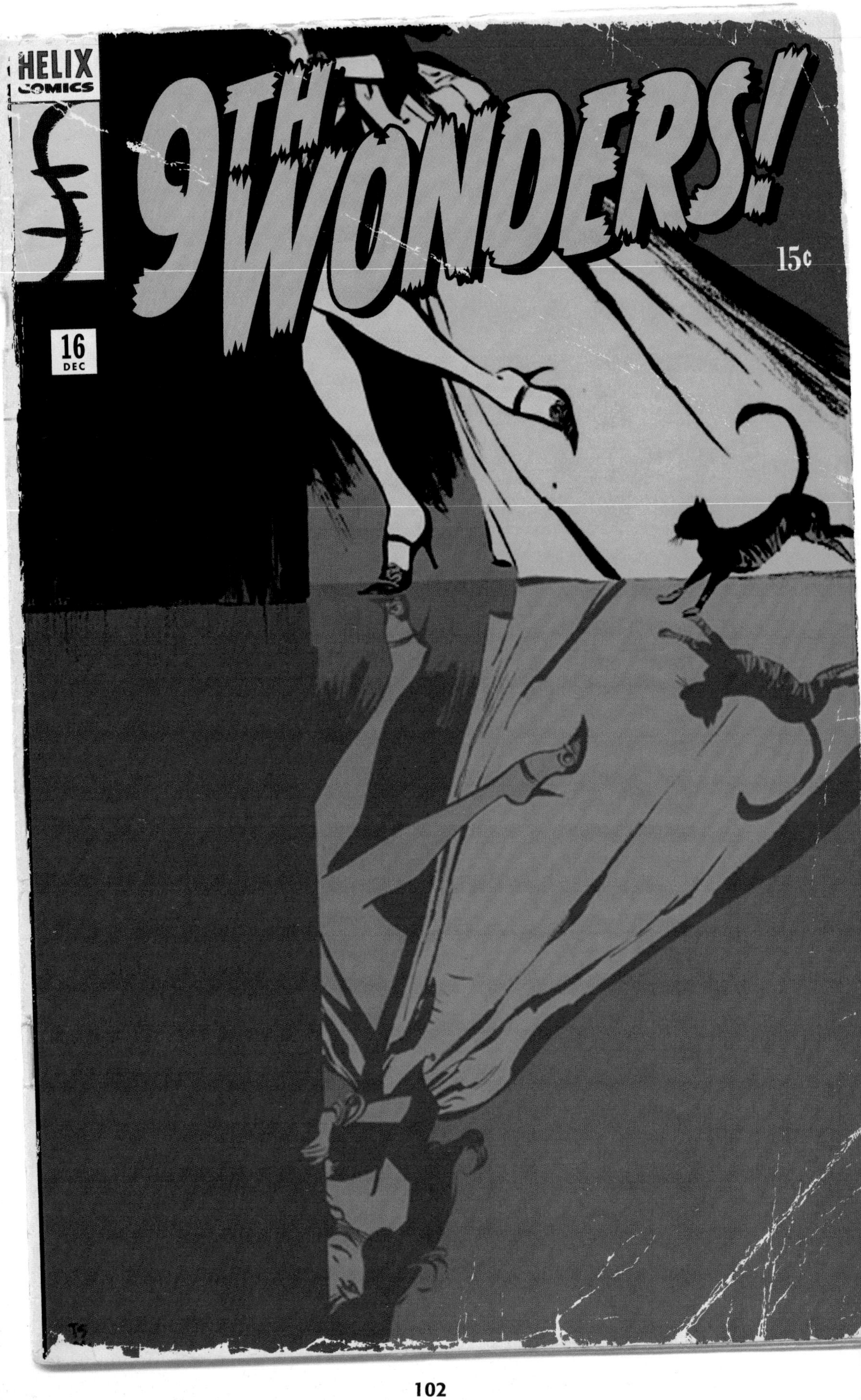
HELIX
COMICS
9TH WONDERS!
15¢
16
DEC

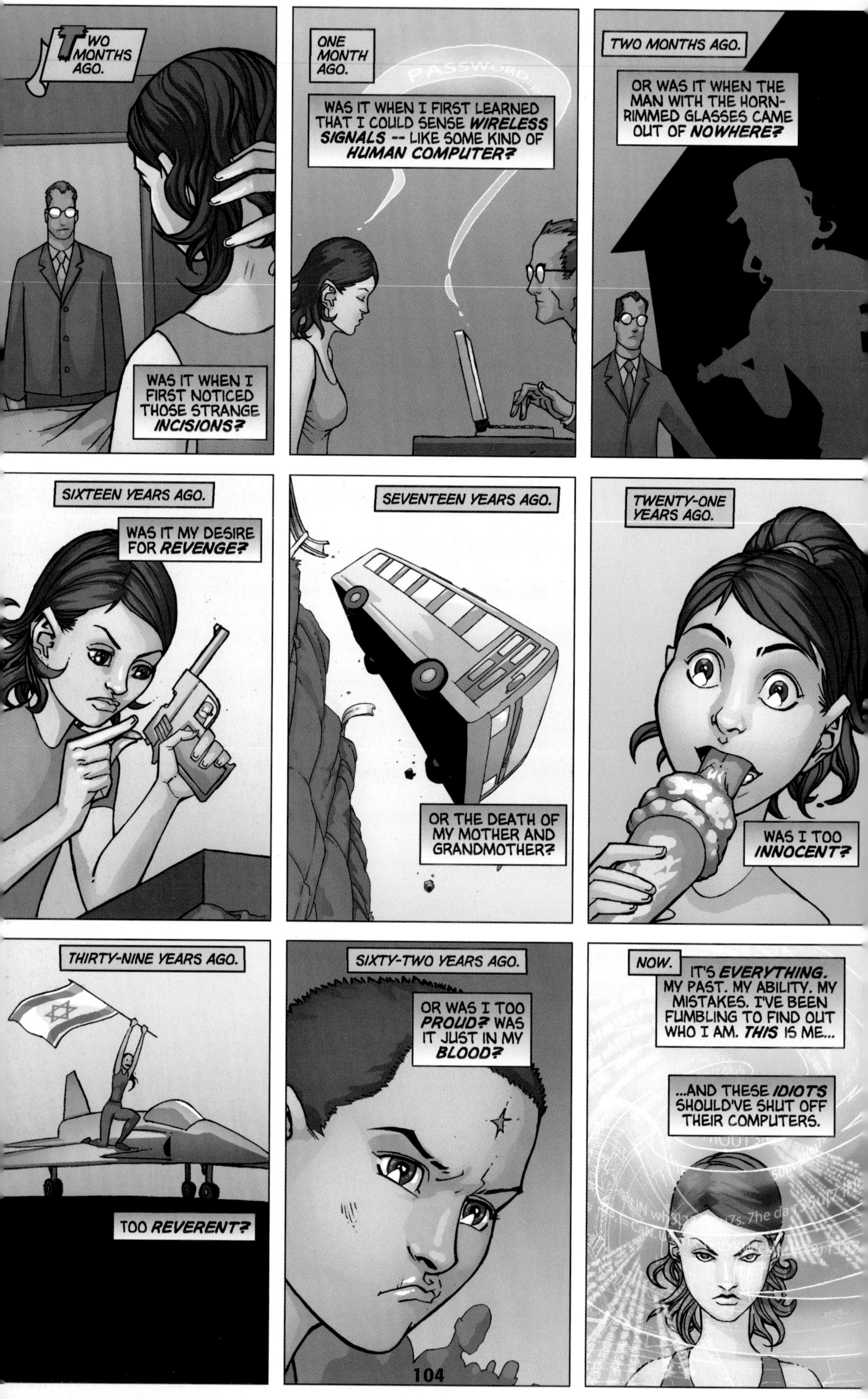
TWO MONTHS AGO.
WAS IT WHEN I FIRST NOTICED THOSE STRANGE INCISIONS?
ONE MONTH AGO.
WAS IT WHEN I FIRST LEARNED THAT I COULD SENSE WIRELESS SIGNALS -- LIKE SOME KIND OF HUMAN COMPUTER?
TWO MONTHS AGO.
OR WAS IT WHEN THE MAN WITH THE HORN-RIMMED GLASSES CAME OUT OF NOWHERE?
SIXTEEN YEARS AGO.
WAS IT MY DESIRE FOR REVENGE?
SEVENTEEN YEARS AGO.
OR THE DEATH OF MY MOTHER AND GRANDMOTHER?
TWENTY-ONE YEARS AGO.
WAS I TOO INNOCENT?
THIRTY-NINE YEARS AGO.
TOO REVERENT?
SIXTY-TWO YEARS AGO.
OR WAS I TOO PROUD? WAS IT JUST IN MY BLOOD?
NOW.
IT'S EVERYTHING. MY PAST. MY ABILITY. MY MISTAKES. I'VE BEEN FUMBLING TO FIND OUT WHO I AM. THIS IS ME...
...AND THESE IDIOTS SHOULD'VE SHUT OFF THEIR COMPUTERS.

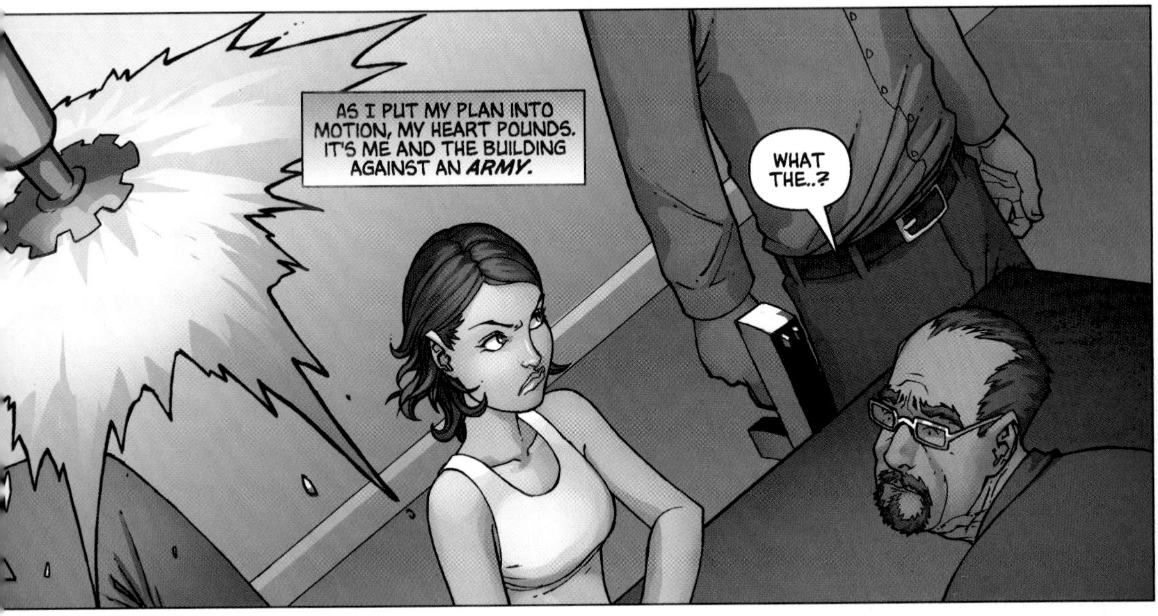
AS I PUT MY PLAN INTO MOTION, MY HEART POUNDS. IT'S ME AND THE BUILDING AGAINST AN *ARMY.*
WHAT THE..?

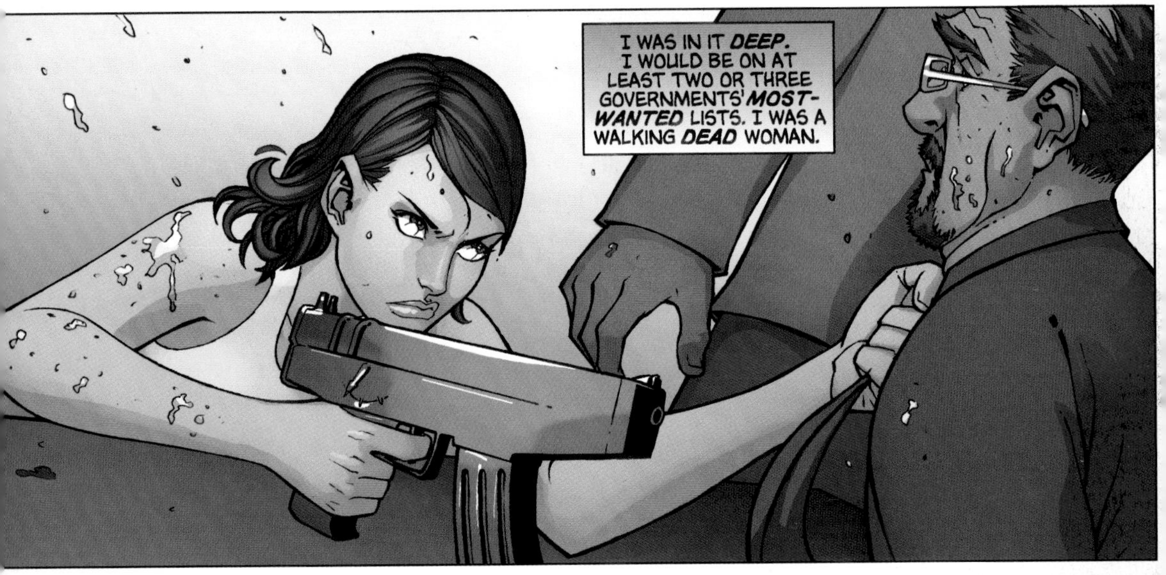
I WAS IN IT *DEEP.* I WOULD BE ON AT LEAST TWO OR THREE GOVERNMENTS' *MOST-WANTED* LISTS. I WAS A WALKING *DEAD* WOMAN.

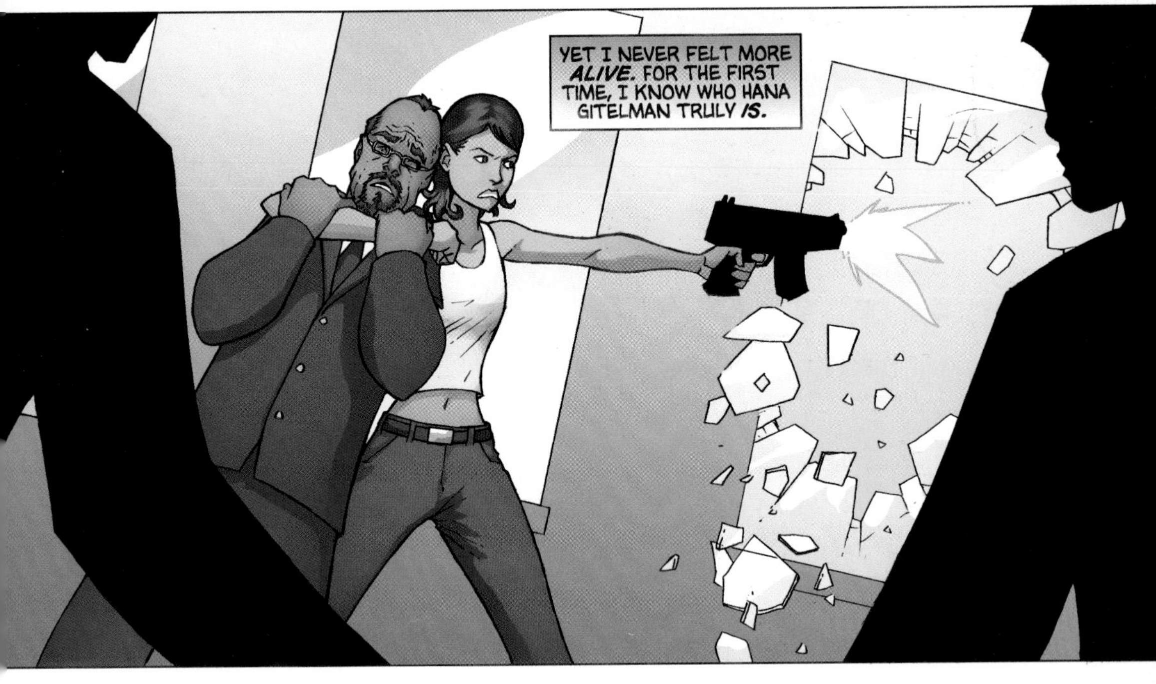
YET I NEVER FELT MORE *ALIVE.* FOR THE FIRST TIME, I KNOW WHO HANA GITELMAN TRULY *IS.*

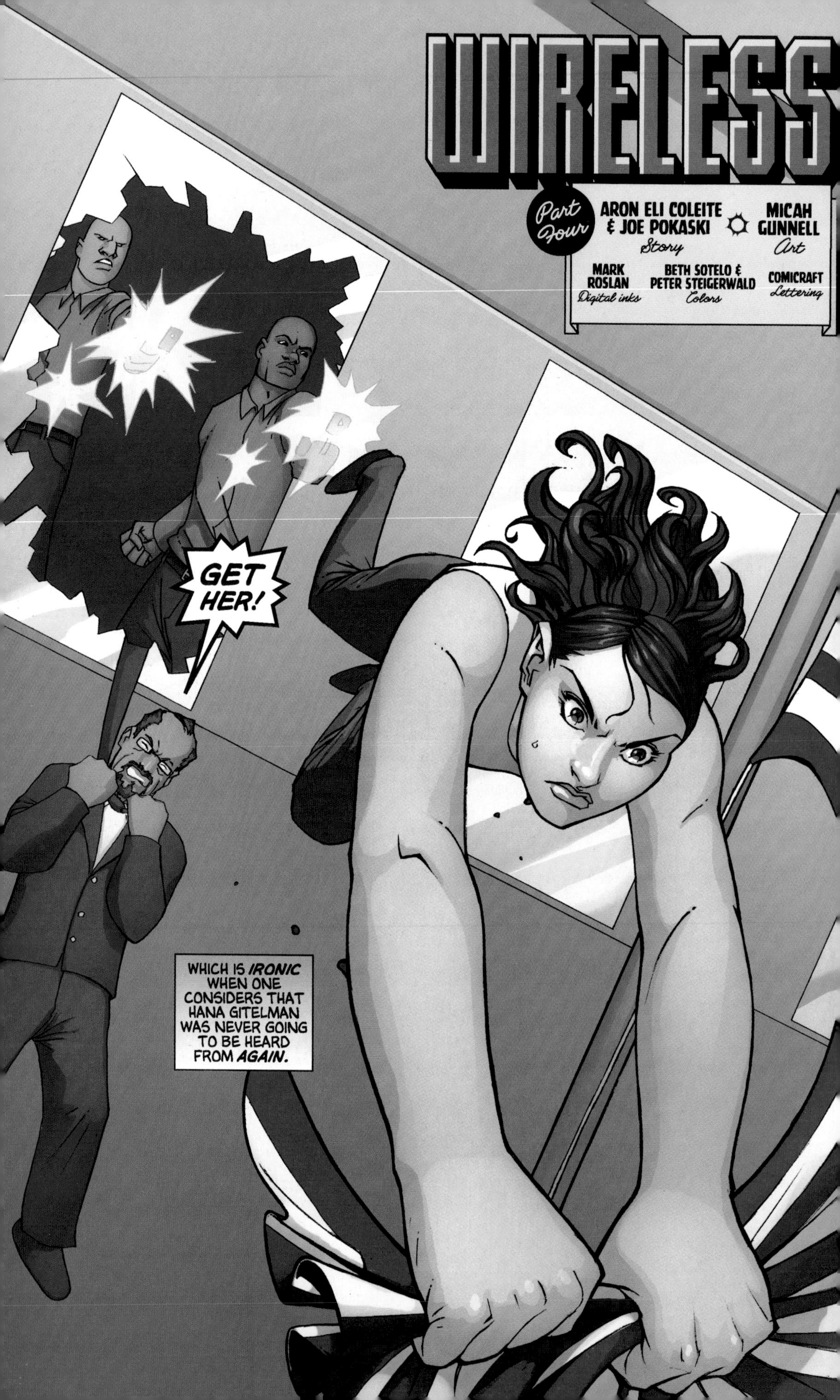

WIRELESS
Part Four
ARON ELI COLEITE & JOE POKASKI Story
MICAH GUNNELL Art
MARK ROSLAN Digital inks
BETH SOTELO & PETER STEIGERWALD Colors
COMICRAFT Lettering
GET HER!
WHICH IS IRONIC WHEN ONE CONSIDERS THAT HANA GITELMAN WAS NEVER GOING TO BE HEARD FROM AGAIN.

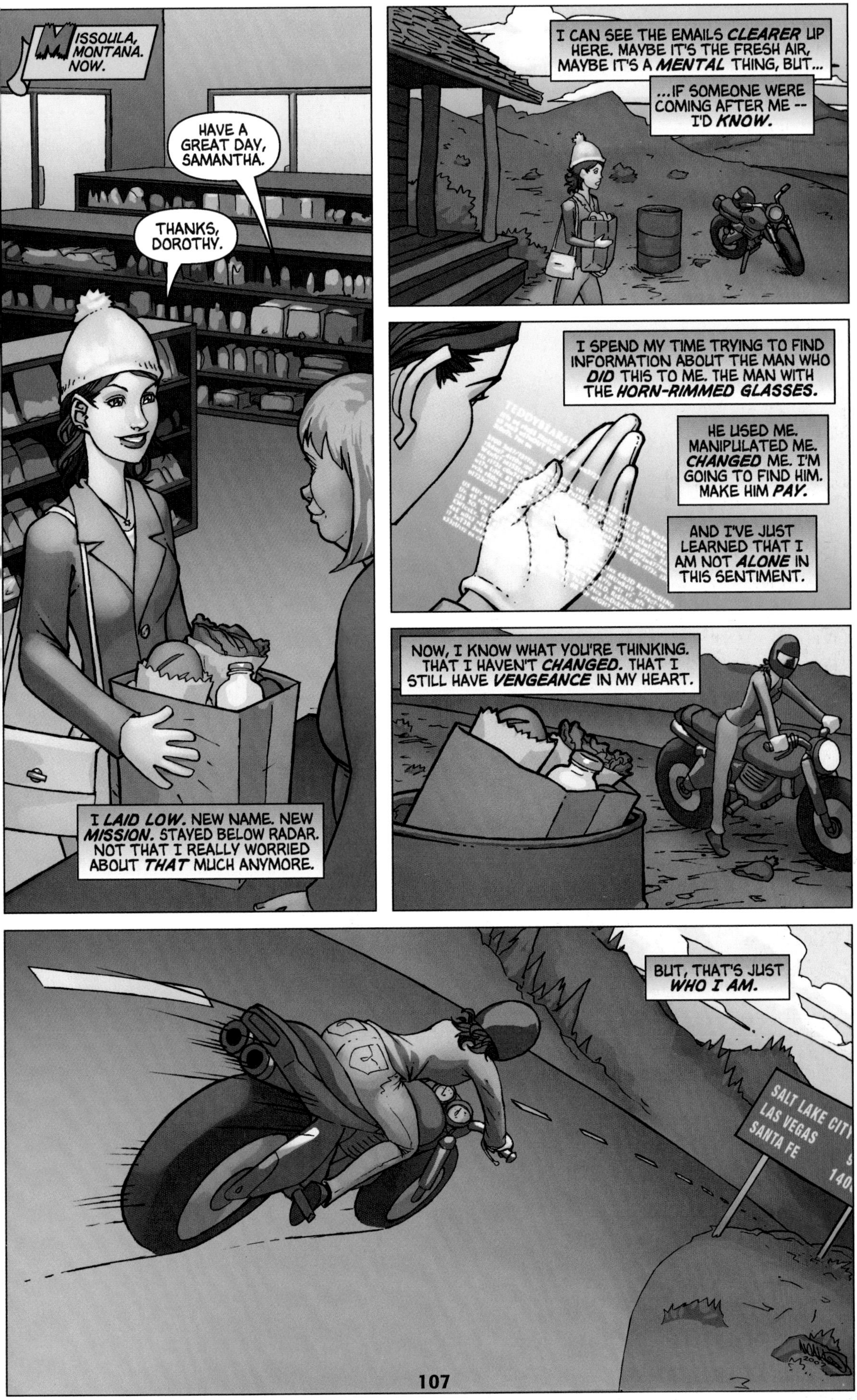

MISSOULA, MONTANA. NOW.
HAVE A GREAT DAY, SAMANTHA.
THANKS, DOROTHY.
I LAID LOW. NEW NAME. NEW MISSION. STAYED BELOW RADAR. NOT THAT I REALLY WORRIED ABOUT THAT MUCH ANYMORE.
I CAN SEE THE EMAILS CLEARER UP HERE. MAYBE IT'S THE FRESH AIR, MAYBE IT'S A MENTAL THING, BUT...
...IF SOMEONE WERE COMING AFTER ME -- I'D KNOW.
I SPEND MY TIME TRYING TO FIND INFORMATION ABOUT THE MAN WHO DID THIS TO ME. THE MAN WITH THE HORN-RIMMED GLASSES.
HE USED ME. MANIPULATED ME. CHANGED ME. I'M GOING TO FIND HIM. MAKE HIM PAY.
AND I'VE JUST LEARNED THAT I AM NOT ALONE IN THIS SENTIMENT.
NOW, I KNOW WHAT YOU'RE THINKING. THAT I HAVEN'T CHANGED. THAT I STILL HAVE VENGEANCE IN MY HEART.
BUT, THAT'S JUST WHO I AM.
SALT LAKE CITY
LAS VEGAS
SANTA FE

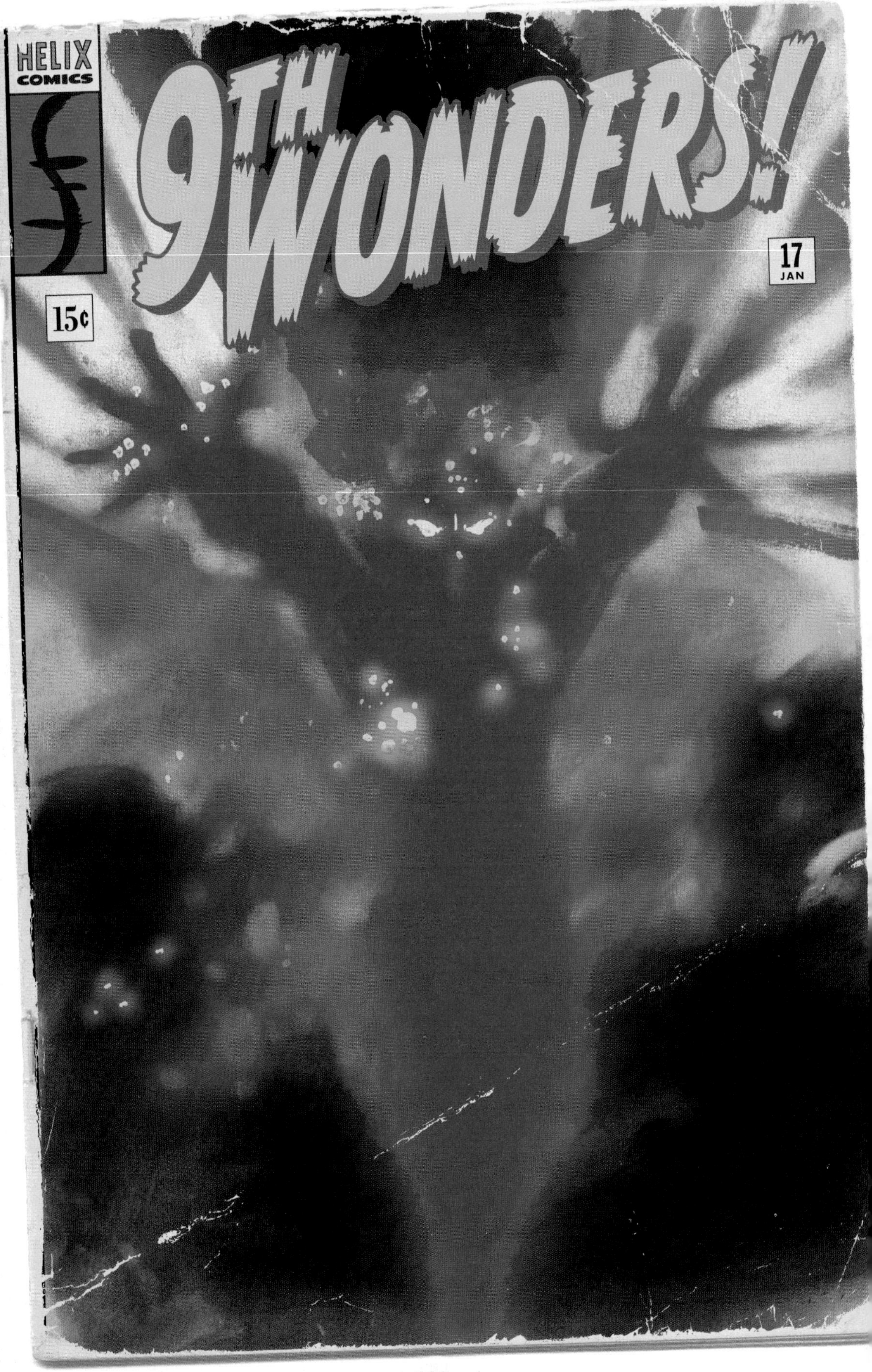
HELIX
COMICS
9TH WONDERS!
17
JAN
15¢

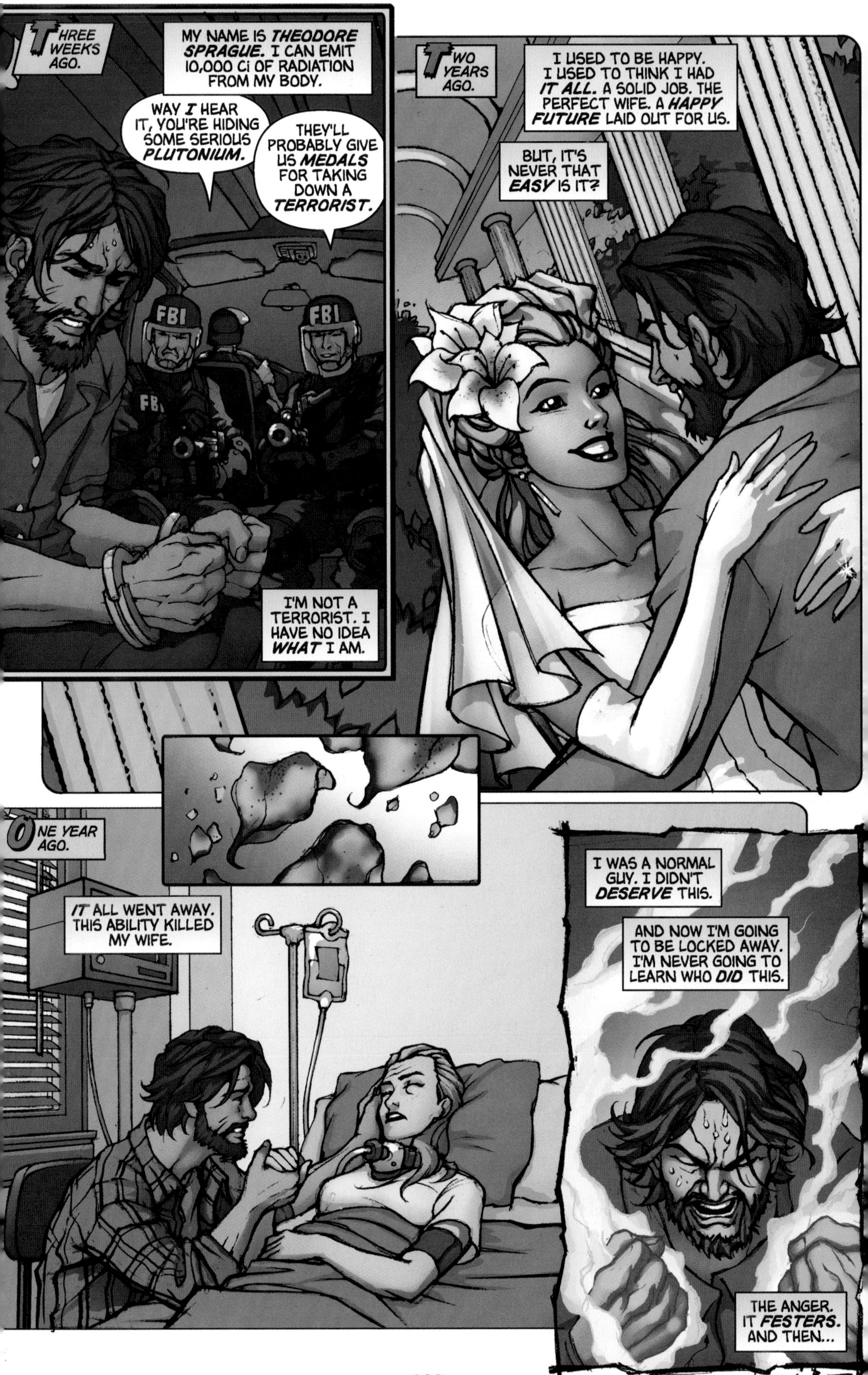
THREE WEEKS AGO.
MY NAME IS THEODORE SPRAGUE. I CAN EMIT 10,000 Ci OF RADIATION FROM MY BODY.
WAY I HEAR IT, YOU'RE HIDING SOME SERIOUS PLUTONIUM.
THEY'LL PROBABLY GIVE US MEDALS FOR TAKING DOWN A TERRORIST.
FBI
FBI
FBI
I'M NOT A TERRORIST. I HAVE NO IDEA WHAT I AM.
TWO YEARS AGO.
I USED TO BE HAPPY. I USED TO THINK I HAD IT ALL. A SOLID JOB. THE PERFECT WIFE. A HAPPY FUTURE LAID OUT FOR US.
BUT, IT'S NEVER THAT EASY IS IT?
ONE YEAR AGO.
IT ALL WENT AWAY. THIS ABILITY KILLED MY WIFE.
I WAS A NORMAL GUY. I DIDN'T DESERVE THIS.
AND NOW I'M GOING TO BE LOCKED AWAY. I'M NEVER GOING TO LEARN WHO DID THIS.
THE ANGER. IT FESTERS. AND THEN...

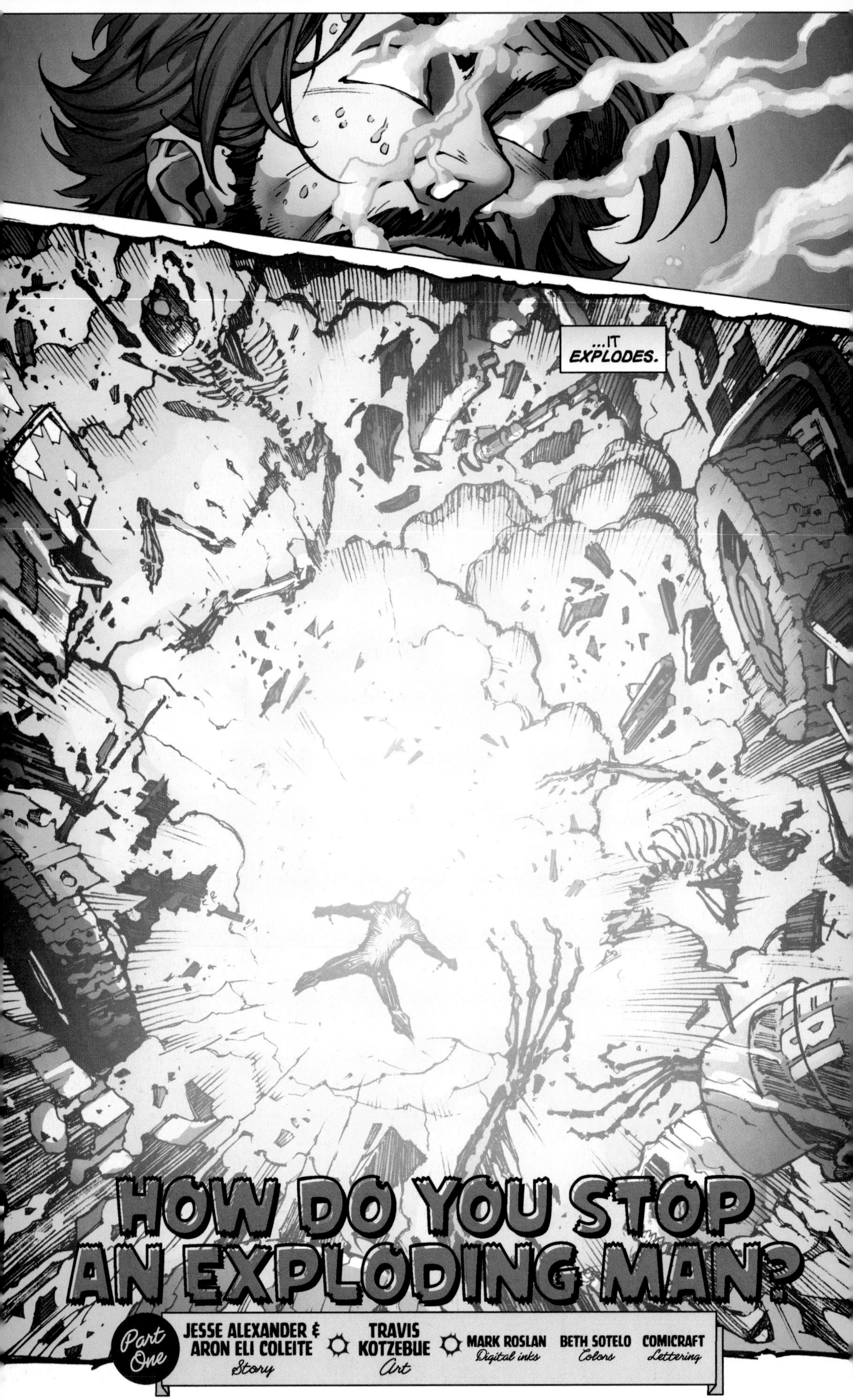
...IT EXPLODES.
HOW DO YOU STOP AN EXPLODING MAN?
Part One
JESSE ALEXANDER & ARON ELI COLEITE Story
TRAVIS KOTZEBUE Art
MARK ROSLAN Digital inks
BETH SOTELO Colors
COMICRAFT Lettering

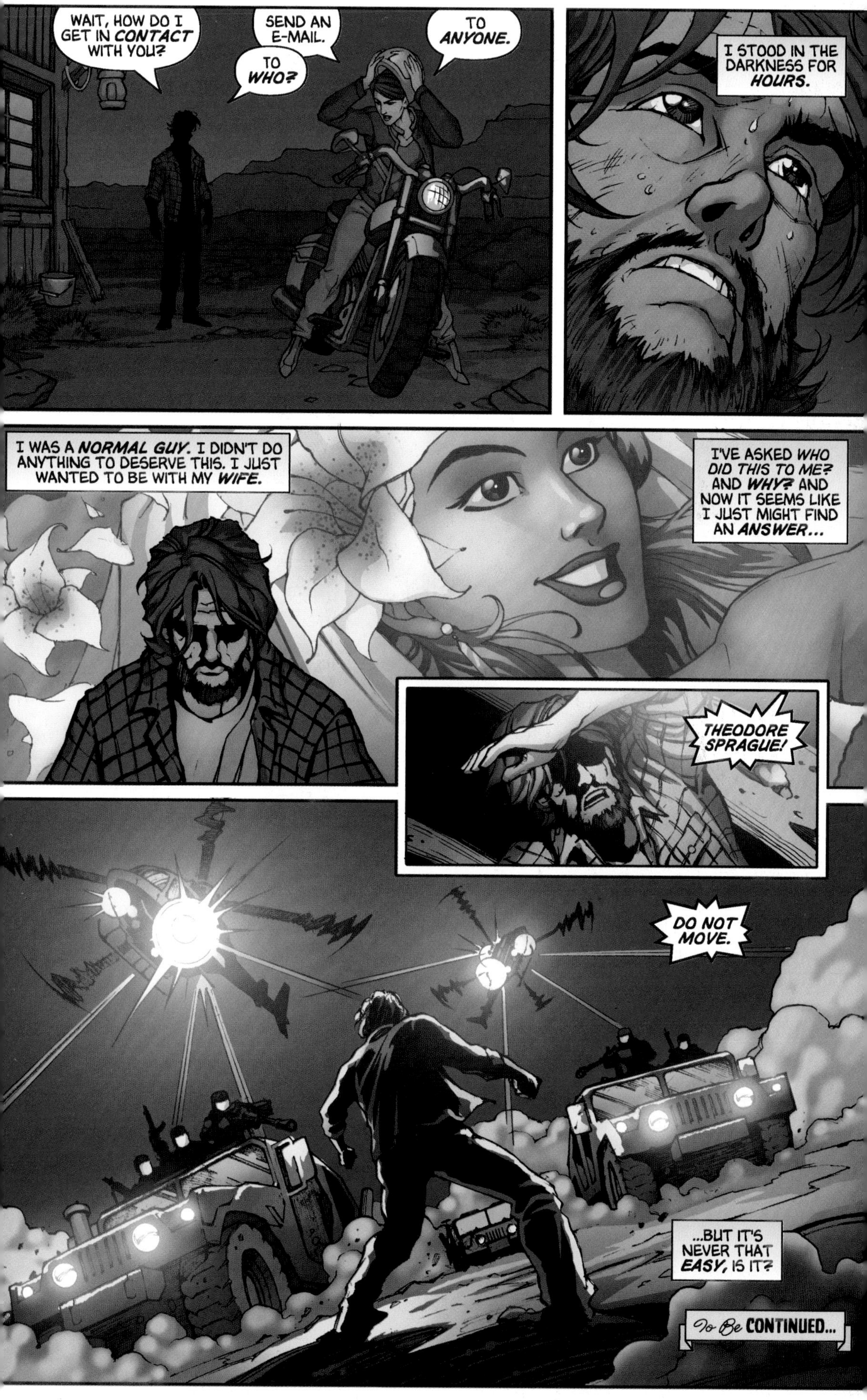

WAIT, HOW DO I GET IN CONTACT WITH YOU?
SEND AN E-MAIL.
TO WHO?
TO ANYONE.
I STOOD IN THE DARKNESS FOR HOURS.
I WAS A NORMAL GUY. I DIDN'T DO ANYTHING TO DESERVE THIS. I JUST WANTED TO BE WITH MY WIFE.
I'VE ASKED WHO DID THIS TO ME? AND WHY? AND NOW IT SEEMS LIKE I JUST MIGHT FIND AN ANSWER...
THEODORE SPRAGUE!
DO NOT MOVE.
...BUT IT'S NEVER THAT EASY, IS IT?
To Be CONTINUED...

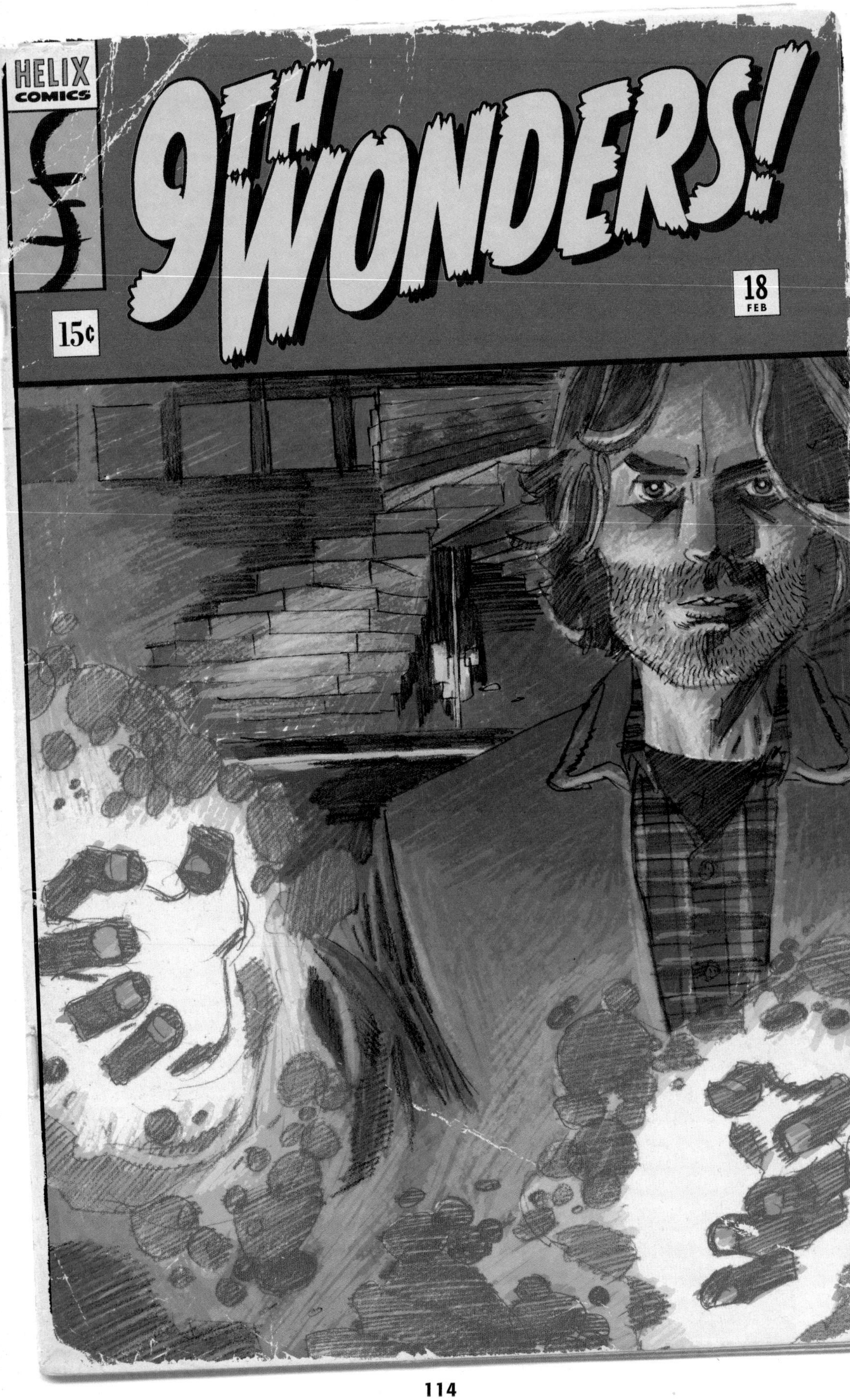
HELIX
COMICS
9TH WONDERS!
18
FEB
15¢

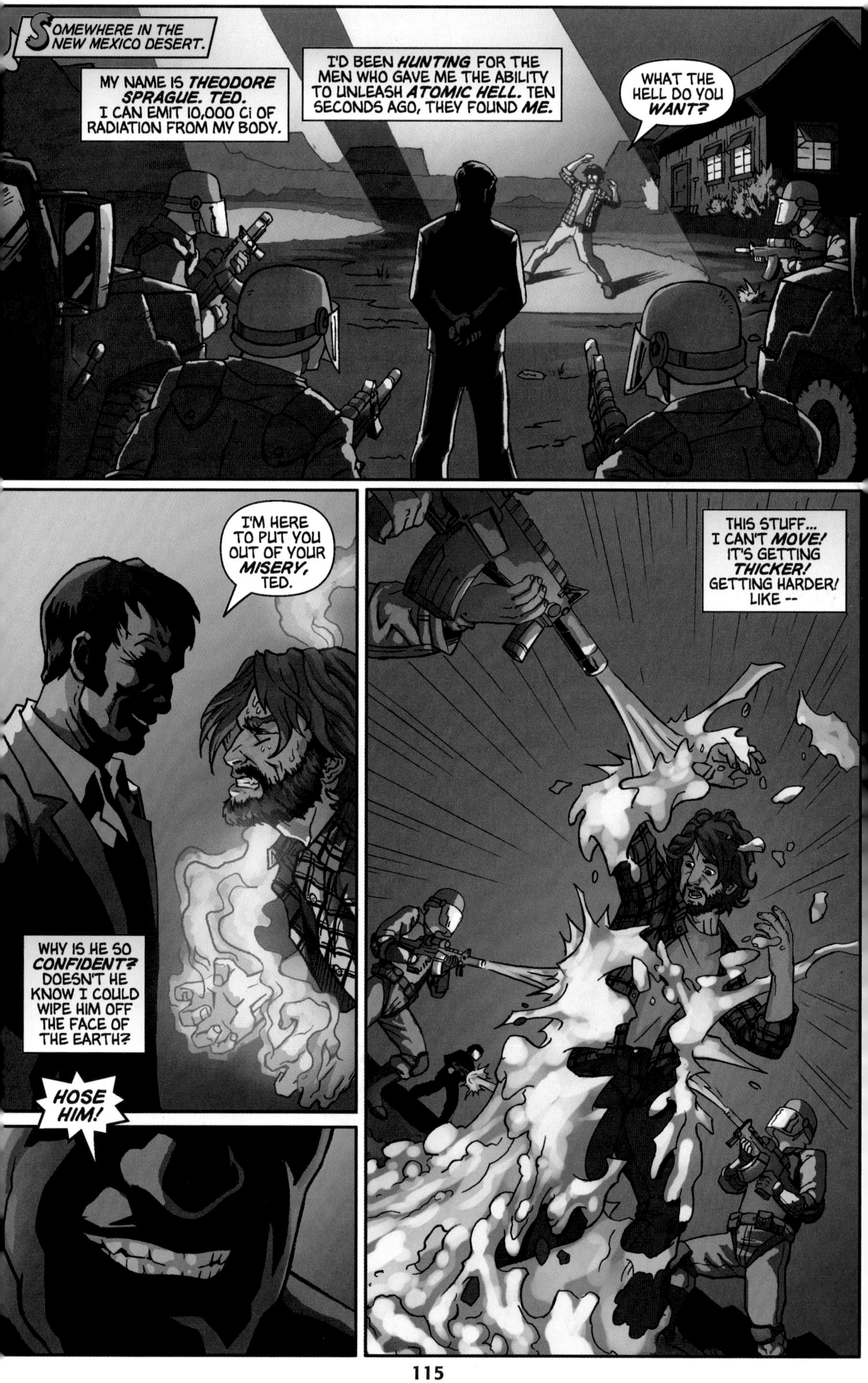
SOMEWHERE IN THE NEW MEXICO DESERT.
MY NAME IS THEODORE SPRAGUE. TED. I CAN EMIT 10,000 Ci OF RADIATION FROM MY BODY.
I'D BEEN HUNTING FOR THE MEN WHO GAVE ME THE ABILITY TO UNLEASH ATOMIC HELL. TEN SECONDS AGO, THEY FOUND ME.
WHAT THE HELL DO YOU WANT?
I'M HERE TO PUT YOU OUT OF YOUR MISERY, TED.
WHY IS HE SO CONFIDENT? DOESN'T HE KNOW I COULD WIPE HIM OFF THE FACE OF THE EARTH?
HOSE HIM!
THIS STUFF... I CAN'T MOVE! IT'S GETTING THICKER! GETTING HARDER! LIKE --

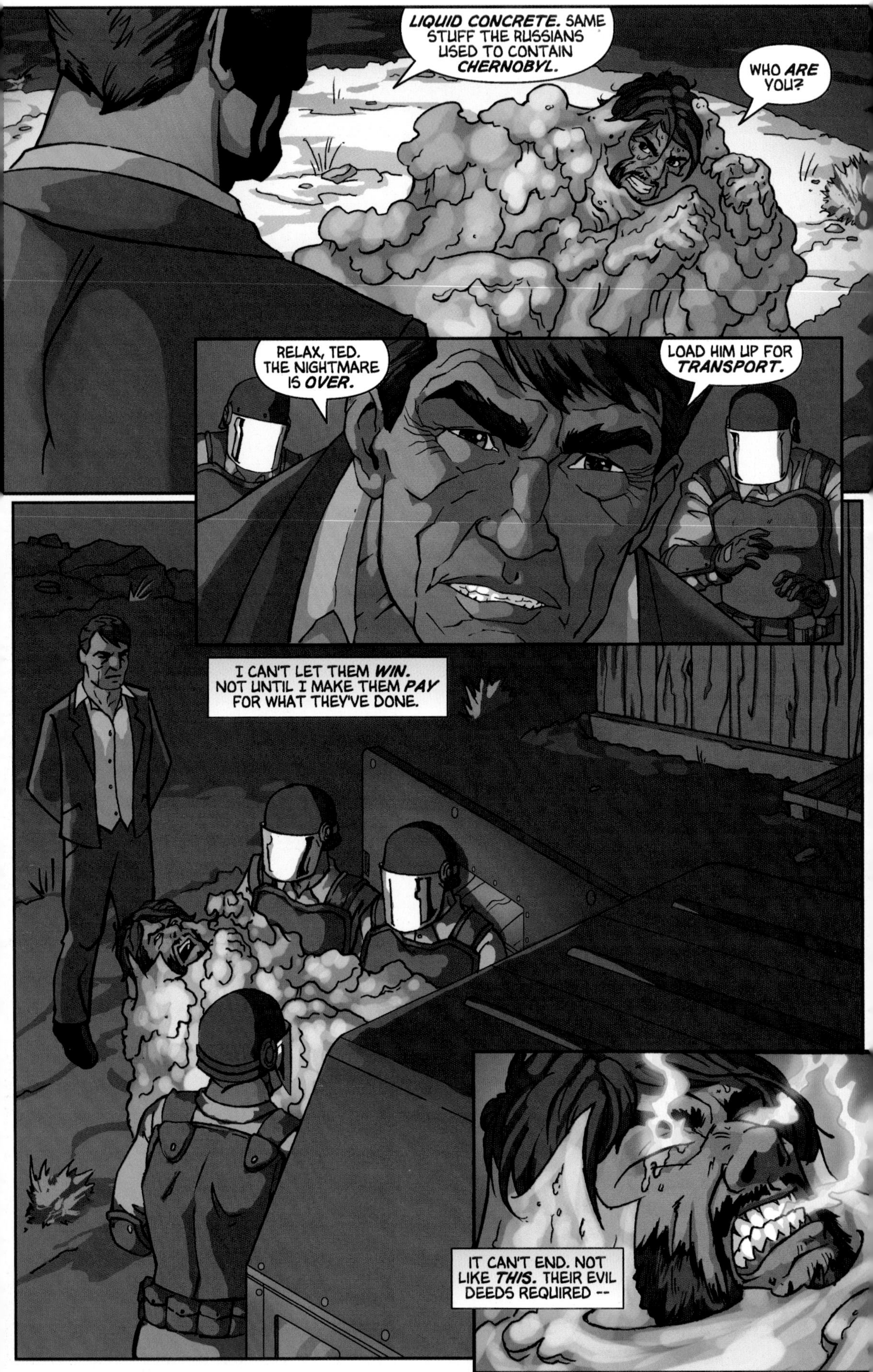
LIQUID CONCRETE. SAME STUFF THE RUSSIANS USED TO CONTAIN CHERNOBYL.
WHO ARE YOU?
RELAX, TED. THE NIGHTMARE IS OVER.
LOAD HIM UP FOR TRANSPORT.
I CAN'T LET THEM WIN. NOT UNTIL I MAKE THEM PAY FOR WHAT THEY'VE DONE.
IT CAN'T END. NOT LIKE THIS. THEIR EVIL DEEDS REQUIRED --

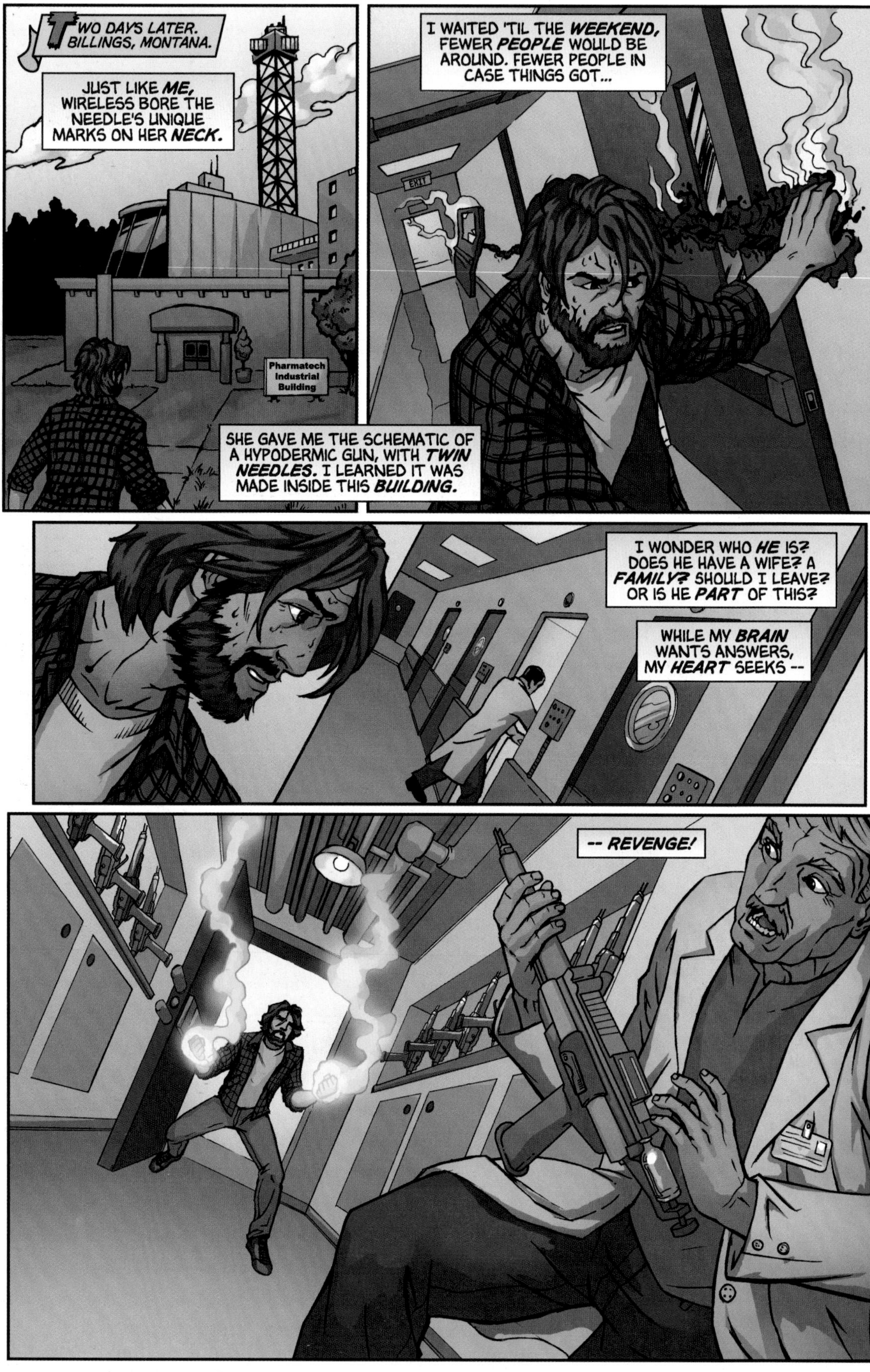
TWO DAYS LATER. BILLINGS, MONTANA.
JUST LIKE ME, WIRELESS BORE THE NEEDLE'S UNIQUE MARKS ON HER NECK.
Pharmatech Industrial Building
SHE GAVE ME THE SCHEMATIC OF A HYPODERMIC GUN, WITH TWIN NEEDLES. I LEARNED IT WAS MADE INSIDE THIS BUILDING.
I WAITED 'TIL THE WEEKEND, FEWER PEOPLE WOULD BE AROUND. FEWER PEOPLE IN CASE THINGS GOT...
EXIT
I WONDER WHO HE IS? DOES HE HAVE A WIFE? A FAMILY? SHOULD I LEAVE? OR IS HE PART OF THIS?
WHILE MY BRAIN WANTS ANSWERS, MY HEART SEEKS --
-- REVENGE!

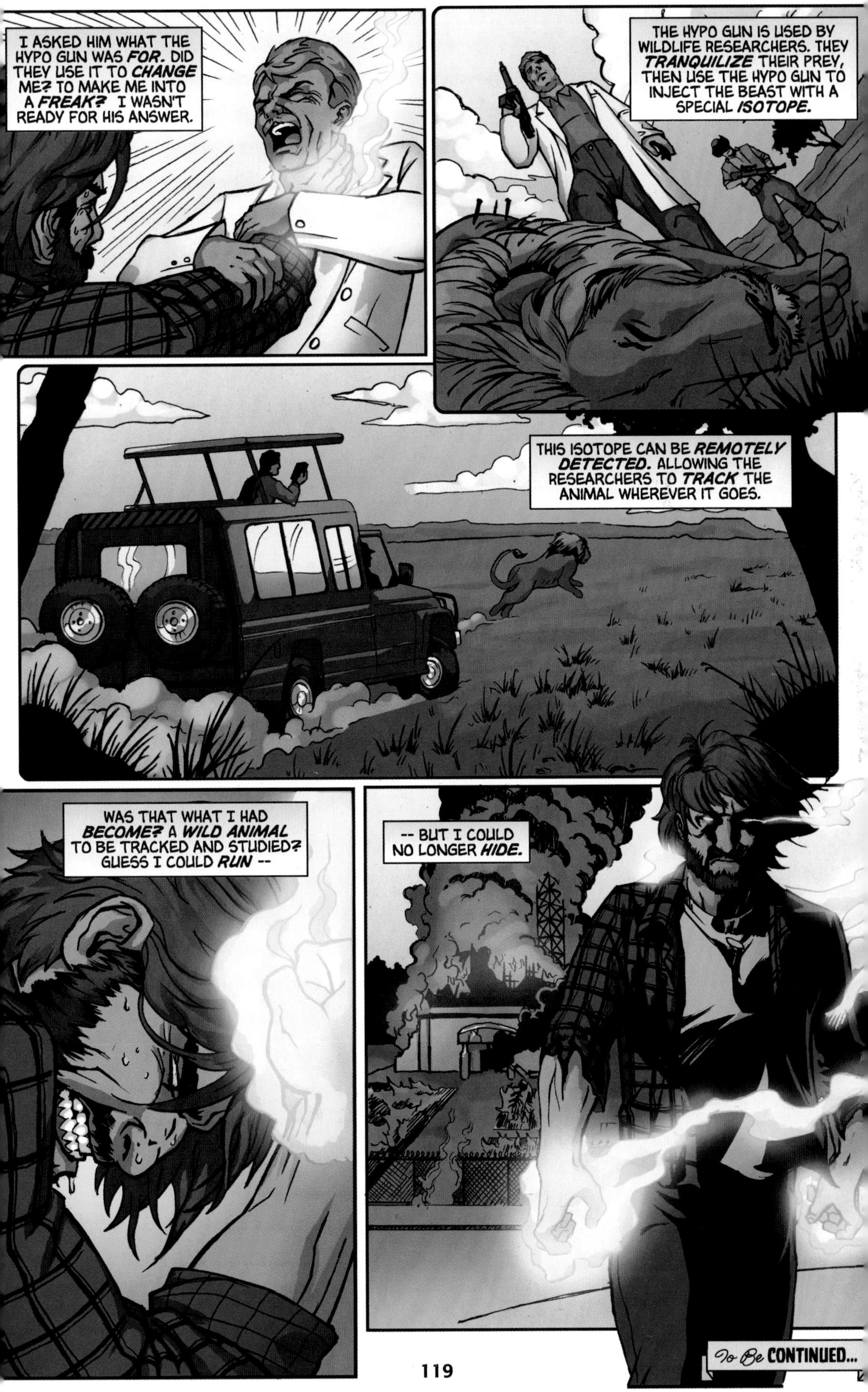
I ASKED HIM WHAT THE HYPO GUN WAS *FOR.* DID THEY USE IT TO *CHANGE* ME? TO MAKE ME INTO A *FREAK?* I WASN'T READY FOR HIS ANSWER.
THE HYPO GUN IS USED BY WILDLIFE RESEARCHERS. THEY *TRANQUILIZE* THEIR PREY, THEN USE THE HYPO GUN TO INJECT THE BEAST WITH A SPECIAL *ISOTOPE.*
THIS ISOTOPE CAN BE *REMOTELY DETECTED.* ALLOWING THE RESEARCHERS TO *TRACK* THE ANIMAL WHEREVER IT GOES.
WAS THAT WHAT I HAD *BECOME?* A *WILD ANIMAL* TO BE TRACKED AND STUDIED? GUESS I COULD *RUN* --
-- BUT I COULD NO LONGER *HIDE.*
To Be CONTINUED...

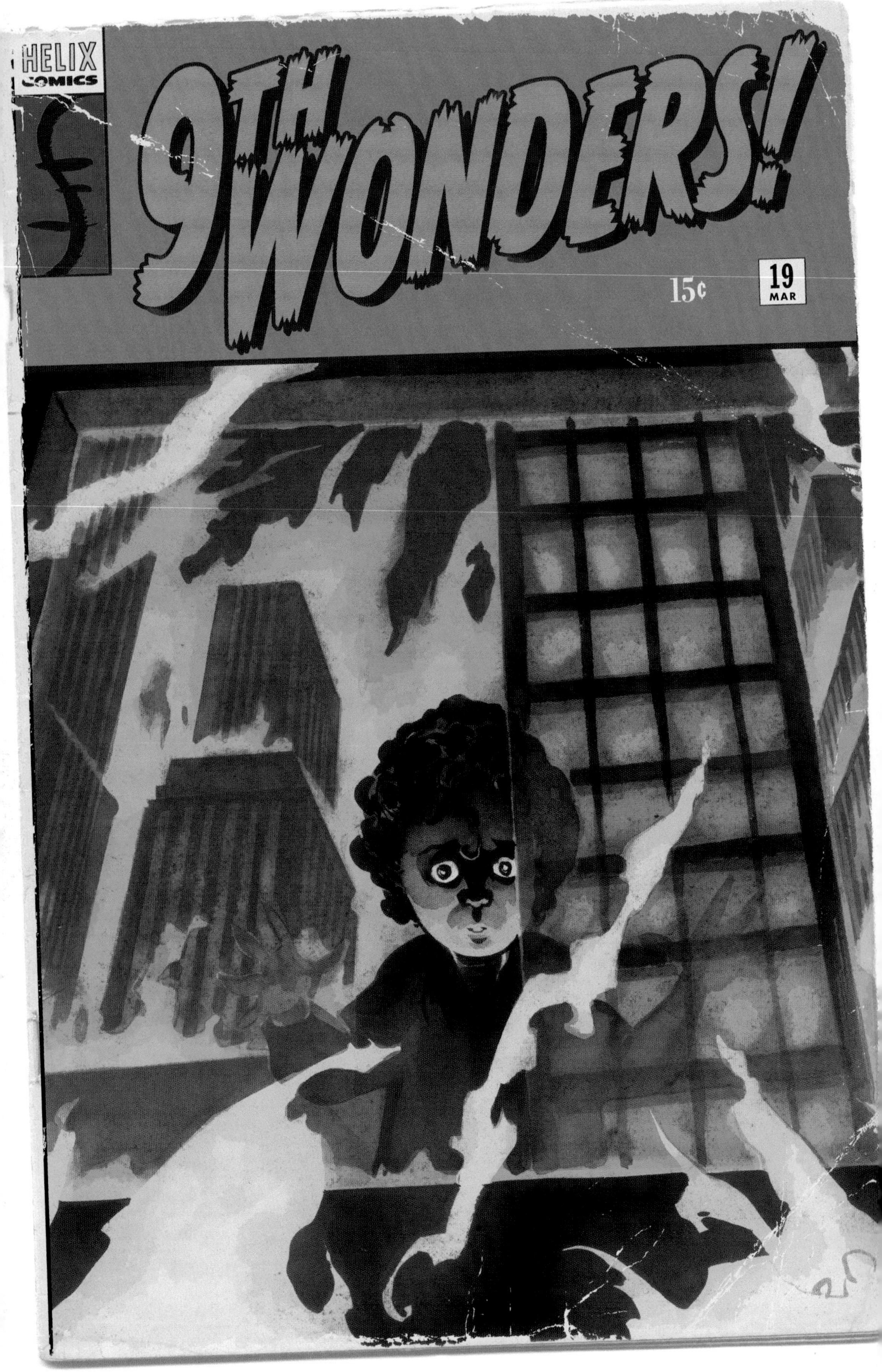
HELIX
COMICS
9TH WONDERS!
15¢
19
MAR

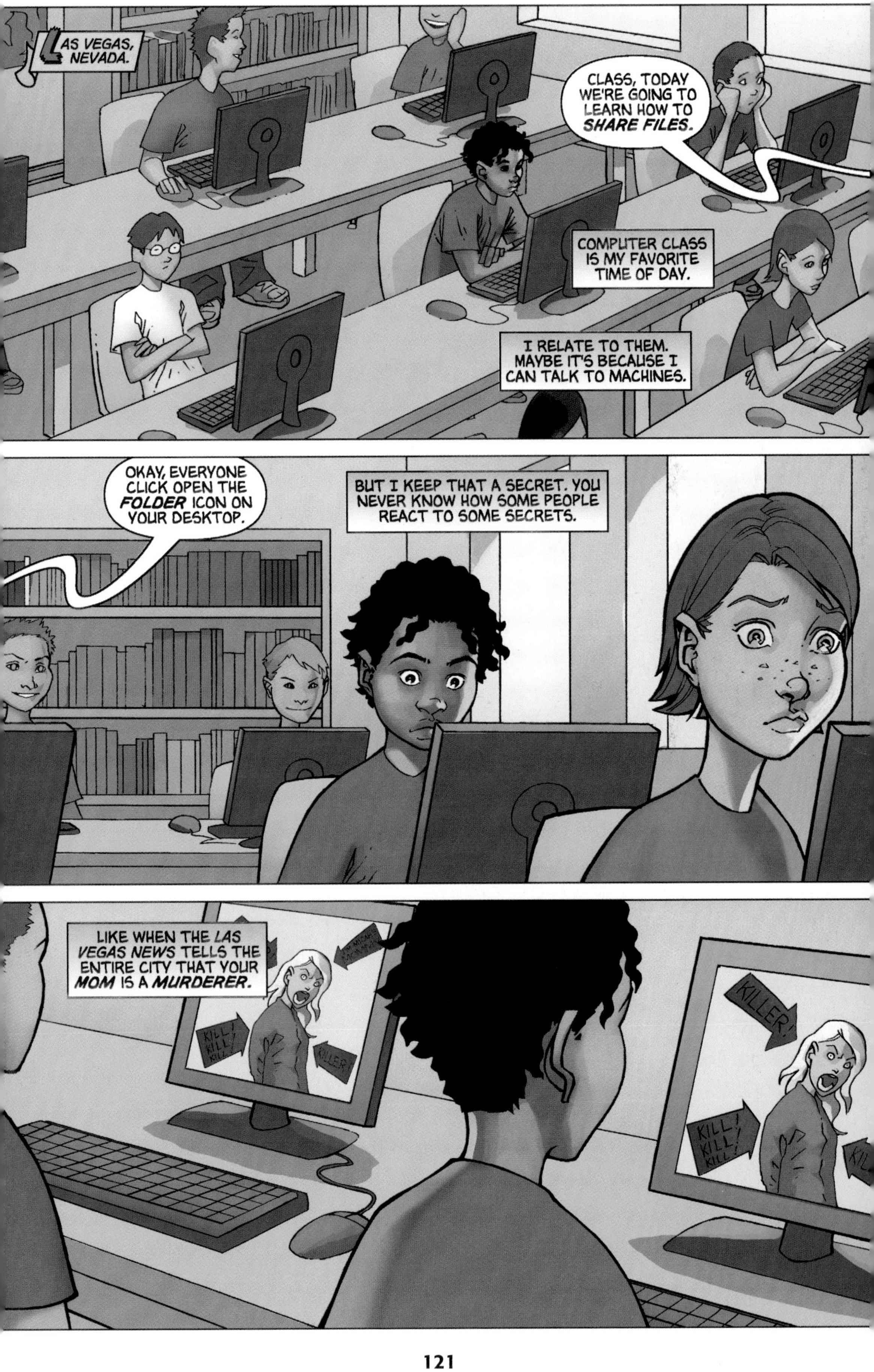
LAS VEGAS, NEVADA.
CLASS, TODAY WE'RE GOING TO LEARN HOW TO SHARE FILES.
COMPUTER CLASS IS MY FAVORITE TIME OF DAY.
I RELATE TO THEM. MAYBE IT'S BECAUSE I CAN TALK TO MACHINES.
OKAY, EVERYONE CLICK OPEN THE FOLDER ICON ON YOUR DESKTOP.
BUT I KEEP THAT A SECRET. YOU NEVER KNOW HOW SOME PEOPLE REACT TO SOME SECRETS.
LIKE WHEN THE LAS VEGAS NEWS TELLS THE ENTIRE CITY THAT YOUR MOM IS A MURDERER.
KILL! KILL! KILL!
KILLER!
KILLER!
KILL! KILL! KILL!

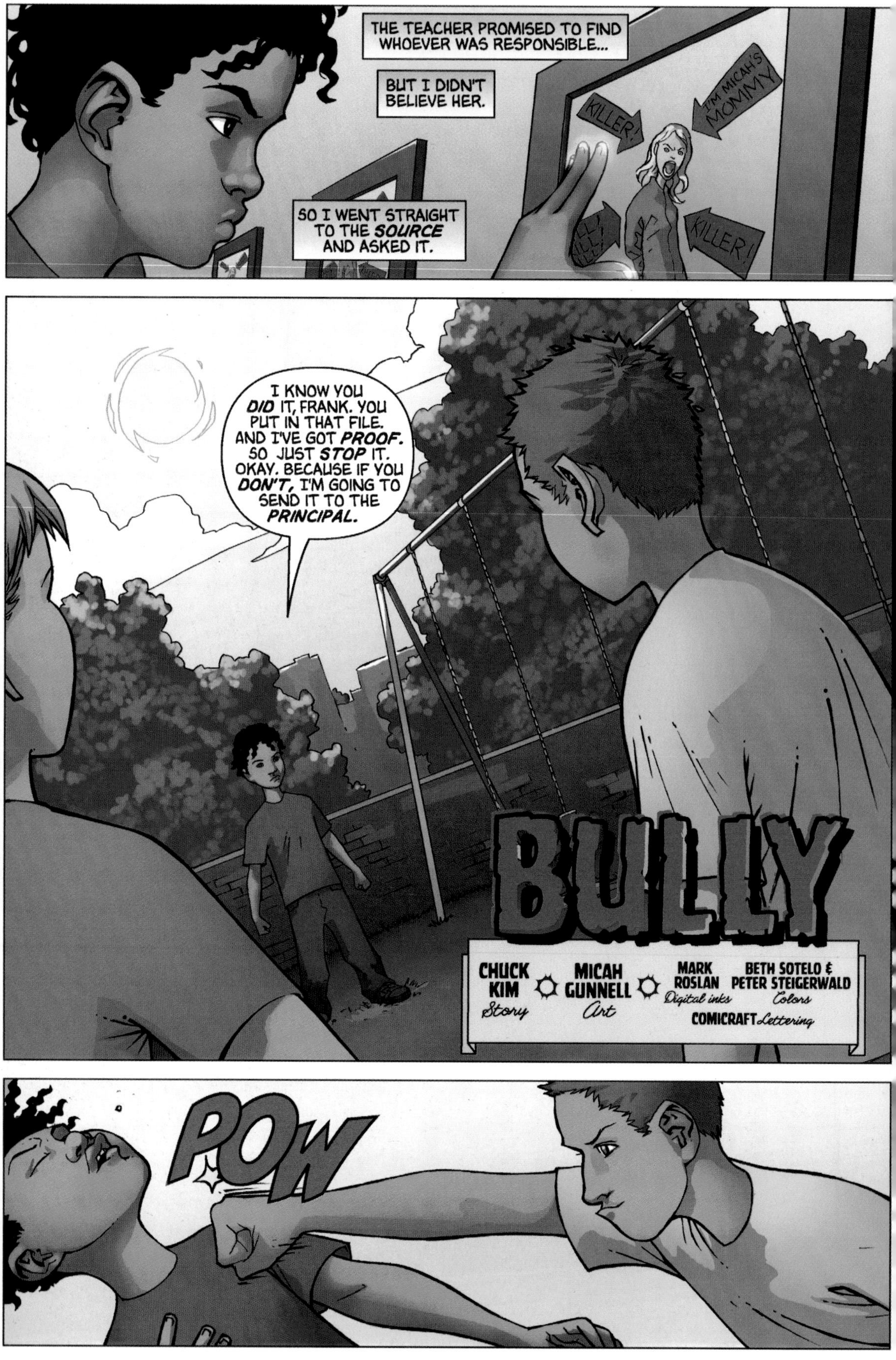

THE TEACHER PROMISED TO FIND WHOEVER WAS RESPONSIBLE...
BUT I DIDN'T BELIEVE HER.
KILLER!
I'M MICAH'S MOMMY
KILLER!
SO I WENT STRAIGHT TO THE SOURCE AND ASKED IT.
I KNOW YOU DID IT, FRANK. YOU PUT IN THAT FILE. AND I'VE GOT PROOF. SO JUST STOP IT. OKAY. BECAUSE IF YOU DON'T, I'M GOING TO SEND IT TO THE PRINCIPAL.
BULLY
CHUCK KIM Story
MICAH GUNNELL Art
MARK ROSLAN Digital inks
BETH SOTELO & PETER STEIGERWALD Colors
COMICRAFT Lettering
POW

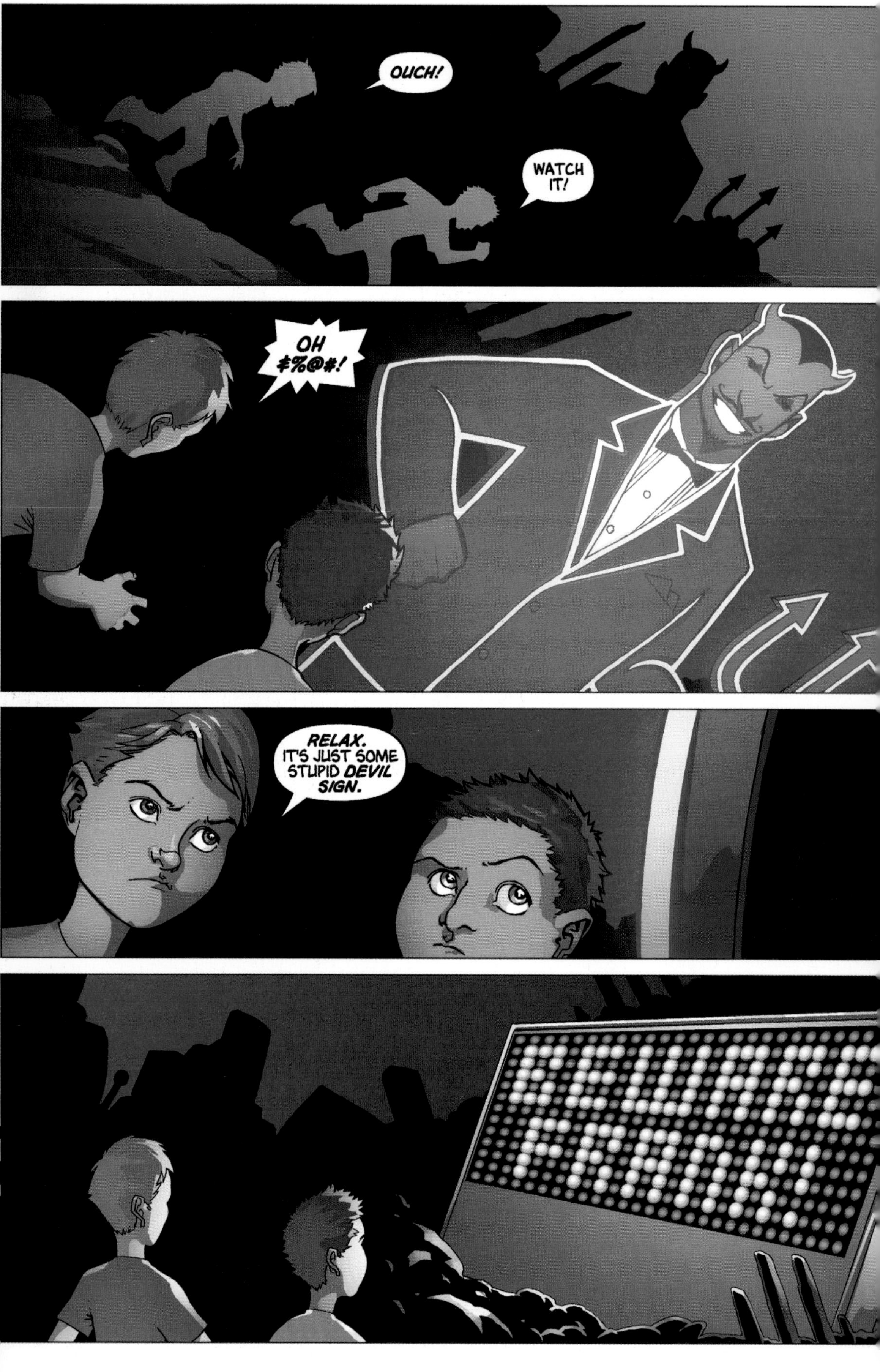
OUCH!
WATCH IT!
OH ≠%@#!
RELAX. IT'S JUST SOME STUPID DEVIL SIGN.

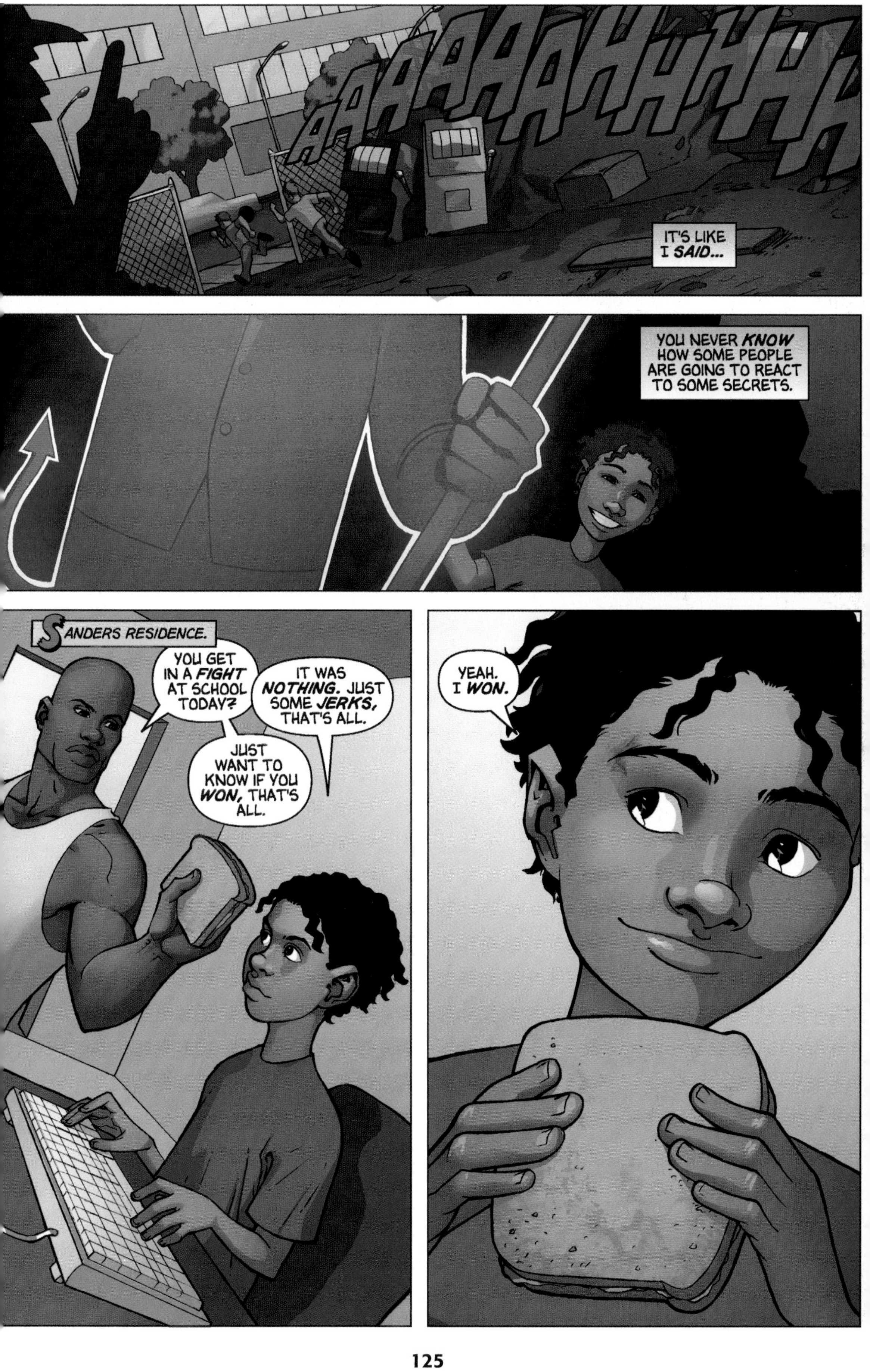
AAAAAAHHHHH
IT'S LIKE I SAID...
YOU NEVER KNOW HOW SOME PEOPLE ARE GOING TO REACT TO SOME SECRETS.
SANDERS RESIDENCE.
YOU GET IN A FIGHT AT SCHOOL TODAY?
IT WAS NOTHING. JUST SOME JERKS, THAT'S ALL.
JUST WANT TO KNOW IF YOU WON, THAT'S ALL.
YEAH. I WON.

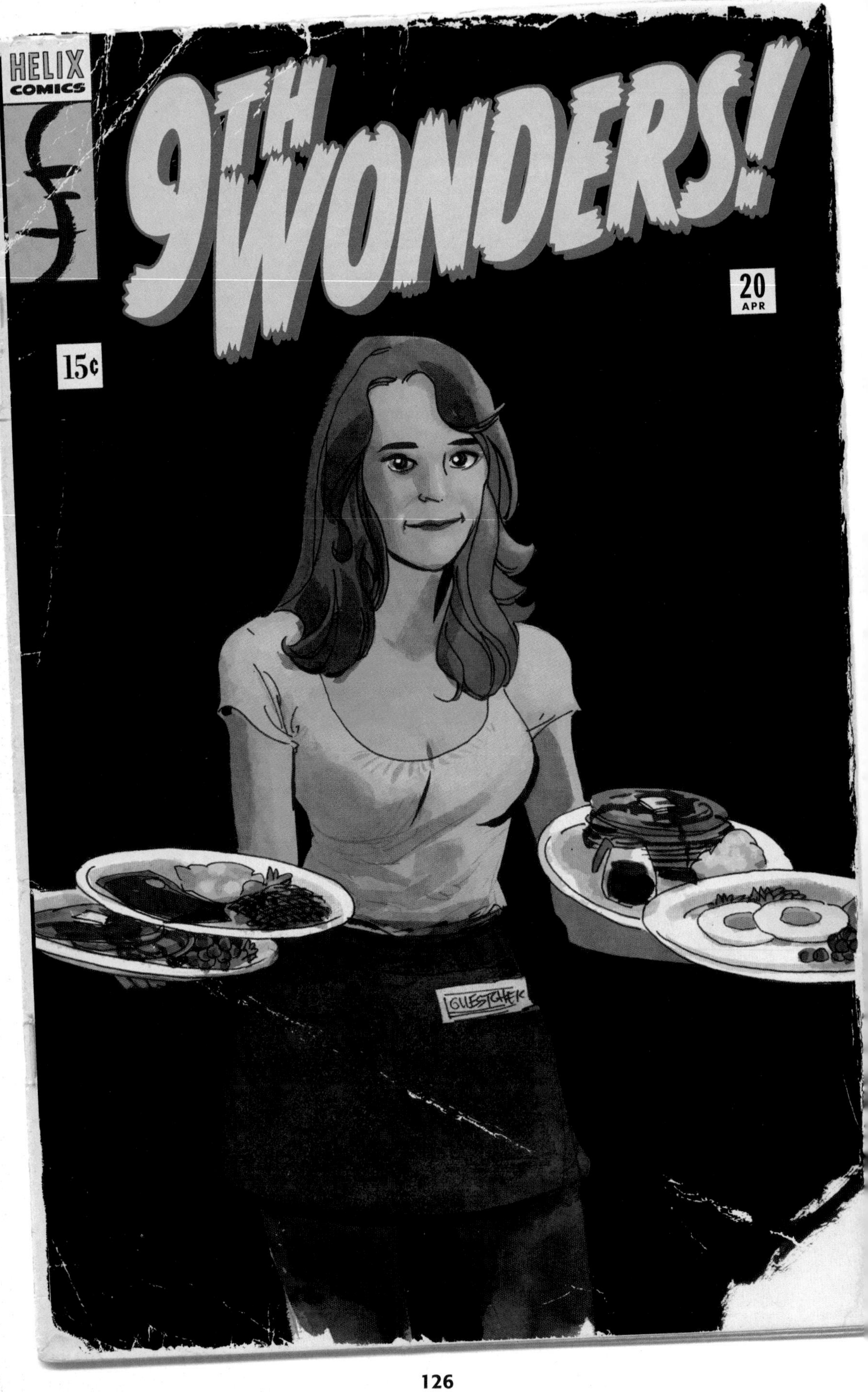
HELIX
COMICS
9TH WONDERS!
20
APR
15¢
GUESTCHECK

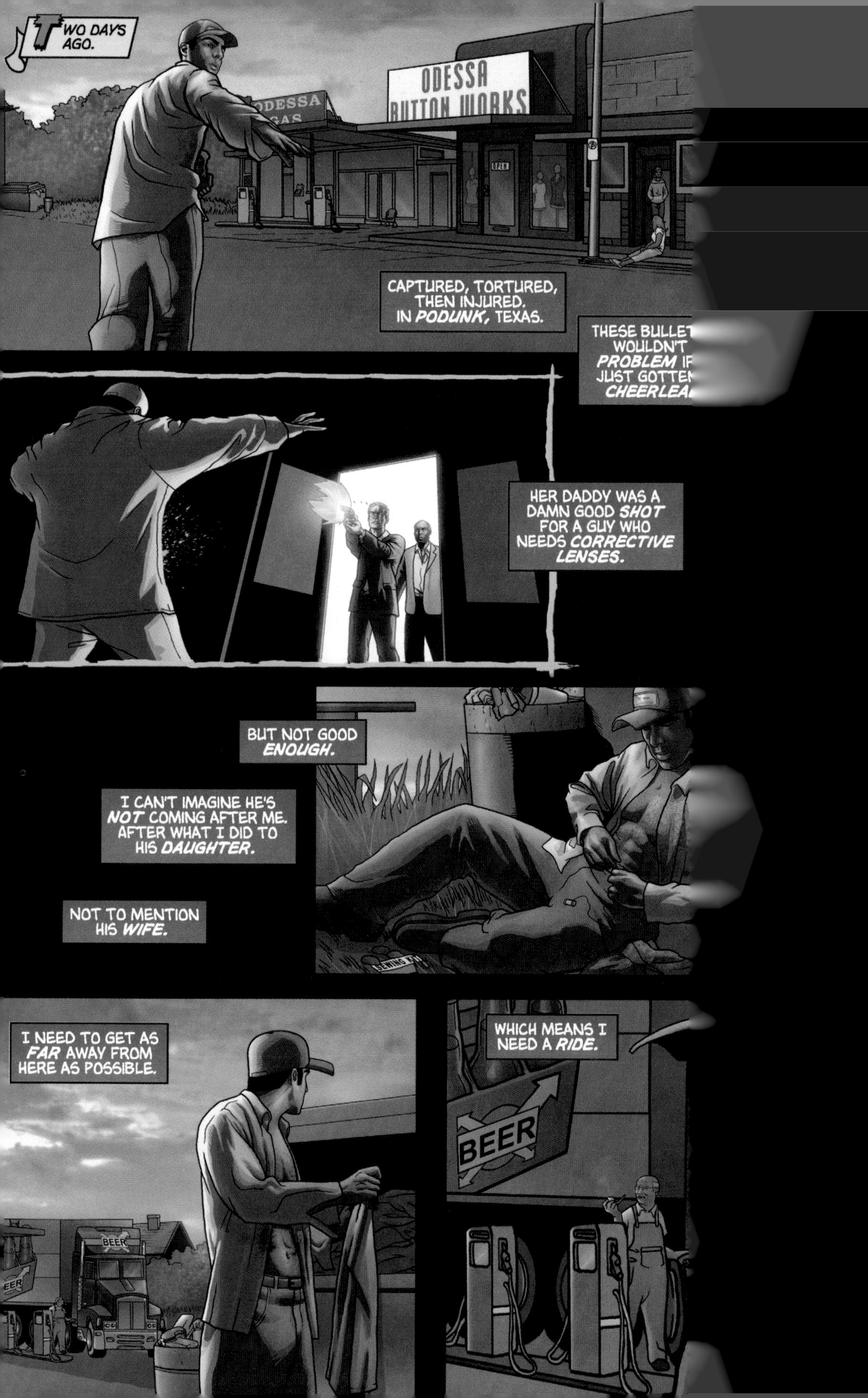
TWO DAYS AGO.
ODESSA GAS
ODESSA BUTTON WORKS
OPEN
CAPTURED, TORTURED, THEN INJURED. IN PODUNK, TEXAS.
THESE BULLET WOULDN'T PROBLEM IF JUST GOTTEN CHEERLEA
HER DADDY WAS A DAMN GOOD SHOT FOR A GUY WHO NEEDS CORRECTIVE LENSES.
BUT NOT GOOD ENOUGH.
I CAN'T IMAGINE HE'S NOT COMING AFTER ME. AFTER WHAT I DID TO HIS DAUGHTER.
NOT TO MENTION HIS WIFE.
I NEED TO GET AS FAR AWAY FROM HERE AS POSSIBLE.
WHICH MEANS I NEED A RIDE.
BEER
BEER

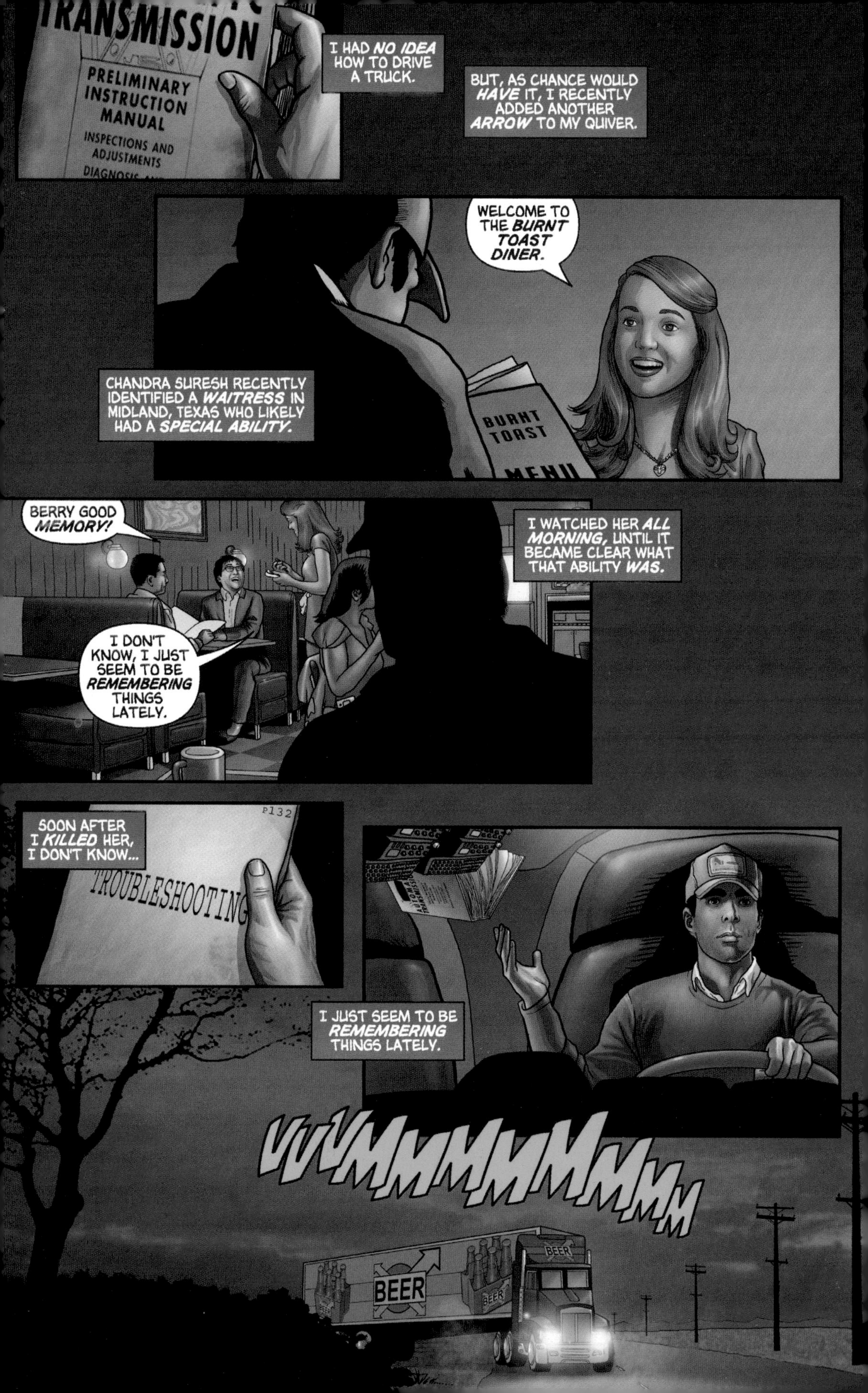
TRANSMISSION
PRELIMINARY INSTRUCTION MANUAL
INSPECTIONS AND ADJUSTMENTS
I HAD NO IDEA HOW TO DRIVE A TRUCK.
BUT, AS CHANCE WOULD HAVE IT, I RECENTLY ADDED ANOTHER ARROW TO MY QUIVER.
WELCOME TO THE BURNT TOAST DINER.
CHANDRA SURESH RECENTLY IDENTIFIED A WAITRESS IN MIDLAND, TEXAS WHO LIKELY HAD A SPECIAL ABILITY.
BURNT TOAST
BERRY GOOD MEMORY!
I WATCHED HER ALL MORNING, UNTIL IT BECAME CLEAR WHAT THAT ABILITY WAS.
I DON'T KNOW, I JUST SEEM TO BE REMEMBERING THINGS LATELY.
P132
SOON AFTER I KILLED HER, I DON'T KNOW...
TROUBLESHOOTING
I JUST SEEM TO BE REMEMBERING THINGS LATELY.
VVVMMMMMMMMMMM
BEER
BEER
BEER

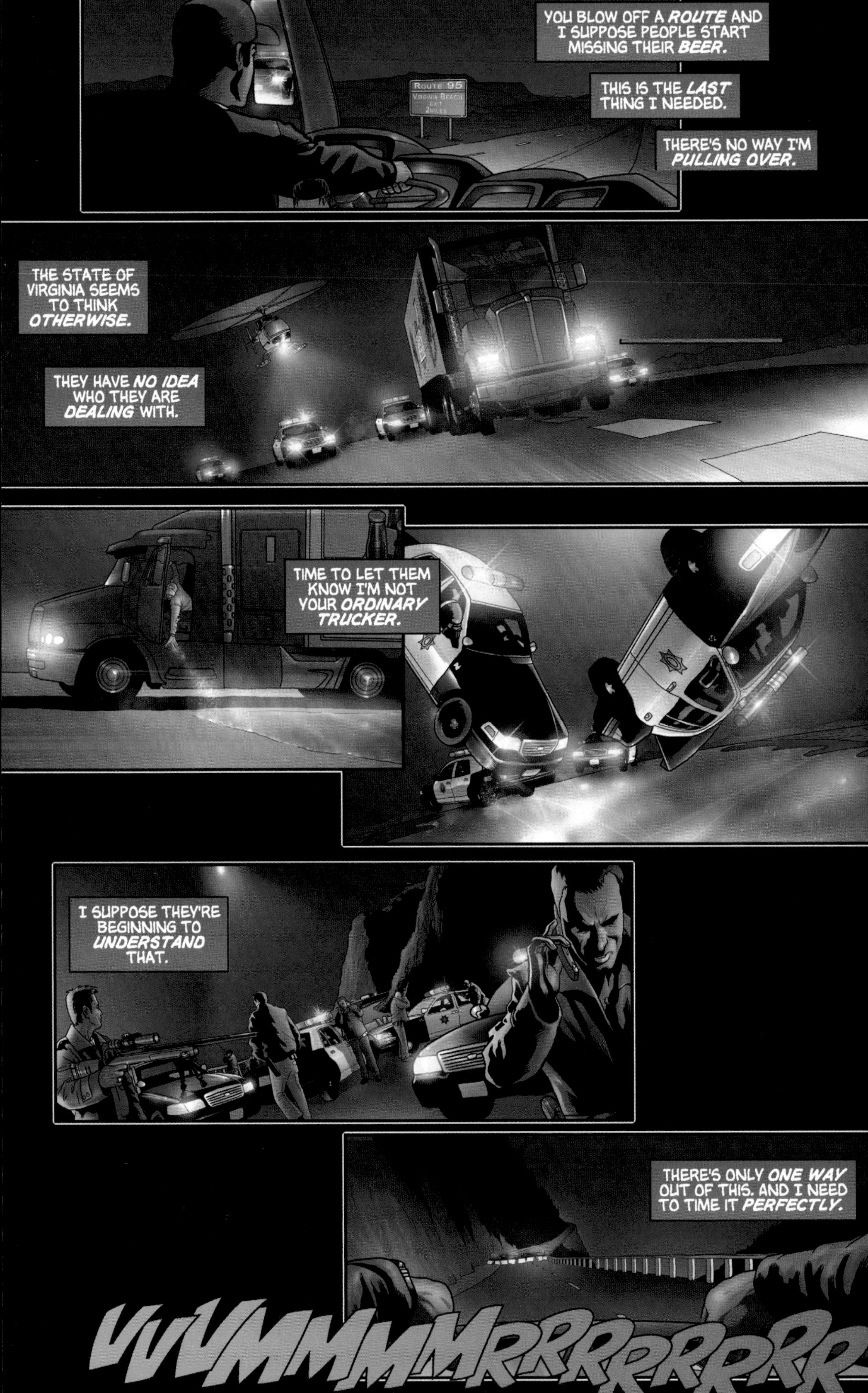
YOU BLOW OFF A ROUTE AND I SUPPOSE PEOPLE START MISSING THEIR BEER.
THIS IS THE LAST THING I NEEDED.
THERE'S NO WAY I'M PULLING OVER.
ROUTE 95
VIRGINIA BEACH
EXIT
2 MILES
THE STATE OF VIRGINIA SEEMS TO THINK OTHERWISE.
THEY HAVE NO IDEA WHO THEY ARE DEALING WITH.
TIME TO LET THEM KNOW I'M NOT YOUR ORDINARY TRUCKER.
I SUPPOSE THEY'RE BEGINNING TO UNDERSTAND THAT.
THERE'S ONLY ONE WAY OUT OF THIS. AND I NEED TO TIME IT PERFECTLY.
VVUMMMMRRRRRRRR

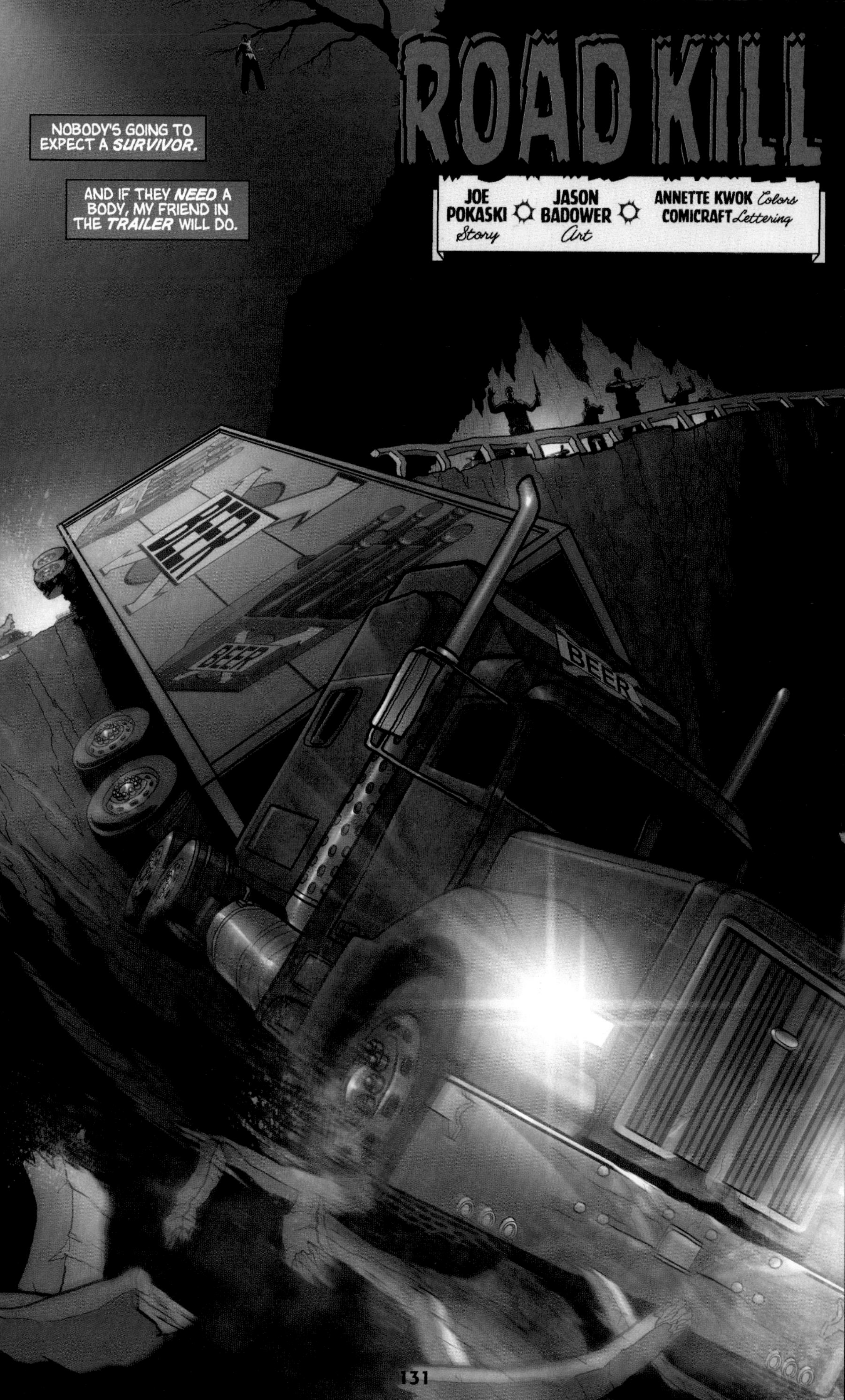

ROAD KILL
NOBODY'S GOING TO EXPECT A SURVIVOR.
AND IF THEY NEED A BODY, MY FRIEND IN THE TRAILER WILL DO.
JOE POKASKI Story
JASON BADOWER Art
ANNETTE KWOK Colors
COMICRAFT Lettering
BEER

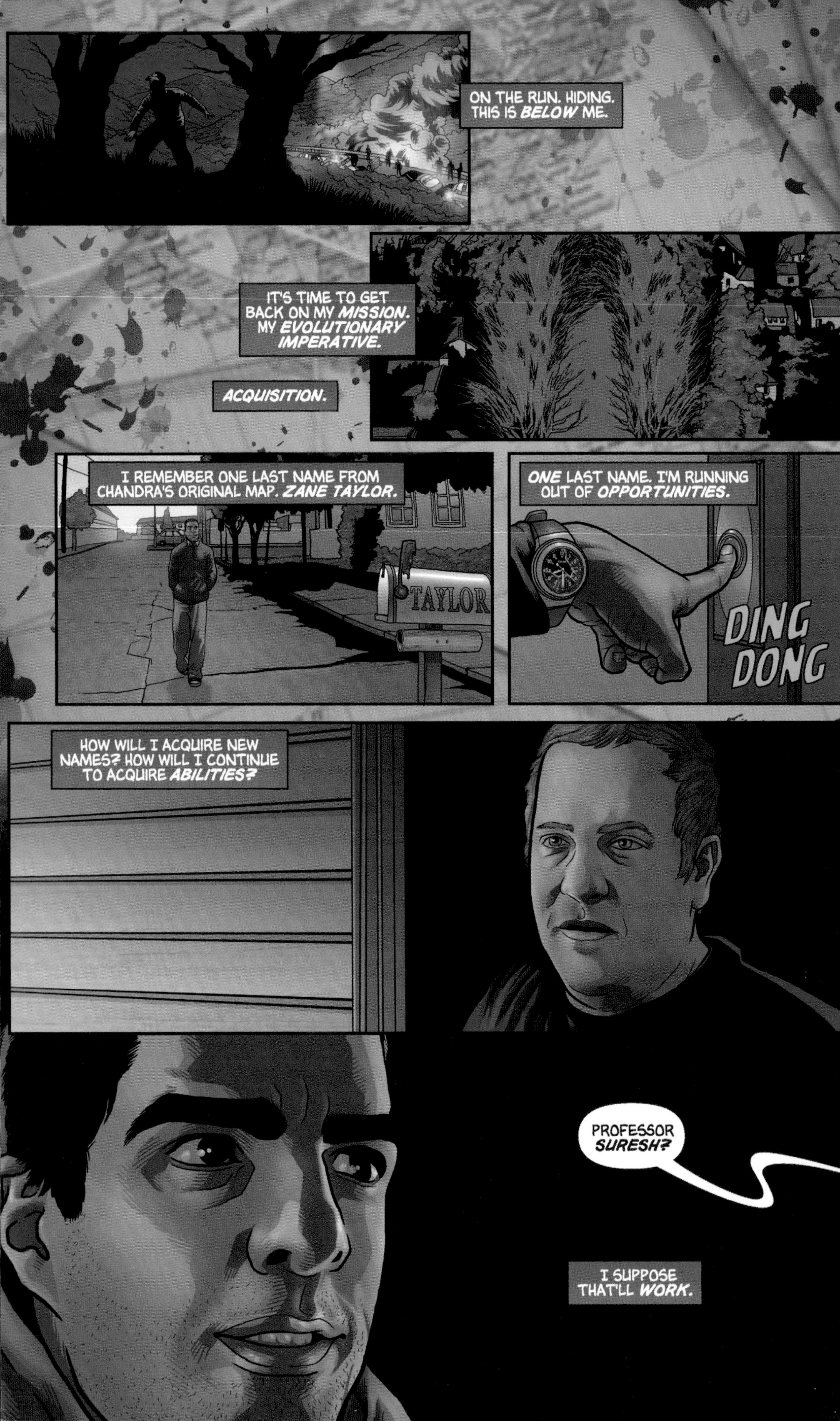
ON THE RUN. HIDING. THIS IS BELOW ME.
IT'S TIME TO GET BACK ON MY MISSION. MY EVOLUTIONARY IMPERATIVE.
ACQUISITION.
I REMEMBER ONE LAST NAME FROM CHANDRA'S ORIGINAL MAP. ZANE TAYLOR.
TAYLOR
ONE LAST NAME. I'M RUNNING OUT OF OPPORTUNITIES.
DING DONG
HOW WILL I ACQUIRE NEW NAMES? HOW WILL I CONTINUE TO ACQUIRE ABILITIES?
PROFESSOR SURESH?
I SUPPOSE THAT'LL WORK.

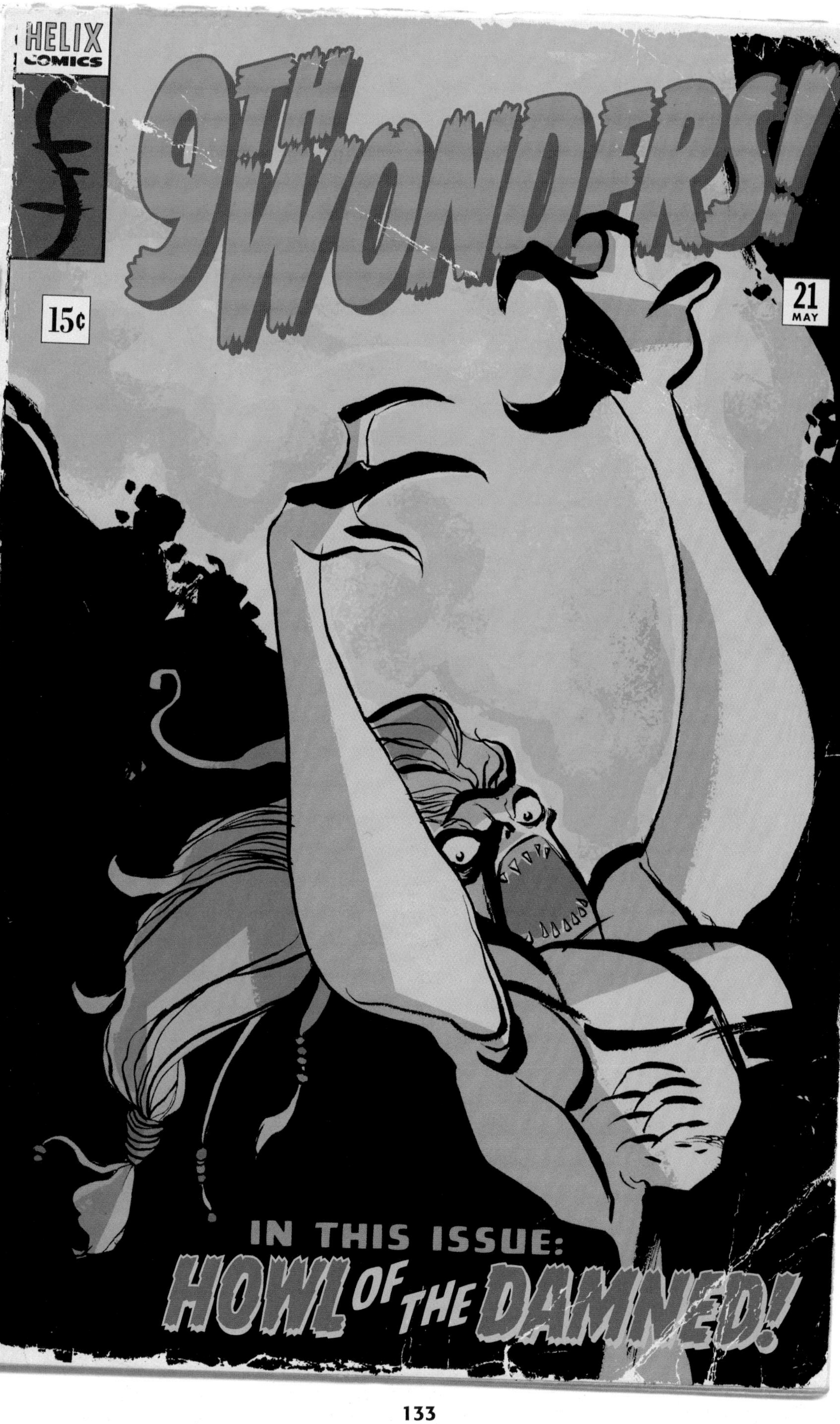
HELIX
COMICS
9TH WONDERS!
15¢
21
MAY
IN THIS ISSUE:
HOWL OF THE DAMNED!

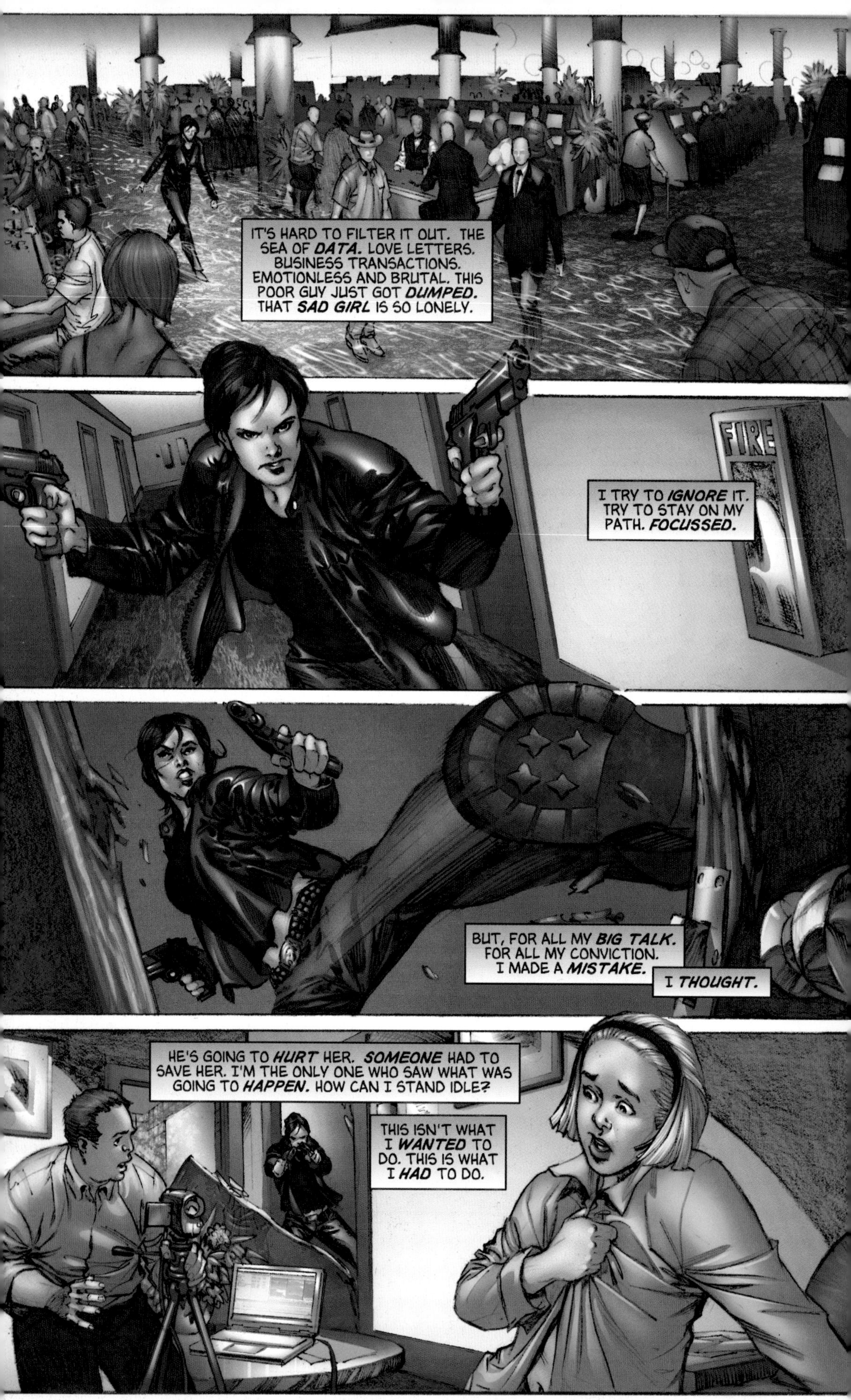
IT'S HARD TO FILTER IT OUT. THE SEA OF *DATA.* LOVE LETTERS. BUSINESS TRANSACTIONS. EMOTIONLESS AND BRUTAL. THIS POOR GUY JUST GOT *DUMPED.* THAT *SAD GIRL* IS SO LONELY.
FIRE
I TRY TO *IGNORE* IT. TRY TO STAY ON MY PATH. *FOCUSSED.*
BUT, FOR ALL MY *BIG TALK.* FOR ALL MY CONVICTION. I MADE A *MISTAKE.*
I *THOUGHT.*
HE'S GOING TO *HURT* HER. *SOMEONE* HAD TO SAVE HER. I'M THE ONLY ONE WHO SAW WHAT WAS GOING TO *HAPPEN.* HOW CAN I STAND IDLE?
THIS ISN'T WHAT I *WANTED* TO DO. THIS IS WHAT I *HAD* TO DO.

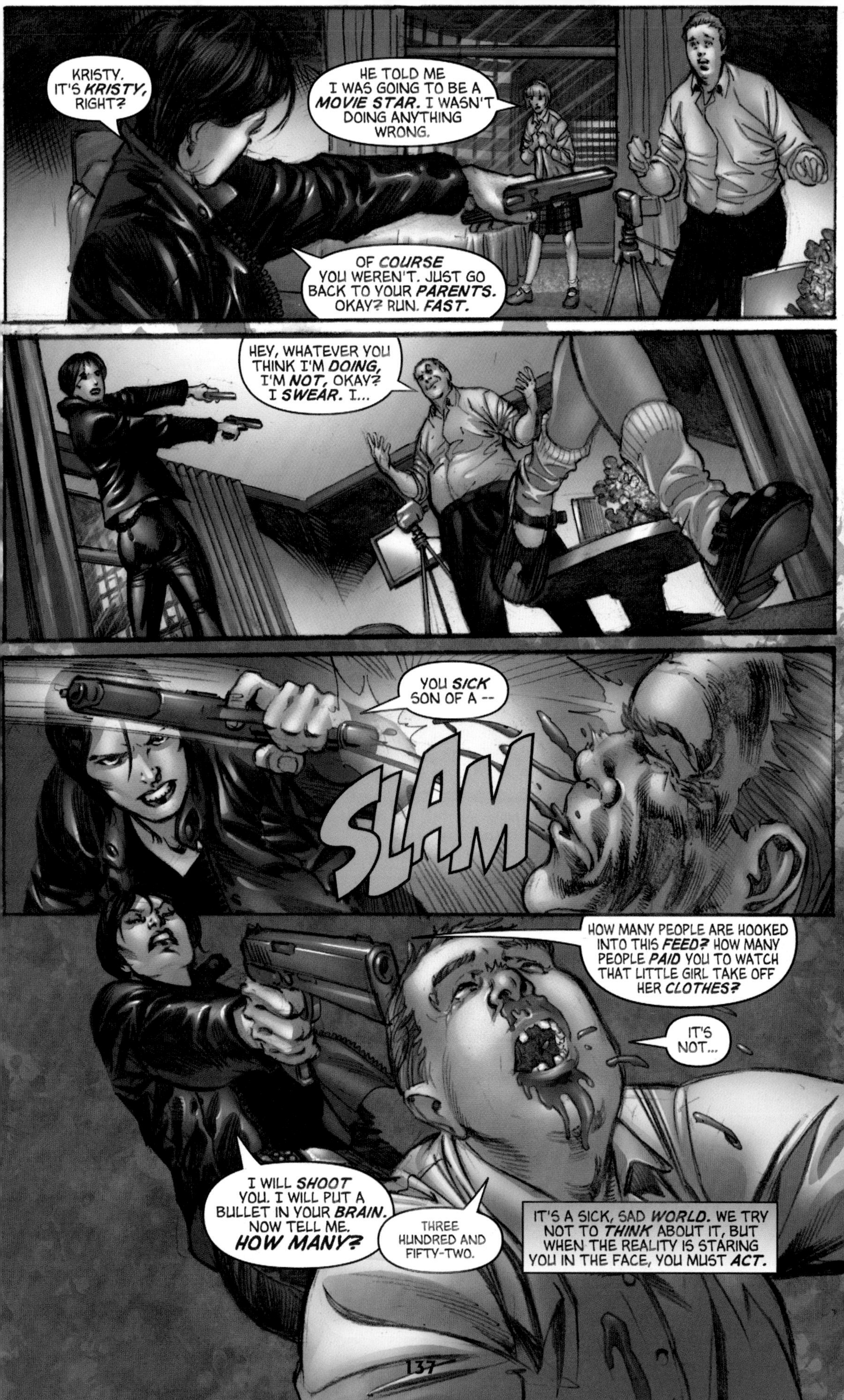
KRISTY. IT'S KRISTY, RIGHT?
HE TOLD ME I WAS GOING TO BE A MOVIE STAR. I WASN'T DOING ANYTHING WRONG.
OF COURSE YOU WEREN'T. JUST GO BACK TO YOUR PARENTS. OKAY? RUN. FAST.
HEY, WHATEVER YOU THINK I'M DOING, I'M NOT, OKAY? I SWEAR. I...
YOU SICK SON OF A --
SLAM
HOW MANY PEOPLE ARE HOOKED INTO THIS FEED? HOW MANY PEOPLE PAID YOU TO WATCH THAT LITTLE GIRL TAKE OFF HER CLOTHES?
IT'S NOT...
I WILL SHOOT YOU. I WILL PUT A BULLET IN YOUR BRAIN. NOW TELL ME. HOW MANY?
THREE HUNDRED AND FIFTY-TWO.
IT'S A SICK, SAD WORLD. WE TRY NOT TO THINK ABOUT IT, BUT WHEN THE REALITY IS STARING YOU IN THE FACE, YOU MUST ACT.

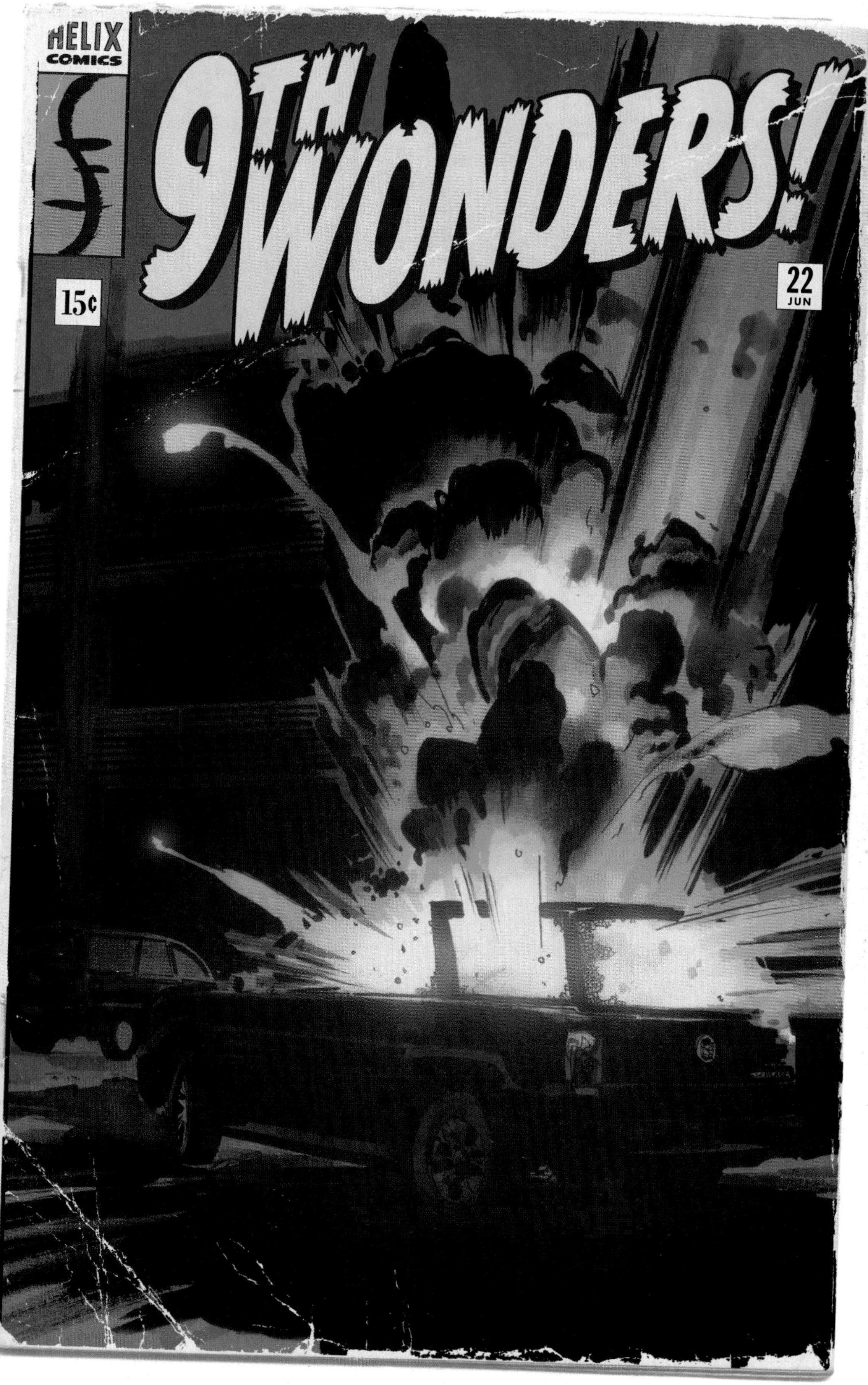
HELIX COMICS
9TH WONDERS!
15¢
22 JUN

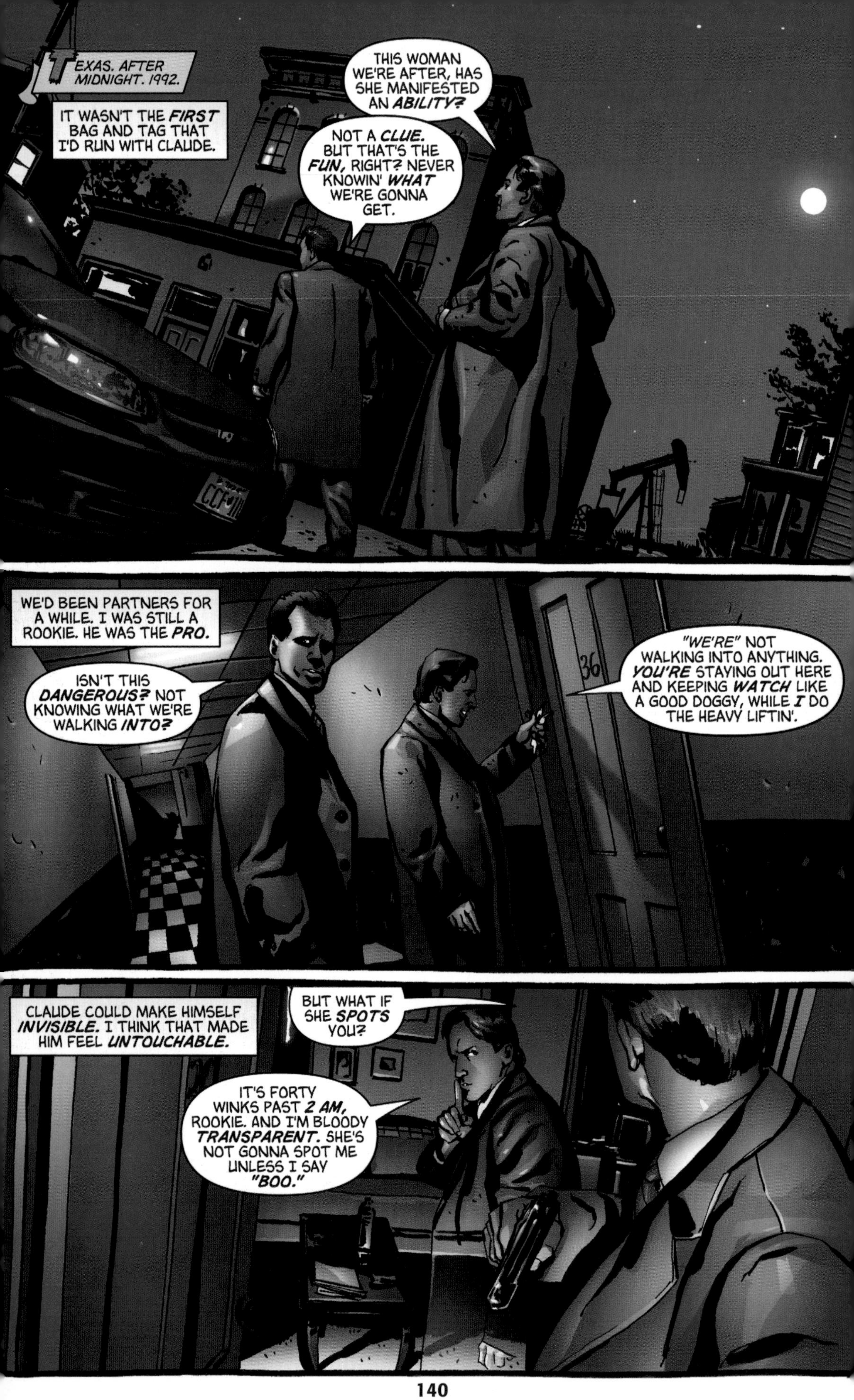
TEXAS. AFTER MIDNIGHT. 1992.
IT WASN'T THE FIRST BAG AND TAG THAT I'D RUN WITH CLAUDE.
THIS WOMAN WE'RE AFTER, HAS SHE MANIFESTED AN ABILITY?
NOT A CLUE. BUT THAT'S THE FUN, RIGHT? NEVER KNOWIN' WHAT WE'RE GONNA GET.
WE'D BEEN PARTNERS FOR A WHILE. I WAS STILL A ROOKIE. HE WAS THE PRO.
ISN'T THIS DANGEROUS? NOT KNOWING WHAT WE'RE WALKING INTO?
"WE'RE" NOT WALKING INTO ANYTHING. YOU'RE STAYING OUT HERE AND KEEPING WATCH LIKE A GOOD DOGGY, WHILE I DO THE HEAVY LIFTIN'.
CLAUDE COULD MAKE HIMSELF INVISIBLE. I THINK THAT MADE HIM FEEL UNTOUCHABLE.
BUT WHAT IF SHE SPOTS YOU?
IT'S FORTY WINKS PAST 2 AM, ROOKIE. AND I'M BLOODY TRANSPARENT. SHE'S NOT GONNA SPOT ME UNLESS I SAY "BOO."

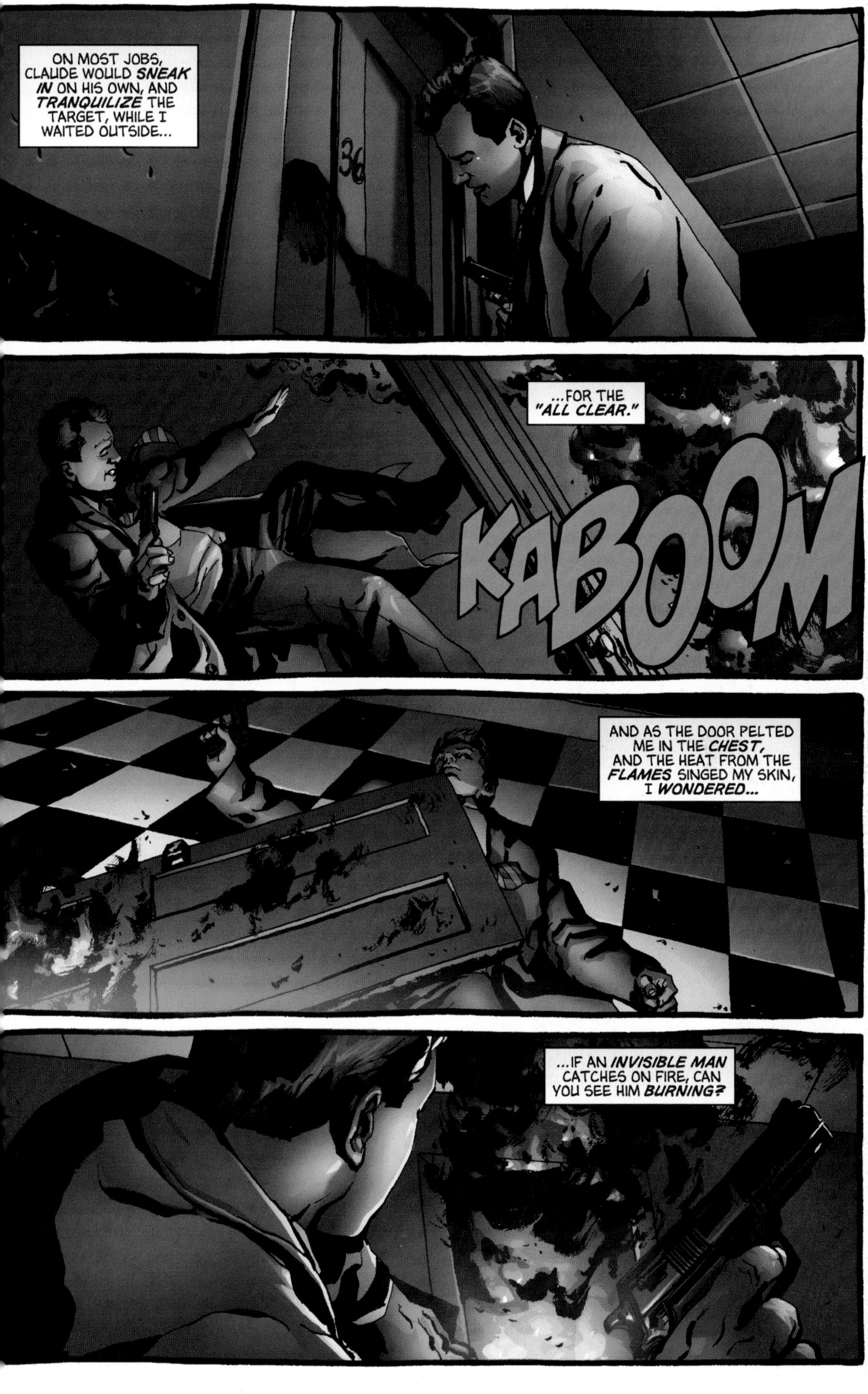

ON MOST JOBS, CLAUDE WOULD SNEAK IN ON HIS OWN, AND TRANQUILIZE THE TARGET, WHILE I WAITED OUTSIDE...
...FOR THE "ALL CLEAR."
KABOOM
AND AS THE DOOR PELTED ME IN THE CHEST, AND THE HEAT FROM THE FLAMES SINGED MY SKIN, I WONDERED...
...IF AN INVISIBLE MAN CATCHES ON FIRE, CAN YOU SEE HIM BURNING?

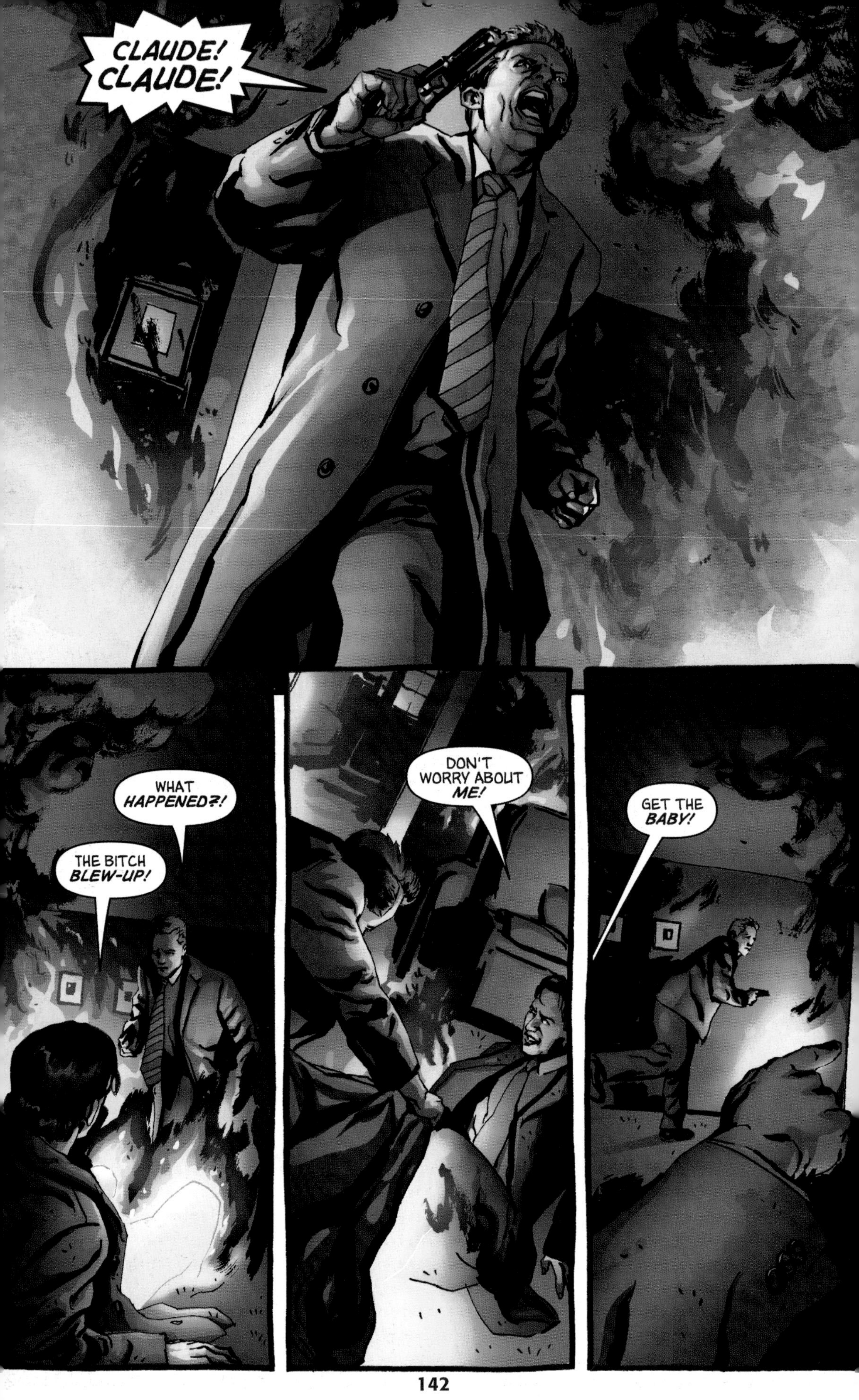
CLAUDE! CLAUDE!
WHAT HAPPENED?!
THE BITCH BLEW-UP!
DON'T WORRY ABOUT ME!
GET THE BABY!

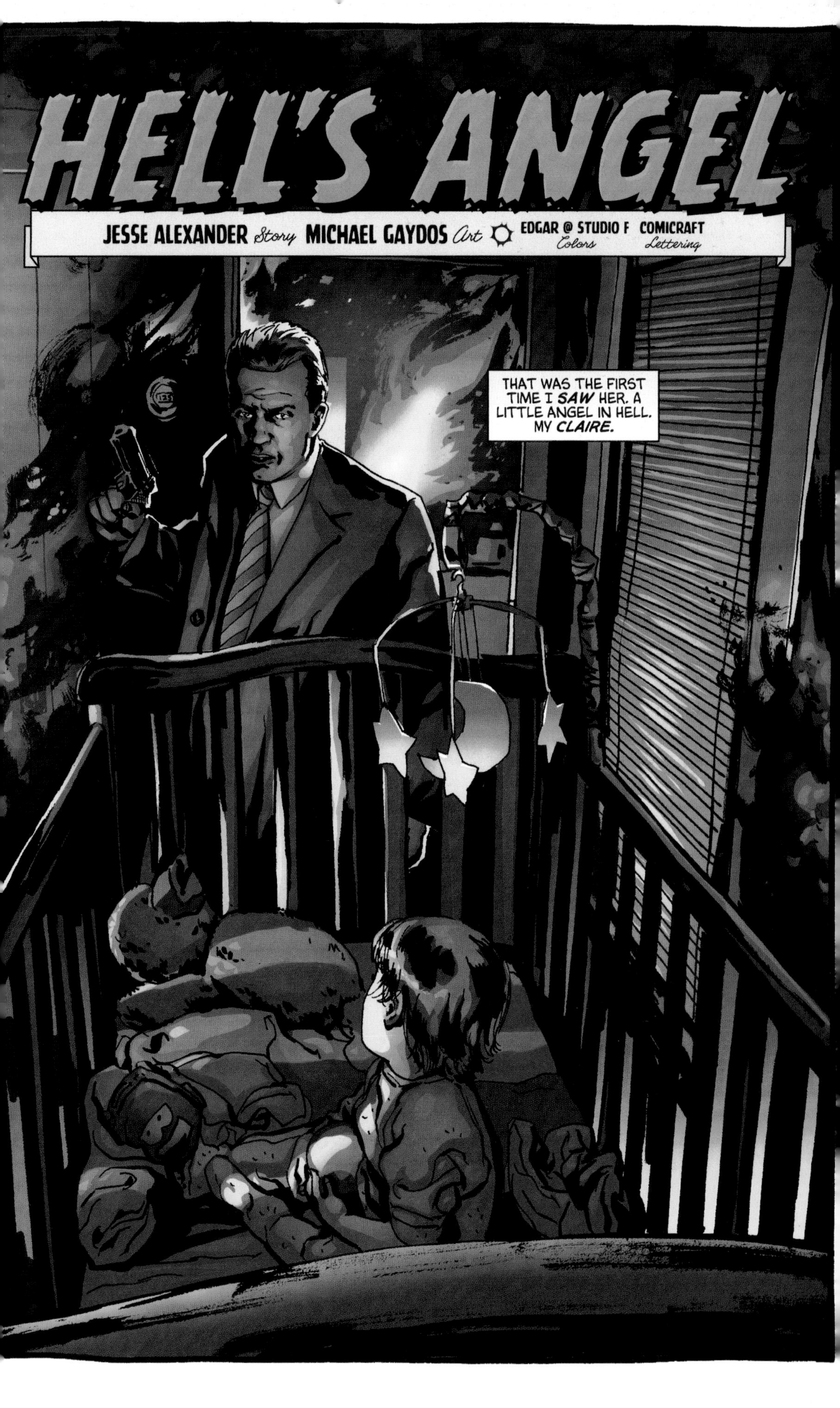
HELL'S ANGEL
JESSE ALEXANDER Story MICHAEL GAYDOS Art EDGAR @ STUDIO F Colors COMICRAFT Lettering
THAT WAS THE FIRST TIME I SAW HER. A LITTLE ANGEL IN HELL. MY CLAIRE.

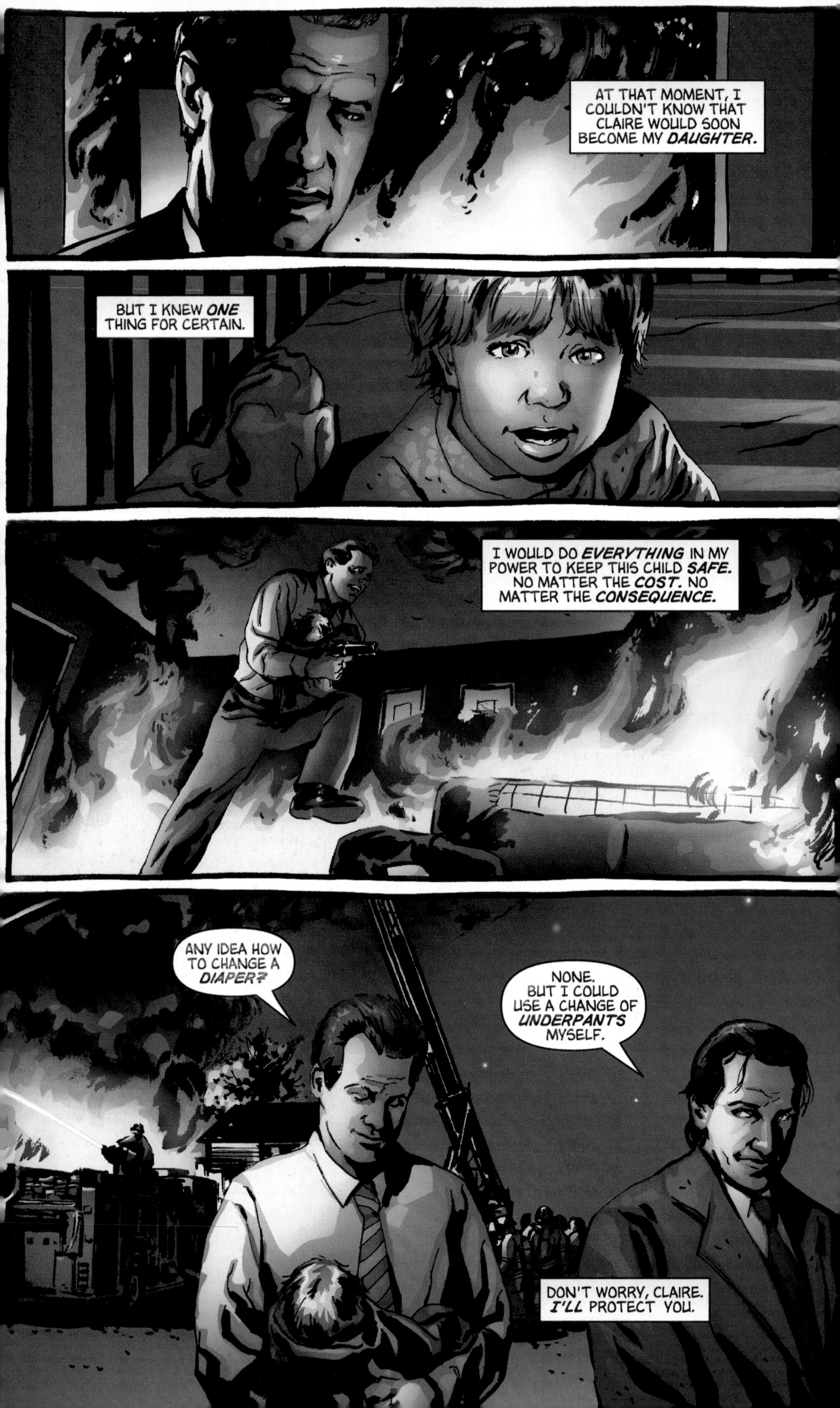
AT THAT MOMENT, I COULDN'T KNOW THAT CLAIRE WOULD SOON BECOME MY *DAUGHTER.*
BUT I KNEW *ONE* THING FOR CERTAIN.
I WOULD DO *EVERYTHING* IN MY POWER TO KEEP THIS CHILD *SAFE.* NO MATTER THE *COST.* NO MATTER THE *CONSEQUENCE.*
ANY IDEA HOW TO CHANGE A *DIAPER?*
NONE. BUT I COULD USE A CHANGE OF *UNDERPANTS* MYSELF.
DON'T WORRY, CLAIRE. *I'LL* PROTECT YOU.

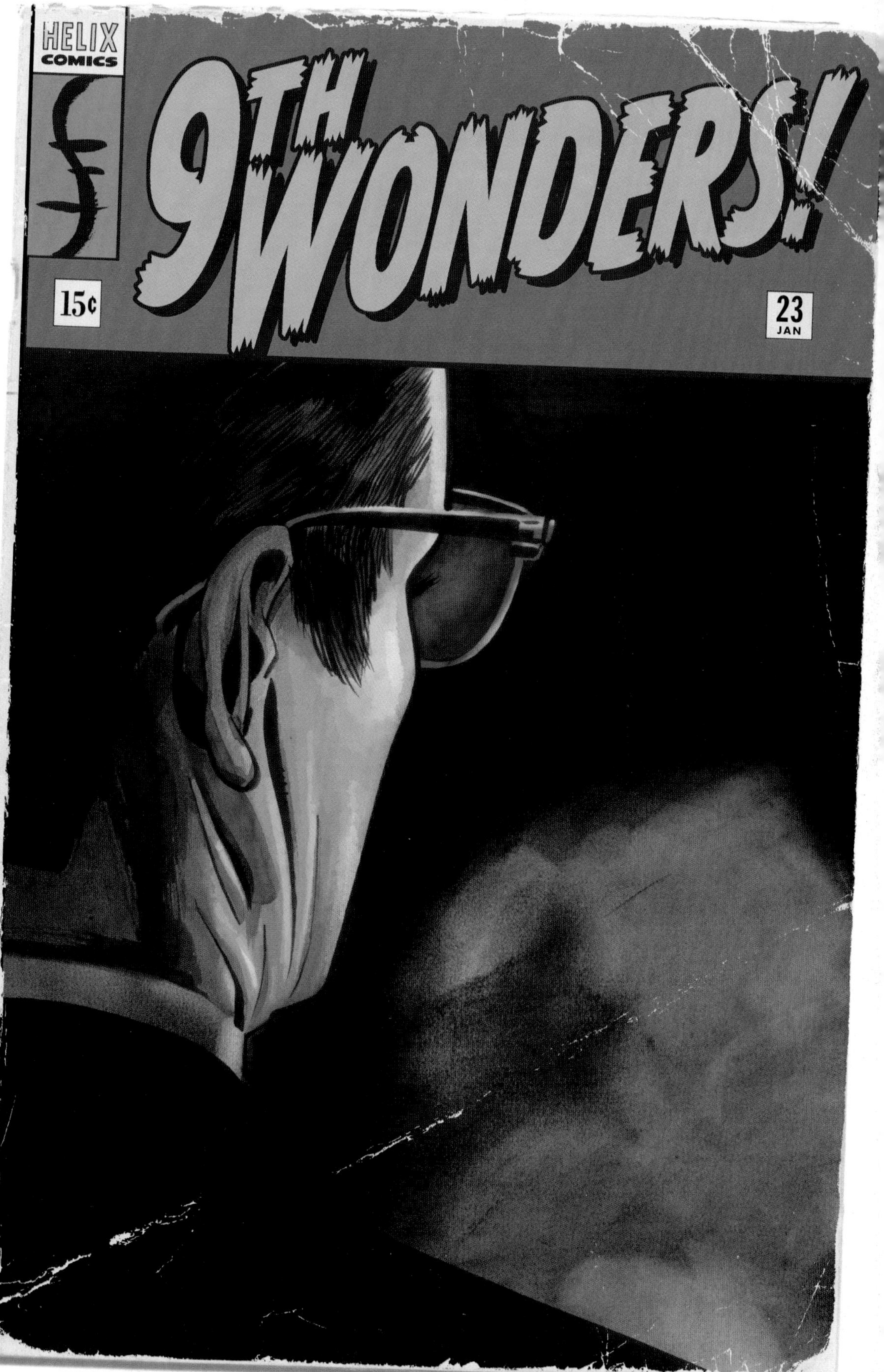

HELIX
COMICS
9TH WONDERS!
15¢
23
JAN

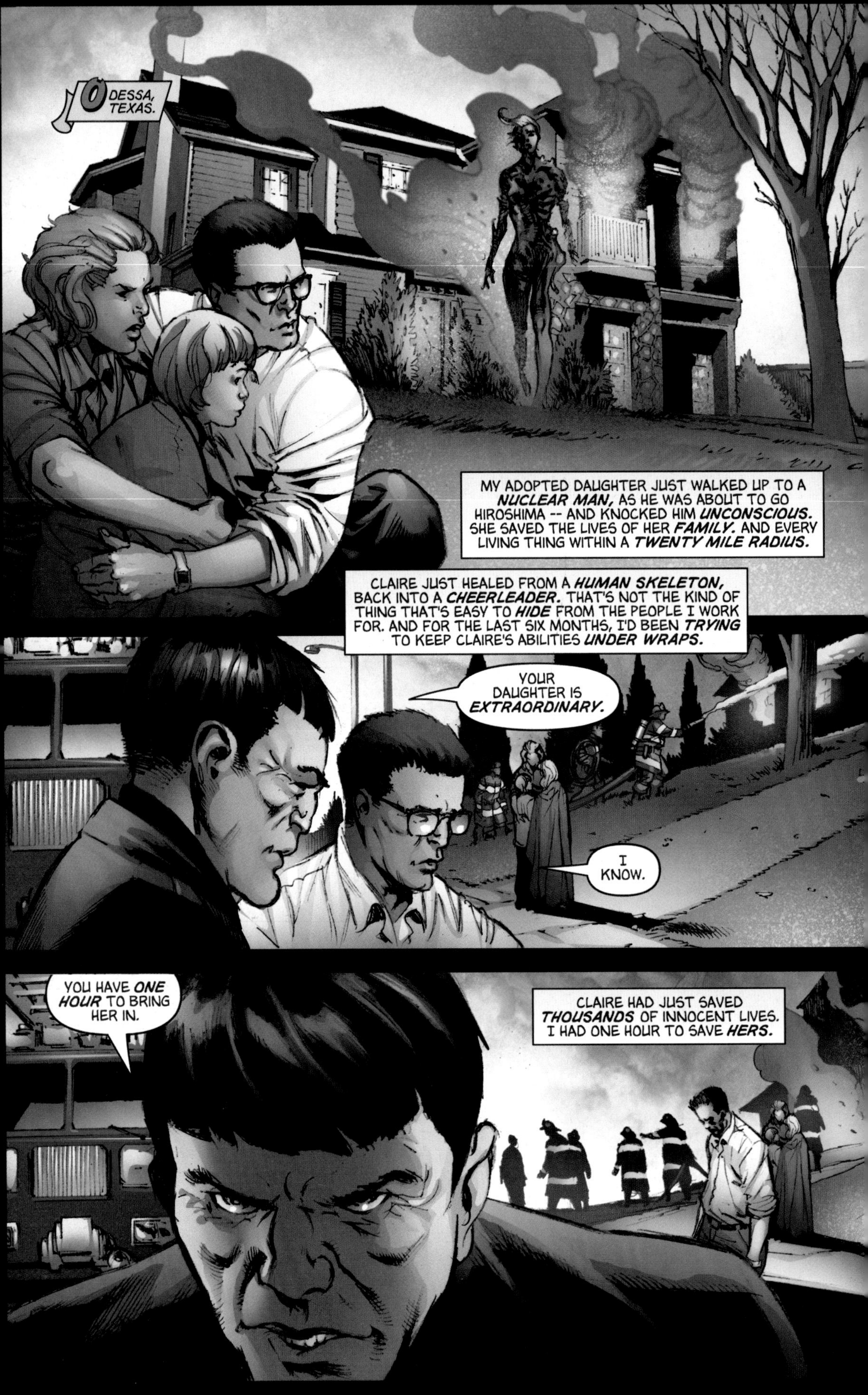
ODESSA, TEXAS.
MY ADOPTED DAUGHTER JUST WALKED UP TO A *NUCLEAR MAN,* AS HE WAS ABOUT TO GO HIROSHIMA -- AND KNOCKED HIM *UNCONSCIOUS.* SHE SAVED THE LIVES OF HER *FAMILY.* AND EVERY LIVING THING WITHIN A *TWENTY MILE RADIUS.*
CLAIRE JUST HEALED FROM A *HUMAN SKELETON,* BACK INTO A *CHEERLEADER.* THAT'S NOT THE KIND OF THING THAT'S EASY TO *HIDE* FROM THE PEOPLE I WORK FOR. AND FOR THE LAST SIX MONTHS, I'D BEEN *TRYING* TO KEEP CLAIRE'S ABILITIES *UNDER WRAPS.*
YOUR DAUGHTER IS *EXTRAORDINARY.*
I KNOW.
YOU HAVE *ONE HOUR* TO BRING HER IN.
CLAIRE HAD JUST SAVED *THOUSANDS* OF INNOCENT LIVES. I HAD ONE HOUR TO SAVE *HERS.*

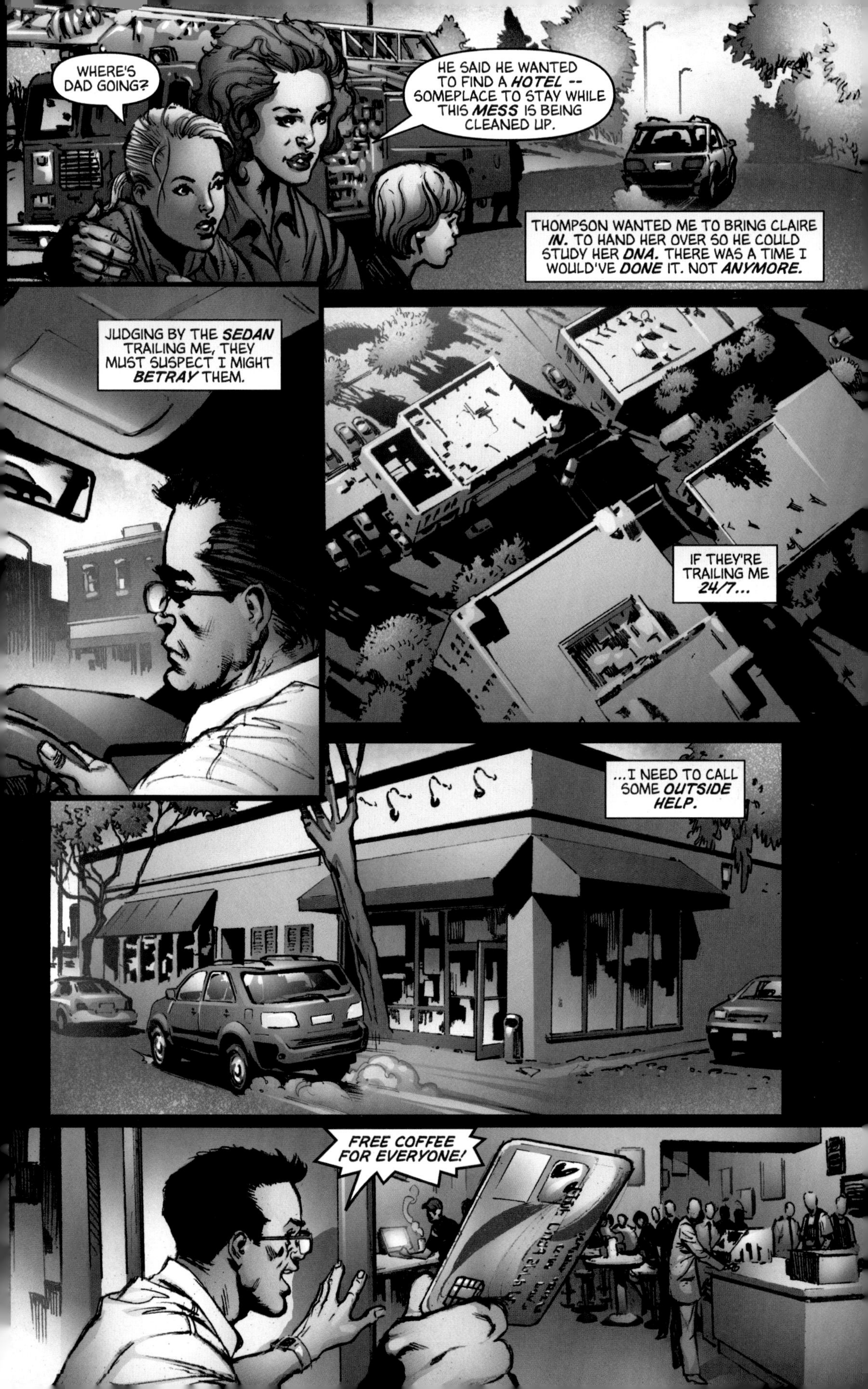
WHERE'S DAD GOING?
HE SAID HE WANTED TO FIND A HOTEL -- SOMEPLACE TO STAY WHILE THIS MESS IS BEING CLEANED UP.
THOMPSON WANTED ME TO BRING CLAIRE IN. TO HAND HER OVER SO HE COULD STUDY HER DNA. THERE WAS A TIME I WOULD'VE DONE IT. NOT ANYMORE.
JUDGING BY THE SEDAN TRAILING ME, THEY MUST SUSPECT I MIGHT BETRAY THEM.
IF THEY'RE TRAILING ME 24/7...
...I NEED TO CALL SOME OUTSIDE HELP.
FREE COFFEE FOR EVERYONE!

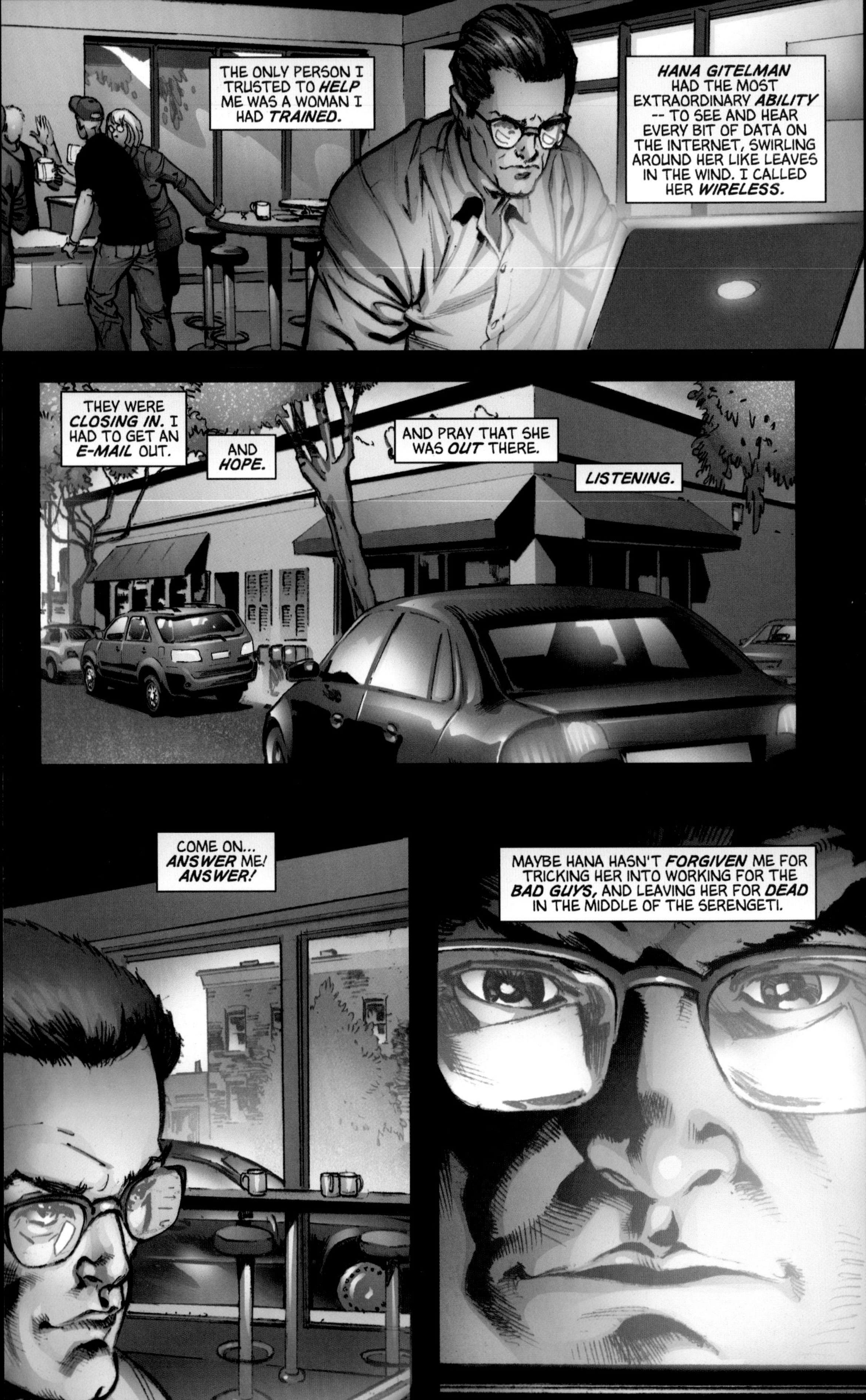

THE ONLY PERSON I TRUSTED TO *HELP* ME WAS A WOMAN I HAD *TRAINED.*
HANA GITELMAN HAD THE MOST EXTRAORDINARY *ABILITY* -- TO SEE AND HEAR EVERY BIT OF DATA ON THE INTERNET, SWIRLING AROUND HER LIKE LEAVES IN THE WIND. I CALLED HER *WIRELESS.*
THEY WERE *CLOSING IN.* I HAD TO GET AN *E-MAIL* OUT.
AND *HOPE.*
AND PRAY THAT SHE WAS *OUT* THERE.
LISTENING.
COME ON... *ANSWER* ME! *ANSWER!*
MAYBE HANA HASN'T *FORGIVEN* ME FOR TRICKING HER INTO WORKING FOR THE *BAD GUYS,* AND LEAVING HER FOR *DEAD* IN THE MIDDLE OF THE SERENGETI.

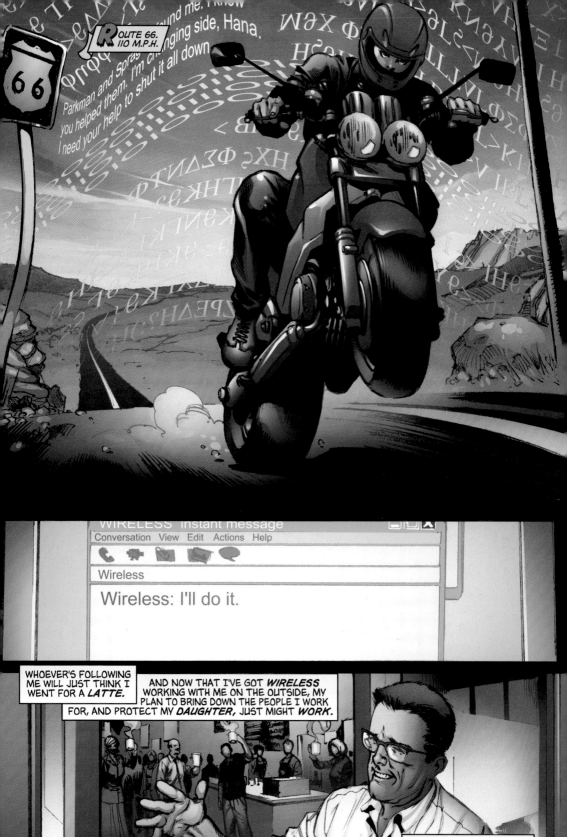

ROUTE 66.
110 M.P.H.

Parkman and Spray... ...und me. I know you helped them. I'm ch...nging side, Hana. I need your help to shut it all down

66

WIRELESS Instant message

Conversation   View   Edit   Actions   Help

Wireless

Wireless: I'll do it.

WHOEVER'S FOLLOWING ME WILL JUST THINK I WENT FOR A *LATTE.*

AND NOW THAT I'VE GOT *WIRELESS* WORKING WITH ME ON THE OUTSIDE, MY PLAN TO BRING DOWN THE PEOPLE I WORK FOR, AND PROTECT MY *DAUGHTER,* JUST MIGHT *WORK.*

AS LONG AS MY PARTNER CAN *SHOOT* STRAIGHT...

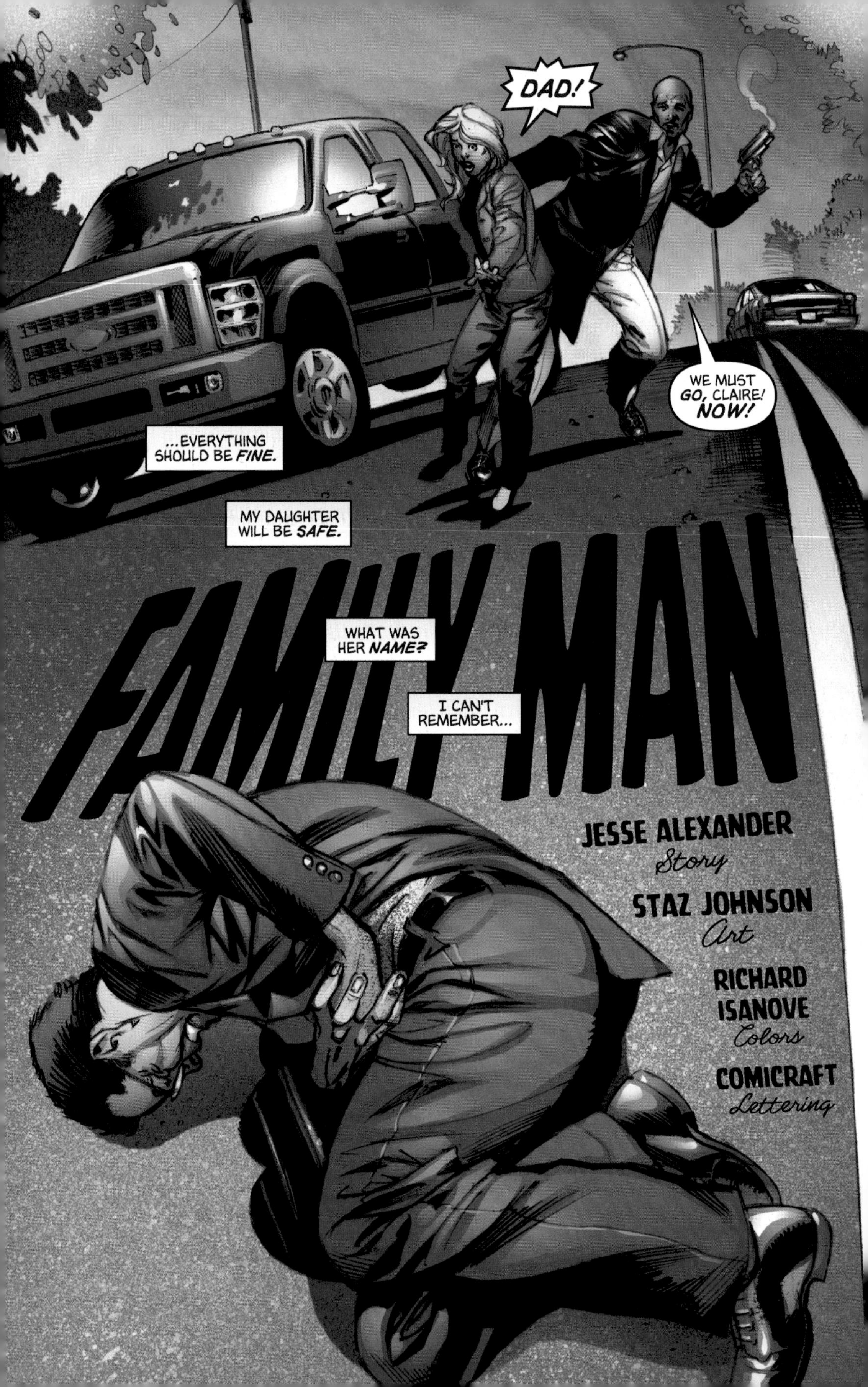
DAD!
WE MUST GO, CLAIRE! NOW!
...EVERYTHING SHOULD BE FINE.
MY DAUGHTER WILL BE SAFE.
FAMILY MAN
WHAT WAS HER NAME?
I CAN'T REMEMBER...
JESSE ALEXANDER
Story
STAZ JOHNSON
Art
RICHARD ISANOVE
Colors
COMICRAFT
Lettering

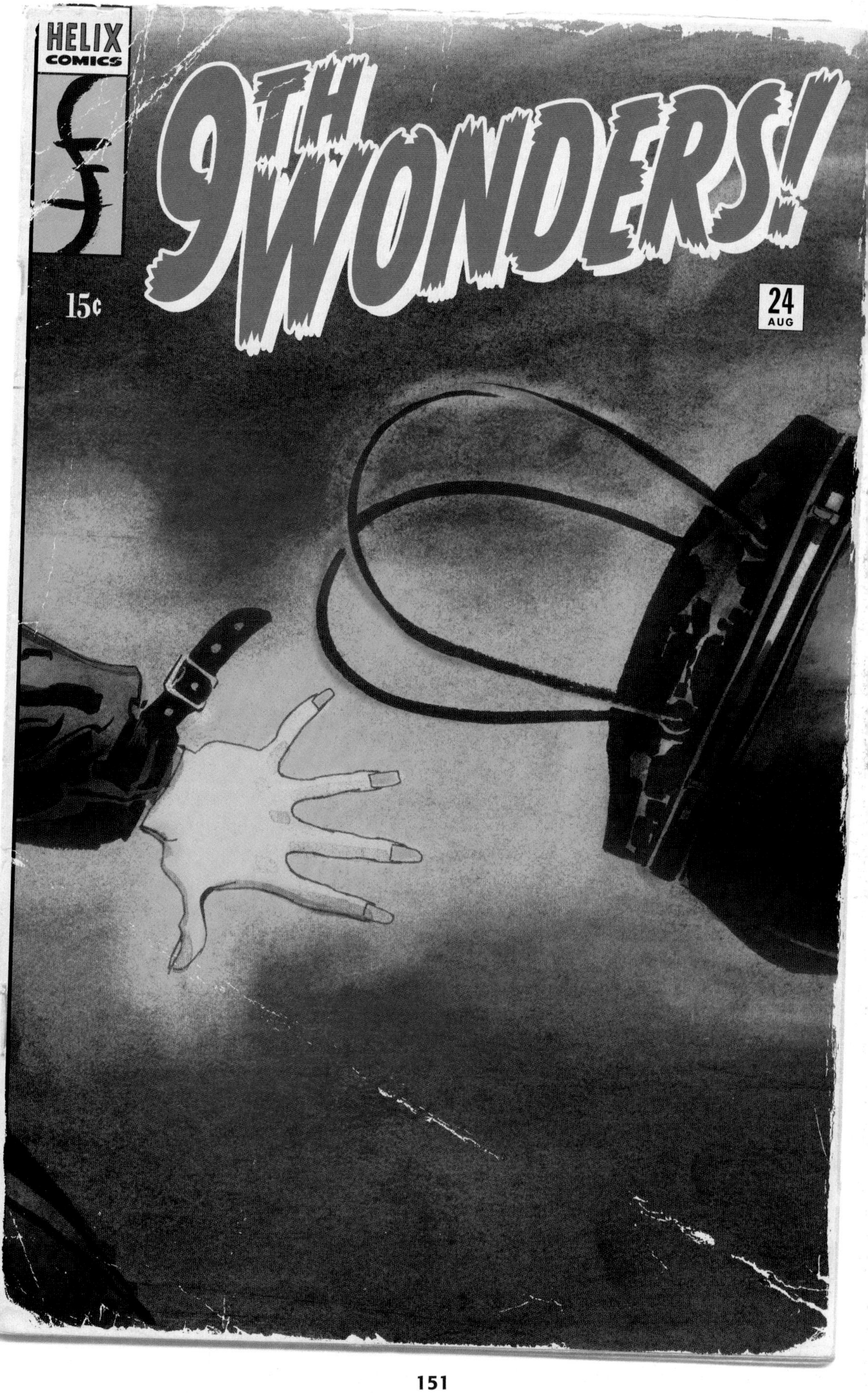
HELIX
COMICS
9TH WONDERS!
15¢
24
AUG

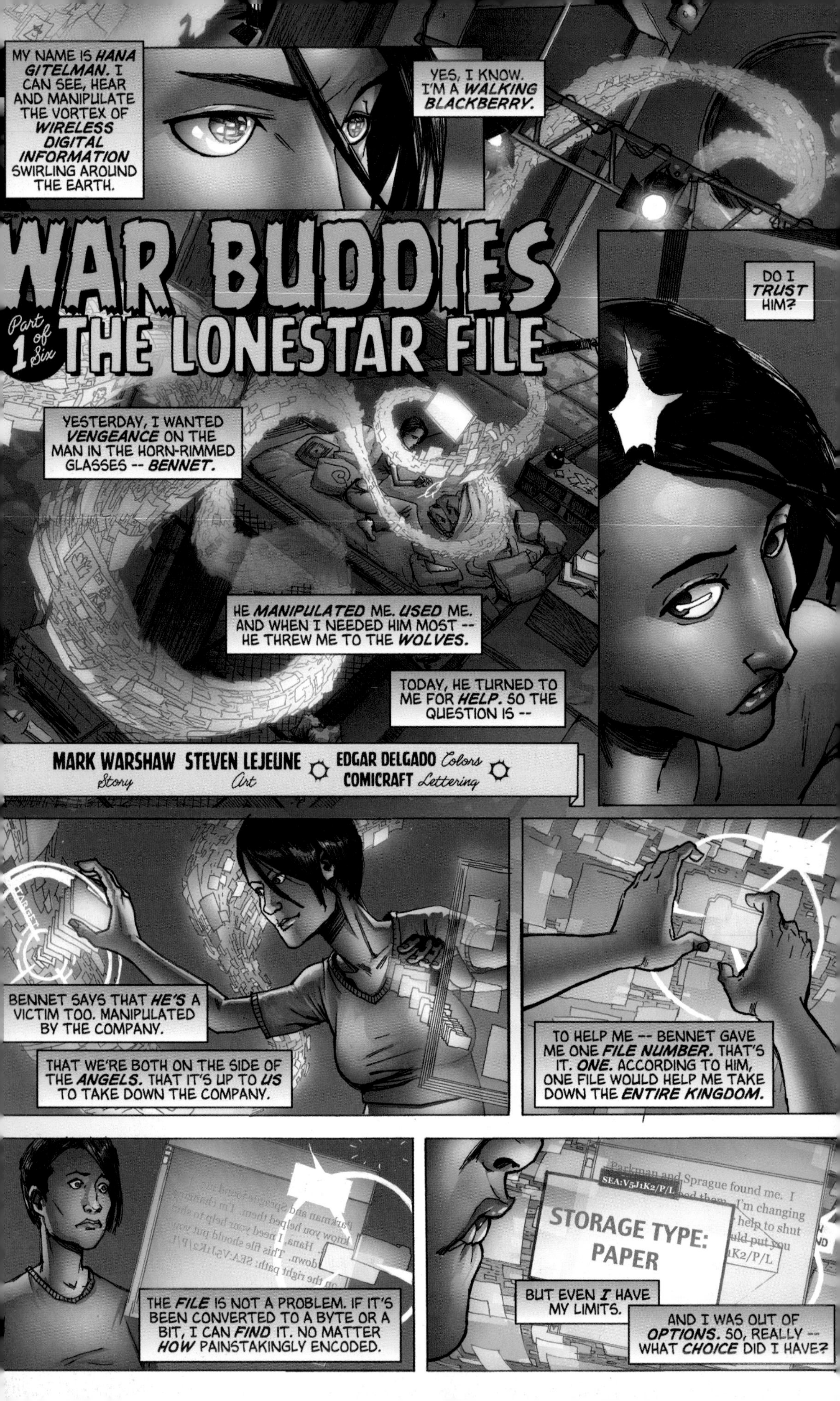

MY NAME IS HANA GITELMAN. I CAN SEE, HEAR AND MANIPULATE THE VORTEX OF WIRELESS DIGITAL INFORMATION SWIRLING AROUND THE EARTH.
YES, I KNOW. I'M A WALKING BLACKBERRY.
WAR BUDDIES
Part 1 of Six
THE LONESTAR FILE
YESTERDAY, I WANTED VENGEANCE ON THE MAN IN THE HORN-RIMMED GLASSES -- BENNET.
HE MANIPULATED ME. USED ME. AND WHEN I NEEDED HIM MOST -- HE THREW ME TO THE WOLVES.
TODAY, HE TURNED TO ME FOR HELP. SO THE QUESTION IS --
DO I TRUST HIM?
MARK WARSHAW Story
STEVEN LEJEUNE Art
EDGAR DELGADO Colors
COMICRAFT Lettering
TARGET
BENNET SAYS THAT HE'S A VICTIM TOO. MANIPULATED BY THE COMPANY.
THAT WE'RE BOTH ON THE SIDE OF THE ANGELS. THAT IT'S UP TO US TO TAKE DOWN THE COMPANY.
TO HELP ME -- BENNET GAVE ME ONE FILE NUMBER. THAT'S IT. ONE. ACCORDING TO HIM, ONE FILE WOULD HELP ME TAKE DOWN THE ENTIRE KINGDOM.
THE FILE IS NOT A PROBLEM. IF IT'S BEEN CONVERTED TO A BYTE OR A BIT, I CAN FIND IT. NO MATTER HOW PAINSTAKINGLY ENCODED.
SEA:V5J1K2/P/L
Parkman and Sprague found me. I
STORAGE TYPE: PAPER
BUT EVEN I HAVE MY LIMITS.
AND I WAS OUT OF OPTIONS. SO, REALLY -- WHAT CHOICE DID I HAVE?

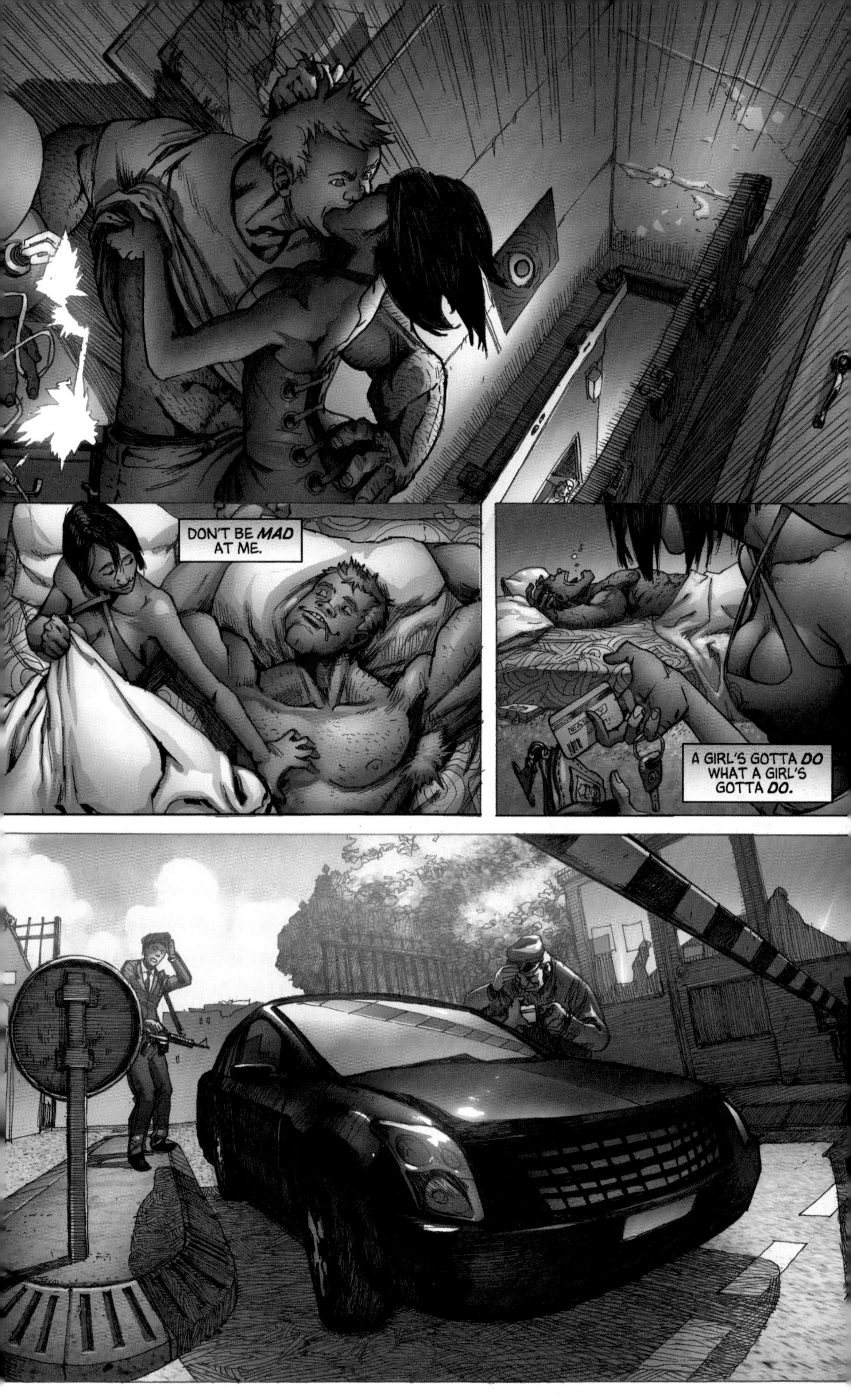
DON'T BE *MAD* AT ME.
A GIRL'S GOTTA *DO* WHAT A GIRL'S GOTTA *DO*.

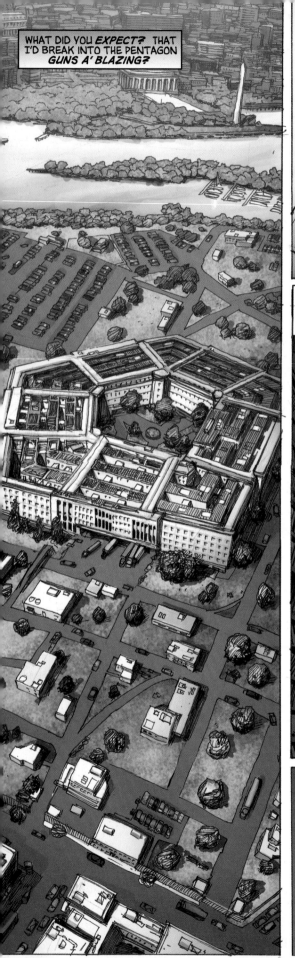

WHAT DID YOU *EXPECT?* THAT I'D BREAK INTO THE PENTAGON *GUNS A' BLAZING?*

I NEED TO ACCOMPLISH THIS *MISSION.*

I NEED *ANSWERS* TO MY QUESTIONS.

LOOKS LIKE I'M OFF TO A *GOOD START.*

To Be Continued...

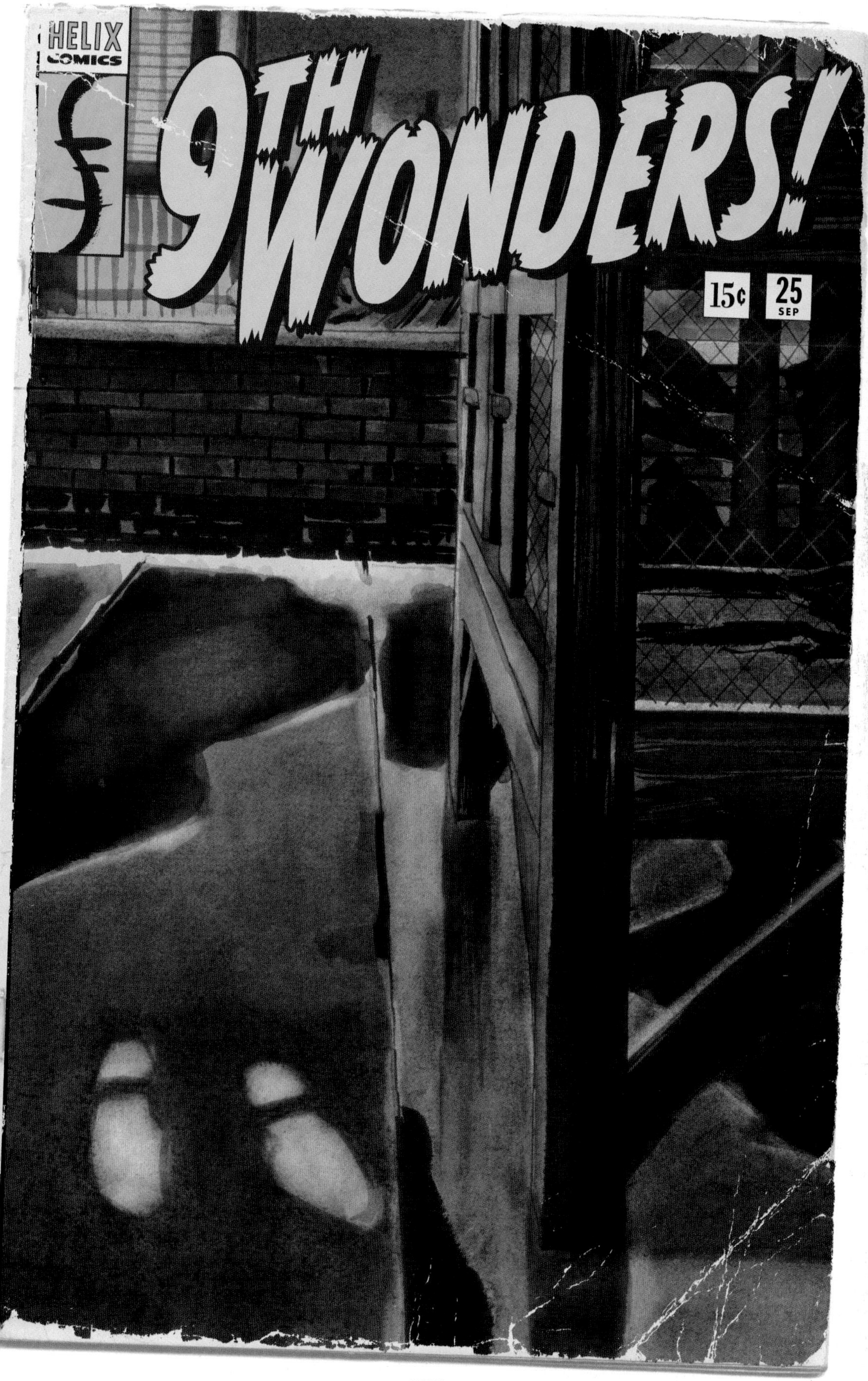
HELIX COMICS
9TH WONDERS!
15¢
25 SEP

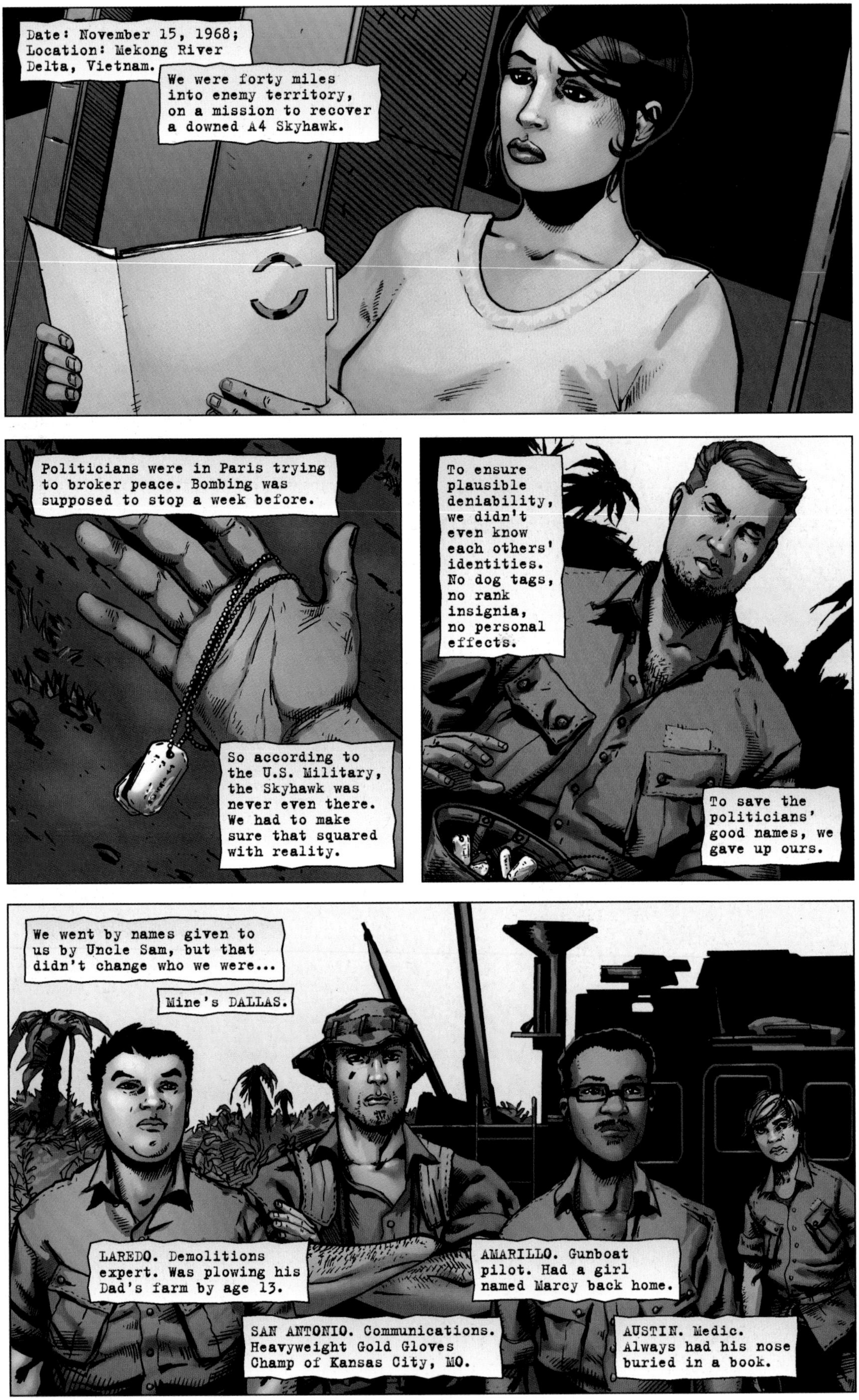
Date: November 15, 1968; Location: Mekong River Delta, Vietnam.
We were forty miles into enemy territory, on a mission to recover a downed A4 Skyhawk.
Politicians were in Paris trying to broker peace. Bombing was supposed to stop a week before.
So according to the U.S. Military, the Skyhawk was never even there. We had to make sure that squared with reality.
To ensure plausible deniability, we didn't even know each others' identities. No dog tags, no rank insignia, no personal effects.
To save the politicians' good names, we gave up ours.
We went by names given to us by Uncle Sam, but that didn't change who we were...
Mine's DALLAS.
LAREDO. Demolitions expert. Was plowing his Dad's farm by age 13.
SAN ANTONIO. Communications. Heavyweight Gold Gloves Champ of Kansas City, MO.
AMARILLO. Gunboat pilot. Had a girl named Marcy back home.
AUSTIN. Medic. Always had his nose buried in a book.

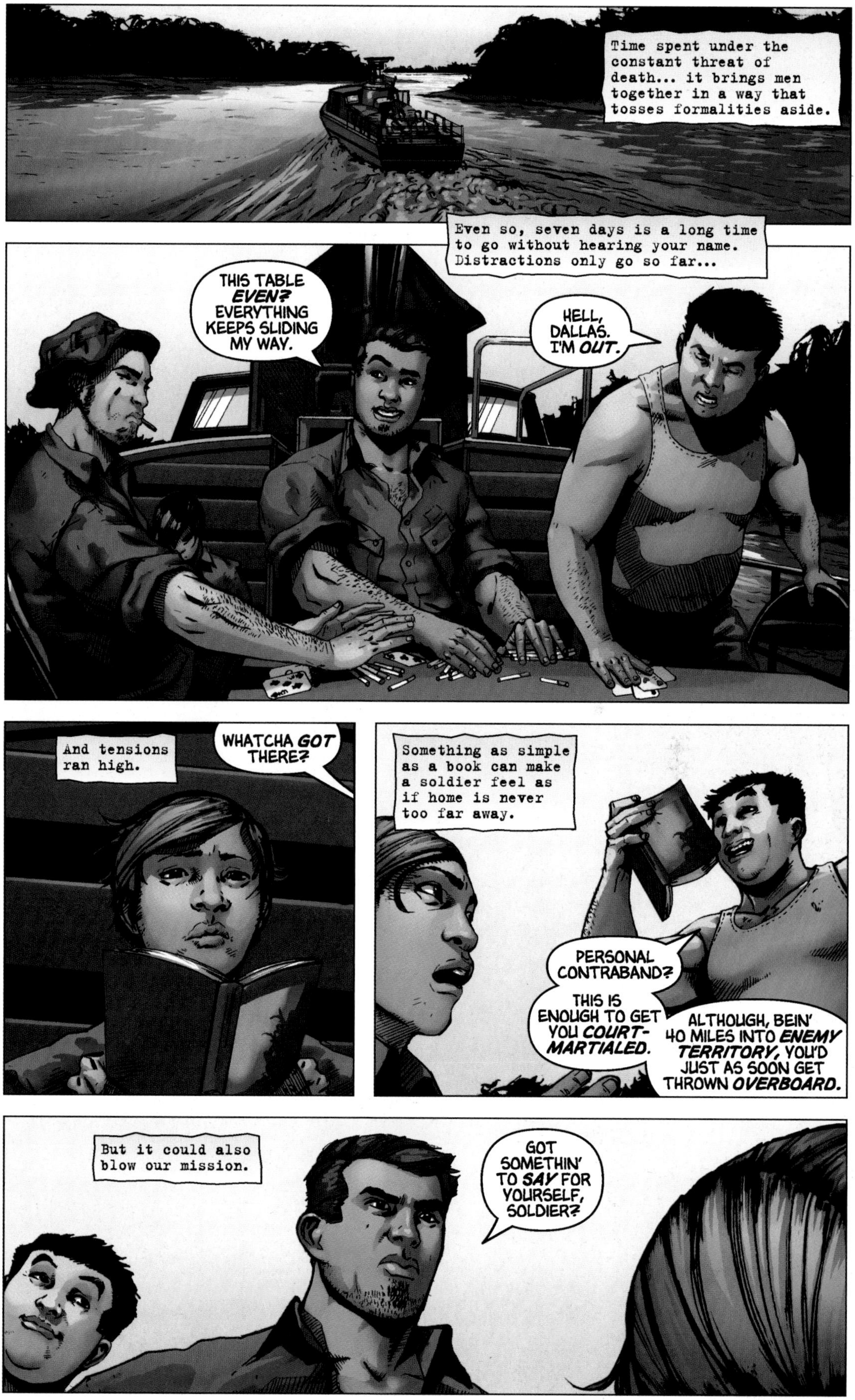

Time spent under the constant threat of death... it brings men together in a way that tosses formalities aside.
Even so, seven days is a long time to go without hearing your name. Distractions only go so far...
THIS TABLE EVEN? EVERYTHING KEEPS SLIDING MY WAY.
HELL, DALLAS. I'M OUT.
And tensions ran high.
WHATCHA GOT THERE?
Something as simple as a book can make a soldier feel as if home is never too far away.
PERSONAL CONTRABAND?
THIS IS ENOUGH TO GET YOU COURT-MARTIALED.
ALTHOUGH, BEIN' 40 MILES INTO ENEMY TERRITORY, YOU'D JUST AS SOON GET THROWN OVERBOARD.
But it could also blow our mission.
GOT SOMETHIN' TO SAY FOR YOURSELF, SOLDIER?

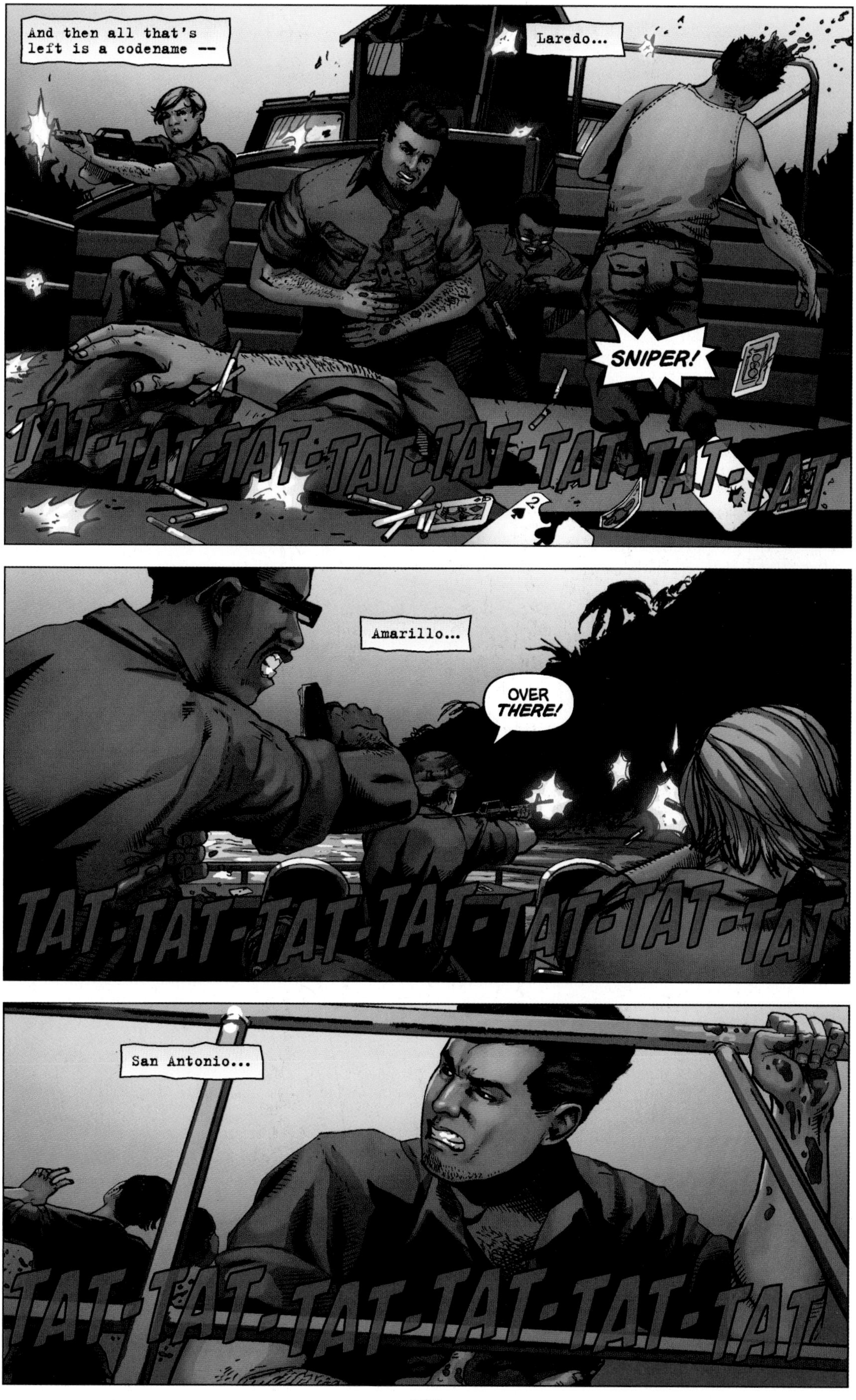
And then all that's left is a codename --
Laredo...
SNIPER!
TAT-TAT-TAT-TAT-TAT-TAT-TAT-TAT
Amarillo...
OVER THERE!
TAT-TAT-TAT-TAT-TAT-TAT-TAT
San Antonio...
TAT-TAT-TAT-TAT-TAT-TAT

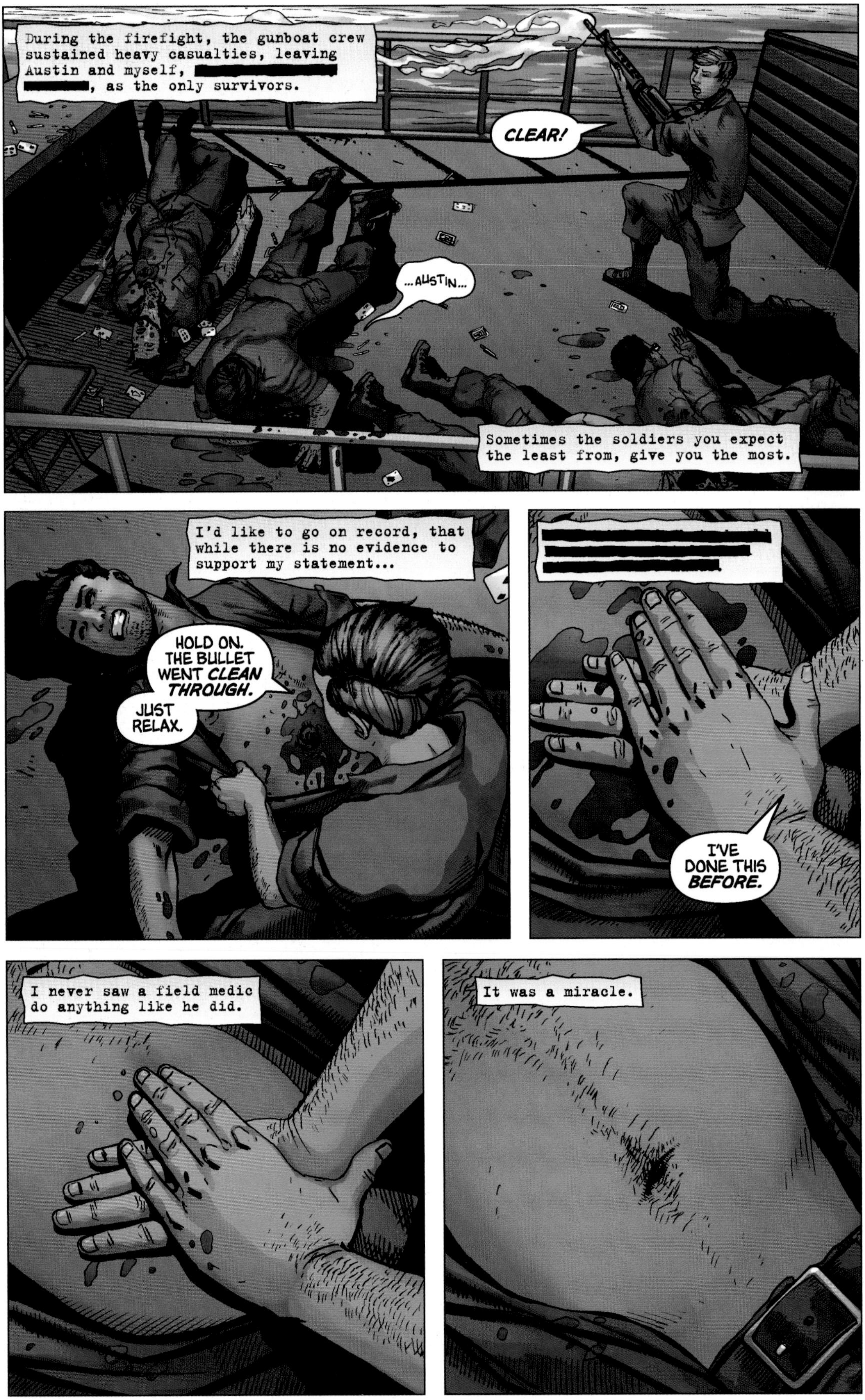

During the firefight, the gunboat crew sustained heavy casualties, leaving Austin and myself, [redacted], as the only survivors.
CLEAR!
...AUSTIN...
Sometimes the soldiers you expect the least from, give you the most.
I'd like to go on record, that while there is no evidence to support my statement...
HOLD ON. THE BULLET WENT *CLEAN THROUGH.*
JUST RELAX.
[redacted]
I'VE DONE THIS *BEFORE.*
I never saw a field medic do anything like he did.
It was a miracle.

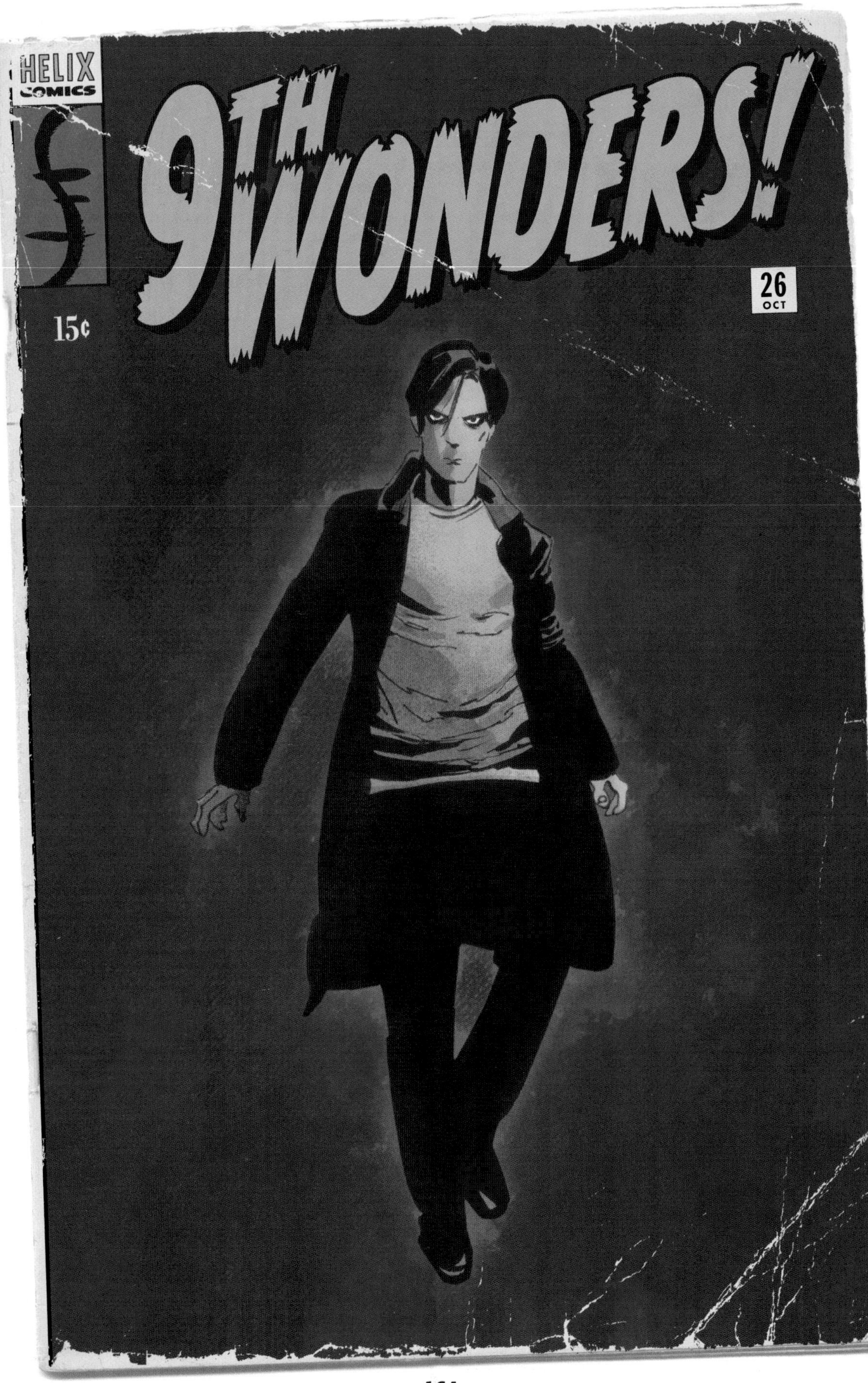
HELIX COMICS
9TH WONDERS!
26 OCT
15¢

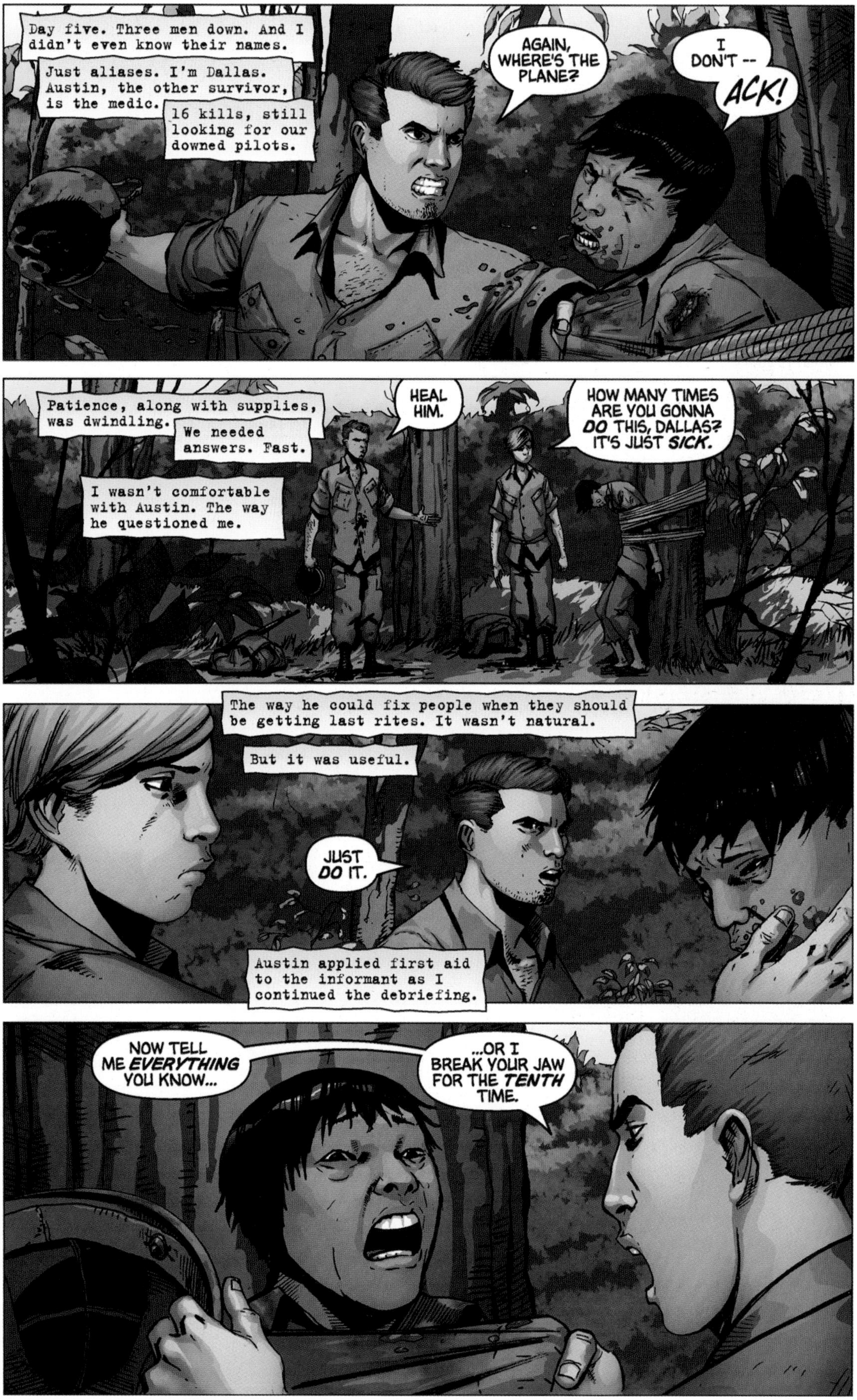

Day five. Three men down. And I didn't even know their names.
Just aliases. I'm Dallas. Austin, the other survivor, is the medic.
16 kills, still looking for our downed pilots.
AGAIN, WHERE'S THE PLANE?
I DON'T -- ACK!
Patience, along with supplies, was dwindling.
We needed answers. Fast.
I wasn't comfortable with Austin. The way he questioned me.
HEAL HIM.
HOW MANY TIMES ARE YOU GONNA DO THIS, DALLAS? IT'S JUST SICK.
The way he could fix people when they should be getting last rites. It wasn't natural.
But it was useful.
JUST DO IT.
Austin applied first aid to the informant as I continued the debriefing.
NOW TELL ME EVERYTHING YOU KNOW...
...OR I BREAK YOUR JAW FOR THE TENTH TIME.

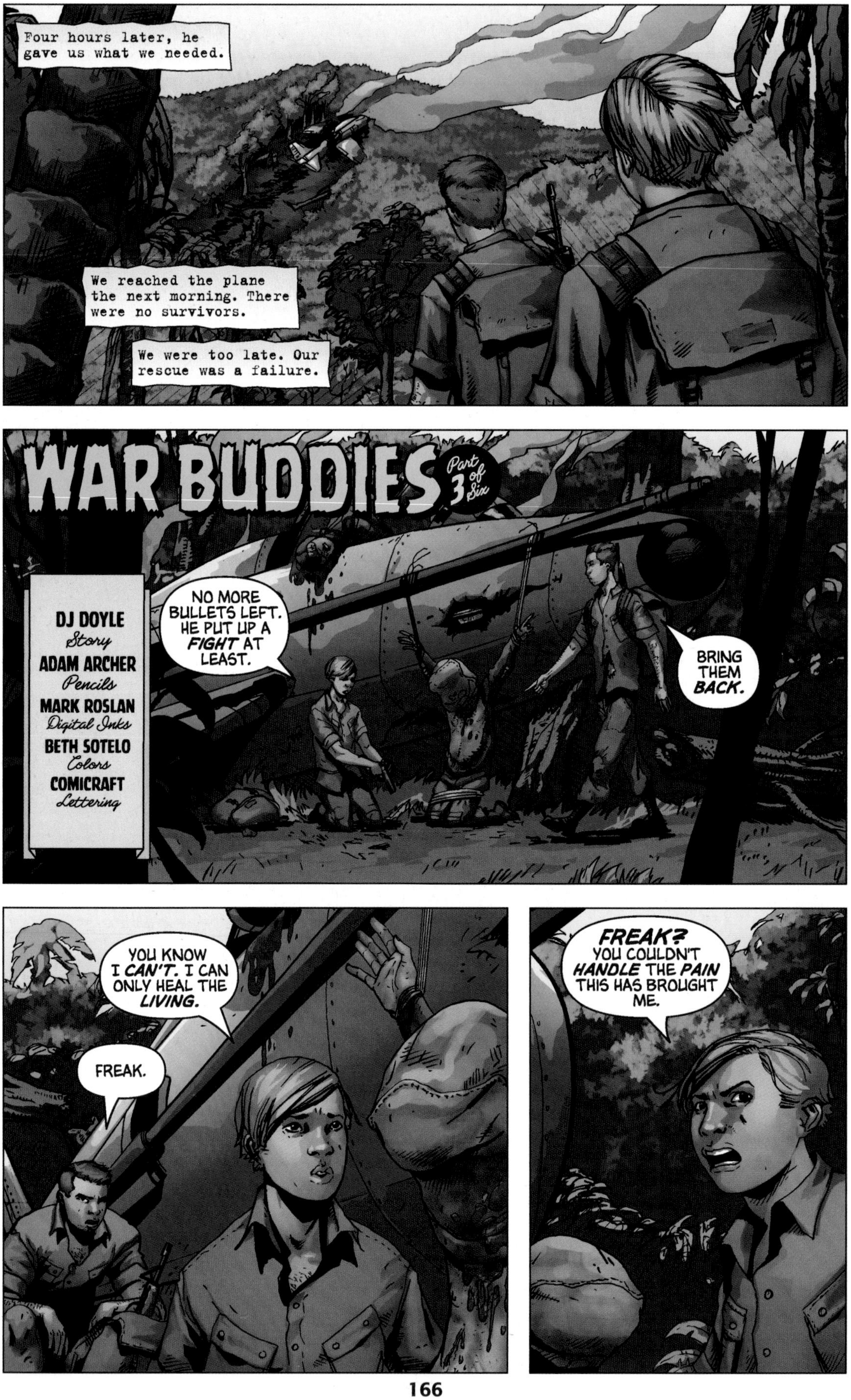

Four hours later, he gave us what we needed.
We reached the plane the next morning. There were no survivors.
We were too late. Our rescue was a failure.
WAR BUDDIES Part 3 of Six
DJ DOYLE Story
ADAM ARCHER Pencils
MARK ROSLAN Digital Inks
BETH SOTELO Colors
COMICRAFT Lettering
NO MORE BULLETS LEFT. HE PUT UP A FIGHT AT LEAST.
BRING THEM BACK.
YOU KNOW I CAN'T. I CAN ONLY HEAL THE LIVING.
FREAK.
FREAK? YOU COULDN'T HANDLE THE PAIN THIS HAS BROUGHT ME.

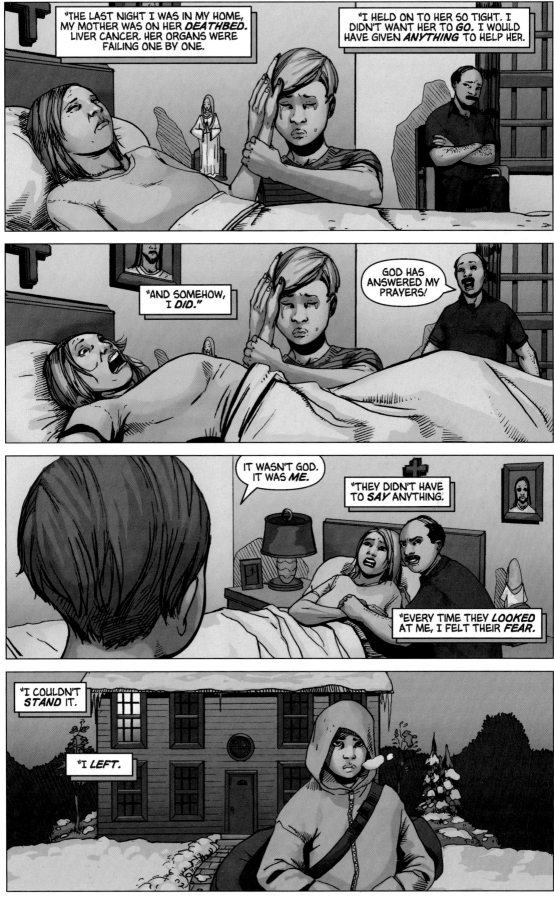

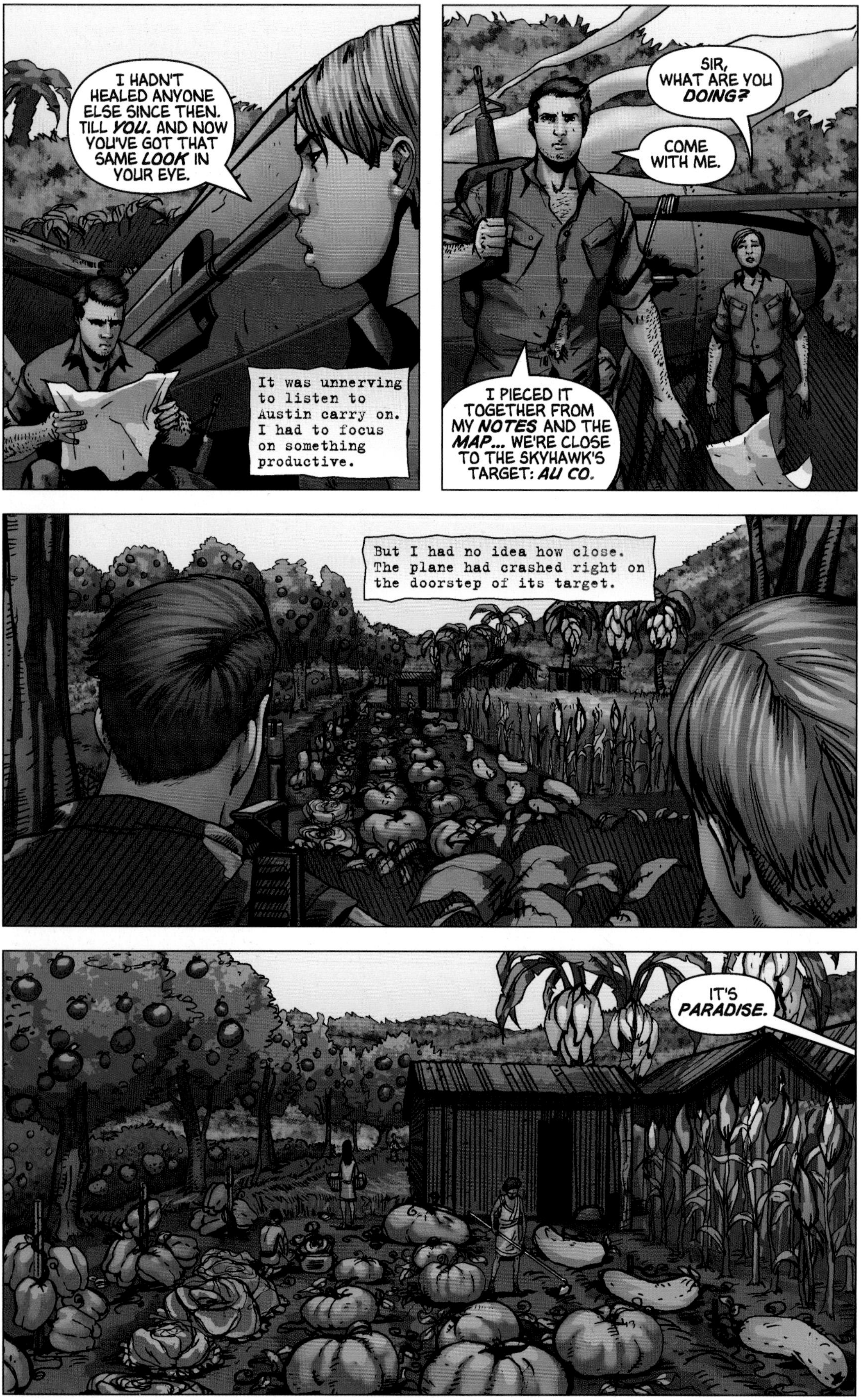
I HADN'T HEALED ANYONE ELSE SINCE THEN. TILL YOU. AND NOW YOU'VE GOT THAT SAME LOOK IN YOUR EYE.
It was unnerving to listen to Austin carry on. I had to focus on something productive.
SIR, WHAT ARE YOU DOING?
COME WITH ME.
I PIECED IT TOGETHER FROM MY NOTES AND THE MAP... WE'RE CLOSE TO THE SKYHAWK'S TARGET: AU CO.
But I had no idea how close. The plane had crashed right on the doorstep of its target.
IT'S PARADISE.

169

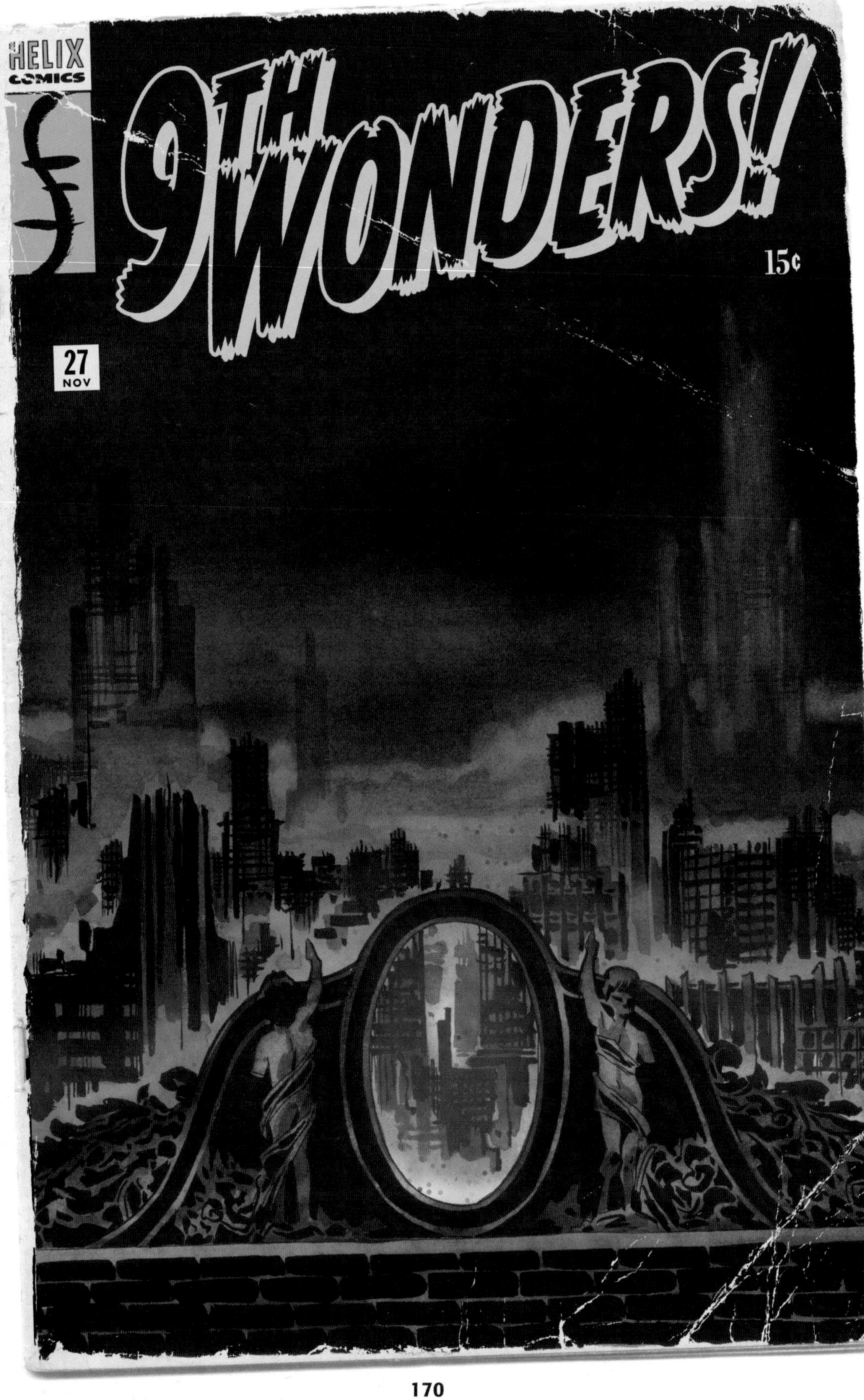
HELIX
COMICS
9TH WONDERS!
15¢
27
NOV

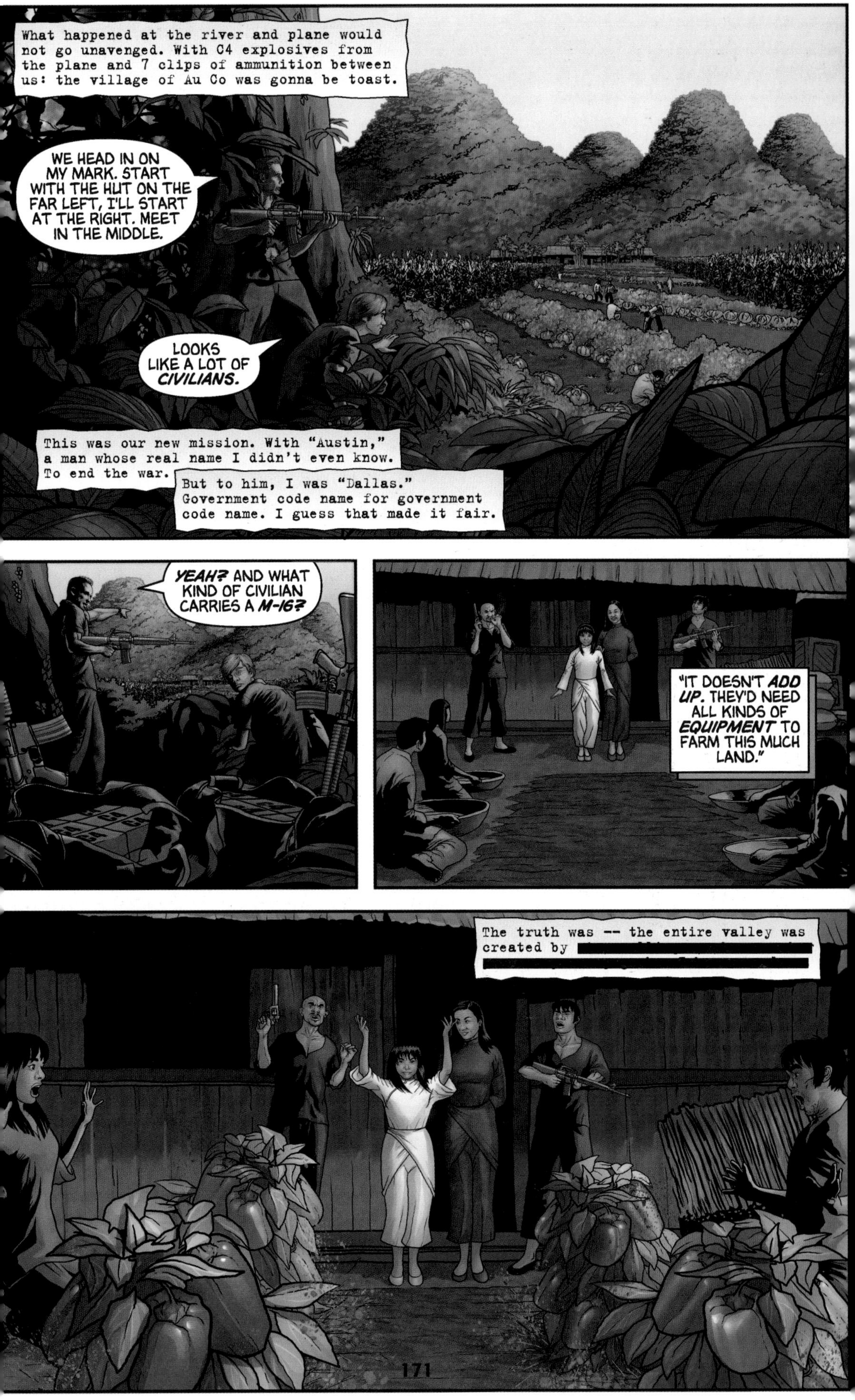
What happened at the river and plane would not go unavenged. With C4 explosives from the plane and 7 clips of ammunition between us: the village of Au Co was gonna be toast.
WE HEAD IN ON MY MARK. START WITH THE HUT ON THE FAR LEFT, I'LL START AT THE RIGHT. MEET IN THE MIDDLE.
LOOKS LIKE A LOT OF *CIVILIANS.*
This was our new mission. With "Austin," a man whose real name I didn't even know. To end the war.
But to him, I was "Dallas." Government code name for government code name. I guess that made it fair.
YEAH? AND WHAT KIND OF CIVILIAN CARRIES A *M-16?*
"IT DOESN'T *ADD UP.* THEY'D NEED ALL KINDS OF *EQUIPMENT* TO FARM THIS MUCH LAND."
The truth was -- the entire valley was created by [redacted]

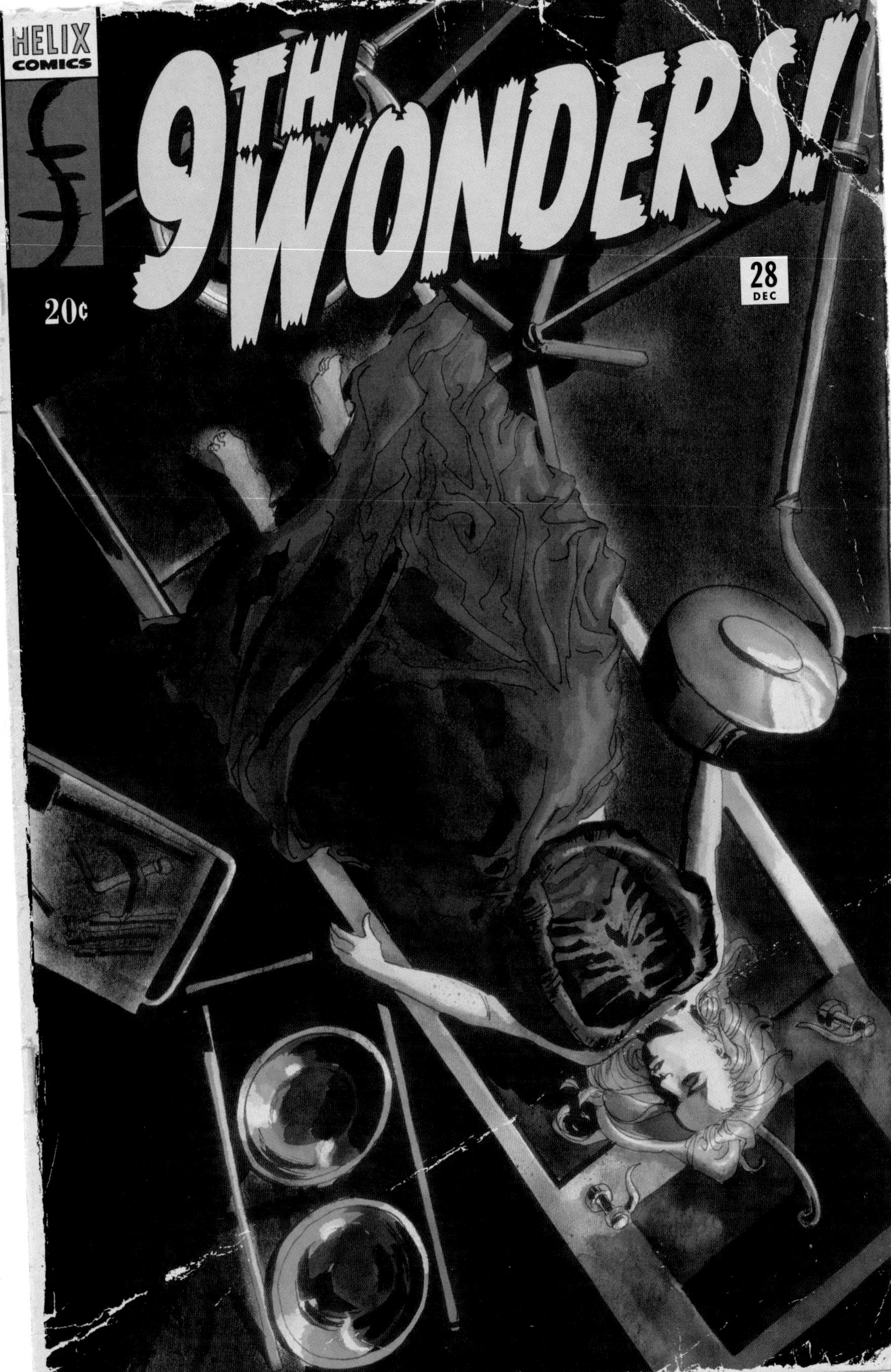
HELIX
COMICS
9TH WONDERS!
20¢
28
DEC

A secret mission to find one of
our downed jets turned into taking
out an entire enemy village. We all
thought Au Co was the name of the
village. It wasn't. It was a girl.
I had to kill her.

Au Co, ████████████ with
just a wave of her arms.

WAR BUDDIES
Part 5 of Six
INTRODUCTIONS

HARRISON WILCOX
& OLIVER GRIGSBY ◇ **JASON BADOWER**
Story *Pencils*

ANNETTE KWOK ◇ **COMICRAFT**
Digital Inks & Colors *Lettering*

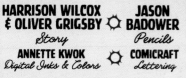

Days earlier, most of the unit was gunned down. Only Austin the medic and I were left. I was shot in the chest.

I should have died.

Austin ████████ No scars, no blood. Nothing. I should be dead.

He didn't want to go through with the mission. To kill Au Co. Understandable. ████████ she was special.

But Austin couldn't see the bigger picture.

Au Co had to die. I wouldn't let him save her. Not like he saved me.

YOU'LL THANK ME FOR THIS ONE DAY. WE JUST SAVED A LOT OF LIVES.

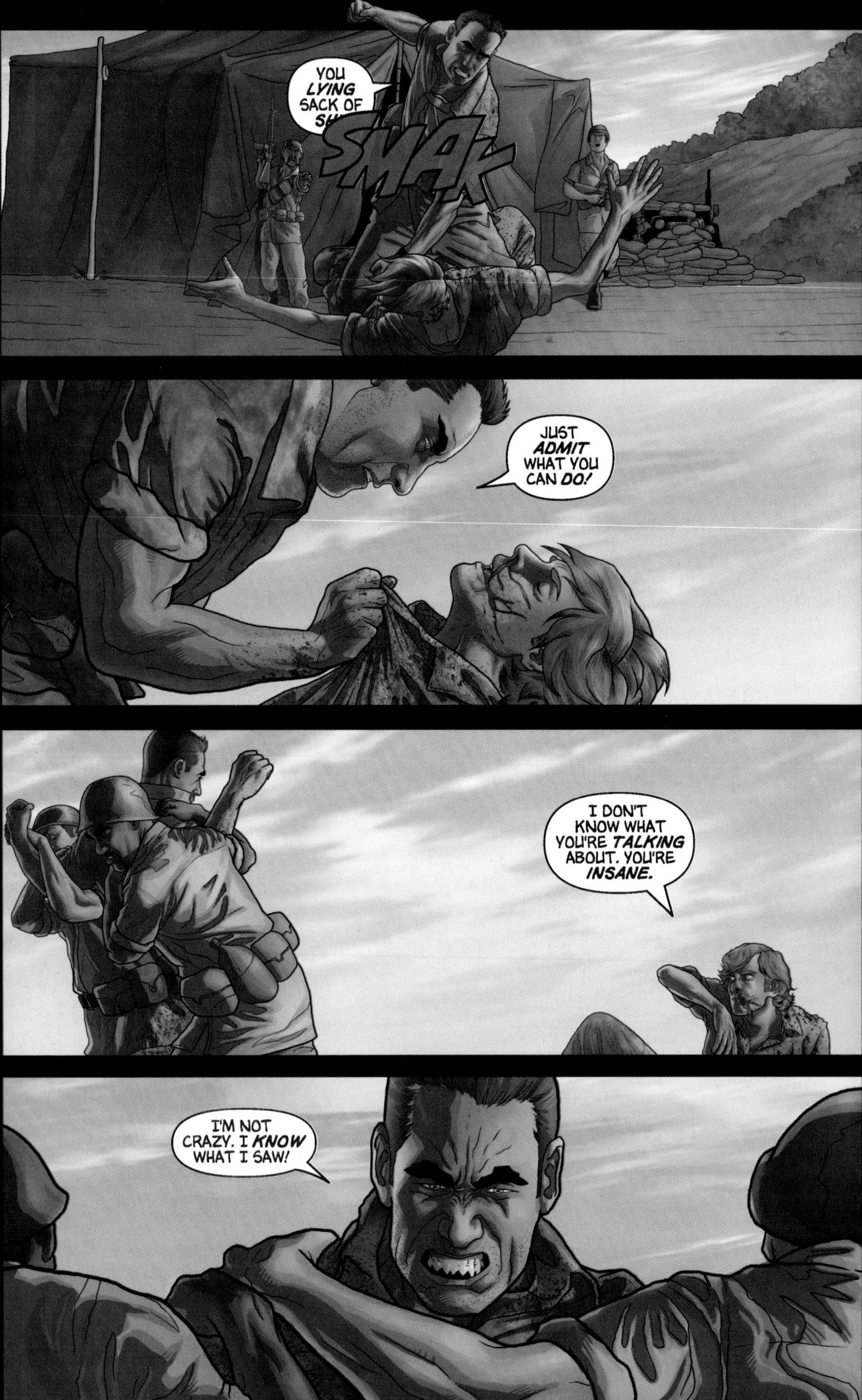
YOU *LYING* SACK OF SH--
SMAK
JUST *ADMIT* WHAT YOU CAN *DO!*
I DON'T KNOW WHAT YOU'RE *TALKING* ABOUT. YOU'RE *INSANE.*
I'M NOT CRAZY. I *KNOW* WHAT I SAW!

Austin's refusal to admit the truth ended up costing me greatly.

Silenced. Discharged. Ignored. The desire to ▮▮▮▮▮▮▮▮▮▮▮▮▮▮ ▮▮▮▮▮▮▮▮▮▮▮▮▮▮ destroyed everything I had built for myself in the military.

My life, my family, for what it was, had become...pointless.

DING DONG

Until Austin showed up at my home. Older and different. With what appeared to be a change of heart.

I OWE YOU AN APOLOGY.

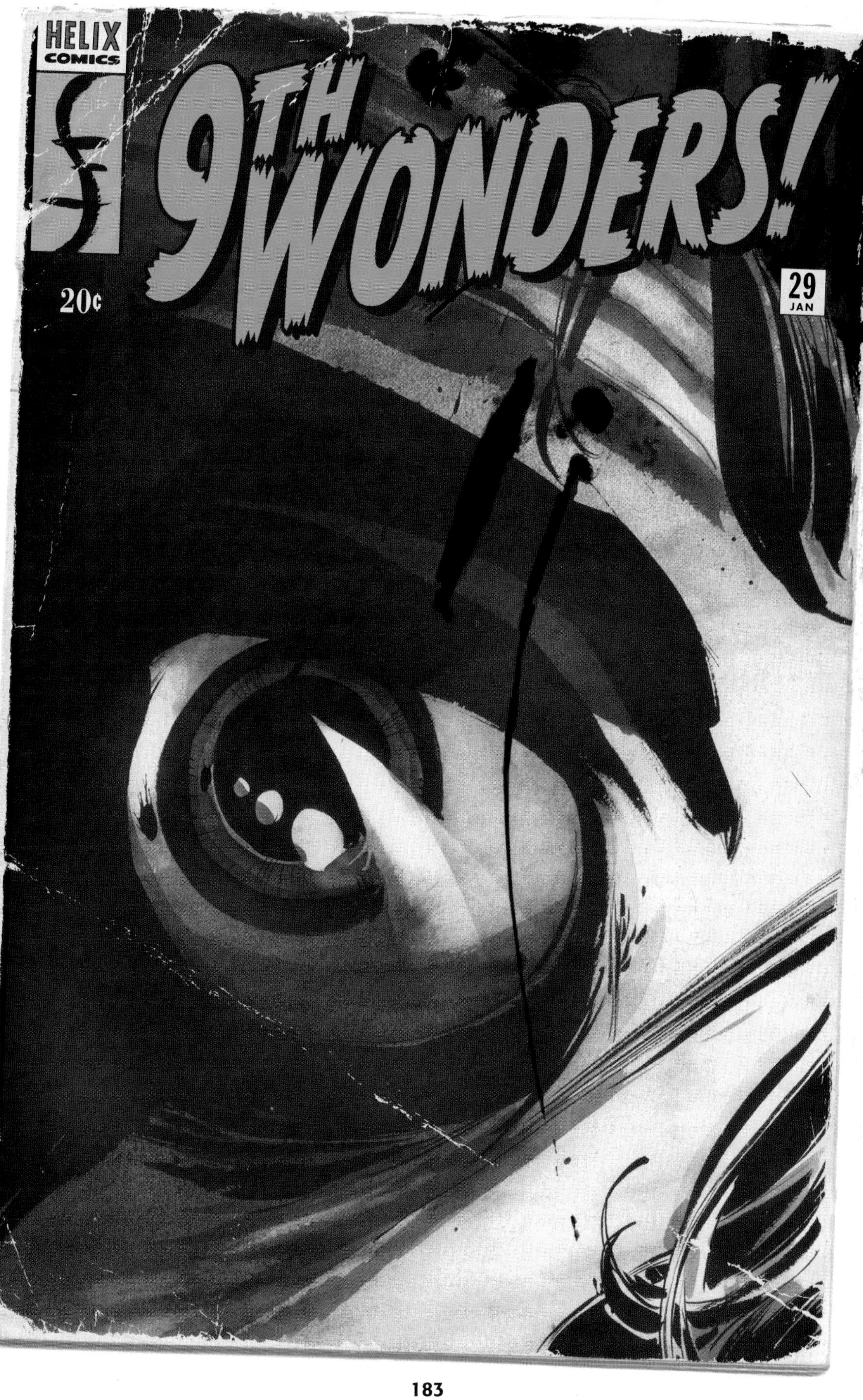
HELIX
COMICS
9TH WONDERS!
20¢
29
JAN

BENNET LED ME TO THIS FILE.

WAR BUDDIES *Part 6 of Six* CALL TO ARMS

HE SAID FINDING IT WOULD PUT US ON THE PATH TO *ANSWERS*.

SEEMS HE WANTED ME TO SEE THE *CONNECTION* BETWEEN THESE TWO MEN.

MARK WARSHAW *Story*
STAZ JOHNSON *Pencils*
EDGAR AT STUDIO F *Digital Inks & Colors*
COMICRAFT *Lettering*

I JUST DID A SEARCH FOR THIS *LINDERMAN* GUY.

LOOKS LIKE HE IS A *BIG SHOT* OUT OF *VEGAS*.

GUESS WE KNOW WHERE ALL THOSE *ENCODED MESSAGES* OUT OF ODESSA WERE HEADED.

Codename "Dallas": Petrelli.
Codename "Austin": Linderman.

At date of filing, the two men remain close friends.

GUESS WE KNOW WHERE I'M HEADED *NEXT*.

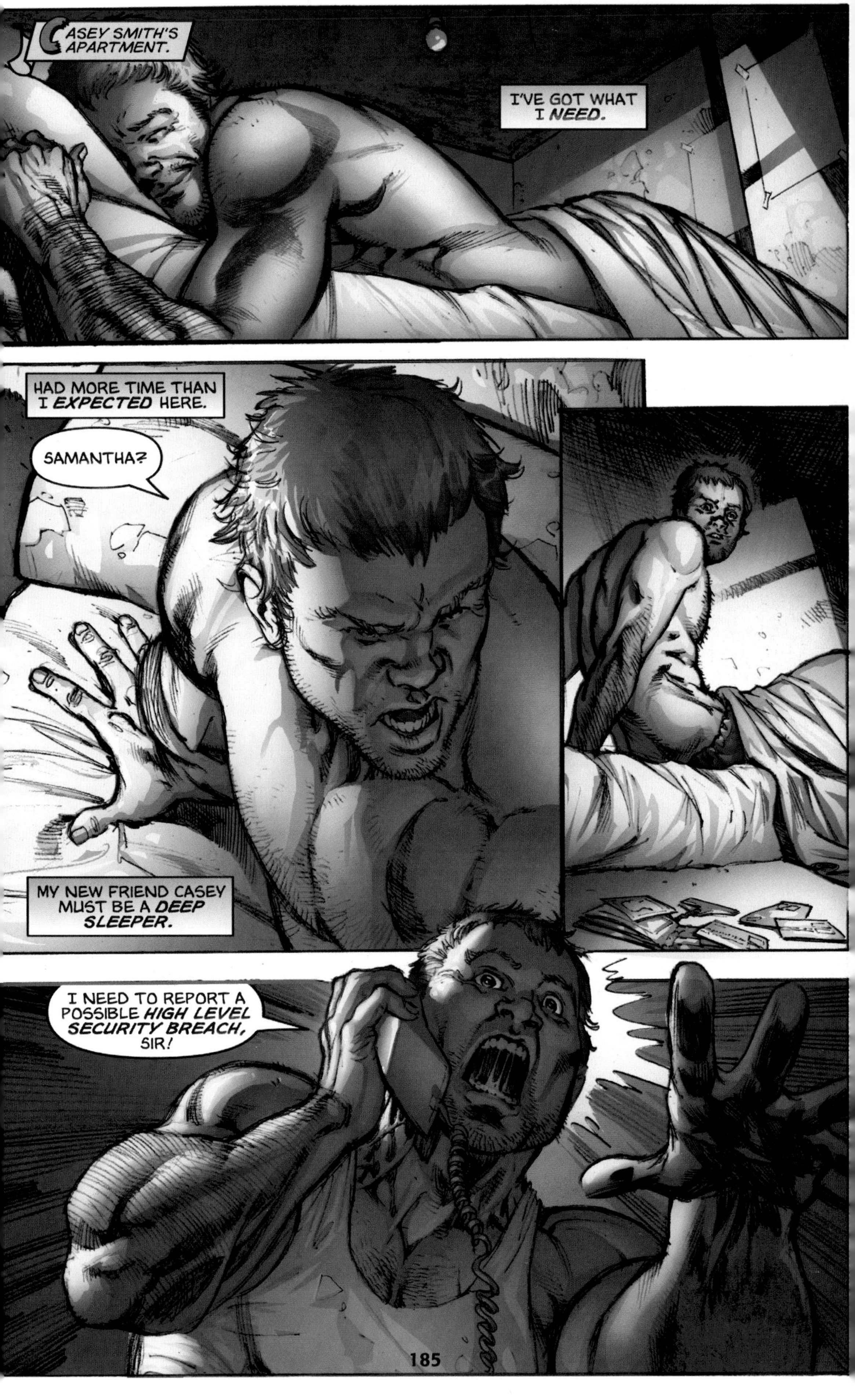
CASEY SMITH'S APARTMENT.
I'VE GOT WHAT I NEED.
HAD MORE TIME THAN I EXPECTED HERE.
SAMANTHA?
MY NEW FRIEND CASEY MUST BE A DEEP SLEEPER.
I NEED TO REPORT A POSSIBLE HIGH LEVEL SECURITY BREACH, SIR!

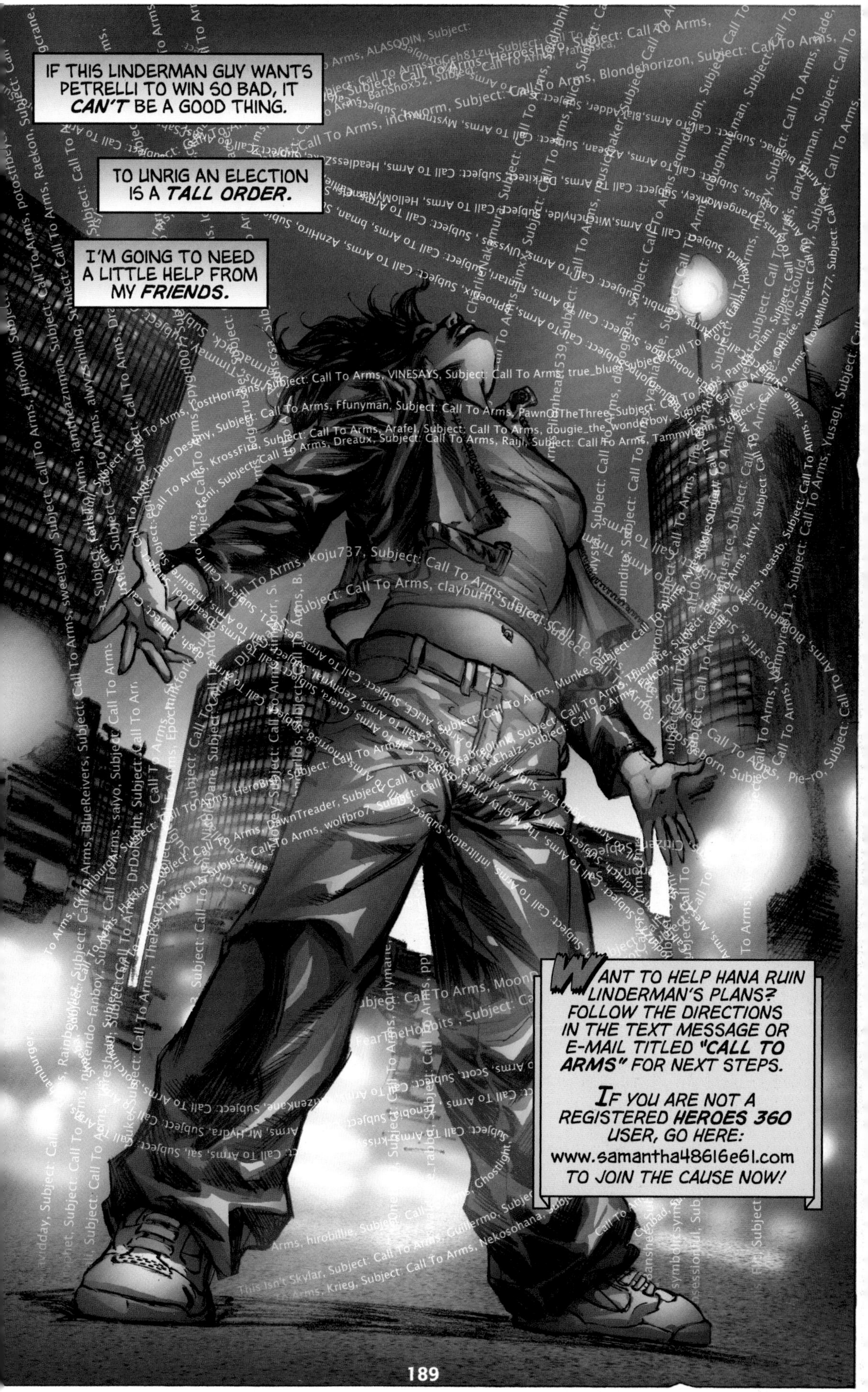
IF THIS LINDERMAN GUY WANTS PETRELLI TO WIN SO BAD, IT CAN'T BE A GOOD THING.
TO UNRIG AN ELECTION IS A TALL ORDER.
I'M GOING TO NEED A LITTLE HELP FROM MY FRIENDS.
WANT TO HELP HANA RUIN LINDERMAN'S PLANS? FOLLOW THE DIRECTIONS IN THE TEXT MESSAGE OR E-MAIL TITLED "CALL TO ARMS" FOR NEXT STEPS.
IF YOU ARE NOT A REGISTERED HEROES 360 USER, GO HERE: www.samantha48616e61.com TO JOIN THE CAUSE NOW!

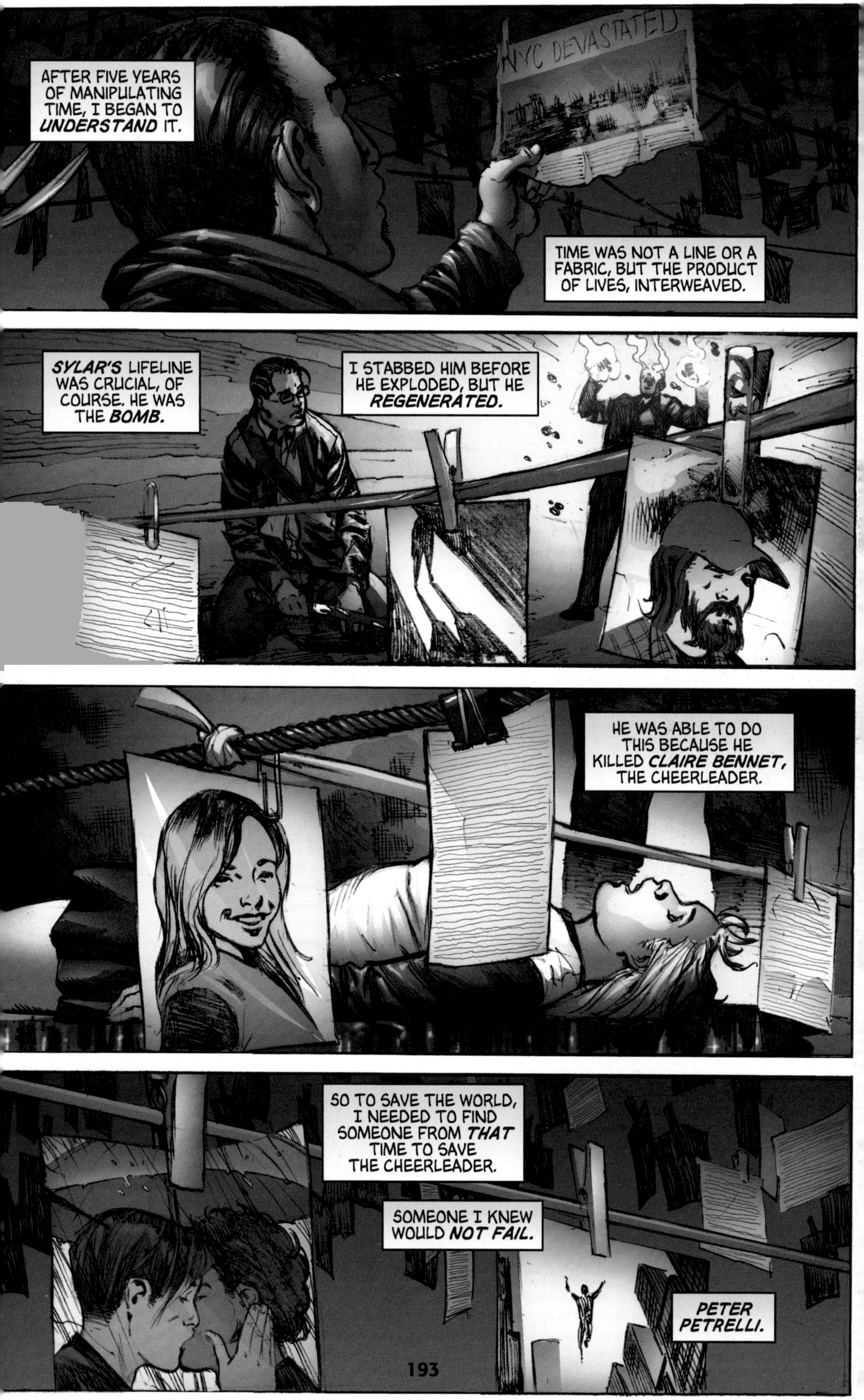
NYC DEVASTATED
AFTER FIVE YEARS OF MANIPULATING TIME, I BEGAN TO *UNDERSTAND* IT.
TIME WAS NOT A LINE OR A FABRIC, BUT THE PRODUCT OF LIVES, INTERWEAVED.
SYLAR'S LIFELINE WAS CRUCIAL, OF COURSE. HE WAS THE *BOMB.*
I STABBED HIM BEFORE HE EXPLODED, BUT HE *REGENERATED.*
HE WAS ABLE TO DO THIS BECAUSE HE KILLED *CLAIRE BENNET,* THE CHEERLEADER.
SO TO SAVE THE WORLD, I NEEDED TO FIND SOMEONE FROM *THAT* TIME TO SAVE THE CHEERLEADER.
SOMEONE I KNEW WOULD *NOT FAIL.*
PETER PETRELLI.

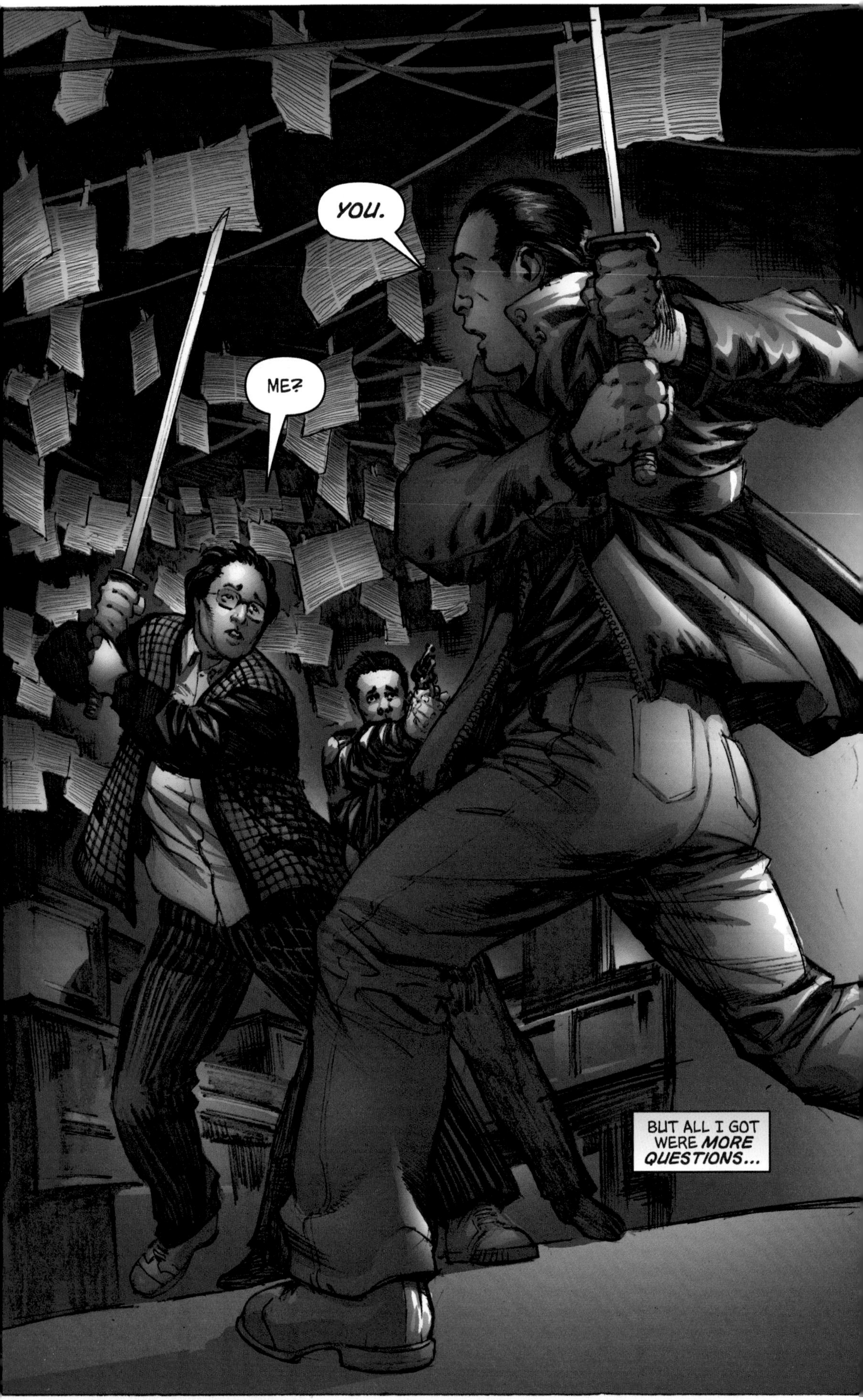
YOU.
ME?
BUT ALL I GOT WERE MORE QUESTIONS...

WALLS Part 1

JOE POKASKI
Story

TOM GRUMMETT
Art

CHRIS SOTOMAYOR Colors
COMICRAFT Lettering

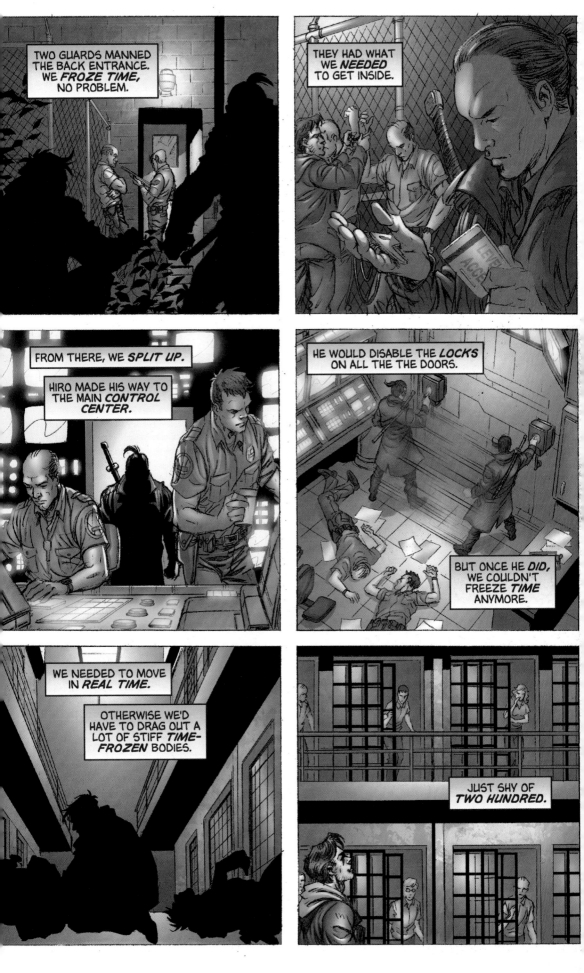

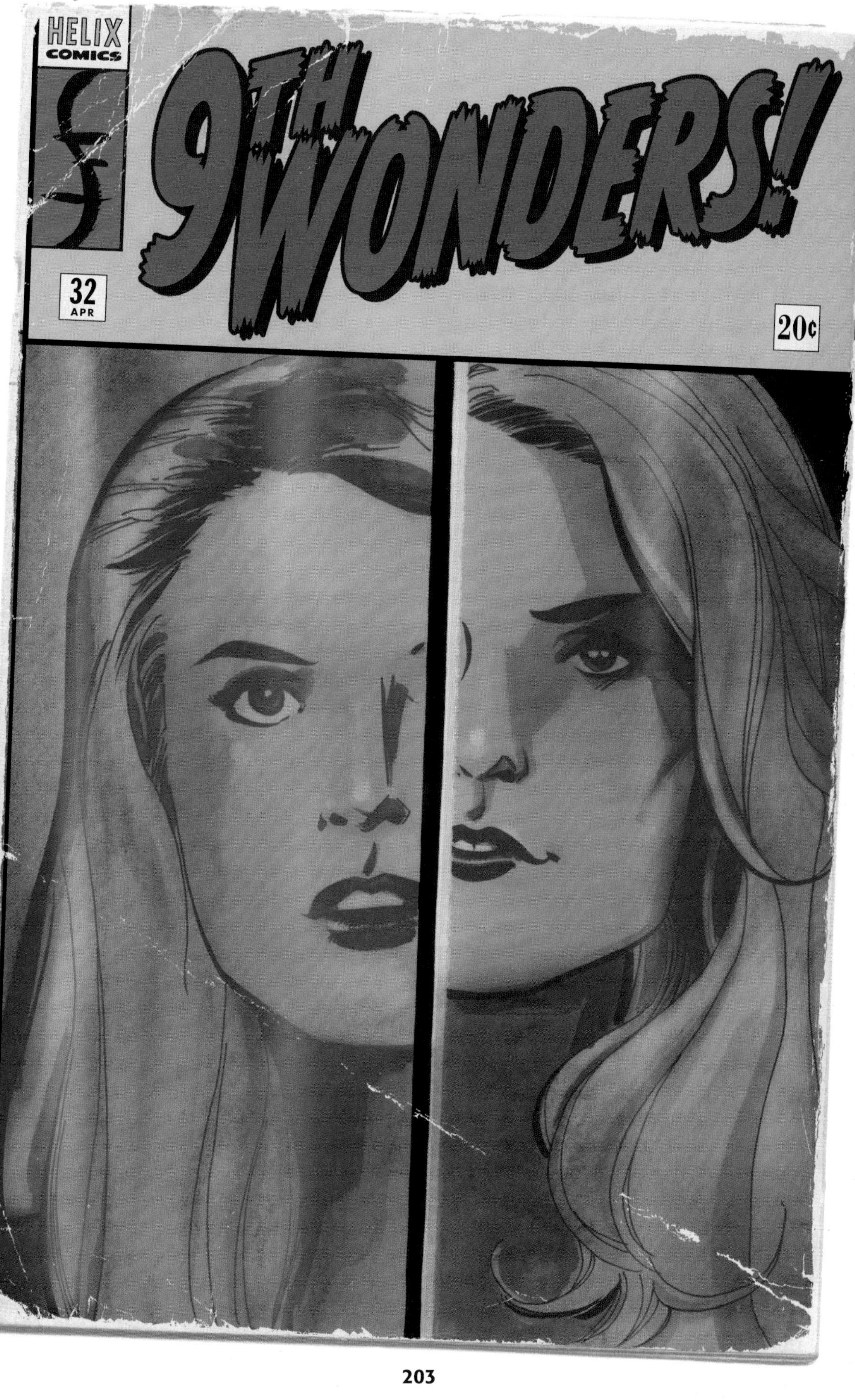

HELIX
COMICS
9TH WONDERS!
32
APR
20¢

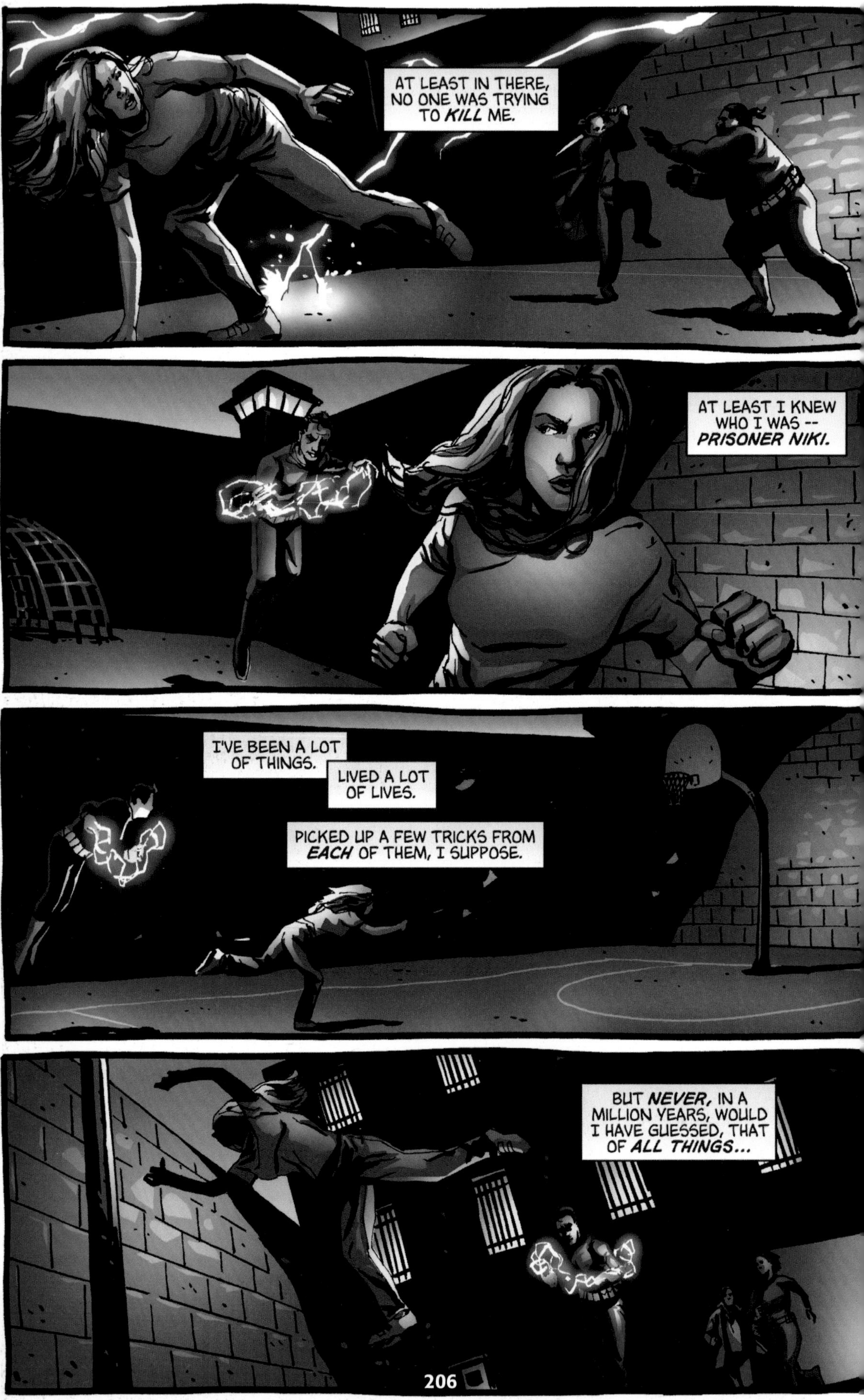
AT LEAST IN THERE, NO ONE WAS TRYING TO *KILL* ME.
AT LEAST I KNEW WHO I WAS -- ***PRISONER NIKI.***
I'VE BEEN A LOT OF THINGS.
LIVED A LOT OF LIVES.
PICKED UP A FEW TRICKS FROM ***EACH*** OF THEM, I SUPPOSE.
BUT ***NEVER,*** IN A MILLION YEARS, WOULD I HAVE GUESSED, THAT OF ***ALL THINGS...***

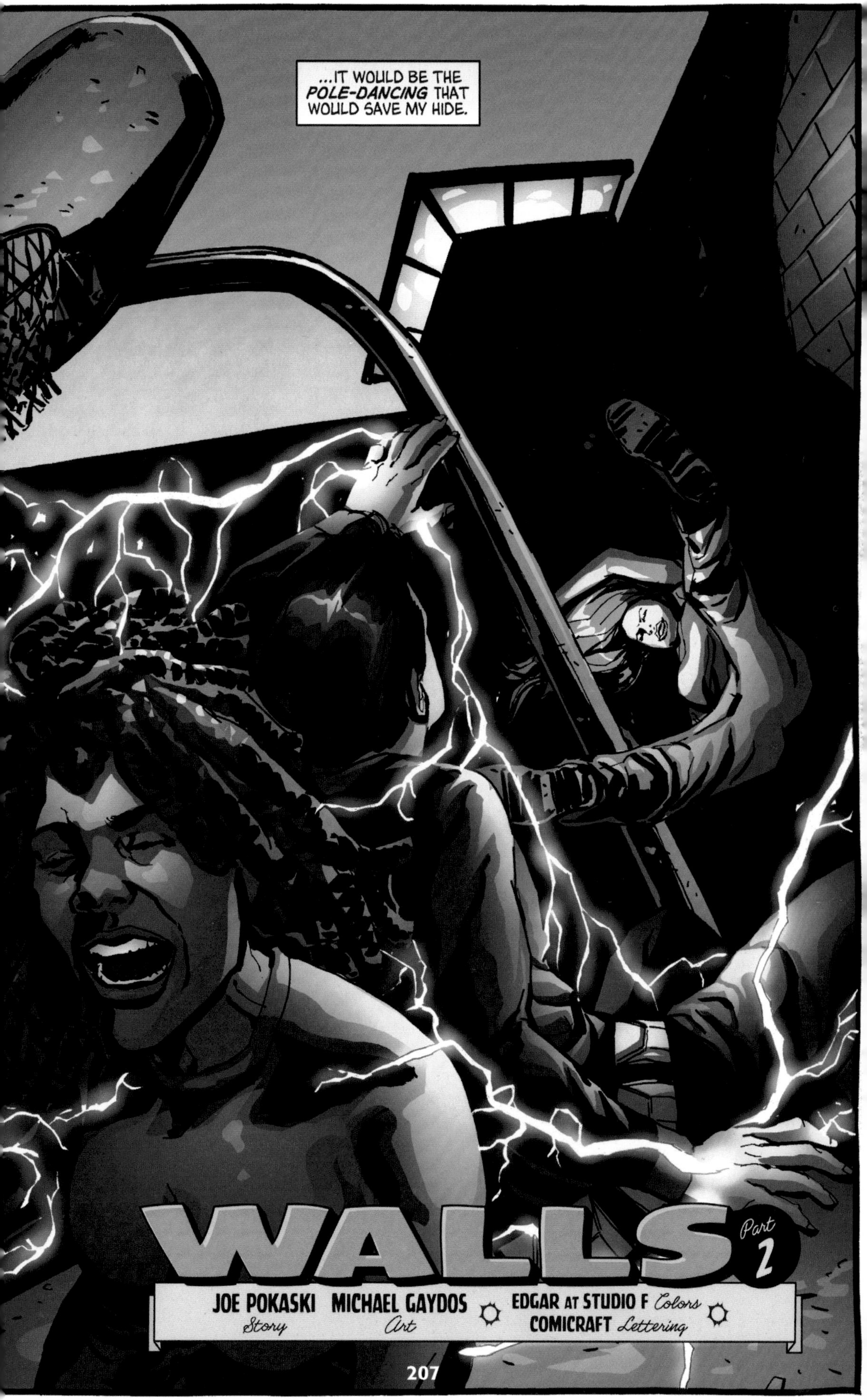
...IT WOULD BE THE POLE-DANCING THAT WOULD SAVE MY HIDE.
WALLS Part 2
JOE POKASKI Story
MICHAEL GAYDOS Art
EDGAR AT STUDIO F Colors
COMICRAFT Lettering

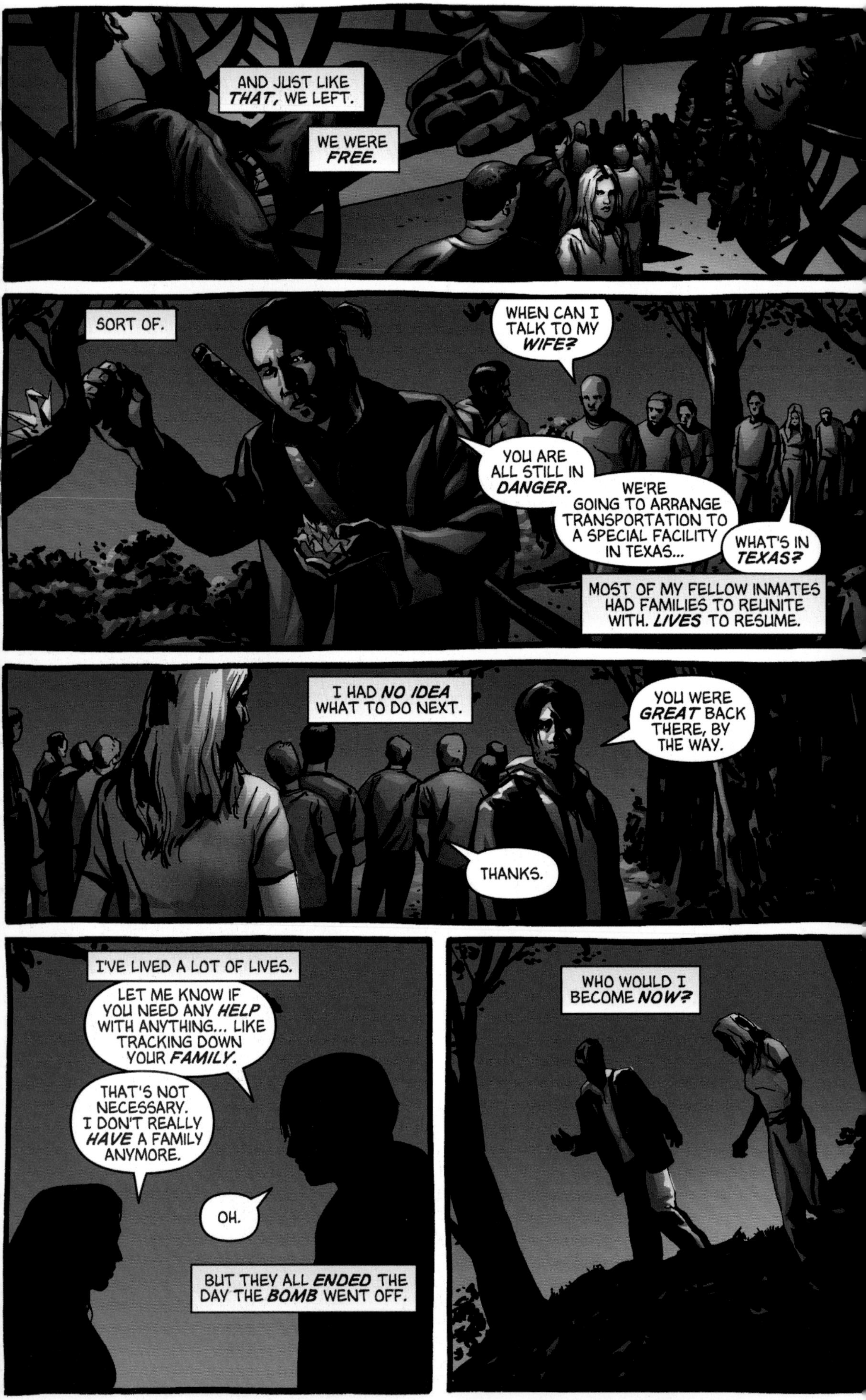

AND JUST LIKE THAT, WE LEFT.
WE WERE FREE.
SORT OF.
WHEN CAN I TALK TO MY WIFE?
YOU ARE ALL STILL IN DANGER.
WE'RE GOING TO ARRANGE TRANSPORTATION TO A SPECIAL FACILITY IN TEXAS...
WHAT'S IN TEXAS?
MOST OF MY FELLOW INMATES HAD FAMILIES TO REUNITE WITH. LIVES TO RESUME.
I HAD NO IDEA WHAT TO DO NEXT.
YOU WERE GREAT BACK THERE, BY THE WAY.
THANKS.
I'VE LIVED A LOT OF LIVES.
LET ME KNOW IF YOU NEED ANY HELP WITH ANYTHING... LIKE TRACKING DOWN YOUR FAMILY.
THAT'S NOT NECESSARY. I DON'T REALLY HAVE A FAMILY ANYMORE.
OH.
BUT THEY ALL ENDED THE DAY THE BOMB WENT OFF.
WHO WOULD I BECOME NOW?

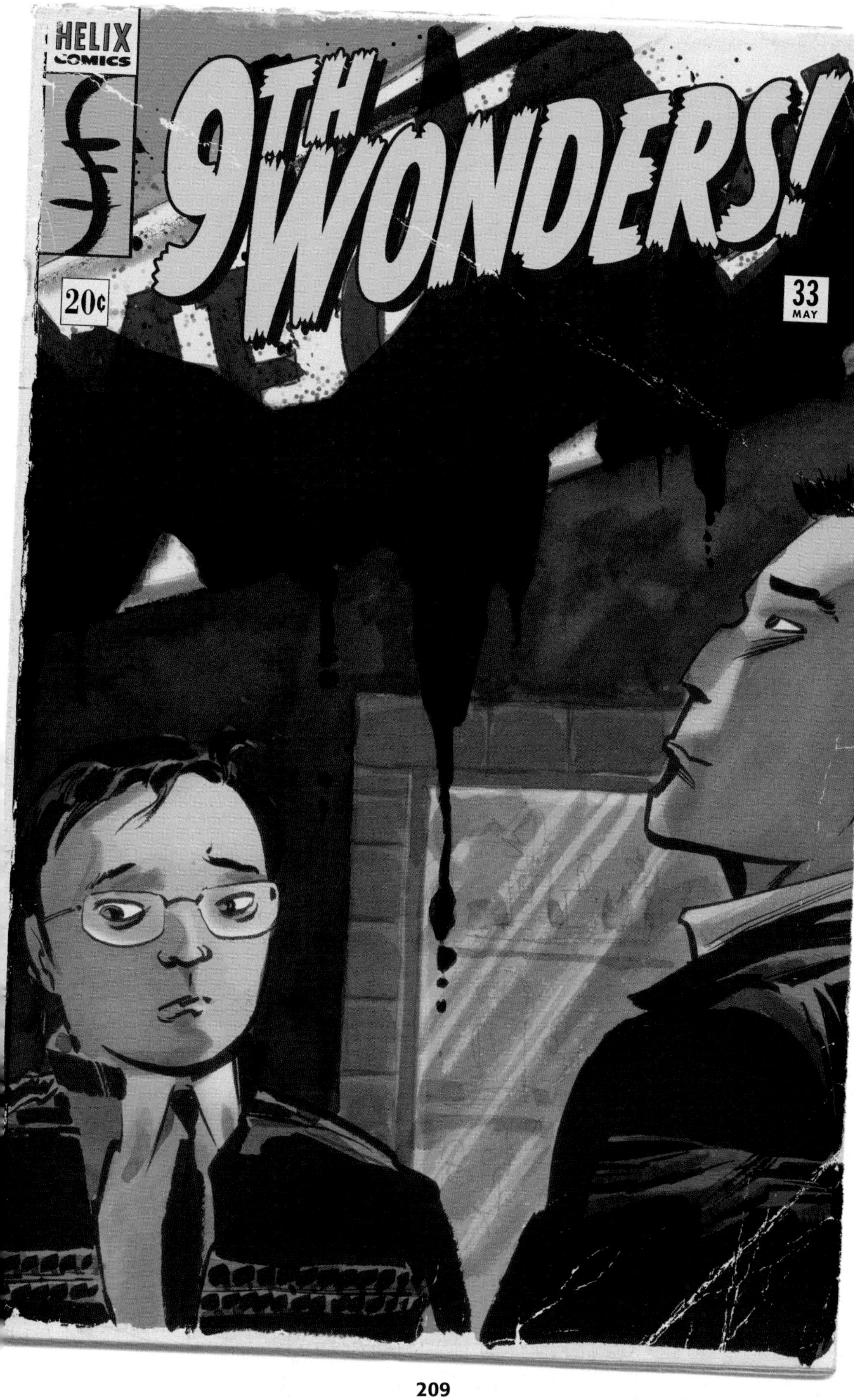
HELIX COMICS
9TH WONDERS!
20¢
33
MAY

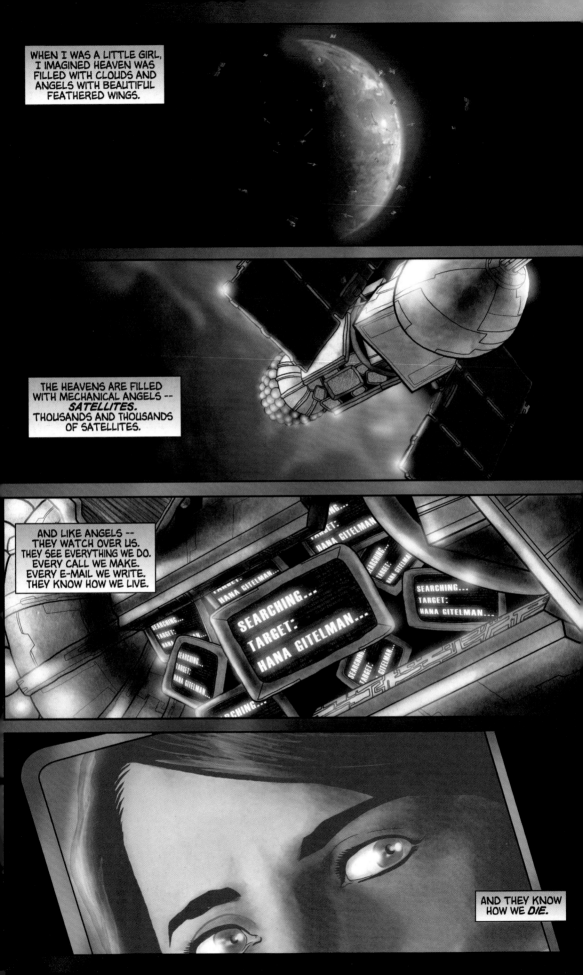

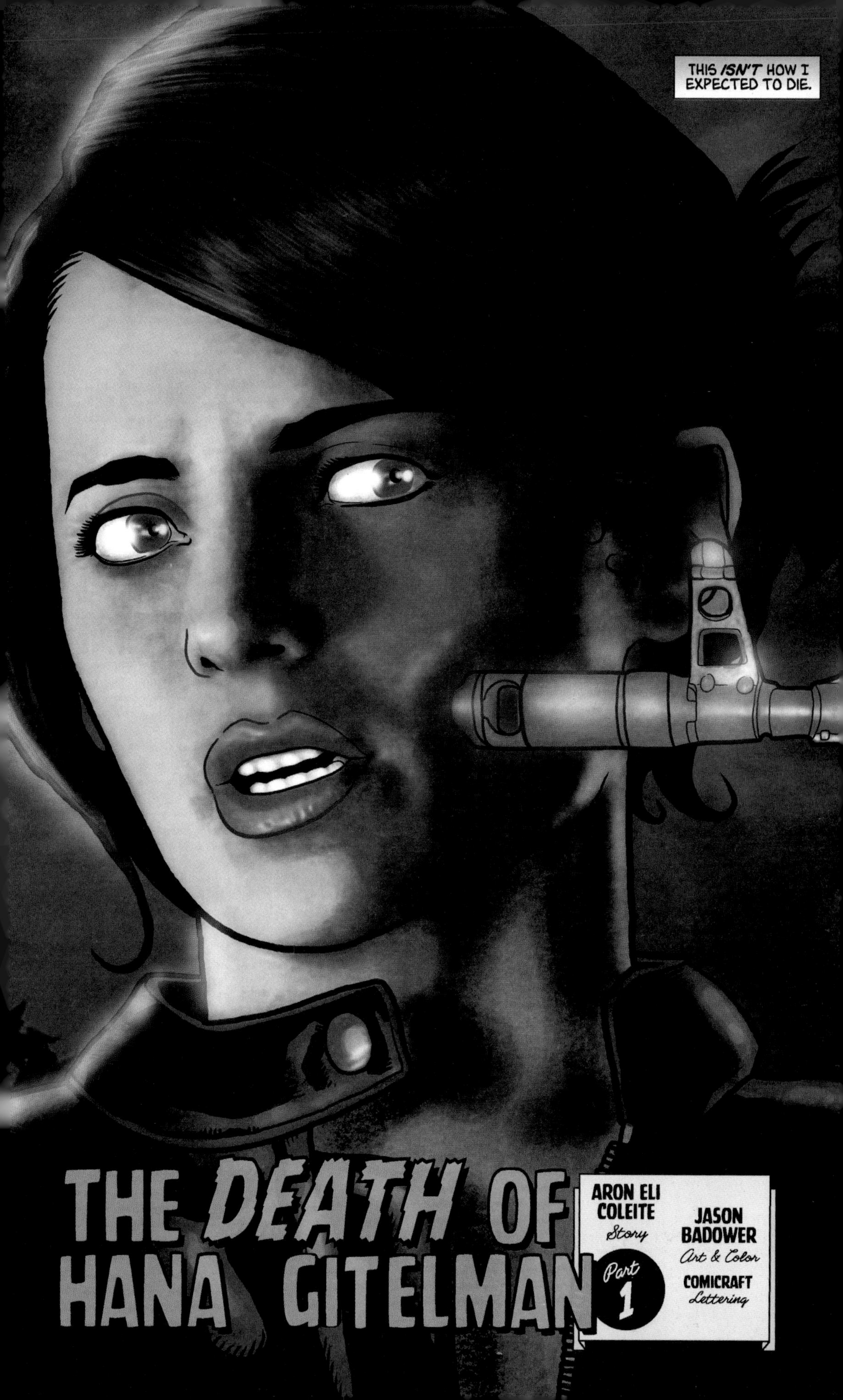
THIS ISN'T HOW I EXPECTED TO DIE.
THE DEATH OF HANA GITELMAN
Part 1
ARON ELI COLEITE Story
JASON BADOWER Art & Color
COMICRAFT Lettering

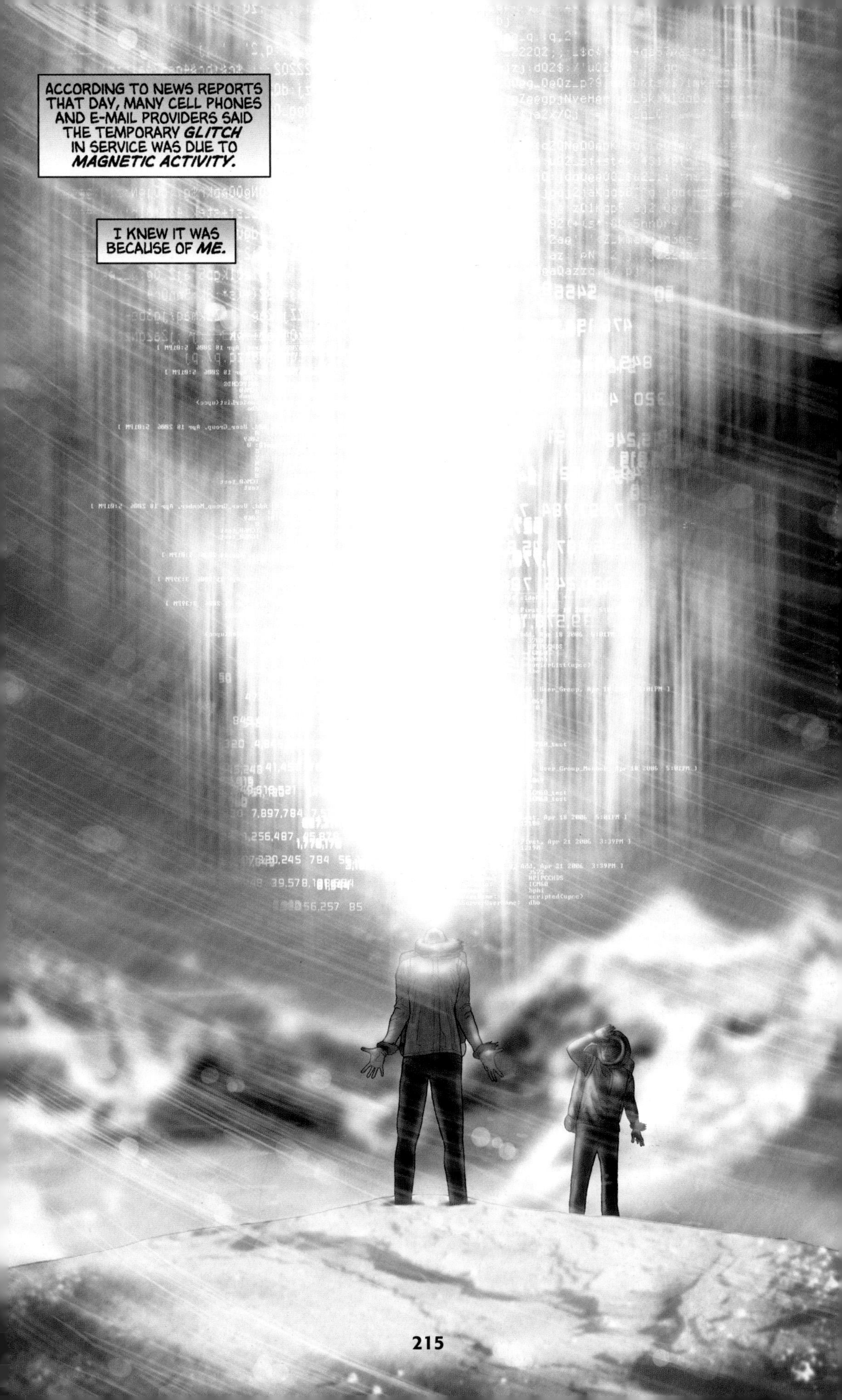
ACCORDING TO NEWS REPORTS THAT DAY, MANY CELL PHONES AND E-MAIL PROVIDERS SAID THE TEMPORARY GLITCH IN SERVICE WAS DUE TO MAGNETIC ACTIVITY.
I KNEW IT WAS BECAUSE OF ME.

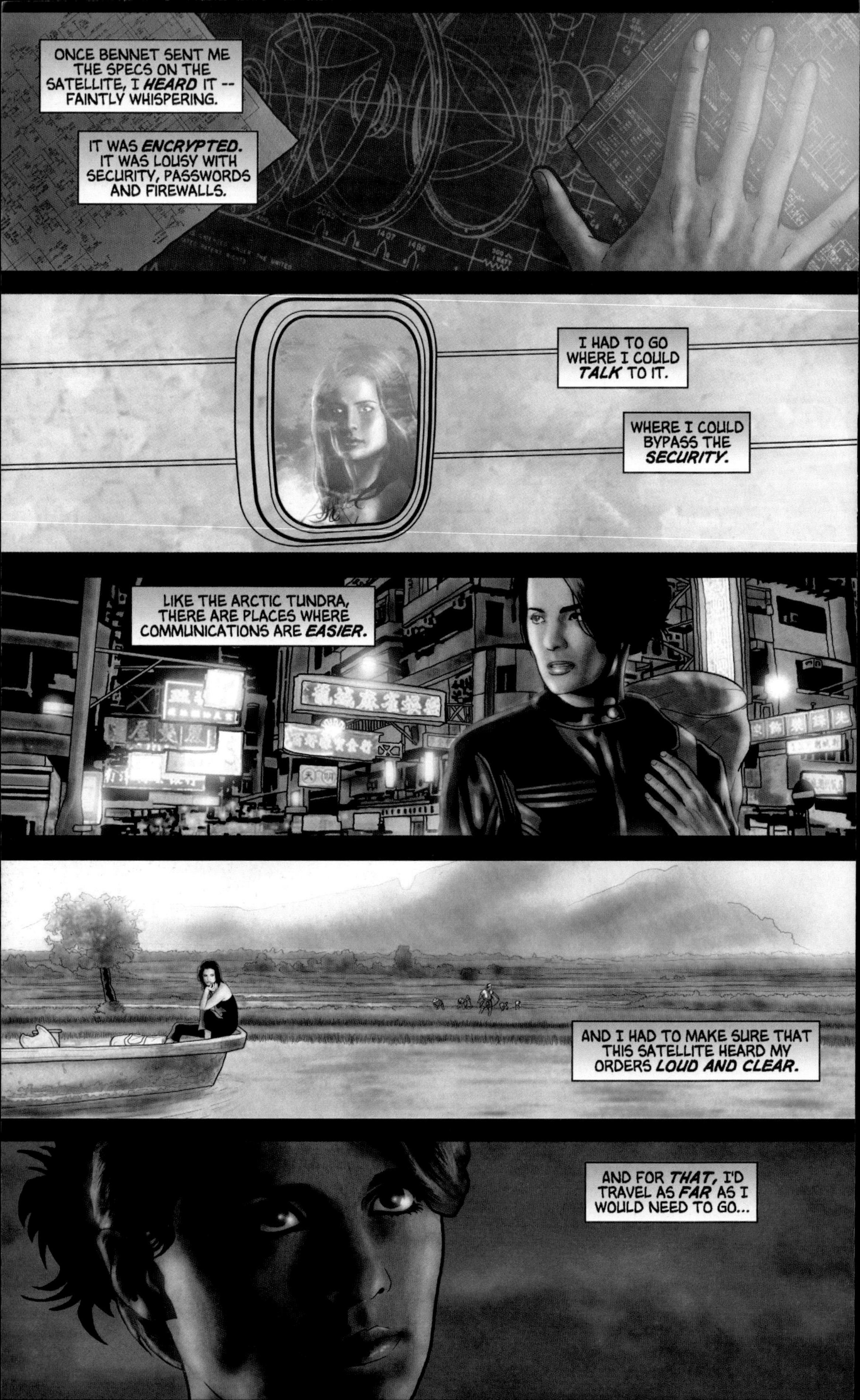
ONCE BENNET SENT ME THE SPECS ON THE SATELLITE, I *HEARD* IT -- FAINTLY WHISPERING.
IT WAS *ENCRYPTED.* IT WAS LOUSY WITH SECURITY, PASSWORDS AND FIREWALLS.
I HAD TO GO WHERE I COULD *TALK* TO IT.
WHERE I COULD BYPASS THE *SECURITY.*
LIKE THE ARCTIC TUNDRA, THERE ARE PLACES WHERE COMMUNICATIONS ARE *EASIER.*
AND I HAD TO MAKE SURE THAT THIS SATELLITE HEARD MY ORDERS *LOUD AND CLEAR.*
AND FOR *THAT,* I'D TRAVEL AS *FAR* AS I WOULD NEED TO GO...

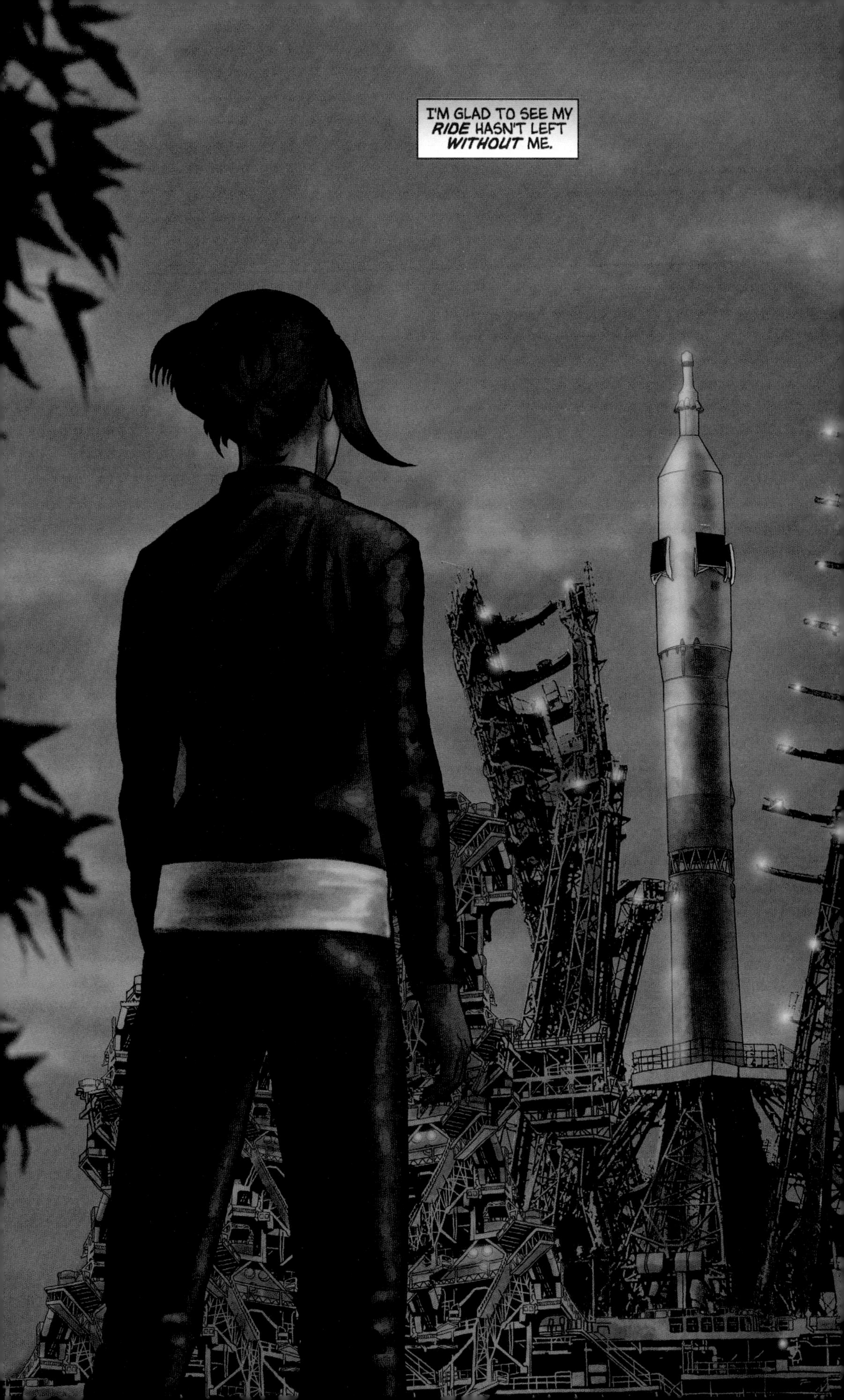
I'M GLAD TO SEE MY RIDE HASN'T LEFT WITHOUT ME.

221

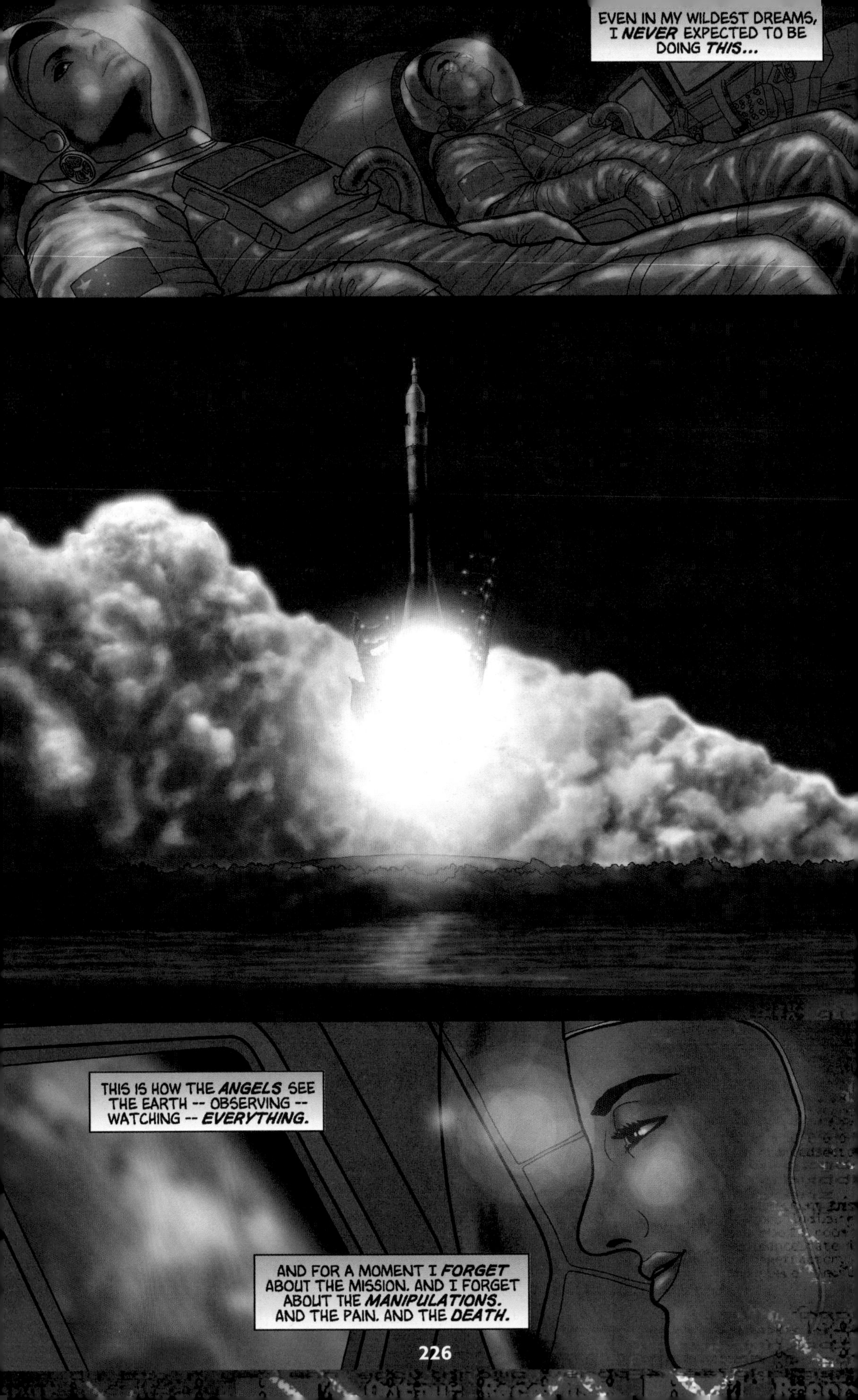
EVEN IN MY WILDEST DREAMS, I NEVER EXPECTED TO BE DOING THIS...
THIS IS HOW THE ANGELS SEE THE EARTH -- OBSERVING -- WATCHING -- EVERYTHING.
AND FOR A MOMENT I FORGET ABOUT THE MISSION. AND I FORGET ABOUT THE MANIPULATIONS. AND THE PAIN. AND THE DEATH.

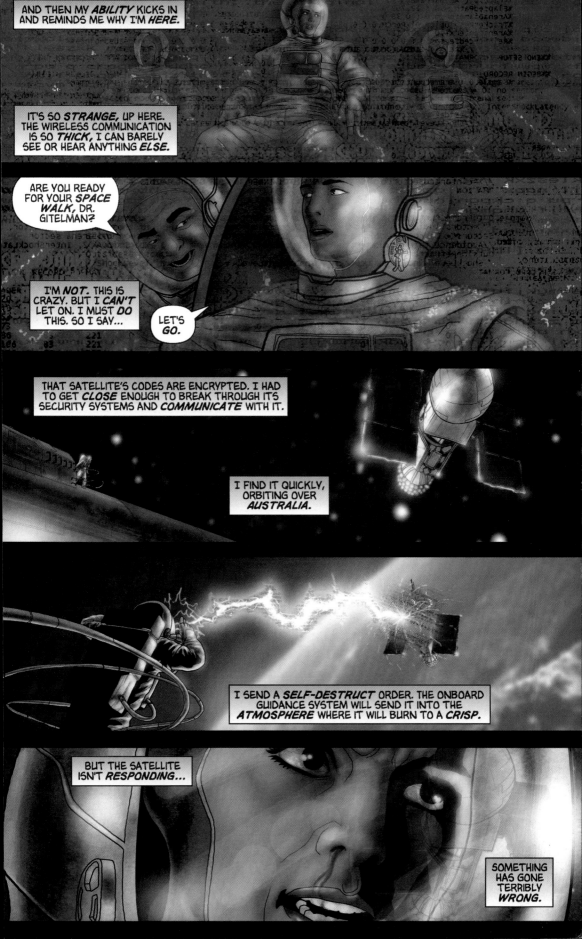

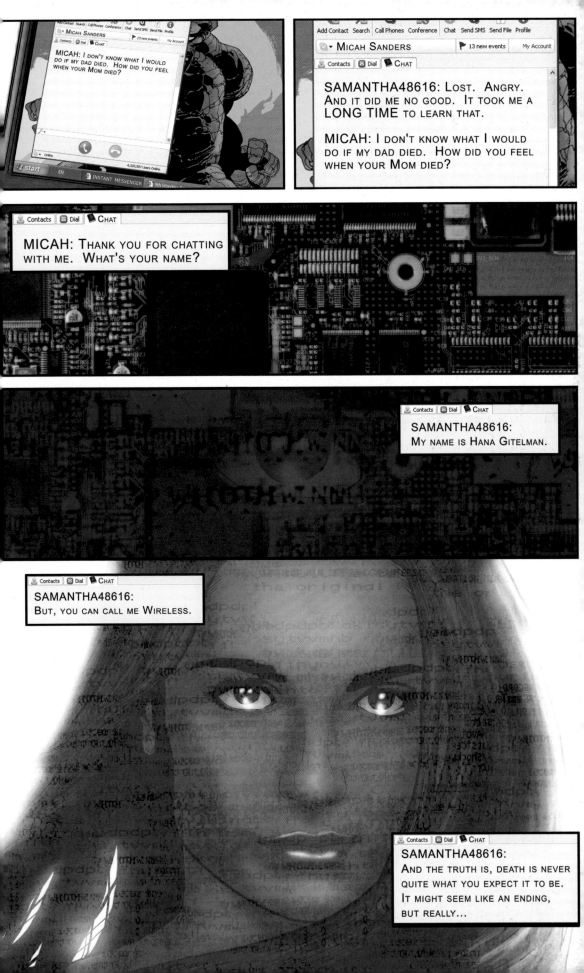

THE HEROES INTERVIEW

EXECUTIVE PRODUCER **JEPH LOEB** TALKS WITH SERIES WRITERS **ARON ELI COLEITE** AND **JOE POKASKI**

JEPH: A comic book version of HEROES seems like a no-brainer, but how did it come about?

ARON & JOE: If Tim Kring was the general who ordered a strike on the American zeitgeist with this crazy show called "Heroes"—I guess you could consider us to be some of the first boots on the ground. Before the Pilot was even picked up, we talked extensively with Tim about the online component of the show. How to extend the storytelling from one hour on a Monday into an immersive fan experience.

The online comic was one of the first ideas that came to mind. We had so many stories to tell and there was only so much room in the TV show—so we decided that we could tell these alternate stories in the comics. The stories could be deeper, broader and reveal more secrets about our characters. It was also a way to tell stories that would be otherwise unproduceable on our show.

But this is different from traditional comics, right? It's online and only 5 or 6 pages a shot.

The goal was to put out 22 pages a month, like most comics, but to come out weekly like a television show. So the math dictated 5 or 6 pages per installment and we lucked into the perfect length for a Heroes Webcomic.

Like the scenes or stories in the pilot or in subsequent episodes—the webcomic would be what we called "Haiku," short but purposeful. Every panel meaning something.

It actually forced us to be better, more concise storytellers—we weren't allowed to ramble or wander. We had to tell unique, exciting and fulfilling stories in 5 pages.

You've filled in some of the gaps in the stories from the show. Do you feel like people who watch the show have to read these to know what's going on?

Not at all. In fact, our first rule going in was that you didn't have to read the comic to enjoy the show, but it created an enhanced experience if you did.

On the other side, we wanted people who did watch the show and read the comic to feel rewarded—that they were taking part of something larger and give them real emotional and important stories—not just fluff or filler.

233

Michael Turner, Phil Jimenez, Aspen, Nanci Quesada, Alex Ross, and Jim Lee—and those are just for starters. How did the comic book community get involved with what could otherwise be seen as just another licensed property?

For starters, we had a big gun—this guy named Jeph Loeb. It's not a stretch to call him a living legend. And on top of that, a ridiculously large amount of people in the industry who love him—and would jump in front of a train for him. We're not sure if it was that, or his ability to sell a good idea, but soon we had an amazing bullpen of writers and artists working for us.

The short format had a little to do with it too. Many comic book artists pour their hearts and soul onto each page. At 22 pages per comic that is a lot of soul pouring. It's easier to get a top-notch artist for 5 or 6 pages. It's like keeping a friend out at a bar by saying "one more drink." Who doesn't want one more?

Are there new writers we can look forward to next season?

We've already got a bunch of great writers from the show. We've also been joined by veterans like Steven Seagle, Joe Kelly and Duncan Rouleau. But, we've also been fortunate to get some young comic book scribes to join our crew like Mark Sable and Christine Boylen.

On top of that, we've got an amazing staff of up and coming brilliant minds that help us with the impossible task of writing one of these a week. Writers like Harry Wilcox, Oliver Grigsby, Chris Zatta, Jim Martin, Pierluigi Cothran, Timm Keppler and Andrew Chambliss. Watch out for these names—you will see them in the future.

And rumor has it that a certain writer whose name rhymes with SCHMEPH SCHMOEB will introduce a new character called "Rachel Red, Robogirl."

You had to start even before anyone had seen the show. What was that like?

In a lot of ways, it was liberating. As with the show, all we could do is tell the most exciting stories that you would want to experience yourself. Just go for it, because there was no audience reaction to be reactionary towards.

But of course, in the back of your head, for the show and the webcomic, there's the whole "what if you threw a Television Show and nobody arrives" concern eating at the back of your head.

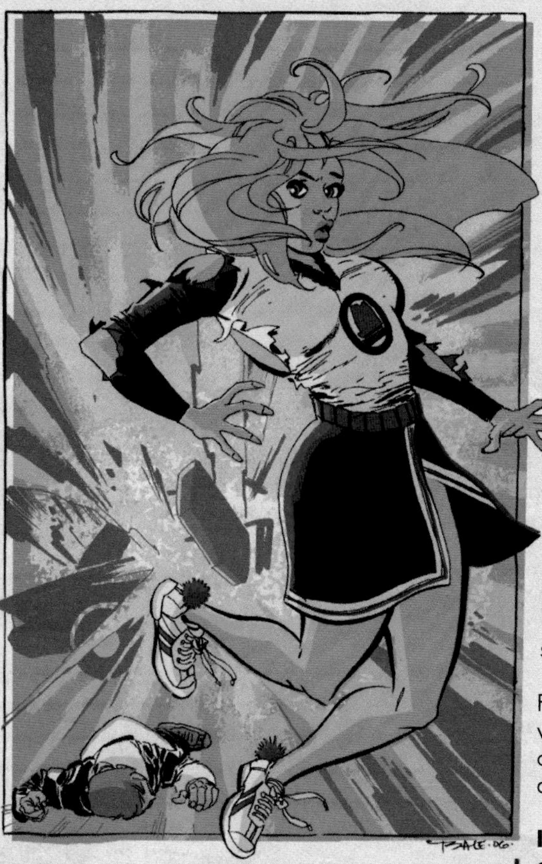

Are there some stories you CAN'T or WON'T tell as comics?

We don't want to touch anything that should be seen on the television. For example, we were tempted to tell the webcomic of how H.R.G. got assigned to be Claire's father—but we knew that would be better served on the show—as everyone finally saw in "Company Man."

There's a new online story up every week! How do you do that when some monthly comics -koff-*Ultimates*-koff- sometimes can't make shipping!

Most of that lies with a guy named Mark Warshaw. And Chuck Kim. They keep the trains running on time. Sometimes we run right up to the wire and deliver the pages moments before they need to go live, but even so—we have yet to miss a deadline.

Fortunately we're able to line up the stories with the episodes so we can try to keep ahead of the curve and have scripts generated quickly and early.

If you could have a crossover with any of the DC characters, what would your dream team-up be?

I think everyone would want to see the Supergirl/Claire team up. A Peter/Superman throwdown might be fun as well. And of course Green Lantern/Ando would be a classic matchup.

So...are you comic book writers or graphic novelists? Remember, this is how you'll be defined for the rest of your lives...

Is there a third choice?

You're both pretty big comic geeks. What's it like now, creating your own universe? What do you read? Do you buy comics on a weekly basis?

Each Wednesday (ideally) we actually make our trek to the local store. A big shout-out to our friends at Meltdown who take good care of us every week. We read a lot of everything. Bendis. Millar. Johns. And of course everything that Loeb puts out. It's one of the rare pleasures in life to go to a comic book store with Jeph Loeb and see the fans pointing and whispering.

Are there stories that you can tell only in this graphic novel form?

There are certainly ones that are easier—because there are no production restraints. For example, when Hana Gitelman went to China to stow away on the Space Shuttle so she could spacewalk to a satellite and ride it down into the burning atmosphere. That would have been difficult to produce.

Fire. Space. Polar Ice Caps. Jungles of Africa. Battles with Indian gods and confrontations with Australian rock formations. There is no limit in this format. It's very rewarding.

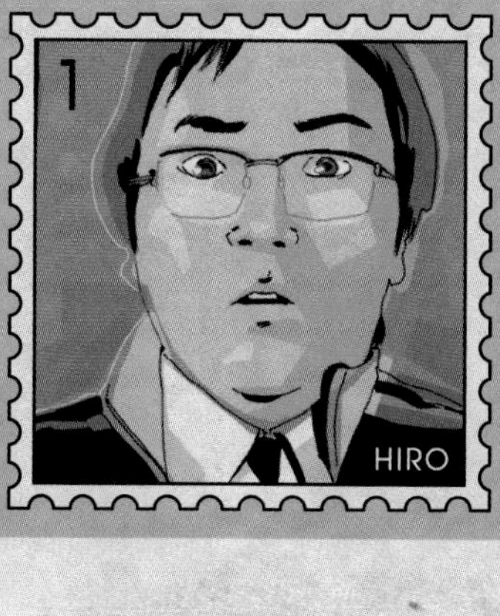
1
HIRO

THIS IS IT! YOUR

HEROES VALUE STAMP

FOR THIS ISSUE! CLIP 'EM AND COLLECT 'EM!

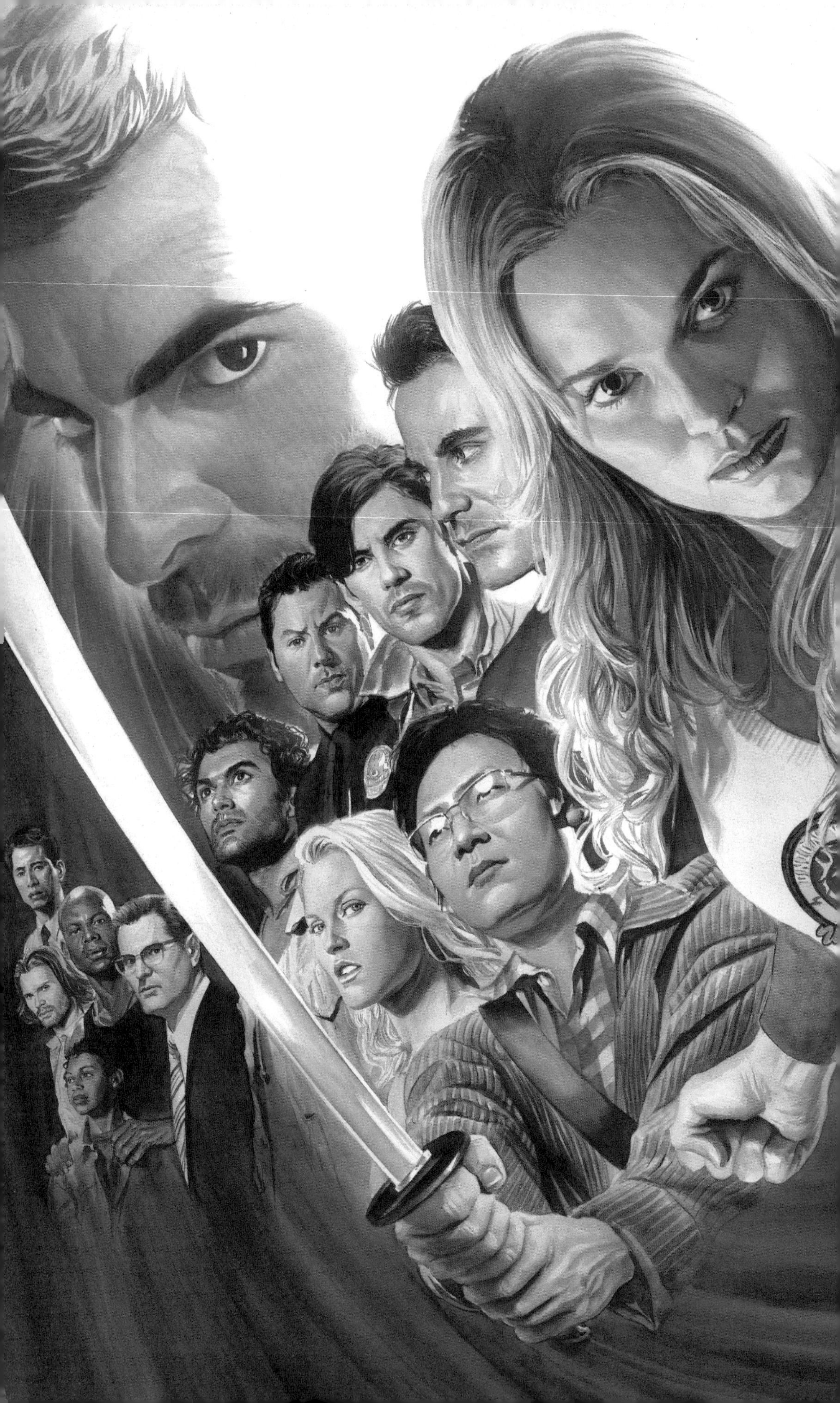

FROM THE CREATORS FEATURED ON

HEROES

JEPH LOEB & TIM SALE

Superman
For All Seasons
Jeph Loeb
Tim Sale
with Bjarne Hansen

The catalyst for the *Smallville* television program, SUPERMAN FOR ALL SEASONS is an emotional and insightful examination of Clark Kent's transformation from a powerful boy into a heroic man. Told through the course of four seasons in the Man of Steel's adolescent life, this coming-of-age tale humanizes the alien from another planet so that he is not only realistic but also relatable. Featuring in-depth characterizations of Lana Lang, Lex Luthor, Lois Lane and the Kents, this groundbreaking story of a simple Midwestern boy with awesome abilities illustrates that it is the man, not the powers, that make Clark Kent a hero.

ADDITIONAL COLLABORATIONS STARRING GOTHAM'S FINEST...

BATMAN: LONG HALLOWEEN

JEPH LOEB TIM SALE
BATMAN
THE LONG HALLOWEEN
JAN 1
OCT 31

BATMAN: DARK VICTORY

From the Eisner Award-winning creators
JEPH LOEB TIM SALE
BATMAN
Dark Victory

CATWOMAN: WHEN IN ROME

Jeph Loeb Tim Sale
CATWOMAN
When in Rome
From the
Eisner Award-winning
creative team
that created
BATMAN: THE LONG
HALLOWEEN
and
BATMAN:
DARK VICTORY

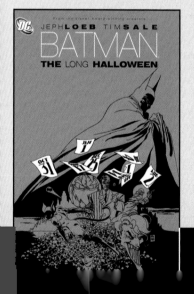

ALAN MOORE

TAKES ON A WHOLE NEW UNIVERSE!

In 1992 Jim Lee and Brandon Choi ushered in a new era of in comics with the release of WildC.A.Ts #1. It introduced readers to the WildStorm Universe and was a runaway sensation. Several years later Alan Moore and Travis Charest tried their hands at the WildStorm flagship title and the results were astounding; Moore's unique stories coupled with Charest's masterful visuals set a new bar for the title.

Now, for the first time, Moore's complete story is collected in one handsome volume, telling the entire WildC.A.T.s saga that he envisioned from start to finish. It's a tale of honor, adventure and betrayal, as only the writer of WATCHMEN, V FOR VENDETTA and THE LEAGUE OF EXTRAORDINARY GENTLEMEN could tell it!

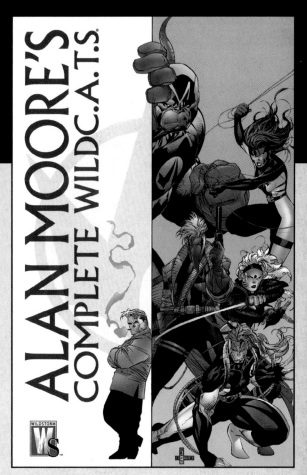

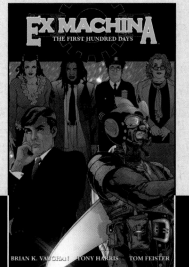

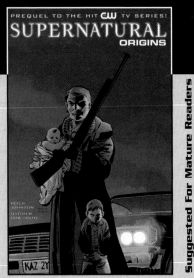

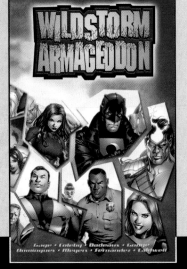

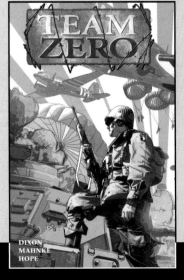